Anthony Trollope

The Macdermots of Ballycloran

Anthony Trollope

The Macdermots of Ballycloran

ISBN/EAN: 9783743306288

Manufactured in Europe, USA, Canada, Australia, Japa

Cover: Foto ©ninafisch / pixelio.de

Manufactured and distributed by brebook publishing software (www.brebook.com)

Anthony Trollope

The Macdermots of Ballycloran

BY ANTHONY TROLLOPE.

Price 2s. Picture Boards.

- EYE FOR AN EYE.
- SIR HARRY HOTSPUR.
- DOCTOR THORNE.
- THE MACDERMOTS.
- RACHEL RAY.
- THE KELLYS.
- TALES OF ALL COUNTRIES.
- CASTLE RICHMOND.
- THE BERTRAMS.

- COUSIN HENRY.
- RALPH THE HEIR.
- MISS MACKENZIE.
- THE BELTON ESTATE.
- IS HE POPENJOY?
- AN EDITOR'S TALES.
- LA VENDEE.
- LADY ANNA.
- VICAR OF BULLHAMPTON.

Price Half-a-Crown.

- ORLEY FARM.
- CAN YOU FORGIVE HER?
- PHINEAS FINN.

- EUSTACE DIAMONDS.
- PHINEAS REDUX.
- THE PRIME MINISTER.

HE KNEW HE WAS RIGHT.

London : CHAPMAN & HALL (LIMITED), 193 Piccadilly.
And at all Booksellers and Railway Bookstalls.

CONTENTS.

CHAP.		PAGE
I.	Ballycloran House as first seen by the Author	1
II.	The Macdermot Family	4
III.	The Tenantry of Ballycloran	7
IV.	Myles Ussher	15
V.	Father John	23
VI.	The Brother and Sister	37
VII.	The Priest's Dinner Party	51
VIII.	Miss Macdermot at Home	60
IX.	Mohill	72
X.	Mr. Keegan	84
XI.	Pat Brady	99
XII.	The Wedding	108
XIII.	How the Wedding Party was concluded	124
XIV.	Denis McGovery's Tidings	140
XV.	The McKeons	148
XVI.	Promotion	162
XVII.	Sport in the West	174
XVIII.	How Pat Brady and Joe Reynolds were eloquent in vain	186
XIX.	The Races	194
XX.	How Captain Ussher succeeded	210
XXI.	The Coroner's Inquest	220

CONTENTS.

CHAP.		PAGE
XXII.	THE ESCAPE	231
XXIII.	AUGHACASHEL	243
XXIV.	THE SECOND ESCAPE	250
XXV.	RETROSPECTIVE	257
XXVI.	THE DUEL	269
XXVII.	FEEMY RETURNS TO BALLYCLORAN	280
XXVIII.	ASSIZES AT CARRICK-ON-SHANNON	293
XXIX.	THADY'S TRIAL IS COMMENCED	306
XXX.	THE PRISONER'S DEFENCE	322
XXXI.	THE LAST WITNESS	339
XXXII.	THE VERDICT	349
XXXIII.	THE END	355

THE
MACDERMOTS OF BALLYCLORAN.

CHAPTER I.

BALLYCLORAN HOUSE AS FIRST SEEN BY THE AUTHOR.

In the autumn, 184—, business took me into the West of Ireland, and, amongst other places, to the quiet little village of Drumsna, which is in the province of Connaught, County Leitrim, about 72 miles w.n.w. of Dublin, on the mail-coach road to Sligo. I reached the little inn there in the morning by the said mail, my purpose being to leave it late in the evening by the day coach; and as my business was but of short duration, I was left, after an early dinner, to amuse myself. Now, in such a situation, to take a walk is all the brightest man can do, and the dullest always does the same. There is a kind of gratification in seeing what one has never seen before, be it ever so little worth seeing; and the gratication is the greater if the chances be that one will never see it again. Now Drumsna stands on a bend in the Shannon; the street leads down to a bridge, passing over which one finds oneself in the County Roscommon; and the road runs by the well-wooded demesne of Sir G— K—; moreover there is a beautiful little hill, from which the demesne, river, bridge, and village can all be seen; and what farther *agremens* than these could be wanted to make a pretty walk? But, alas! I knew not of their existence then. One cannot ask the maid at an inn to show one where to find the beauties of nature. So, trusting to myself, I went directly away from river, woods, and all,—along as dusty, ugly, and disagreeable a road as is to be found in any county in Ireland.

After proceeding a mile or so, taking two or three turns to look for improvement, I began to perceive evident signs on the part of the road of retrograding into lane-ism; the county had evidently deserted it, and though made for cars and coaches, its traffic appeared to be now confined to donkeys carrying turf home from the bog, in double kishes on their back. Presently the fragments of a

B

bridge presented themselves, but they too were utterly fallen away from their palmy days, and in their present state afforded but indifferent stepping-stones over a bog stream which ran, or rather crept, across the road. These, however, I luckily traversed, and was rewarded by finding a broken down entrance to a kind of wood on the right hand. In Ireland, particularly in the poorer parts— to rank among which, County Leitrim has a right which will not be disputed—a few trees together are always the recognised sign of a demesne, of a gentleman's seat, or the place where a gentleman's seat has been ; and I directly knew that this must be a demesne. But ah! how impoverished, if one might judge from outward appearances. Two brick pillars, from which the outside plaster had peeled off and the coping fallen, gave evidence of former gates; the space was closed up with a loose built wall, but on the outer side of each post was a little well worn footpath, made of soft bog mould. I of course could not resist such temptation, and entered the demesne. The road was nearly covered with that short dry grass which stones seem to throw up, when no longer polished by the wealthier portion of man or brute kind.

About thirty feet from the gap a tall fir had half fallen, and lay across the road, so that a man should stoop to walk under it; it was a perfect barrier to any equipage, however humble, and the roots had nearly refixed themselves in their reversed position, showing that the tree had evidently been in that fallen state for years.

The usual story, thought I, of Connaught gentlemen; an extravagant landlord, reckless tenants, debt, embarrassment, despair, and ruin. Well, I walked up the deserted avenue, and very shortly found myself in front of the house. Oh, what a picture of misery, of useless expenditure, unfinished pretence, and premature decay!

The house was two stories high, with large stone steps up to the front door, with four windows in the lower, and six in the upper story, and an area with kitchens, &c., below. The entire roof was off; one could see the rotting joists and beams, some fallen, some falling, the rest ready to fall, like the skeleton of a felon left to rot on an open gibbet. The stone steps had nearly dropped through into the area, the rails of which had been wrenched up. The knocker was still on the door,—a large modern lion-headed knocker; but half the door was gone ; on creeping to the door-sill, I found about six feet of the floor of the hall gone also—stolen for fire wood. But the joists of the flooring were there, and the whitewash of the walls showed that but a few, a very few years back, the house had been inhabited. I leaped across the gulf, at great risk of falling into the cellar, and reached the bottom of the stairs; here my courage failed me; all that was left was so damp and so rotten, so again, and down the ruined steps, and walked round the mansion; not only was there not a pane of glass in the whole, but the window frames were all gone; everything that wanted keeping was gone; everything that required care to preserve it had perished. Time had not touched it. Time had evidently not yet had leisure to do his work. He is sure, but slow. Ruin works fast enough unaided, where once he puts his foot. Time would have pulled down the chimneys—Ruin had taken off the slates; Time would have bulged the walls—Ruin brought in the rain, rotted the timbers, and assisted the thieves. Poor old Time will have but little left him at Ballycloran! The gardens had been large; half were now covered by rubbish heaps, and the other half consisted of potato patches; and round the out-houses I saw clustering a lot of those wretched cabins which the poor Irish build against a deserted wall, when they can find one, as jackdaws do their nests in a superannuated chimney. In the front there had been, I presume, a tolerably spacious lawn, with a drive through it, surrounded on all sides, except towards the house, by thick trees. The trees remained, but the lawn, the drive, and the flower patches, which of course once existed there, were now all alike, equally prolific in large brown dock weeds and sorrels. There were two or three narrow footpaths through and across the space, up to the cabins behind the house, but other marks of humanity were there none.

A large ash, apparently cut down years ago, with the branches still on it, was stretched somewhat out of the wood: on this I sat, lighted a cigar, and meditated on this characteristic specimen of Irish life. The sun was setting beautifully behind the trees, and its imperfect light through the foliage gave the unnatural ruin a still stronger appearance of death and decay, and brought into my mind thoughts of the wrong, oppression, misery, and despair, to which some one had been subjected by what I saw before me.

I had not been long seated, when four or five ragged boys and girls came through the wood, driving a lot of geese along one of the paths. When they saw me, they all came up and stood round me, as if wondering what I could be. I could learn nothing from them—the very poor Irish children will never speak to you; but a middle aged man soon followed them. He told me the place was called Ballycloran: "he did not know who it belonged to; a gintleman in Dublin recaved the rints, and a very stiff gintleman he was too; and hard it was upon them to pay two pound tin an acre for the garden there, and that half covered with the ould house and the bricks and rubbish, only on behalf of the bog that was convaynient, and plinty of the timber, tho' that was rotten, and illigant outhouses for the pigs and the geese, and the ould bricks of the wall wor good manure for the praties" (this, in all my farming, I had never dreamt of); "but times was very hard on the poor, the praties being ninepence a stone in Carrick all last summer; God help the poor, the crayturs! for the gintlemin, their raal frinds, that should be, couldn't help thimselves now, let alone others"— and so on, now speaking of his sorrow and poverty, and again descanting on the "illigance" of his abode. I could only learn that a family called the Macdermots had lived there some six or seven years back, that they were an unfortunate people, he had heard tell, but he had not been in the country then, and it was a bloody story, &c. &c. &c. The evening was drawing on, and the time for my coach to come was fast approaching; so I was obliged to leave Ballycloran, unsatisfied as to its history, and to return to Drumsna.

Here I had no time to make further inquiries, as Mr. Hartley's servants always keep their time; and very shortly the four horses clattered down the hill into the village. I got up behind, for McC—, the guard, was an old friend of mine; and after the usual salutations and strapping of portmanteaus, and shifting down into places, as McC— knows everything, I began to ask him if he knew anything of a place called Ballycloran.

"'Deed then, Sir, and I do," said he, "and good reason have I to know; and well I knew those that lived in it, ruined, and black, and desolate, as Ballycloran is now:" and between Drumsna and Boyle, he gave me the heads of the following story. And, reader, if I thought it would ever be your good fortune to hear the history of Ballycloran from the guard of the Boyle coach, I would recommend you to get it from him, and shut my book forthwith.

CHAPTER II.

THE MACDERMOT FAMILY.

McC—'s story runs thus. About sixty years ago, a something Macdermot, true Milesian, pious Catholic, and descendant of king somebody, died somewhere, having managed, through all the troubles of his poor country, to keep a comfortable little portion of his ancestors' royalties to console him for the loss of their sceptre. He having two sons, and disdaining to make anything but estated gentlemen of them, made over in some fictitious manner (for in those righteous days a Roman Catholic could make no legal will) to his eldest, the estate on which he lived, and to the youngest, that of Ballycloran—about six hundred as bad acres as a gentleman might wish to call his own. But Thaddeus, otherwise Thady Macdermot, being an estated gentleman, must have a gentleman's residence on his estate, and the house of Ballycloran was accordingly built. Had Thady Macdermot had ready money, it might have been well built; but though an estated gentleman, he had none. He had debts even when his father died; and though he planned, ordered, and agreed for a house, such as he thought the descendant of a Connaught Prince might inhabit without disgrace, it was ill built, half finished, and paid for by long bills. This, however, is so customary in poor Ireland that it but little harassed Thady. He had a fine, showy house, with stables, &c., gardens, an avenue, and a walk round his demesne; and his neighbours had no more. It was little he cared for comfort, but he would not be the first of the Macdermots that would not be respectable. When his house was finished, Thady went into County Galway, and got himself a wife with two thousand pounds fortune, for which he had to go to law with his brother-in-law. The lawsuit, the continual necessity of renewing the bills with which the builder in Carrick on Shannon every quarter attacked him, the fruitless endeavour to make his tenants pay thirty shillings an acre for half-reclaimed bog, and a somewhat strongly developed aptitude for potheen, sent poor Thady to another world rather prematurely, and his son and heir, Lawrence, came to the throne at the tender age of twelve. The Galway brother-in-law compromised the lawsuit; the builder took a mortgage on the property from the boy's guardian; the mother gave new leases to the tenants; Larry went to school at Longford; and Mrs. Mac kept up the glory of Ballycloran.

At the age of twenty, Lawrence, or Larry, married a Milesian damsel, portionless, but of true descent. The builder from Carrick had made overtures about a daughter he had at home, and offered poor Larry his own house, as her fortune. But the blood of the Macdermots could not mix with the lime and water that flowed in a builder's veins; he therefore made an enemy where he most wanted a friend, and brought his wife home to live with his mother. In order that we may quickly rid ourselves of encumbrances, it may be as well to say that during the next twenty-five years his mother and wife died; he had christened his only son Thaddeus, after his grandfather, and his only daughter had been christened Euphemia, after her grandmother. He had never got over that deadly builder, with his horrid percentage coming out of the precarious rents; twice, indeed, had writs been out against him for his arrears, and once he had received notice from Mr. Hyacinth Keegan, the oily attorney of Carrick, that Mr. Flannelly meant to foreclose. Rents were greatly in arrear, his credit was very bad among the dealers in Mohill, with Carrick he had no other dealings than those to which necessity compelled him with Mr. Flannelly the builder, and Larry Macdermot was anything but an easy man.

Thady was at this time about twenty-four. As had been the case with his father, he had been educated at a country school; he could read and write, but could do little more : he was brought up to no profession or business; he acted as his father's agent over the property—by which I mean to signify that he occupied himself in harrowing the tenantry for money which they had no means of paying; he was occasionally head driver and ejector; and he considered, as Irish landlords are apt to do, that he had an absolute right over the tenants, as feudal vassals. Still, they respected and to a certain extent loved him; "for why? wasn't he the masther's son, and wouldn't he be the masther hisself?" And he had a regard, perhaps an affection, for the poor creatures; against any one else he would defend them; and would they but coin their bones into pounds, shillings, and pence, he would have been as tender to them as a man so nurtured could be. With all his faults, Thady was perhaps a better man than his father; he was not so indomitably idle; had he been brought up to anything, he would have done it; he was more energetic, and felt the degradation of his position; he felt that his family was sinking lower and lower daily; but as he knew not what to do, he only became more gloomy and more tyrannical. Beyond this, he had acquired a strong taste for tobacco, which he incessantly smoked out of a dhudheen; and was content to pass his dull life without excitement or pleasure.

Euphemia, or Feemy, was about twenty; she was a tall, dark girl, with that bold, upright, well-poised figure, which is so peculiarly Irish. She walked as if all the blood of the old Irish Princes was in her veins : her step, at any rate, was princely. Feemy, also, had large, bright brown eyes, and long, soft, shining dark hair, which was divided behind, and fell over her shoulders, or was tied with ribands; and she had a well-formed nose, as all coming of old families have; and a bright olive complexion, only the olive was a little too brown, the skin a little too coarse; and then Feemy's mouth was, oh! half an inch too long; but her teeth were white and good, and her chin was well turned and short, with a dimple on it large enough for any finger Venus might put there. In all, Feemy was a fine girl in the eyes of a man not too much accustomed to refinement. Her hands were too large and too red, but if Feemy got gloves sufficient to go to mass with, it was all she could do in that way; and though Feemy had as fine a leg as ever bore a pretty girl, she was never well shod,—her shoes were seldom clean, often slipshod, usually in holes; and her stockings—but no! I will not further violate the mysteries of Feemy's wardrobe. But if the beautiful girls of this poor country knew but half the charms which neatness has, they would not so often appear as poor Feemy too usually appeared.

Like her brother, she was ardent and energetic, if she had aught to be ardent about; she was addicted to novels, when she could get them from the dirty little circulating library at Mohill; she was passionately fond of dancing, which was her chief accomplishment; she played on an old spinnet which had belonged to her mother; and controlled the motions and actions of the two barefooted damsels who officiated as domestics at Ballycloran.

Such was the family at Ballycloran in the summer of 183—, and though not perfect, I hope they have charms enough to make a further acquaintance not unacceptable.

CHAPTER III.

THE TENANTRY OF BALLYCLORAN.

"THADY," said old Macdermot, as he sat eating stirabout and thick milk, over a great turf fire, one morning about the beginning of October, "Thady, will you be getting the money out of them born divils this turn, and they owing it, some two, some three years this November, bad cess to them for tenants? Thady, I say," shouted, or rather screamed, the old man, as his son continued silently eating his breakfast, "Thady, I say; have they the money, at all at all, any of them; or is it stubborn they are? There's Flannelly and Keegan with their d—d papers and bills and costs; will you be making out the £142 7s. 6d. before Christmas for the hell-hounds; or it's them 'll be masters in Ballycloran? Then let the boys see the landlord they'll have over them, that time!"

"Well, Larry," said the son (unless in a passion, he always called his father by his baptismal name, or rather by its abbreviation), "what's the use going on that way before the girls there, and Feemy too." Feemy, however, was reading the "Mysterious Assassin," and paying little heed to her father's lamentations. "When we're done, and the things is out, we'll have a look at the rent-book, and send for the boys to come in; and if they haven't it, why, Pat Brady must go round agin, and see what he can do with the potatoes and oats, and the pigs; but the times, Larry, is very hard on them; too hard entirely, so it is, poor things—"

"Poor things!" said the father, "and aint I a poor thing? and won't you and Feemy be poor things? Hard times, too! who is the times hardest on? See that sneaking ould robber, Flannelly, that cozened my father—good father for him—with such a house as this, that's falling this day over his son's head, and it not hardly fifty years built, bad luck to it for a house! See that ould robber, Flannelly, who has been living and thriving on it for all them years, and a stone or stick not as good as paid for yet; and he getting two hundred a year off the land from the crayturs of tenants."

True enough it was, that Mr. Joe Flannelly, of Carrick-on-Shannon, whatever might have been the original charge of building the Ballycloran mansion, now claimed £200 a year from that estate, to which his ingenious friend and legal adviser, Mr. Hyacinth Keegan usually managed to add certain mysterious costs and ceremonious expenses, which made each half year's rent of Larry Macdermot's own house about £140, before the poor man had managed to scrape it together To add to this annoyance, Mr. Macdermot had continually before his eyes the time, which he could not but foresee was not distant, when this hated Flannelly would come down on the property itself, insist on being paid his principal, and probably not only sell, but buy, Ballycloran itself. And whither, then, would the Macdermots betake themselves?

Often and often did Larry, in his misfortunes, regret the slighted offers of Sally Flannelly's charms and cash. Oh, had he but then condescended to have married the builder's daughter, he would not now have been the builder's slave. But Sally Flannelly was now Sally Keegan, the wife of Hyacinth Keegan, Esq., Attorney; who, if he had not the same advantages as Larry in birth and blood, had compensation for his inferiority in cash and comforts. When the poor man thought of these things—and he did little else now but think of them—bitterly, though generally in silence, he cursed him whom he looked upon as his oppressor and incubus. It never occurred to him that if Mr. Flannelly built the house he lived in, he should be paid for it. He never reflected that he had lived to the extent of, and above his precarious income, as if his house had been paid for; that, instead of passing his existence in hating the Carrick tradesman, he should have used his industry in finding the means to pay him. He sometimes blamed his father, having an indefinite feeling that he ought not to have permitted Flannelly to have anything to do with Ballycloran, after building it; but himself he never blamed; people never do; it is so much easier to blame others,—and so much more comfortable. Mr. Macdermot thus regarded his creditor as a vulgar, low-born blood-sucker, who, having by chicanery obtained an unwarrantable hold over him, was determined, if possible, to crush him. The builder, on the other hand, who had spent a long life of constant industry, but doubtful honesty, in scraping up a decent fortune, looked on his debtor as one who gave himself airs to which his poverty did not entitle him; and was determined to make him feel that though he could not be the father, he could be the master of a "rale gintleman."

After the short conversation between father and son the breakfast passed over in silence. The father finished his stirabout, and turned round to the blazing turf, to find consolation there. Feemy descended into the kitchen, to scold the girls, give out the dinner,— if there was any to give out; and to do those offices, whatever they be, in performing which all Irish ladies, bred, born, and living in moderate country-houses, pass the first two hours after breakfast in the kitchen. Thady took his rent-book and went into an outhouse, which he complimented by the name of his office, at the door of which he was joined by Pat Brady. Now Pat was an appendage, unfortunately very necessary in Ireland to such an estate as Macdermot's; and his business was not only to assist in collecting the rents, by taking possession of the little crops, and driving the cows, or the pig; but he was, moreover, expected to know who could, and who could not, make out the money; to have obtained, and always have ready, that secret knowledge of the affairs of the estate, which is thought to be, and is so, necessary to the managing of the Irish peasantry in the way they are managed. Pat Brady was all this; moreover, he had as little compunction in driving the cow or the only pig from his neighbour or cousin, and in selling off the oats or potatoes of his uncle or brother-in-law, as if he was doing that which would be quite agreeable to them. But still he was liked on the estate; he had a manner with him which had its charms to them; he was a kind of leader to them in their agrarian feelings and troubles; and though the tenants of Ballycloran half feared, they all liked and courted Pat Brady.

The most remarkable feature in his personal appearance was a broken nose; not a common, ordinary broken nose, such as would give it an apparent partiality to the right or left cheek, nor such as would, by indenting it, give the face that good-natured look which Irish broken noses usually possess. Pat Brady's broken nose was all but flattened on to his face, as if it had never lifted its head after the fatal blow which had laid it low. He was strong-built, round-shouldered, bow-legged, about five feet six in height, and he had that kind of external respectability about him, which a tolerably decent hat, strong brogues, and worsted stockings give to a man, when those among whom he lives are without such luxuries. When I add to the above particulars that Pat was chief minister, adviser, and confidential manager in young Macdermot's affairs, I have said all that need be said. The development of his character must be left to disclose itself.

"Well, Pat," began his master, seating himself on the solitary old chair, which, with a still older looking desk on four shaking legs, comprised the furniture of Macdermot's rent-office, "what news from Mohill to-day? was there much in the fair at all?"

"Well, yer honor, then, for them as had money to buy, the fair was good enough; but for them as had money to get, it was as bad as them that wor afore it, and as them as is likely to come afther it."

"Were the boys in it, Pat?"

"They wor, yer honor, the most of 'em."

"Well, Pat?"

"Oh, they wor just there, that's all."

"Tim Brady should have got the top price for that oats of his, Pat."

"Maybe he might, Masther Thady."

"What did he get? there should be twelve barrels there."

"Eleven, or thereabouts, yer honor."

"Did he sell it all, yesterday?"

"Divil a grain, then, at all at all, he took to the fair yesterday."

"Bad manners to him, and why didn't he? why he owes" (and Thady turned over the old book) "five half years this gale, and there's no use gammoning; father must get the money off the land, or Flannelly will help himself."

"I knows, Masther Thady; I knows all about it. Tim has between five and six acres, and he owes twenty-two pound tin; his oats is worth, maybe, five pound fifteen,—from that to six pound, and his cow about six pound more; that's all Tim has, barring the brats and the mother of them. An' he knows right well, yer honor, if he brings you the price of the oats, you wouldn't let him off that way; for the cow should folly the oats, as is nathural; the cabin would be saized next; so Tim ses, if you choose to take the corn yourself, you can do so;—well an' good, and save him the throuble of bringin' it to Mohill."

"Did the widow Reynolds sell her pig?"

"She did, yer honor, for two pound tin."

"And she owes seven pound. And Dan Coulahan—"

"Dan didn't cut the oats, good or bad."

"I'll cut it for him, then. Was ould Tierney there?"

"He war, yer honor; and I was tellin' him yer honor 'id be wantin' the money this week, an' I axed him to stip up o' Friday mornin'; an', sis I, 'Misthur Tierney'—for since he made out the mare and the ould car, it's Misthur Tierney he goes by—'it's a fine saison any way for the corn,' sis I, 'the Lord be praised; an' the hay all saved on thim illigant bottoms of yours, Misthur Tierney. The masther was glad to hear the cocks was all up afore the heavy rain was come.' 'Well, Pat,' sis he, 'I'll be at Ballycloran o' Friday, plase God, but it's little I'll have with me but myself; an' if the masthur likes the corn an' the hay, he may just take them av' it's plazin' to him, for the divil a cock or grain will I sell, an' the prices so bad.'"

"Obstinate ould fool! why, Pat, he must have the money."

"Money, to be shure he has the money, Misthur Thady; but maybe he'd be the bigger fool if he gave it to your father."

"Do the boys mane to say they won't pay the rent at all?"

"They mane to say they can't; an' it's nearly thrue for them."

"Was Joe Reynolds at the fair, Pat?"

"He wor not; that's to say, he wor not at the fair, but I seen him in the evening, with the other boys from Drumleesh, at Mrs. Mulready's."

"Them boys has always the money when they want a drop of whiskey. By dad, if they go to Mulready's with the money in their pockets on a Tuesday, where's the wonder they come here with them empty on a Friday? Fetch me a coal for the pipe, Pat."

Whilst Pat walked into the kitchen for a lighted piece of turf (*Hibernice*, coal) to kindle his patron's pipe, Thady stuck the said pipe in his jaw, and continued poring over the unsatisfactory figures of the Ballycloran rent-book.

"I tell you what it is, Pat," said he, after finishing the process of blowing, and drawing, and throwing the coal on the earthen floor, and pressing down the hot burning tobacco with the top of his forefinger repeatedly, "Misthur Joe Reynolds will out of that. I told him so last April, and divil a penny of his we've seen since; he don't do the best he can for us; and my belief is, he hinders the others; eh, Brady?" and he looked up into Brady's face for confirmation or refutation of this opinion. But that gentleman, contrary to his usual wont, seemed to have no opinion on the matter; he continued scratching his head, and swinging one leg, while he stood on the other. Thady, finding that his counsellor said nothing, continued,

"Joe Reynolds will out of that this time, d'you hear? what has he on that bit of land of his?"

"Pratees mostly, Misthur Thady. He had half an acre of whate; he parted that on the ground to ould Tierney; he owed Tierney money."

"An' so the tenants buy the crops from one another, and yet won't pay their own rents. Well, my father's to blame himself; av he'd put a man like Keegan over them, or have let the land to some rough hand as would make them pay, divil a much he need care for Flannelly this day."

"An' you'd be for puttin' a stranger over thim, Misthur Thady; an' they that would stand between you an' all harum, or the masthur, or the old masthur afore him; becaze of the dirthy money, and becaze a blagguard and a black ruffian like Flannelly has an ould paper signed by the masthur, or the like? An' as for Mr. Hyacinth Keegan,—I'm thinking, the first time he goes collectin' on the lands of Drumleesh, it's a warm welcome he'll be gettin'; at any rate, he'd have more recates in his carcass than in his pocket, that day."

"That's very fine talk, Pat; but if Keegan had them, he'd tame them, as he has others before; not but I'd be sorry they should be in his hands, the robber, bad as they are. But it'll come to that, whether or no. How's my father to get this money for Flannelly?"

"D—n Flannelly!" was Brady's easy solution of the family difficulties. "Let him take the house he built, and be d—d to him; and if we can't build a betther one for the masthur and Miss Feemy and you, without his help, may praties choke me!"

"By dad, if he'd take the house, and leave the ground, he's my welcome, and ceade mille faltha, Pat. But the land will stick to the house; and mark me, when ould Flannelly dies (an' the divil die along with him), Mr. Keegan of Carrick will write himself, Hyacinth Keegan, Esquire, of Ballycloran."

"May I nivir see that day, an' he an' I alive, amen," said Brady, as he crossed himself in sign of the sacred truth of his wish; "but I think, Misthur Thady, when you come to consider of it, you'll find plenty of manes of keepin' Mr. Keegan and Mrs. Keegan out of the parlour of Ballycloran. But about Joe Reynolds, yer honor was sayin'—"

"I was saying that divil another potato he should dig in

Drumleesh, nor another grain of corn shall he sow or rape; that's what I was saying."

"Well, Misthur Thady, you're the masthur, thank God, an' if you say so, it must be done. But Joe Reynolds is not that bad either: he was sayin' tho' at Mrs. Mulready's that he expected little from yer honor, but just leave to go where he liked, and lave the cow and the praties behind him."

"What wor they saying at Mulready's, Pat?"

"They were only jist passin' their remarks, yer honor, about how thick you war this time back with Captain Ussher; an' Miss Feemy too, an' the masthur; an' that when the likes of him wor as one of the family, it's little the likes of them would be gettin' now from Ballycloran, only hard words, and maybe a help to Carrick Gaol."

"Because Captain Ussher visits at Ballycloran, is that any reason why he should interfere between my father and his tenants?"

"Sorra a one av me knows then, Misthur Thady; only that the tenants is no good frinds to the Captain; nor why should they, an' he going through the counthry with a lot of idle blagguards, with arms, an' guns, sazin' the poor divils for nothin' at all, only for thryin' to make out the rint for yer honor, with a thrifle of potheen? That's quare friendship; ay, an' it's the truth I'm tellin' you, Misthur Thady, for he's no frind to you or yours. Shure isn't Pat Reynolds in Ballinamore Bridewell on his account, an' two other boys from the mountains behind Drumleesh, becaze they found a thrifle of half malted barley up there among them? an' be the same token, Joe was sayin', if the frind of the family war parsecuting them that way, an' puttin' his brother in gaol, whilst the masthur wouldn't rise a finger, barrin' for the rint, the sooner he an' his were off the estate, the betther he'd like it; for Joe sed he'd not be fightin' agin his own masthur, but whin you war not his masthur any more,—then let every one look to hisself."

Whilst Brady was giving this short *exposé* of the feelings displayed at the little whiskey shop in Mohill on the previous fair day, young Macdermot was pulling hard at the dhudheen, as if trying to hide his embarrassment in smoke. Brady paused for some time, and then added,

"Joe mostly leads those boys up at Drumleesh, an' hard to lead they are; I'm thinking Captain Ussher, with all his revenue of peelers an' his guns, may meet his match there yit. They'll hole him, av he goes on much farthur, as shure as my name's Pat."

"They'll get the worst of that, Brady—not that I care a thrawneen for him and his company. It's true for you; he is persecuting them too far; what with revenue police, constabulary police, and magistrates' warrants, they won't let them walk to mass quietly next. I didn't care what they did to Master Myles, but they'd have the worst of it in the end."

"And it's little you ought to care for the same Captain, Misthur Thady, av you heard all. It's little he's making of Miss Feemy's name with the police captain, and the young gauger, and young James Fitzsimon, when they're over there at Ballinamore together —and great nights they have of it too; though they all have it in Mohill he's to marry Miss Feemy. If so, indeed! but then isn't he a black Protestant, sorrow take them for Protestants! There's Hyacinth Keegan calls himself a Protestant now; his father warn't ashamed of the ould religion, when he sarved processes away to Drumshambo."

"And what wor the gentlemen saying about Feemy, Pat?"

"Oh, yer honor, how could I know what gentlemin is saying over their punch, together? only they do be sayin' in Ballinamore, that the Captain doesn't spake that dacently of Miss Feemy, as if they wor to be man and wife: sorrow blister his tongue the day he'd say a bad word of her!"

"Faith he'd better take care of himself, if it's my sister he's playing his game with; he'll find out, though there aint much to be got worth having at Ballycloran now, as long as there's a Macdermot in it, he may still get the traitment a blackguard desarves, if he plays his tricks with Feemy!"

Pat saw that his object had been gained; he suspected that no warm feelings of friendship existed in his master towards the aforesaid Captain, and he was determined there should be none if he could help it. He was not wrong in his surmises; for, from the constant visits of Myles Ussher to Ballycloran, people had for some time been saying that he meant to marry Feemy. They now began to say that he ought to do so.

While her brother and his minister are discussing that subject, and others—settling who could pay, or who should pay, at the convocation of the tenants to be held on the coming Friday, and who couldn't, and who should be ejected, and who not—we will obtain a little insight into Captain Ussher's affairs, and account for the residence of so gallant a gentleman in the little town of Mohill.

CHAPTER IV.

MYLES USSHER.

EVERY one knows that Ireland, for her sins, maintains two distinct, regularly organised bodies of police; the duties of the one being to prevent the distillation of potheen or illicit whiskey, those of the other to check the riots created by its consumption. These forces, for they are in fact military forces, have each their officers, sub-officers, and privates, as the army has; their dress, full dress, and half dress; their arms, field arms, and house arms; their barracks, stations, and military regulations; their captains, colonels, and commander-in-chief, but called by other names; and, in fact, each body is a regularly disciplined force, only differing from the standing army by being carried on in a more expensive manner.

The first of these—that for preventing the distillation of potheen, commonly called the revenue police—was, at the time of our story, honoured by the services of Myles Ussher. He held the office of one of the sub-inspectors in the county of Leitrim, and he resided in the town of Mohill; he had a body of about five-and-twenty men under him, with a sergeant; and his duty was, as I have before said, to prevent the distillation of potheen. This was only to be done by seizing it when made, or in the process of making; and, as a considerable portion of the fine levied in all cases possible from the dealers in the trade, became the perquisite of the sub-inspector or officer effecting the seizure, the situation in a wild lawless district was one of considerable emolument; consequently gentlemen of repute and good family were glad to get their sons into the service, and at the present time, a commission in the revenue police is considered, if not a more fashionable, at any rate a more lucrative appointment than a commission in the army. Among these officers some of course would be more active than others, and would consequently make more money; but it will be easily imagined, that however much the activity of a sub-inspector of revenue police might add to his character and standing at head-quarters, it would not be likely to make him popular in the neighbourhood in which he resided.

Myles Ussher was most active in the situation which he filled; whether an impartial judge would have said that he was too much so, would be a question difficult to settle, as I have no impartial judge on the subject to whom I can refer; but the persons among whom he lived thought that he was. At the time I allude to, about ten years ago, a great deal of whiskey was distilled in the mountains running between the counties of Leitrim and Cavan, and in different parts of the County Leitrim. Father Mathew's pledge was then unknown; the district is a wild country, not much favoured by gentlemen's residences, and very poor; and, though it may seem to be an anomaly, it will always be found to be the case that the poorer the people are the more they drink; and, consequently, Captain Ussher, as he was usually called in the neighbourhood, found sufficient occupation for himself and his men.

Now the case is different; the revenue police remain, but their duties have, in most districts, gone; and they may be seen patrolling the roads with their officers accompanying them, being bound to walk so many miles a day. It is very seldom one hears of their effecting a seizure, and their inactivity is no doubt owing to the prevalence of Father Mathew's pledge of total abstinence.

Myles Ussher was a Protestant, from the County Antrim in the north of Ireland, the illegitimate son of a gentleman of large property, who had procured him the situation which he held; he had been tolerably well educated; that is, he could read and write sufficiently, understood somewhat of the nature of figures, and had learnt, and since utterly forgotten, the Latin grammar. He had natural abilities somewhat above par; was good-looking, strongly made, and possessed that kind of courage, which arises more from animal spirits, and from not having yet experienced the evil effects of danger, than from real capabilities of enduring its consequences. Myles Ussher had never yet been hit in a duel, and would therefore have no hesitation in fighting one; he had never yet been seriously injured in riding, and would therefore ride any horse boldly; he had never had his head broken in a row, and therefore would readily go into one; he cared little for bodily pain if it did not incapacitate him,—little at least for any pain he had as yet endured, and his imagination was not strong enough to suggest any worse evil. And this kind of courage, which is the species by far most generally met with, was sufficient for the life he had to lead.

But the quality in which Ussher chiefly excelled, and which was most conducive to give him the character which he certainly held in the country for courage, talent, and gallantry, was his self-confidence and assurance. He believed himself inferior to none in powers of body and mind, and that he could accomplish whatever he perseveringly attempted. He had, moreover, an overwhelming contempt for the poor, amongst whom his duties so constantly brought him, and it is not therefore wonderful that he was equally feared and execrated by them. I should also state that Myles Ussher had had sagacity enough to keep some of the money which he had received, and this added not a little both to his reputation and standing in the country, and also to the real power which he possessed; for in Connaught ready money is scarce, and its scarcity creates its importance.

This, then, was Feemy's lover, and she certainly did love him dearly; he had all the chief ornaments of her novel heroes—he was handsome, he carried arms, was a man of danger, and talked of deeds of courage; he wore a uniform; he rode more gracefully, talked more fluently, and seemed a more mighty personage, than any other one whom Feemy usually met. Besides, he gloried in the title of Captain, and would not that be sufficient to engage the heart of any girl in Feemy's position? let alone any Irish girl, to whom the ornaments of arms are always dear. But whether he loved her as truly, might, I fear, be considered doubtful; if so, why were they not married?

Larry Macdermot was too broken-hearted a man, and too low-spirited, to have objected to Myles on the ground of his being a Protestant: it was not that he was indifferent about his religion, but he had not heart enough left to be energetic on any subject. In other respects, Myles was more than a match for his daughter, in the present fallen condition of the family. But the matter had not even been mentioned to him by his daughter or her lover. Ussher was constantly at Ballycloran,—was in the habit of riding over from Mohill, only three miles, almost daily, when disengaged, giving his horse to Patsy, the only male attendant at Ballycloran, and staying the whole morning, or the evening, there, without invitation; and Larry, if he never seemed particularly glad, at any rate never evinced any dislike to his visits.

Whatever war the sub-inspector might wage against run spirits in the mountains and bogs, he always appeared on good terms with it at Ballycloran, and as the Macdermots had but little else to give in the way of hospitality, this was well.

Young Thady could not but see that his sister was attached to Ussher; but he knew that she could not do better than marry him, and if he considered much about it, he thought that she was only taking her fun out of it, as other girls did, and that it would all come right. Thady was warmly attached to his sister; he had had no one else really to love; he was too sullen at his prospects, too gloomy from his situation, to have chosen for himself any loved one on whom to expend his heart; he was of a disposition too saturnine, though an Irishman, to go and look for love when it did not fall in his way, and all that he had to give he gave to his sister. But it must be remembered that poor Thady had no refinement; how should he? And though he would let no one injure Feemy if he could help it, he hardly knew how effectually to protect her. His suspicions were now aroused by his counsellor Pat Brady; but the effect was rather to create increased dislike in him against Ussher, than to give rise to any properly concerted scheme for his sister's welfare.

On the evening previous to the fair at Mohill mentioned in the last chapter, Captain Ussher with a party of his men had succeeded in making a seizure of some half-malted barley in a cabin on the margin of a little lake on the low mountains, which lay between Mohill and Cashcarrigan. He had, as in these cases was always his practice, received information from a spy in his pay, who accompanied him, dressed as one of his own men, to prevent any chance of his being recognised; this man's name was Cogan, and he had been in the habit of buying illicit whiskey from the makers at a very cheap rate, and carrying it round to the farmers' houses and towns for sale, whereby he obtained considerable profit,—but at considerable risk. With this employment Captain Ussher had made himself acquainted, and instead of seizing the man whilst in possession of the whiskey, he had sounded him, and finding him sufficiently a villain, had taken him into his pay as a spy; this trade Cogan found more lucrative even than the former, but also more dangerous; as if detected he might reckon on his death as certain. He still continued to buy the spirits from the people, but in smaller quantities; he offered lower prices; and though he nominally kept up the trade, it was more for the purpose of knowing where the potheen was, than of buying and selling it.

It was not wonderful therefore that more seizures than ever had been lately made, and that the men were getting more cautious, and at the same time more irate and violent in their language. In the present instance the party had come on the cabin in question unawares; not that they might not have been noticed, but that the people were confident of not being suspected. No whiskey had been run there; and the barley had only lately been brought in turf kishes from another cabin where it was not thought to be safe.

Three men and an old woman were found in the cabin when Captain Ussher entered with three of his own men. On being questioned they denied the existence of either whiskey, malt, or barley; but on searching, the illicit article was found in the very kishes in which it had been brought; they were easily discovered shoved into the dark chimney corner farthest from the door.

"Dat I may never see the light," began the old woman, " if I thought it wor anything but the turf, and jist the kishes that Barney Smith left there, the morn; and he to say nothing of the barley, and bring all these throubles on me and yer honer,—the like of him, the spalpeen!"

"Never mind my trouble, my dear," said Ussher; "it is little we think of the trouble of casing you; and who's Barney Smith, ma'am?"

"Oh, then, Barney's jist my daughter's own son; and he coming down from the mountains with turf, and said he must lave the kishes here, till he just went back round Loch Sheen with the ass, he'd borrowed from Paddy Byrne, and he'd be—"

"And very good natured it was of him to leave you the malt instead of the turf; and who are you, my good men?"

The men had continued smoking their pipes quietly at the fire without stirring.

"We be sthrangers here, yer honer," said one; "that is, not sthrangers jist, but we don't live here, yer honer."

"Where do you live, and what's your names?"

"I and Joe Smith live down away jist on the road to Cash, about half a mile out of this; and Tim Reynolds, he lives away at Drumleesh, on Mr. Macdermot's land; and my name's Paddy Byrne."

"Oh, oh; so one of you is father of the lad who brought the donkey, and the other the owner of it; and you neither of you knew what was in the kishes."

"Sorrow a know, yer honer; ye see Barney brought them down here from the mountains when we warn't in it; and it war some of the boys up there was getting him to get away the malt unknownst, hearing of yer honer, maybe."

"Ah, yes I see—whose land is this on?"

"Counseller Webb's, yer honer."

"Who holds the cabin and potato garden?"

"I do, your honer, jist for my wife's mother, ye see; but I live down towards Cash."

"Ah, very good-natured of you to your wife's mother. I hope the three of you have no objection to take a walk to Mohill this evening."

"Ochone, ochone, and it's ruined we'll be, yer honer; and that I may never see the light if the boys knew it; and yer honer wouldn't have the death of an ould woman on ye!" the old woman was exclaiming, while the police began seizing the malt and making prisoners of the men.

"Carol, see and get an ass to put these kishes on," said Ussher. "Killeen, pass a rope across these fellows' arms; I suppose they'll go quiet."

It was now full time for the men to arise when they found that the rope was to be fastened across their arms; which meant that a rope was to be fastened on the right arm of one, passed behind his back, fastened to the arm of the second, and so behind his back to the third. Smith and Byrne, the former of whom in spite of his protestations to the contrary was the inhabitant of the cabin, had given the matter up as lost; but as the other, Tim Reynolds, did in fact reside at Drumleesh, he thought he might still show some cause why he should not be arrested for visiting his friend Joe Smith.

"Yer honer won't be afther taking an innocent boy like me," began Tim, "that knows nothing at all at all about it. Shure yer honer knows the masther, Mr. Thady down at Ballycloran; he will tell yer honer I'd nothing in life to do in it. Then don't you know yourself I live with Joe Reynolds down at Drumleesh, and war only up here jist gagging with the ould woman and the boys, and knew nothing in life—how could I?—about the malt, Captain Ussher."

"Oh no, Mr. Reynolds, of course you could not; how could you, as you justly observe,—particularly being the brother of that inoffensive character Mr. Joe Reynolds, and you living too on Mr. Macdermot's property. You and your brother never ran whiskey at Drumleesh, I suppose. Why should a tenant of the Macdermots escape any more than one of Counsellor Webb's?"

"No, yer honer, in course not; only you being so thick with the masther, and that like; and av he'd spake a good word for me—as why shouldn't he?—and I knowing nothing at all at all about it, perhaps yer honer—"

"I'm sorry, Mr. Reynolds, I cannot oblige you in this little matter, but that's not the way I do business. Come along, Killeen; hurry, it's getting d—d cold here by the water."

With this Captain Ussher walked out of the cabin, and the two men followed, each having an end of the rope. Smith and Byrne followed doggedly, but silently; but poor Reynolds, though no lawyer, could not but feel that he was unjustly treated.

"And will I go to gaol then, jist for coming up to see ould widow Byrne, Captain?"

"Yes, Mr. Reynolds, as far as I can foresee, you will."

"Then, Captain Ussher, it's you'll be sorry for the day you were trating that way an innocent boy that knows nothing at all at all about it."

"Do you mean to be threatening me, you ruffian?"

"No, Captain Ussher, I doesn't threaten you, but there is them as does; and it's this day's work, or this night's that's all the same, will be the black night work to you. It's the like of you that makes ruffians of the boys about; they isn't left the manes of living, not even of getting the dhry pratees; and when they tries to make out the rint with the whiskey, which is not for themselves but for them as is your own friends, you hunts them through the mountains and bogs like worried foxes; and not that only; but for them as does it, and them as does not be doing it, is all the same; and it's little the masther, or, for the like of that, the masther's daughter either, will be getting from being so thick with sich as you,— harrowing and sazing his tenants jist for your own fun and divarsion. Mind I am not threatening you, Captain Ussher, but it's little good you or them as is in Ballycloran will be getting for the work you're now doing—What are you pulling at, misther? D'ye think I can't walk av myself, without your hauling and pulling like a gossoon at a pig's hind leg."

The last part of Tim's eloquence was addressed to the man who held the foremost end of the rope, and who was following his officer at a rapid pace.

Captain Ussher made no further answer to his remonstrating prisoner, but marched on rapidly towards Carrick after the advanced party, with whom was Cogan the informer. He, after having pointed out the cabin, of course did not wait to be recognised by its occupiers. This capture was the subject of the discussion held on the fair-day at Mulready's whiskey-shop in Mohill, at which Joe Reynolds the prisoner's brother had presided, as Brady informed Thady Macdermot,—or at any rate had taken the most noisy part. To tell the truth, our friend Pat himself had been present all the evening at Mulready's, and if he did not talk so loud, he had said full as much as Joe. The latter was naturally indignant at the capture of his brother, who, in fact, at the time was living in his cabin, though he did hold an acre or two of ground in the same town-land as Joe Smith and the widow Byrne. He was not, however, engaged in the potheen making there; and though at the moment of the entrance of the police, the party were all talking of the malt, which had, in fact, been brought from Byrne's cabin to that of his mother and brother-in-law, Reynolds had really nothing to do with the concern.

His known innocence made the party more indignant, and they consequently swore that among them they'd put an end to our poor friend Ussher, or as Joe Reynolds expressed it, " we'll hole him till there ar'nt a bit left in him to hole." Now, for the benefit of the ignorant, I may say that, " holing a man," means putting a bullet through him.

The injuries done by the police were not, however, the only subject discussed at Mulready's that night.

Ribbonism, about 183—, was again becoming very prevalent in

parts of Ireland, at any rate so said the stipendiary magistrates and the inspectors of police ; and if they said true, County Leitrim was full of ribbonmen, and no town so full as Mohill. Consequently the police sub-inspector at Ballinamore, Captain Greenough, had his spies as well as Captain Ussher, and Joe Reynolds was a man against whom secret information had been given. Joe was aware that he was a marked man, and consequently, if not actually a ribbonman, was very well inclined to that or anything else, which might be inimical to gaols, policemen, inspectors, gaugers, or any other recognised authority; in fact, he was a reckless man, originally rendered so by inability to pay high rent for miserably bad land, and afterwards becoming doubly so from having recourse to illegal means to ease him of his difficulties.

He, and many others in the neighbourhood of Mohill somewhat similarly situated, had joined together, bound themselves by oaths, and had determined to become ribbonmen ; their chief objects, however, at present, were to free themselves from the terrors of Captains Ussher and Greenough, and to prevent their landlords ejecting them for non-payment of rent. It would be supposed a man of Pat Brady's discernment, station, and character, would not have wished to belong to, or have been admitted by, so desperate a society ; but he, nevertheless, was not only of them, but one of their leaders, and it can only be supposed that "he had his rasons."

All these things were fully talked over at Mulready's that night. The indignities offered to humanity by police of every kind, the iniquities of all Protestants, the benefits likely to accrue to mankind from an unlimited manufacture of potheen, and the injustice of rents, were fully discussed ; on the latter head certainly Brady fought the battle of his master, and not unsuccessfully ; but not on the head that he had a right to his own rents, but what he was to do about Flannelly, if he did not get them.

"And shure, boys, what would the ould masther do, and what would Mr. Thady do without the rint among ye,—an' ould Flannelly dunning about him with his bonds, and his bills and morgidges? How'd ye like to see the good ould blood that's in it now, driven out by the likes of Flannelly and Keegan, and them to be masthers in Ballycloran ? "

"That's all very well, Pat, and we'd be sorry to see harum come to Mr. Larry and the young masther along of such born robbers as them ; but is them dearer to us than our own flesh and blood ? As long as they and the like of them'd stand between us and want, the divil a Keegan of them all'd dare put a foot in Ballycloran. But who is it now rules all at Ballycloran ? Who, but that bloody robber, Ussher? They'd go through the country for him, the born ruffian,—may food choke him!—and he making little of them all the time. Bad manners to the like of him! they say he never called an honest woman his mother. Will I, Mr. Brady, be giving my blood for them, and he putting my brother in gaol, and all for sitting up warming his shins at Loch Sheen? No; may this be my curse if I do!" and Joe Reynolds swallowed a glass of whiskey; "and you may tell Mr. Thady, Pat, if he wants the boys to stick to him, let him stick to them, and not be helping a d—d ruffian to be dhriving the lives out of them he should befriend. And maybe he will want us, and that soon; and if he'll stick to us now, as his fathers always did, sure it's little he need be fearing Flannelly and Keegan. By G—, the first foot they set in Ballycloran they shall leave there for ever, if Thady Macdermot will help rid his father's land of that bloody ruffian."

"It's little Mr. Thady loves the Captain, Joe, and it's little he ever will, I think; however, you can come up, you know, on Friday, and say your own say about your brother, and the rint and all."

"And so I will come, Pat; but there's all the rint I have, and Mrs. Mulready, I think, 'll have the best part of that," and he jingled a few halfpence in his pocket. So ended the meeting previous to the conversation in Macdermot's rent-office.

CHAPTER V.

FATHER JOHN.

The Rev. John McGrath was priest of the parish of Drumsna at the time of which we write. This parish contains the post town of Drumsna and the country adjacent, including the town-land and demesne of Ballycloran. At this time the spacious chapel which now stands on the hill about two miles out of Drumsna had not been built, and Father John's chapel was situated on the road from Drumsna to Ballycloran. Near this he had built himself a small cottage in the quasi-Gothic style, for Father John was a man of taste; he rented also about twenty acres of land, half of this being on the Macdermots' estate.

The Rev. Mr. McGrath is destined to appear somewhat prominently in this history, and I must therefore be excused in giving a somewhat elaborate description of him.

He had been, like many of the present parish priests in Ireland, educated in France; he had been at college at St. Omer, and afterwards at Paris, and had officiated as a curé there; he had consequently seen more of French manners and society than usually falls to the lot of Irish theological students in that capital. He was, also, which is equally unusual, a man of good family, and from his early avocations was more fitted than is generally the case with those of his order, to mix in society. He possessed also very considerable talents, and much more than ordinary acquirements, great natural *bonhommie*, and perpetual good temper. He was a thorough French scholar, and had read the better portion of their modern literature. On leaving Paris he had gone to Rome on a begging expedition, to raise funds for building chapels in his own country, and there too he had been well received; and from thence he had returned to take possession of a populous parish in one of the very poorest parts of Ireland.

With all his acquirements, however, in many things Father John was little better than a child. Though his zeal had enabled him to raise money for the church, he could never keep any of his own; he had always his little difficulties, and though he sedulously strove to live within his income, and never really much outstripped it, he was always in want of money. He had built his house, and, unlike his neighbour, had managed to pay for it; but he was always in trouble about it; the rats were in the roof, and his flooring was all warped, and his windows would neither open nor shut, and the damp would get to his books. Therefore, though his cottage was, exteriorly, the prettiest house in his parish, interiorly, it was discomfort personified.

A more hospitable man than Father McGrath never lived even in Connaught; he took a look in at dinner time as a personal favour; and whatever might be the state of his larder, his heart was always full, and the emptiness of the former never troubled him. He had not the slightest shame at asking any one to eat potatoes and cold mutton. They all knew him, and what they were likely to get at his house, and if they did not choose, they need not come. Whoever did come had as good as he had himself. A more temperate man never lived; but he had as much pleasure in seeing another man drink a tumbler of punch, as any one else would in drinking it himself. He kept under his own bed a great stone jar, always, partly at least, full of whiskey of native manufacture; and though, were he alone, the jar would long have remained untouched, as it was, it very often had to be refilled. Tumblers he had only two; when his guests exceeded that, the tea-cups made their appearance, and he would naïvely tell his friends that he meant to buy tumblers when he got any money; but, heaven help them! if he got in debt, the people would never be paid.

His whole domestic arrangements were on a par: his crockery was of a most heterogeneous and scanty description; his furniture of the most common kind, put in bit by bit, as it was found indispensable. In two things only did Father John show his extravagance; in the first, too, his expenditure was only so to be called, in comparison with that of others round him, of the same profession. It was this—he was always dressed like a gentleman; Father John's black coat was always black, never rusty brown; his waistcoat, his trowsers, his garters, even shoes, the same; and not only did his clothes always look new, but they were always well made, as far as his figure would allow; his hat was neat, and his linen clean; his hands, too, were always clean, and, when he was from home, always gloved; even his steady cob, whom he called Paul (it was rumoured that he had called him St. Paul, but the bishop objected), together with his saddle and bridle, was always neat; this particular was nearly all that the polish of French society had left him, and those who are accustomed to see Irish priests will know that this peculiarity would be striking. His other expensive taste was that of books; he could not resist the temptation to buy books, books of every sort, from voluminous editions of St. Chrysostom to Nicholas Nicklebys and Charles O'Malleys; and consequently he had a great many. But alas! he had no book-shelves, not one; some few volumes, those of every day use, were piled on the top of one another in his little sitting-room; the others were closely packed in great boxes in different parts of the cottage—his bed-room, his little offertory, his parlour, and many in a little drawing-room, as he called it, but in which was neither chair nor table, nor ever appeared the sign of fire! No wonder the poor man complained the damp got to his books.

In all other respects Father John was a fair specimen of the Irish priesthood. He must have been an eloquent man, for he had been sent on different foreign missions to obtain money for building chapels by preaching sermons. But his appearance was anything but dignified; he was very short, and very fat, and had little or no appearance of neck; his face, however was intelligent; he had bright, small black eyes, a fine, high forehead, very white teeth, and short thick, curling, dark hair.

As I am on the subject of the church, I might as well say now that his curate, Father Cullen, was unlike him in everything but his zeal for the church. He was educated at Maynooth, was the son of a little farmer in the neighbourhood, was perfectly illiterate, —but chiefly showed his dissimilarity to the parish priest by his dirt and untidiness. He was a violent politician; the Catholic Emancipation had become law, and he therefore had no longer that grievance to complain of; but he still had national grievances, respecting which he zealously declaimed, when he could find a hearer. Repeal of the Union was not, at that time, the common topic, morning and night, at work and at rest, at table and even at the altar, as it afterwards became; but there were, even then, some who maintained that Ireland would never be herself, till the Union was repealed; and among these was Father Cullen. He was as zealous for his religion as for his politics; and he could become tolerable intimate with no Protestant, without thinking he was specially called on to convert him. A disciple less likely to make converts than Father Cullen it would be difficult to imagine, seeing that in language he was most violent and ungrammatical—in appearance most uncouth—in argument most unfair. He was impatient if any one spoke but himself. He relied in all such arguments on his power of proving logically that his own church was the true church, and as his education had been logical, he put all his arguments into syllogisms. If you could not answer him in syllogisms, he conceived that you must be, evidently to yourself, in the wrong, and that obstinacy alone prevented you from owning it. Father Cullen's redeeming point was his earnestness,—his reality; he had no humbug about him; whatever was there, was real; he had no possible appreciation for a joke, and he understood no ridicule. You might gull him, and dupe him for ever, he would never find you out; his heart and mind were full of the Roman Catholic church and of his country's wrongs; he could neither think nor speak of aught beside.

Ussher was the only Protestant whom this poor man was in the habit of meeting, and he was continually attempting to convert him; in which pursuit Ussher rather encouraged him with the purpose of turning him into ridicule.

Such were the spiritual guides of the inmates of Ballycloran and its neighbourhood.

On the Wednesday morning after the fair, Father John was sitting eating his breakfast in his little parlour, attending much more to a book on the table before him than to the large lumps of bread and butter which he unconsciously swallowed, when the old woman servant, Judy McCan, opened the door and said,

"Father John, plase, there's Denis McGovery wanting to see yer riverence, below then."

People in Connaught always call the hall, door, and passage "below," the parlour, or sitting-room, "above," though, in nine cases out of ten, they are on the same floor.

"Why, then, Judy," said Father John, with his mouth full, "bad manners to them; mayn't I eat a bit of breakfast in peace and quiet? There was I at the widow Byrne's all night, destroyed with the cold, and nothing the matter with her at last, and now I must lose my breakfast, as well as my sleep."

"It's nothing of that sort, I'm thinking, Father John, but Denis McGovery is afther going to get married, I hear."

"Oh," exclaimed Father John, "that's a horse of another colour; going to get married, is he? and why shouldn't he, and he able to support a wife? let him come in, Judy."

It will be remembered that the "above" and "below" in the priest's house were only terms of compliment, and, as Denis McGovery was standing in the hall,—that is, at the open door of the very room in which Judy McCan had been announcing his attendance,—he, of course, had heard what had passed; therefore, when Father John said "let him come in," he wanted no further introduction, but, thrusting himself just through the door, and taking hold of a scanty lock of hair on his forehead, by way of reverential salutation, he said, "Iss, yer honor."

Now, laconic as this was, it was intended to convey, and did convey, a full assent not only to Judy's assertion that he was "afther going to get married," but also to the priest's remark, that there was no good reason on earth why he shouldn't, seeing that he was able to support a family.

"Iss, yer honor," said Denis McGovery.

"Well, Denis—that'll do, Judy," meaning that Judy need not listen any longer, at any rate within the room—"so you are going to get married, are you?"

"Didn't Father Cullen say anything to your riverence about it, then?"

"Oh, yes, he did then; I didn't remember it just at first, when Judy mentioned your name."

"Iss, yer riverence; if ye plaze, I am going to be married."

The bridegroom in this case was a man about forty years of age, who seemed, certainly, never to have eaten the bread of idleness, for he was all gristle and muscle; nor had he; he was a smith living in Drumsna, and the reputed best shoer of horses in the neighbourhood; and consequently was, as the priest had said, able to maintain a family: in fact, Denis had the reputation of hoarded wealth, for it was said he had thirty or forty pounds in the Loan Fund Office at Carrick-on-Shannon. He was a hard-working, ill-favoured, saving man; but, as he was able to keep a comfortable home over a wife, he had no difficulty in getting one.

"Oh then it pleases me entirely, because you are the boy that's both able and willing to pay your clergyman respectably as you should—"

"In course, your riverence, though the likes of a poor boy like me hasn't much, I wouldn't not be married dacently, Father John; and in course I couldn't expect yer riverence to be doing it for nothing."

"For nothing indeed! Where would I be getting the coat on my back, and the roof over my head?—no, the poor themselves always make out something for me; and you, Denis, that are comfortable, would of course be sorry to set a bad example to those that are not so."

"Oh then, yer riverence is poking yer fun at me."

"No fun at all, Denis. If you that have the money don't pay your priest, who is to, I'd like to know. Fun indeed! no, but it's good earnest I'm talking; and if you have a character that you wish to support, and to give your children after you, it's now you should be looking to it."

Denis McGovery began twirling his hat round in his hand, and bending his knees, as if nonplussed. He had known well enough, beforehand, what the priest would say to him, and the priest too, what answer he would get. The question in these cases is, which would cajole the other the best, and of course the priest would have the best of it. This may seem odd to those who do not know the country; but did he not do so, the Roman Catholic clergyman could not get even the moderate remuneration which he does receive for his laborious services.

"Oh, yer riverence," continued Denis, attempting a grim smile, "you know it's the young woman, or her friends, as always pays the priest mostly."

"And who is the young woman, Denis; Betsy Cane, isn't it?"

"No, Father John," said Denis, blushing almost black through his dark skin; "it ain't Betsy."

"Not Betsy Cane! why she told me three weeks ago you were to be married to her."

"And so I was, yer riverence, only ye see for a mistake as happened."

"A mistake! Was it she made the mistake or you?"

"Why it warn't exactly herself thin as did it; it war her mother."

"Her mother made a mistake! What mistake did her mother make?"

"Along of the cow, yer riverence." Denis seemed very slow of explaining, and Father John began to be impatient.

"What cow, Denis? How did the mother's making a mistake about the cow prevent your marrying her daughter?"

"Why, yer riverence, then, if you'll let me, I'll jist explain the matter. Ould Betsy Cane—that's her mother you know—promised me the brown cow, yer riverence may know, as is in the little garden behint the cabin, for her dater's fortin; and says I to her, 'Well, may be she may be worth four pound tin, Mrs. Cane.' 'Four pound tin,' says she, 'Mr. McGovery; and you to know no better than that, and she to calve before Christmas! well then, four pound tin indeed,'—jist in that manner, yer riverence. Well then I looks at the cow, and she seemed a purty sort of a cow, and I agreed to the bargain, yer honer, purviding the cow turned out to be with calf. Well, yer honer, now it's no such thing, but it's sticking me she was entirely about the cow: so now she got the cow and her daughter both at home; and likely to for me."

"And so, Denis, you broke your promise, and refused to marry the girl you were engaged to, because a cow was not in calf?"

"No I didn't, yer honer; that is, I did refuse to marry the girl; why wouldn't I? But I didn't break my promise, becase I only promised, purviding—; and you see, Father John, they was only decaving me."

"Well, Denis; and who is it after all that you are going to have?"

"Well, then, it's jist Mary Brady."

"What! Pat Brady's sister is it?"

"Iss, yer honer."

"And is her cow really in the family way?"

"Now yer riverence 'll make a handle of that agin me!"

"Never mind, Denis, how I handle the cow, so long as you handle the calf; but has Mary a cow?"

"No, Father John, she aint got a cow then, as I knows on."

"Well, Denis, and what fortune are you to get? You are not the man would take a wife unless she brought something with her."

"Well then, it's only jist a pair of young pigs and a small thrifle of change."

"A trifle of change, eh! Then, Mr. McGovery, I take it, it wasn't only along of the mistake about a cow that you left poor Betsy Cane, but you found you could do better, I suppose."

"Well then, it might be jist a little of both; but you see, Father John, they war the first to decave me."

"Well, Denis, and when's the wedding to be?"

"Oh—then, to-morrow evening, if yer riverence plazes."

"What! so soon, Denis? Take care; perhaps after all Betsy Cane's cow may calve; see; would you be too much in a hurry after the pigs?"

"Sorrow to the tongue of me then that I tould yer riverence a word about it!"

"But what are you in such a hurry about? Won't the pigs do as well at Pat Brady's as they will down at Drumsna?"

"Why you see, Father John, after to-morrow is Friday, which wouldn't do for the two legs of mutton Pat brought from Carrick with him yesterday, and the fine ham, yer riverence, Mrs. McKeon, long life to her, has sent us up from Drumsna; and Saturday wouldn't shute at all, seeing the boys will mostly be dhrunk, which may be yer honer wouldn't like on the morning of the blessed Sabbath."

"Nor on any other morning. Can't they take their fun without getting drunk, like beasts? But drunk they'll be. of course. And why would not Monday do?"

"Why that's next week, yer riverence!"

"You've remained single all this time, and only jilted poor Betsy Cane last week; and are you so hot after Mary Brady that you can't wait till next Monday to be married? Or is it the pigs, Denis? Are you afraid Pat may change his mind about the pigs, as you did about the cow?"

"Oh, drat the cow now, Father McGrath! and will ye never be aisy with yer joke agin a poor boy? It was not about the pigs then, nor nothing of the kind, but jist that I heard as how, but—" and Denis began scratching his head—"yer honer 'll be after twisting what I'll be tellin' yer, and poking your fun at me."

"Not I, my boy; out with it. You know nothing goes farther with me."

"Then it war just this, yer riverence, as makes me so hurried about getting the thing done. I heard tell that Tom Ginty, the pig-jobber, has comed home to Dromod from where he was away tiv' Athlone; and they do be telling me, he brought a thrifle of money with him; and yer honer knows Mary had half given a promise to Ginty afore he went; and so, yer riverence, lest there be any scrimmage betwixt Ginty and I, ye see it's as well to get the marriage done off hand."

"Oh yes, I see; you were afraid Tom Ginty would be taking Mary Brady's pigs to Athlone. That was it, was it?"

"No, yer honer, I war not afraid of that; but it might be as well there should be no scrimmage betwixt us, as in course there would not be. and we oncet man and wife. But as in course Mary has promised me now, she could not go and act like that."

"Why no, Denis, not well; unless, you know, she was to find your cow would not have any calf; eh?"

"Oh, bother it for a calf then!"

"No; for not being a calf, Denis."

"Well then, yer honer, I'll jist go and spake to Father Cullen.

Though he is not so good-humoured like,—at least, he don't be always laughing at a boy."

"Come back, McGovery, and don't be a fool. Father Cullen's gone to Dromod. I think I heard him say Tom Ginty wanted him."

"Is it Tom Ginty? but shure what would Tom be doing with Father Cullen? wouldn't he be going to his own priest? Well, what time will yer riverence come up to Pat Brady's to-morrow?"

"Well, get the mutton done about seven to-morrow evening, and I'll be with you. But you'll ask Tom Ginty, eh?"

"Sorrow a foot, then!"

"Nor Betsy Cane, Denis?"

"It ar'nt for me to ax the company, Father John, but if Betsy likes to come up and shake her feet and take her sup, she's welcome for me."

"That's kind of you; and you know you could be asking after the—"

"Well then, Father John, may it be long before I spake another word to you, barring my sins!"

"Well, Denis, I've done. But, look ye now you've a good supper for the boys, and lots of the stuff, I'll go bail. Let there be plenty of them in it, and don't let them come with their pockets empty. By dad, they think their priest can live on the point without the potatoes."

"Oh, Father John, Pat says there'll be plenty of them in it, and a great wedding he says he'll make it: there's a lot of the boys over from Mohill is to be there."

"From Mohill, eh? then they've my leave to stay away; I don't care how little I see of the boys from Mohill. Why can't he get his company from Drumsna and the parish?"

"Oh shure, yer riverence, an' he'll do that too; won't there be all the Ballycloran tenants, and the boys and girls from Drumleesh?"

"Oh, yes, Drumleesh; Drumleesh is as bad as Mohill; I'm thinking it's those fellows in Drumleesh that make Mohill what it is; but I suppose Pat Brady would tell me he has a right to choose his own company."

"Oh, Pat would not tell your riverence the like of that."

"And he's the boy that would do it, directly. And mind this, McGovery, you've the name of a prudent fellow—when you're once married, the less you see of your brother-in-law the better, and stick to your work in Drumsna."

"And so I manes. Oh, yer riverence, they won't be making me be wasting my hard arned wages at Mrs. Mulready's. Pat wanted me to be there last night of all, as I was coming out of the fair; but, no, says I; if ye'd like to see yer sister respectable, don't be axing me to go there; if ye'd like her to be on the roads, and me in Carrick Gaol, why that's the way, I take it."

"Stick to that, Denis, and you'll be the better of it. Well, I'll be down with you to-morrow evening; but mind now, two thirties is the very least; and you should make it more, if you want any luck in your marriage."

"I'll spake to Pat, Father John; you know that's his business; but your riverence, Father John, you'll not be saying anything up there before the boys and girls about you know—Betsy Cane, you know."

"Oh! the cow!—only, you see, if you don't come down with the money as you should, it might be an excuse for your poverty. But, Denis, I'll take care; and if any one should say anything about the price of cows or the like, I'll tell them all it isn't Betsy Cane's cow, who wouldn't have the calf, though she was engaged."

Denis McGovery now hurried off. Father John called for Judy to take away the cold tea, and prepared to sally forth to some of his numerous parochial duties.

But Father McGrath was doomed to still further interruptions. He had not walked above a mile on his road,—he was going by Ballycloran,—when, coming down the avenue, he saw Pat Brady with his master, Mr. Thady, and of course he didn't pass without waiting to speak to them.

"Well, Thady," and "Well, Father John," as they shook hands; and, "Well, Pat Brady," and "Well, yer riverence," as the latter made a motion with his hand towards his hat, was the first salutation.

It will be remembered that Thady and the other had just been talking over affairs in the rent-office, and Thady did not seem as though he were exactly in a good humour.

'So, Pat, your sister is getting married to Denis McGovery. I'll tell you what—she might do a deal worse."

"She might do what she plased for me, Father John. But, faix, I was tired enough of her myself; so, you see, Denis is welcome to his bargain."

"What! are you going to bring a wife of your own home then?"

"Devil a wife, then, axing your riverence's pardon. What'd I be doing with a wife?"

'Who'll keep the house over you now, Pat, your sister's as good as gone?"

"I won't be axing a woman to keep the house over me; so

Mary's welcome to go; or, she wor welcome to stay, too, for me. I didn't ax her to have him, and, by the 'postles, when Denis is tired of his bargain, he'll be recollecting I wasn't axing him to have her."

"Well, Thady, I suppose you and Feemy 'll be at the wedding, eh? and, Pat, you must make them bring Captain Ussher. Mrs. McGovery, as is to be, must have the Captain at her wedding; you'll be there, Thady?"

"Oh, Pat's been telling me about it, and I suppose I and Feemy must go down. If Brady chooses to ask the Captain, I've nothing to say; it's not for me to ask him, and, as he'd only be quizzing at all he saw, I think he might as well be away."

"Ah! Thady, but you never think of your priest; think of the half-crown it would be to me. Never mind, Pat, you ask him; he'll come anywhere, where Miss Feemy is likely to be; eh, Thady?"

"Then I wish Feemy had never set eyes on him, Father John; and can't you be doing better than coupling her name with that of his, that way? and he a black ruffian and a Protestant, and filling her head up with nonsense: I thought you had more respect for the family. Well, Pat, jist go down to them boys, and do as I was telling you:"—and Pat walked off.

"And what more respect for the family could I have, Thady, than to wish to see your sister decently married?" and Father John turned round to walk back with young Macdermot the way he was going, "what better respect could I have? If Captain Ussher were not a proper young man in general, your father and you, Thady, wouldn't be letting him be so much with Feemy; and, now we're on it, if you did not mean it to be a match, and if you did not mean they should marry, why have you let him be so much at Ballycloran, seeing your father doesn't meddle much in anything now?"

"That's just the reason, Father John, I couldn't be seeing all day who was in it and who was not; besides, Feemy's grown now; she's no mother, and must learn to care for herself."

"No, Thady, she's no mother; and no father, poor girl, that can do much for her; and isn't that the reason you should care the more for her? Mind, I'm not blaming you, Thady, for I know you do care for her; and you only want to know how to be a better brother to her; and what could she do better than marry Captain Ussher?"

"But isn't he a black Protestant, Father John; and don't the country hate him for the way he's riding down the poor?"

"He may be Protestant, Thady, and yet not 'black.' Mind, I'm

D

not saying I wouldn't rather see Feemy marry a good Catholic; but if she's set her heart on a Protestant, I wouldn't have you be against him for that: that's not the way to show your religion; it's only nursing your pride; and sure, mightn't she make a Catholic of him too?"

"Oh, Father Cullen has tried that."

"Well, I wouldn't tell him so, but I think your sister would show more power in converting a young fellow like Ussher than poor Cullen. And then, as to his riding down the poor; you know every one must do his duty, and if the boys will be acting against the laws, why, of course, they must bear the consequences. Not but that I think Captain Ussher is too hard upon them. But, Thady, are you telling me the truth in this? Is it not that you fear the young man won't marry Feemy, rather than that he will?"

"Why, Father John?"

"I'll tell you why, Thady: this Captain Ussher has been the intimate friend in your house now for more than six months back; he has been received there willingly by your father, and willingly by yourself, but still more willingly by Feemy; all the country knows this; of course they all said Feemy was to be married to him; and who could say why she shouldn't, if her father and brother agreed? I always thought it would be a match; and though, as I said before, I would sooner have married Feemy to a good Catholic, I should have thought myself much exceeding my duty as her priest, had I said a word to persuade her against it. Now people begin to say—and you know what they say in the parish always comes to my ears—that Captain Ussher thinks too much of himself to take a wife from Ballycloran, and that he has only been amusing himself with your sister; and I must tell you, Thady, if you didn't know more of Captain Ussher and his intentions than you seem to do, it isn't to-day you should be thinking what you ought to do."

· Thady walked on with his head down, and the priest went on.

"I've been meaning to speak to you of this some days back, for your poor father is hardly capable to manage these things now; and it's the respect I have for the family, and the love I have for Feemy,—and, for the matter of that, for you too,—that makes me be mentioning it. You aint angry with your priest, are you, Thady, for speaking of the welfare of your sister? If you are, I'll say no more.".

"Oh no! angry, Father John! in course I aint angry. But what can I do then? Bad luck to the day that Ussher darkened the door of Ballycloran! By dad, if he plays Feemy foul he'll shortly enter no door, barring that of hell fire!"

"Whisht, Thady, whisht! it's not cursing 'll do you any good in life, or Feemy either;"—and then continued the priest, seeing that poor Macdermot still appeared miserably doubtful what to say or do, "come in here awhile," they had just got to the gate of Father John's Gothic cottage, "just come in here awhile, and we'll talk over what will be best to do."

They entered the little parlour in which McGovery had shortly before been discussing his matrimonial engagements, and having closed the door, and, this time, taking care that Judy McCan was not just on the other side of it, and making Macdermot sit down opposite to him, the priest began, in the least disagreeable manner he could, to advise him on the very delicate subject in question.

"You see, Thady, there's not the least doubt in life poor Feemy's very fond of him; and how could she not be, poor thing, and she seeing no one else, and mewed up there all day with your father?—no blame to her—and in course she thinks he means all right; only she doesn't like to be asking him to be naming the day, or talking to you or Larry, or the like, and that's natural too; but what I fear is, that he's taking advantage of her ignorance and quietness, you see; and, though I don't think she would do anything really wrong, nor would he lead her astray altogether—"

"And av he did, Father John, I'd knock the brains out of the scoundrel, though they hung me in Carrick Gaol for it; I would, by G—!"

"Whisht, now, Thady; I don't mean that at all—but you get so hot—but what I really mean is this; though no actual harm might come of it, it doesn't give a girl a good name through the country, for her to be carrying on with a young man too long, and that all for nothing; and Feemy's too pretty and too good, to have a bad word about her. And so, to make a long story short, I think you'd better just speak to her, and tell her, if you like, what I say; and then, you know, if you find things not just as they should be, ask her not to be seeing the Captain any more, except just as she can't help; and do you tell him that he's not so welcome at Ballycloran as he was, or ask him at once what he means about your sister. It's making too little of any girl to be asking a man to marry her, but better that than let her break her heart, and get ill spoken of through the country too."

"I don't think they dare do that yet, poor as the Macdermots now are, or, by heaven—"

"There's your pride,—bad pride, again, Thady. Poor or rich, high or low, don't let your sister leave it to any one to speak bad of her, or put it in any man's power to hurt her character. At any rate, by following my advice, you'll find how the land lies."

"But you see, Father John, she mightn't exactly mind what I say. Feemy has had so much of her own way, and up to this I haven't looked after her ways,—not so much as I should, perhaps; though, for the matter of that there's been little need, I believe; but she's been left to herself, and if she got cross upon me when I spoke of Ussher, it would only be making ill blood between us. I'd sooner a deal be speaking to Captain Ussher."

"Nonsense, Thady; do you mean to say you are afraid to speak to your sister when you see the necessity? By speaking to Captain Ussher you mean quarrelling with him, and that's not what'll do Feemy any good."

"Well, then, I'm sure, I'll do anything you tell me, Father John; but if she don't mind me, will you speak to her?"

"Of course I will, Thady, if you wish it; but go and see her now at once, while it's on your mind, and though Feemy may be a little headstrong, I think you'll find her honest with you."

"I'll tell you another thing, Father John; father is so taken up with Ussher, and—to out with it at once—he's trying to borrow a thrifle of money from him; not that that should stand in my way, but the ould man gets obstinate, you know."

"Oh, then, that'd be very bad, Thady; why doesn't he go to his natural friends for money, and not to be borrowing it of a false friend and a stranger?"

"Nathural friends! and who is his nathural friends! Is it Flannelly, and Hyacinth Keegan? I tell you what it is, Father John, Feemy and her father and I won't have the roof over our heads shortly, with such nathural friends as we have. God knows where I'm to make out the money by next November, even let alone what's to come after."

"Anything better than borrowing from Ussher, my boy; but sure, bad as the time is, the rints more than pay Flannelly's interest money, any how."

"I wish you had to collect them then, Father John, and then you'd see how plentiful they are; besides, little as is spent, or as there is to spend up above there, we can't live altogether for nothing."

"No, Thady, the Lord knows we can none of us do that—and, tell the truth now, only I stopped the words in your throat about poor Feemy's business, weren't you just going to be dunning me for the bit of rent? out with it now."

"It's little heart I have now to be saying to you what I was going to do, for my soul's sick within me, with all the throubles that are on me. An' av it warn't for Feemy then, Father John, bad as I know I've been to her, laving her all alone there at Ballycloran, with her novels and her trash,—av it warn't for her, it's little I'd mind about Ballycloran. There is them still as wouldn't let the ould man want his stirabout, and his tumbler of punch, bad as they all are to us; and for me, I'd sthrike one blow for the counthry, and then, if I war hung or shot, or murthered any way, devil a care But I couldn't bear to see the house taken off her, and she to lose the rispect of the counthry entirely, and the name of Macdermot still on her!"

"Oh, nonsense, Thady, about blows for your country, and getting hung and murthered. You're very fond of being hung in theory, but wait till you've tried it in practice, my boy."

"May be I may! there be many things to try me."

"Oh, bother Thady; stop with your nonsense now. Go up to your sister, and have your talk well' out with her, and then come down to me. Judy McCan has got the best half of a goose, and there's as fine a bit of cold ham—or any way there ought to be—as ever frightened a Jew; and when you get a tumbler of punch in you, and have told me all you've said to Feemy, and all Feemy's said to you, why, then you can begin to dun in earnest, and we'll talk over how we'll make out the rint."

"No, Father John, I'd rather not be coming down."

"But it's yes, Father John, and I'm not saying what you'd rather do, but showing you your duty; so at five, Thady, you'll be down, and see what sort of a mess Judy makes of the goose."

There was no gainsaying this, so Thady started off for Ballycloran, and Father John once more set about performing his parochial duties.

CHAPTER VI.

THE BROTHER AND SISTER.

At the time that the priest and young Macdermot were talking over Feemy's affairs at the cottage, she and her lover were together at Ballycloran.

Nothing that her brother or Father John had said about her, either for her or against, would give a fair idea of her character.

She was not naturally what is called strong-minded; but her feelings and courage were strong, and they stood to her in the place of mind.

She would have been a fine creature had she been educated, but she had not been educated, and consequently her ideas were ill-formed, and her abilities were exercised in a wrong direction.

She was by far the most talented of her family, but she did not know how to use what God had given her, and therefore, abused it. Her mother had died before she had grown up, and her grandmother had soon followed her mother. Whatever her feelings were,—and for her mother they were strong,—the real effect of this was, that she was freed from the restraint and constant scolding of two stupid women at a very early age; consequently she was left alone with her father and her brother, neither of whom were at all fitting guides for so wayward a pupil. By both she was loved more than any other living creature; but their very love prevented them taking that care of her they should have taken. Her father had become almost like the tables and chairs in the parlour, only much less useful and more difficult to move. What little natural power he had ever had, could not be said to have been impaired by age, for Lawrence Macdermot was not in years an old man—he was not above fifty; but a total want of energy, joined to a despairing apathy, had rendered him by this time little better than an idiot.

Very soon after his coming to his property Flannelly had become a daily and intolerant burthen to him. He had in his prime made some ineffectual fight again this man,—he had made some faint attempts rather to parry blows, than overcome his foe; but from the time that Keegan's cunning had been added to Flannelly's weight, poor Lawrence Macdermot had, as it were, owned himself thoroughly vanquished for this world. Since that time he had done nothing but complain.

Joined to all this—and no wonder—he had taken to drink,—not drinking in the would-be-jolly, rollicking, old Irish style, as his father had done before him; but a slow, desperate, solitary, continual melancholy kind of suction, which left him never drunk and never sober. It had come to that, that if he were left throughout the morning without his whiskey and water, he would cry like a child; whatever power he had of endurance would leave him, and he would sit over the fire whining the names of Flannelly and Keegan, and slobbering over his wrongs and persecutions, till he had again drank himself into silence and passive tolerance.

Not only his hair and his whiskers, but his very face had become grey from the effect of the miserable, torpid life he led. He looked as if he were degenerating into the grub even before he died.

The only visible feeling left to him was a kind of stupid family pride, which solely, or chiefly, showed itself in continual complaints that the descendants and the present family of the Macdermots should be harrowed and brought to the ground by such low-born ruffians as Flannelly and Keegan.

It is odd that though Feemy often thwarted him and Thady rarely did,—and though Thady was making the best fight he could, poor fellow, for the Macdermots and Ballycloran,—the old man always seemed cross to him, and never was so to her. May be he spent more of his time with her, and was more afraid of her; but so it was; and though he certainly loved her better than anything, excepting Ballycloran and his own name, it will be owned that he was no guide for a girl like Feemy, possessed of strong natural powers, stronger passions, and but very-indifferent education.

And from circumstances her brother was not much better. He had been called on at a very early age to bear the weight of the family. From the time of his leaving school he had been subjected to constant vexation; on the contrary, his pleasures were very few and far between; his constant occupation for many years had been hunting for money, which was not to be got. If his heart could have been seen, the word "Rent" would have been found engraved on it. Collecting the rent, and managing the few acres of land which the Macdermots kept in their own hands, were his employments, and hard he laboured at them. He was therefore constantly out of the house; and of an evening after his punch, he spent his hours in totting and calculating, adding and subtracting at his old greasy book, till he would turn into bed, to forget another day's woes, and dream of punctual tenants and unembarrassed properties. Alas! it was only in his dreams he was destined to meet such halcyon things. What could such a man have to say to a young girl that would attract or amuse her? Poor Thady had little to say to any one, except in the way of business, and on that subject Feemy would not listen to him. She constantly heard her father growling about his Carrick foes, and her brother cursing the tenants; but she had so long been used to it, that now she did not think much of it. She knew they were very poor, and that it was with difficulty she now and again got the price of a new dress from her brother; and when she did, it was usually somewhat in this fashion: Pat Kelly owed two years' rent or so, may be five pounds. Mrs. Brennan, the Mohill haberdasher, took Pat's pig or his oats in liquidation of the small bill then due to her from Ballycloran, and Feemy's credit at the shop was good again about to the amount of another pig. It was very rarely ready money found its way to Ballycloran.

On the whole, therefore, she paid little or no attention to the family misfortunes. She had used to confine her desires to occasional visits to Carrick or Mohill; for they still possessed an old car, and sometimes she could take the old mare destined to perform the whole farming work of Ballycloran; and sometimes she coaxed the loan of Paul for a day from Father John; and if she could do that, could always have a novel from Mohill, and see her friends the Miss McKeons at Drumsna two or three times a week, she was tolerably contented and good-humoured. But of late things were altered. Feemy had got a lover. Her novels ceased to interest her; she did not care about going to Carrick, and the Miss McKeons were neglected. It was only quite lately, however, that Feemy had begun to show signs of petulance and ill temper. When her father grumbled she left him to grumble alone, and if her brother asked her to do any ordinary little thing about the house, she would show her displeasure. She did not attend either so closely as she used to do to Biddy and Katty, the two kitchen girls, and consequently the fare at Ballycloran grew worse than ever.

Larry always grumbled, but no one marked his grumbling more than heretofore. Thady had too many causes of real suffering to grumble much at trifles, and usually passed over his sister's petulance in silence: but the truth was, her lover was sometimes cross to her.

Soon after Father John and young Macdermot had turned their backs on Ballycloran, Pat Brady, who stood smoking his pipe, and idly leaning against the gate-post from which, even then, the gate was half wrenched, heard the sounds of Captain Ussher's horse on the road from Mohill. As soon as he came up, Brady very civilly touched his hat: "Well then long life to you, Captain Ussher, and it's you enjoys a fine horse, and it'd be a pity you shouldn't have one. You war with the Carrick harriers last Monday, I'll go bail."

"No doubt, Mr. Brady, you would go bail for that or anything else; but I was not there."

"You war not! faix but you war in the wrong then, Captain, for they had fine sport, right away behind Lord Lorton's new farms—right to Boyle. I wonder yer honer warn't in it."

"Seeing you know very well I was arresting prisoners up at Loch Sheen, Mr. Brady, your wonder is wonderful."

"Sorrow a taste I knew then, Captain. I did hear at the fair poor Paddy Smith was in throuble about a thrifle of sperits, or the like. But I didn't know yer honer'd been at it yerself. If the boys, ye know, will be going agin the laws, why in course they'd be the worse of it, when they is took."

"A very true and moral reflection. Was it a note you were taking to Mr. Keegan's at Carrick from the master, about the money perhaps, on Monday evening?"

"Me in Carrick Monday evening!" said Pat, a little confused;

"so I war shure enough, yer honer, jist to buy the mate for the supper as is to be for McGovery's marriage. You've heard in course, Captain, that Mary—that's my sister—is to be married to Denis McGovery to-morrow night?"

"Why I didn't see it in the Dublin newspapers."

"Oh, yer honer; the newspapers indeed! Perhaps, Captain, you'd not think it too much throuble to come down; Miss Feemy of course has promised Mary to be there,"—and Pat attempted a facetious grin.

"I shall be most proud, Mr. Brady," and the Captain made a mock bow; "but do they sell mutton at Mr. Keegan's little office door?"

Here Brady again seemed confused, and muttered something about Keegan's boy and messages: but he was evidently annoyed.

"Shall I take yer honer's horse round then?" said he; and Ussher dismounted without saying anything further, and ran up the stone steps, at the top of which Feemy opened the hall door for him.

There were two sitting-rooms at Ballycloran, one at each side of the hall; in that on the right as you entered the family breakfasted, dined, and in fact lived; and here also Larry sat throughout the day sipping his grog, and warming his shins over the fire from morning to night. He would every now and again walk to the hall door; and if it were warm, he would slowly creep down the steps, and stand looking at the trees and the lawn till he was cold, when he would creep back again.

The other room seemed to be the exclusive property of Feemy; here she made and mended her clothes, and sometimes even washed and ironed them too; here she read her novels, received the two Miss McKeons, and thought of Captain Ussher; and here also it was, that he would tell her all the soft things which had filled her young heart, and made her dislike Ballycloran.

"Well, Myles," she said as soon as he was in the room, and before the door was shut, "where were you all this time, since Sunday?" and she stood on tiptoe to give him the kiss which she rather offered than he asked. "Who have you got in Mohill then that keeps you away from Feemy? It's Mary Cassidy now; what business had you shopping with Mary Cassidy?"

"And was I shopping with Mary Cassidy, Feemy? 'deed then I forget it. Oh yes, it was fair-day yesterday, and I saw them all in at Brennan's."

"And what did you want at Brennan's, Myles?" said she, playfully shaking his shoulder with her hand; "it's talking to that pretty girl in the shop you're after."

"Oh, of course, Feemy; I was making love to the three Miss Cassidys, and Jane Thompson, and old widow Brennan at once. But why was I there, you say? why then, I was just buying this for Mary Cassidy, and I wanted your opinion, my pet;" and he took from his pocket some article of finery he had bought for his mistress.

"Oh, Myles, how good of you! but why do you be squandering your money; but it is very pretty," and Feemy put the collar over her shoulders.

"Don't toss it now, or Mary Cassidy won't take it from me, and then it would be left on my hands, for Mrs. Brennan wouldn't take it back anyhow," and he put out his hand for the article.

"No fear, Myles; no fear," said the laughing girl, running round the table. "It won't be left on your hands; I'll wear it to-morrow at Mary Brady's wedding."

"But you won't keep it from me without paying me, Feemy?"

"Oh, paying you, Captain Ussher; oh, I'll pay you, bring in your bill;"—and she came round to him, and he took her in his arms and kissed her. Then at least he seemed fondly attached to her.

Her lover was evidently in one of his best humours, and Feemy was quite happy. I won't further violate their conversation, as it is not essential to the tale, and was much such as those conversations usually are.

Feemy told her lover of the wedding, and he told her that he had already been invited, and had promised to go; and then she was more happy, for Feemy dearly loved a dance, though it was only a jig at a country wedding; but a dance with her lover would be delightful; she had only danced with him twice. On the first of these occasions she had met him at a grand gala party, at Mrs. Cassidy's, the wife of Lord Birmingham's agent in Mohill, where first Captain Ussher had made up his mind that Feemy Macdermot was a finer girl than pretty little Mary Cassidy, though perhaps not so well educated; and once again at a little tea-party at Mrs. McKeon's, which had been got up on purpose by Feemy's friends, to ask her husband as was to be—when first people said it was a settled thing. Oh! that was a happy night to Feemy, for her friends then all thought that her intimacy with Ussher was as good a thing as could be wished for; and when Feemy danced the whole night with him, the Miss McKeons all thought what a happy girl she was;—and that night she was happy. Then he first told her she should be his wife, and swore that he never had loved, and never would love any but her; and oh, how truly she believed him! Why should she not? was not she happy to love him, and why should not he be as much so to love her? If any one had whispered a word of caution to her, how she would have hated the whisperer! But there was no one to whisper caution to Feemy, and she had given all she had—her heart, her love, her obedience, her very soul—to him, without having any guarantee that she really had aught in return.

It was not because she began to doubt her lover that she was now occasionally fretful and uneasy. No; the idea to doubt him never reached her, but nevertheless she felt that things were not quite as they should be.

He seldom talked of marriage though he said enough of love; and when he did, it was with vague promises, saying how happy they would be when she was his wife, how much more comfortable her home would be, how nicely she would receive her friends in Mohill. These, and little jokes about their future *ménage* in a married state, were all he had ever said. She never asked him—indeed, she did not dare to ask; she did not like to press him; and Captain Ussher had a frown about him, which, somehow, Feemy had already learnt to fear.

He treated her too a little cavalierly, and her father and brother not a little. He ridiculed openly all that with her, hitherto, had been most sacred—her priest and her religion. She was not angry at this; she was hardly aware of it; and, in fact, was gradually falling into his way of thinking; but the effect upon her was the same—it made her uncomfortable. A girl should never obey her lover till she is married to him; she may comply with his wishes, but she should not allow herself to be told with authority that this or that should be her line of conduct.

Now Feemy had so given herself up to her lover, that she was obedient to him in all things; to him, even in opposition to her brother or her priest, and consequently she was to a degree humiliated even in his eyes. She did not feel the degradation herself, but there was still a feeling within, which she could not define, which usually destroyed her comfort.

Now, however, Myles was in so good a temper, and seemed so kind to her, that that, and her little prospect of pleasure, did make her happy.

She was sitting in this humour on the old sofa close to him, leaning on his arm, which was round her waist, when she heard her brother's footstep at the hall door.

"Here's Thady, Myles; sit off a bit."

Myles got up and walked to the window, and Thady entered with anything but a gay look; he had just left Father John.

"Well, Thady?" said Feemy

"How are you, Thady, this morning?" said the Captain, offering his hand, which the other reluctantly took.

"Good morning, Captain Ussher."

"Did you hear, Thady, I caught another of your boys with malt up at Loch Sheen last Monday,—Joe Reynolds, or Tim Reynolds, or something? He's safe in Carrick."

"I did hear you got a poor boy up there, who was in it by chance, and took him off just for nothing. But he's no tenant of ours, so I have nothing to do with it; his brother Joe lives on our land."

"Do you mean to tell me, Thady, you believe all that d—d nonsense about knowing nothing about it; and he sitting there in the cabin, and the malt hadn't been in it half an hour?"

"I don't know what you call d—d nonsense, Captain Ussher; but I suppose I may believe what I please without going to Carrick Gaol too for it."

"Believe what you please for me, Master Thady. Why you seem to have got out of bed the wrong side this morning; or have you and Keegan been striking up some new tiff about the 'rints?'"

"Mr. Keegan's affairs with me arn't any affairs of yours, Captain Ussher. When I ask you to set them right, then you can talk to me about them."

"Hoity toity, Mr. Macdermot; your affairs, and Mr. Keegan's affairs, and my affairs! Why I suppose you'll be calling me out next for taking up a d—d whining thief of a fellow because his brother is a tenant of your father's, and send me the challenge by Mr. Brady, who invited me to a party at his house just now."

Thady said nothing to this, but stood with his back to the fire, looking as grim as death.

"Oh, Captain Ussher!" said Feemy, "you wouldn't be quarrelling with Thady about nothing? You know he has so much to bother him with the rents and things. Will you come to Mary's wedding to-morrow, Thady?"

"Quarrelling with him! 'Deed then and I will not, but it seems he wants to quarrel with me."

"When I do want to quarrel with you, Captain Ussher,—that is, should I ever want,—you may be quite certain it's not in a round about way I'll be telling you of it."

"No, don't, my boy, for ten to one I shouldn't understand what you'd be after. Didn't you say you'd walk up to Aughermore, Miss Macdermot?"

"I'm sorry to baulk Feemy of her walk, Captain Ussher, if she did say so. It's not very often I ask her to put herself out for me; but this afternoon, I shall feel obliged to her not to go."

Captain Ussher stared, and Feemy opened wide her large bright eyes; for what reason could her brother desire her to stay in doors?

"What can you want me in the house for, Thady, this time of day?"

"Well never mind, Feemy; I do want you, and you'll oblige me by staying."

Feemy still had on the new collar, and she pulled it off and threw it on the table; she evidently imagined that it had something to do with her brother's unusual request. She certainly would not have put it on in that loose way, had she thought he would have seen it; but then he so seldom came in there.

"Well, Captain Ussher," she at last said slowly, "I suppose then I can't go to Aughermore to-day."

Captain Ussher had turned to the window as if not to notice Thady's request, and now came back into the middle of the room, as if Feemy's last sentence had been the first he had heard on the subject.

"Oh! you have changed your mind, then," said he; and his face acquired the look that Feemy dreaded. "Ladies, you know, are at liberty to think twice."

"But, Thady, I did wish to go to Aughermore particularly to-day; wouldn't this evening or to-morrow do?"

"No, Feemy," and Thady looked still blacker than Myles; "this evening won't do, nor to-morrow."

"Well, Captain Ussher, you see we must put it off," and she looked deprecatingly at her lover.

His answering look gave her no comfort; far from it, but he said, "I see no must about it, but that's for you to judge; perhaps you should ask your father's leave to go so far from home."

This was a cruel cut at all the fallen family, the father's incapacity, the sister's helplessness, and the brother's weak authority. Feemy did not feel it so, she felt nothing to be cruel that came from Ussher; but Thady felt it strongly, he was as indignant as if he had lived all his life among those who thought and felt nobly, but, poor fellow, he could not express his indignation as well.

"My sister, Captain Ussher, has long been left her own misthress to go in and out as she plazes, without lave from father, mother, or brother; better perhaps for her that she had not! God knows I have seldom stopped her wishes, though may be not often able to forward them. If she likes she may go now to Aughermore, but if a brother's love is anything to her, she'll stay this day with me."

Feemy looked from one to the other; she knew well by Miles' look, that he still expected her to go, and strange as it may be, she hardly dared to disobey him; but then her brother looked determined and sadly resolute, and it was so unusual in him to speak in that way.

"Well, Miss Macdermot," said Ussher, seeing he could not prevail without causing an absolute break with Thady, "your brother wants you to count the rent for him. I'm glad he has received so much; it must be that, I presume, for he seldom troubles himself on much else, I believe."

"I do what I have to do, and must do; God knows its throuble enough. Do you go and do the same; even that, bad as it is, is better than amusing my sister by laughing at me."

"Oh, Thady, how can you be saying such things! you see I am staying for you, and why can't you be quiet?"

Thady made no reply; the Captain twirled his hat, and ceremoniously bowing to the lady, took his leave.

Thady had screwed his courage to the sticking point while the Captain was the foe with whom he had to contend, and he had carried on the battle manfully while he spoke to Feemy in the Captain's presence; but to tell the truth, when he heard the clatter of his horse's feet he almost wished him back again, or that Feemy was away with him to Aughermore. He was puzzled how to begin; he could not think what he was to say; was he to quarrel with his sister for having a lover without telling him? was he to put it on the ground that her lover was a Protestant? That would have been the easiest line, but then Father John had especially barred that! Was he to scold her because her lover would not marry her at once? That seemed unreasonable. It had never occurred to him, in his indignation, to think of these difficulties, and he now stood with his back to the fire, looking awfully black, but saying nothing.

"Well, Thady, what is it I'll be doing for you, instead of going to Aughermore this morning?" at last said Feemy, the first to begin the disagreeable conversation.

When Thady looked up, thinking what to answer to this plain speech, his eye, luckily for him, fell on the new Mohill collar.

"Where were you getting that collar, Feemy?"

"And are you afther making me stay at home all the blessed day, and sending Captain Ussher all the way back to Mohill, and he having come over here by engagement to walk with me,"—this was a fib of Feemy's,—"and all to ask me where I got a new collar?"

"May be I was, Feemy, and may be I wasn't; but I suppose

there isn't any harum in my asking the question, or in you answering it?"

"Oh no, not the laist; only it ain't usual in you to be asking such questions."

"But if there's no harum, I ask it now; where were you getting the collar?"

"Well, you're very queer; but if you must know, Captain Ussher brought it with him from Mohill."

"And if you wanted a parcel from Mohill, why couldn't you let Brady bring it, who is in it constantly, instead of that upstart policeman, who'd think it more condescension to bring that from Mohill, than I would to be carrying a sack of potatoes so far."

"There then you're wrong; the policeman, as you're pleased to call him, thinks no such thing."

"Well, Feemy, but did you bid him bring it, or did he bring it of his own accord?"

Feemy could now shuffle no longer, so blushing slightly, she said, "Well, if you must know then, it was a present; and there's no such great harm in that, I suppose."

Here Thady was again bothered; he really did not know whether there was any harm in it or not; a week ago he certainly would have thought not, but he was now inclined to think that there was; but he was not sure, and he sadly wished for Father John to tell him what to do.

"Well, Thady, now what was it you were wanting of me?"— and then after a pause, she added, her courage rising as she saw her brother's falling: "Was it anything about Captain Ussher?"

"Yes, it was."

"Well?"

"Is there anything between you and he, Feemy?"

"What do you mean by between us, Thady?" and Feemy made a little fruitless attempt to laugh.

"Well then; you're in love with him, ain't you? there now, that's the long and the short."

"Supposing I was, why shouldn't I?"

"Only this, Feemy, he's not in love with you."

This put Feemy's back up, "'Deed then, it's little you know about it, for he just is; and I love him too with all my heart, and that's all about it; and you might have found that out without sending him back to Mohill."

"I wish then he'd stay at Mohill, and that I might never see him over the door at Ballycloran again!"

"That's kind of you, Thady, after what I just told you; but don't tell him so, that's all."

"But it's just what I mane to tell him, and what I shall go over to Mohill on purpose to tell him, to-morrow."

"Good gracious, Thady! and for why?"

"For why, Feemy! becase I still want to see my father's daughter an honest woman, though she may be soon a beggar; becase I don't want to see my sister crouching under a blackguard's foot; becase I don't want the worst disgrace that can happen a family to blacken the name of Macdermot!"

Feemy was now really surprised; fear at her brother's strange words brought out at once what was ever most present in her mind.

"Oh, heavens, Thady! sure we're to be married."

It must be remembered that this was not an interview between a fashionable brother and an elegant sister, both highly educated, in which the former had considered himself called upon to remonstrate with the latter for having waltzed too often with the same gentleman, and in which any expression of actual blame would highly offend the delicacy of the lady. Thady and his sister had not been accustomed to delicacy; and though she was much shocked at his violence, she hardly felt the strong imputation against herself, as she had so good an answer for it. She therefore exclaimed,

"Oh heavens, Thady, sure we're to be married."

"Well, now, Feemy, jist listen to me. If Captain Ussher manes to marry you, under all circumstances, I don't know you could do better. I don't like him, as how should I, for isn't he a Protestant, and a low-born, impudent ruffian? but you do like him, and I suppose, if he marries you, it's becase he likes you; if not, why should he do it? And when once married, you'll have to fight your own battles, and no joke it'll be for either of you. But if, as I'm thinking, he has no idea on arth of marrying you, no more than he has of Mary Brady, I'll be d—d if I let him come here fooling you, though you haven't sperit enough to prevent it yourself. We're low enough already, Feemy, but for heaven's sake don't be making us lower yet!"

"Well, now, Thady, is that all? and you're wrong then, as you always are, for Captain Ussher has asked me to have him, just as plain as I'm telling you now; and he's no ruffian. It is you're the ruffian to him, snubbing him when he speaks good-naturedly to you. And as for being a Protestant, I suppose he's none the worse for that, if he's none the better. I don't know why you do be hating him so, unless it's because I love him."

"I'm not talking about my hating him, or loving him. If he's honest to you, I'll neither say nor do anything to cross him. But if he does mane to marry you, it's time he did it; that's all. Did he say anything to father about it?"

"What should he be saying to him? Of course, dada would have no objection."

"And would you then be letting him come here as he likes, and settling nothing, and just maning to marry you or not, as he likes, and you and he talked of over the counthry these four months back, and he talking about you, jist as his misthress, through the counthry?"

Feemy was now regularly roused.

"That's a lie for you, Thady! and a black lie—about your own sister too, to say he ever spoke a bad word against me! Pat Brady was telling you that perhaps. It's what he never did, or would do; for he's as true as you are false; and it's from jealousy, and just from your hate, because everybody else likes him, makes you say it. And now we are on it, Thady, I'll just tell you one thing: I'm not to do what you tell me, nor will I, for I'm much more able to manage myself than you are for me. And for all you say about him, I'd attend more to one word from Myles, than to all you say, if you stood talking till night; and talk you may, but I'll not stand and hear you!" And she bounced out of the room, slamming the door in a manner which made Mr. Flannelly's building shake to the foundation.

Poor Thady was signally defeated. There he stood with his back to the fire, his old and dirty hat pulled low over his brow, his hands stuck into the pockets of his much worn shooting coat, his strong brogues and the bottoms of his corduroy trowsers covered with dirt and dry mould, with the same heavy discontented look about his face which he always now wore. He certainly appeared but a sorry Mentor for a young lady in a love affair! He felt that his sister despised him, the more from her being accustomed to the comparatively gentleman-like appearance and refined manners of her lover.

There he stood a long time without stirring, and so he stood in absolute silence. He had put his pipe down when first Captain Ussher left the room, and he had not resumed it, now even that he was alone. With Thady this was a sign that his heart was very full indeed; and so it was, full almost to breaking.

He had come there eager with two high feelings, love for his sister, real fond brotherly affection, and love and respect for his family name; he had wished to protect the former from insult and unhappiness, and to sustain the fallen respectability of the latter; and he had only been scoffed at and upbraided by the sister he loved. For he did love her, though little real communication had ever passed between them; he had always supposed that she loved him; he had taken it for granted, and had asked for no demonstrative affection; but her manner and her words now cut him very deep. He was not aware how very uncouth his own manner had been,; that instead of reasoning with her gently he had began by sneering at her lover, that he had taken the very course to offend her self-love, and that therefore Feemy was quite as convinced at the end of the meeting that she had a right to be angry, as he was that he was the injured party.

At any rate, there he stood perfectly baffled. His object had been to advise her, if Captain Ussher did not at once declare his purpose to her family, to put a stop to his further visits; and if she refused to comply with his advice, to tell her that he should himself ask Captain Ussher his intentions, and that if they were not such as he approved, he should inform him that he was no longer welcome at Ballycloran.

This had seemed, though disagreeable, straightforward and easy enough before the meeting; and now that it was over he could not think why he had not said exactly what he had come there to say. To give him his due, he blamed himself as much as he did his sister; he was very unhappy about it all, but he could not think how he had been so very stupid.

Had he lived more in the world, he would have had recourse to the common resort in cases where speech is difficult; he would have written a letter to his sister. But this never occurred to him; even had it done so, Thady's epistolary powers were very small, and his practice very limited; a memento to the better sort of tenants, as to their "thrifle of rint," or a few written directions to Pat Brady, about seizing crops and driving pigs, was its extent; and these were written on pieces of coarse paper, which had been ruled for accounts, and were smeared rather than fastened with very much salivated wafers. His writing too was very slow, and his choice of language not extensive; a letter on such a subject from a brother to a sister should be well turned, impressive, terse, sententious: that scheme would never have done for Thady.

What then should he do? if he were to go to Captain Ussher now, and tell him to discontinue his visits, he would only be asked if he had his sister's authority for doing so, or his father's. Should he get, or try to get, his father's authority? The old man he knew was moping over the parlour fire, half drunk, half stupid, and half asleep.

After thinking over it alone there in Feemy's sitting-room for an hour, he determined that all he could do was to go back again to his only friend, Father John.

When Feemy slammed the door, as she did at the end of her

violent oration above given, she betook herself to her bedroom, and began to cry.

Though she had so well assumed the air of an injured person, and had to the best of her abilities vindicated her absent lover, still she was very unhappy at what her brother had said to her. Nor, in truth, was it only because Thady had expressed himself unkindly about Myles, but she also could not but feel that there was something wrong. She never for a moment believed that her lover spoke loosely of her behind her back, for she never for a moment doubted his love; but she did feel that it would be more comfortable if Myles would speak, or let her speak to some of her family, if it were only to her father. Though she knew so little of what was usual in the world, still she felt that even his sanction, stupid, tipsy, unconscious as he was, would give to her attachment a respectability which it wanted now; and if a day for her marriage were fixed, though circumstances might require that it should be ever so distant, she would be able to talk much more satisfactorily of her prospects to Mary Cassidy, and the Miss McKeons. Besides, if she could bring matters to this state, she could so triumphantly prove that Thady was wrong in his unhandsome conjectures, and she determined before she had done thinking on the subject, to give Myles a few hints as to her wishes. The next day he would be sure to come to Ballycloran on his way to McGovery's wedding, and he would probably ask why Thady had prevented their walk to Aughermore; and then she would have a good opportunity of saying what she wanted.

CHAPTER VII.

THE PRIEST'S DINNER PARTY.

THADY, as I said, walked off to the priest's cottage, to partake of the relics of a goose, and seek counsel of his friend; but it was not Father John's dinner hour yet, and he found no one in but Judy McCan. He walked into the priest's little parlour, and sat down to wait for him, again meditating on all the evils which hung over his devoted family, and sitting thus he at length fell fast asleep.

Here he slept for above an hour, when he was awakened by the door opening behind him, and in jumping up to meet Father John, as he thought, he encountered the lank and yellow features, much worn dress, and dirty, moist hand of Father Cullen.

"Were you sleeping, then, Mr. Thady, before Father McGrath's fire? 'deed, then, I dare say you've been walking a great sight, for you look jaded. I'm not that fresh myself, for I've been away to Loch Sheen, to widow Byrne's. Bad luck to the cratures, there's nothing but sick calls now, and my heart's broken with them, so it is."

Thady's only answer to this was, "How are you, Father Cullen?" He wished him back at Maynooth.

"Well, I hope Father McGrath isn't far off thin," and he looked at a watch nearly as big as a church clock, "for I'm very hungry, and, my! it's only twenty minutes to six—"

This gave Thady the very unwelcome intelligence that Father Cullen meant to dine at the cottage.

"And now the pony's lamed undher me, I had to walk all the way to Loch Sheen, in the dirt and gutther."

Thady's mind was full of one object, and he could not interest himself about the curate's misfortunes in the lameness of his pony and the dirt of his walk.

"And bad manners to them Commissioners and people they sent over bothering and altering the people! Couldn't we have our own parishes as we like, and fix them ourselves, but they must be sending English people to give us English parishes, altering the meerings just to be doing something? You know, Thady, the far end of Loch Sheen up there?"

"Yes, Father Cullen, I know where Loch Sheen is."

"Well, that used to be Cashcarrigan parish; and Father Comyns —that's the parish priest in Cash—don't live not two miles all out from there; and the widow Byrne's is six miles from where I live out yonder, if it's a step, and yet they must go and put Loch Sheen into this parish."

Father Cullen's misfortunes still did not come home to Macdermot; he sat looking at the fire.

"There's that poor ould woman, too, up there, left to starve by herself, the crature, now they've gone and put her two sons into gaol. I wonder what the counthry'll be the better for all them boys being crammed into gaol. I wish they'd kept that Ussher down in the north when he was there; he's fitter for that place than County Leitrim, any how."

"What's that about Captain Ussher, Father Cullen?"

"Shure didn't you hear he put three more of the boys into gaol Tuesday evening, and one of them off Drumleesh?"

"Heard it! of course I heard it; and more than I'll be hearing it too. Oh, Father Cullen, wherever that Ussher came from, I wish they'd kept him there."

Thady's earnestness in this surprised the young priest.

"Why, I thought you and he were so thick; but I'm glad it's not so much so. Why would the like of you be making so free with a Protestant like him? Did you break with him, then, Mr. Thady?"

Macdermot by no means desired to admit Father Cullen into the conference about his sister; the strong expression of his dislike had fallen from him as it were involuntarily: he therefore turned off the question.

"Oh no; break with him! why would I break with him? But you can't think I like to see him dhriving the boys into the gaol like sheep to the shambles. What business had they sending Tim Reynolds into gaol? There'll be noise enough in the counthry about that yet, Father Cullen."

"There'll never be noise enough about that, and such like cruelties till he and all of the sort is put down intirely in the counthry; and that'll only be when the counthry rights herself as she should do, and, by God's blessing, will still; and that you and I, Mr. Thady, may live to see it—"

The further expression of Father Cullen's favourite political opinions was here interrupted by Father John's quick, heavy step on the little gravel walk.

"Well, boys," said he, sitting down and pulling off his dirty gaiters and shoes before the fire, "waiting for the goose, eh? Egad, when I found what time it was, I thought you'd be bribing Judy to divide it between you. Cullen, you look awfully hungry; I'd better set you at the ham first, or you'll make terrible work at the half bird—for a half is all there is for the three of us. Well, Judy, let's have the stew."

The dinner was now brought in, and Father John talked joyously, as though nothing was on his mind; and yet we know the sad conversation he had had with young Macdermot that very morning, and that Thady was there chiefly to tell the upshot of his mission,—and Thady's face was certainly no emblem of good news. He had also had a sad morning's work with his curate, his parishioners were in great troubles, the times were very bad on them; many of them were in gaol for illegal distillation; more were engaged in the business, and were determined so to continue in open defiance of the police; many of them were becoming ribbonmen, or, at any rate, were joining secret and illegal societies. Driven from their cabins and little holdings, their crops and cattle taken from them, they were everywhere around desperate with poverty, and discontented equally with their own landlords and the restraints put upon them by government. All this weighed heavily on Father John's mind, and he strongly felt the difficulty of his own situation; but he was not the man to allow his spirits to master him when entertaining others in his own house. Had only Cullen or only Thady been there, he would have tuned his own mind to that of his guest; but as their cases were so different, he tried to cheer them both.

"Egad, Thady, here's another leg—come, my boy, we've still a leg to stand upon—Cullen has just finished one, and I could have sworn I ate the other yesterday. See, did Judy put one of her own in the hash—'*ex pede Herculem*'—you'd know it so any way by the toughness. Lend me your fork, Thady, or excuse my own. Well, when I get the cash from Denis's marriage, I'll get a carving-knife and fork from Garley's; not but what I ought to have one. Judy, where's the big fork?"

"Why, didn't yer riverence smash it entirely drawing the cork from the bottle of sherry wine ye got for Doctor Blake the day he was here about the dispinsary business?"

This little explanation Judy bawled from the kitchen.

"It is true for you, Judy; so I did, and bad luck to the day and Doctor Blake, too. That same day, Thady, cost me three good shillings for a bottle of bad wine, my old fork, and a leg of mutton and all; for I thought I'd be able to come round the doctor about his coming down to Drumsna here once a week regular; and when he'd ate my mutton and drank the sherry, he just told me it was not possible."

"He'd sooner be making may be twenty or thirty poor sick craturs be walking five or six miles, than he'd ride over to see them; though it's little he'd think of the distance av he'd a fee to touch."

"For the matter of that, Cullen, I think yourself would go quicker to a wedding than you would to a sick call. 'Deed, and I know myself I like the part of the business where the cash is."

"In course, Mr. McGrath, I'd go with more sperit, but not a foot quicker, nor so quick. May be I'd grumble at the one and not at the other; but what the church tells me, I'll do, if it plazes God to let me."

"Oh, Cullen, you'd make one think I was admonishing you. A fine martyr he'd make, wouldn't he, Thady?"

Cullen, who took everything in downright earnest, clasped his dirty hands, and exclaimed,

"If the church required it, and it was God's will, I hope I would."

"Well, well, but it'll be just at present much more comfortable for all parties you should square round a little, and take your punch. Come, Thady, are you going to be a martyr, too? it's a heathenish kind of penance, though, to be holding your tongue so long. Come, my boy, you were to bring the ticket about the rent with you."

Thady opened his ears at the word rent, but before he'd time to make any suitable reply, Judy was moving the things, Father John was pulling back the table, and pushing Cullen into a corner by the fire.

"Now, Judy, the fire under the pump, you know; out with the groceries,—see, but have I any sugar, then?"

"Sorrow a bit of lump, but moist and plenty, Father John."

"Well, my boys, you must make your punch with brown sugar for once in your life; and what's the harm? what we want in sugar, we'll make up in the whiskey, I'll be bound. Judy, bring the tumblers."

Out came the tumblers—that is, two tumblers, one with a stand, the other with a flat bottom, and a tea-cup with a spoon in it. The tea-cup was put opposite Father John's chair, and the reverend father himself proceeded to pour a tolerable modicum of spirits out of the stone jar into a good-sized milk jug, and placed it on the table.

"Isn't it queer, then, Thady, I can't get a bottle, or a decanter, or anything of glass to remain in the house at all? I'm sure I had a decanter, though I didn't see it these six months."

"And wouldn't it be odd if you did, Father John? wasn't it smashed last February?"

"Smashed! why, I think everything gets smashed."

"Well now, Mr. Thady, to hear his riverence going on the like of that," said the old woman, appealing to Macdermot; "and wasn't it himself sent the broth down in it to Widow Green the latter end of last winter, and didn't the foolish slip of a girl, her grand-dater, go to hait it over the hot coals for the ould woman, jist as it was, and in course the hait smashed the glass, and why wouldn't it, and the broth was all spilt? But isn't the jug just as good for the sperits, yer honers?"

"Well, well; boiling mutton broth over a turf fire, in my cut decanter! '*optat ephippia bos piger.*' That'll do, Judy, that'll do."

And the old woman retreated with a look of injured innocence.

Father John sniffed the whiskey. '*Fumum bibere institutæ;*' it's the right smell of the smoke. Come, Cullen, make your punch; come, Thady, don't be sitting there that way;"—and he proceeded to make a most unpalatable-looking decoction of punch in his tea-cup, to which the moist sugar gave a peculiarly nasty appearance.

But all Father John's attempted jovialities and preparations for enjoyment could not dispel the sadness from Thady's face, or the settled solemnity from Father Cullen's visage; he never joked, and rarely conversed; when he did speak, it was usually to argue or declaim; and Thady, even in his best times, was but a sorry companion for such a man as Father John. There the three of them sat, with their eyes fixed on the fire, all drinking their punch, it is true, but with very little signs of enjoying it.

How long they remained thus, I am unable to say; but Father John was getting very tired of his company, when they were all three startled by a sharp rap at the hall door, and before they had had time to surmise who it was, Captain Ussher walked in.

Now, though neither Father John nor his curate were very fond of Ussher, they both were tolerably intimate with him; indeed, till lately, when the priest began to think the gallant Captain was playing his fair parishioner false, and the opinion was becoming general that he was acting the tyrant among the people, Father John had rather liked Ussher than not. He was lively;—and if not well educated, he had some little general comprehension of which no others of those the priest knew around him could boast. He had met him first very frequently at Ballycloran, had since dined with him at Mohill, and had more than once induced him to join the unpretending festivities of the cottage. There was nothing, therefore, very singular in Captain Ussher's visit; and yet, from what was uppermost in the mind of each of the party, it did surprise them all.

Father John, however, was never taken aback.

"Ah, my darling, and how are you? come to see we are drinking parliament and not cheating the king."

Although they were drinking potheen, and though Ussher might, doubtless, have put a fine of from five to fifty pounds on the priest for doing so, Father John knew that he was safe. It was at that time considered that no revenue officer would notice potheen if he met it, as a guest. People are rather more careful now on the matter.

"Oh, Father John, I never bring my government taster with me when I am not on service; but if you've any charity, give me an air of the fire and a drop of what's going forward, all for love. How are you, Father Cullen?" and he shook hands with the curate. "How are you, Thady, old boy?" and he slapped Macdermot on the back as though they were the best friends in the world.

"How are you, Captain Ussher?" said the former, sitting down again as though the Captain's salutation were a signal for him to do so, and as if he did not dare do it before. Nor would he. Father Cullen had been told that he should stand up when strangers came into a room,—that it was a point of etiquette; and there he would have stood, though it had been ten minutes, if Ussher had not addressed him.

Thady did not get up at all; in fact, he did not know what to do or to say. He had been waiting anxiously, hoping that Father Cullen would go, and now the difficulties in his way were more than doubled.

Captain Ussher, however, took no notice of his silence; but, sitting down by Father John, began rubbing and warming his hands at the fire.

"Well, may I be d—d—begging your reverence's pardon—if this isn't as cold a night as I'd wish to be out in, and as dark as my hat. I say, Thady, this'll be the night for the boys to be running a drop of the stuff; there'd be no seeing the smoke now, anyhow. I was dining early at Carrick, and was getting away home as quick as I could, and my mare threw a shoe, luckily just opposite the forge down there; so I walked up here, Father John, and I told them to bring the mare up when she's shod."

"I'm glad the mare made herself so agreeable. Come, Judy, another tumbler here. By the by, then, Cullen, you must take to a tea-cup like myself—you're used to it; and Captain Ussher, you must take brown sugar in your punch, though you are not used to it. If I could make lump sugar for you, I'd do it myself directly."

"Oh, what's the odds! I'm so cold I shan't feel it;" and without any apology, he took poor Father Cullen's tumbler, who emptied the rest of his punch into a tea-cup.

"Well, Thady, and who do you think there was at Hewson's, but Keegan, your friend, you know? and a very pleasant fellow he is in his way: but how he does abuse you Catholics!"

"Well, Captain, and it's little good you'll hear any of us say of him, so that's all fair," said Father John.

"Take it that way, so it is; but I thought I heard some of you at Ballycloran say he was once a Catholic," said Ussher turning to Thady; " your father was telling me so I think."

He seemed determined to make Thady say something, but he only muttered an affirmative.

"Whoever said so, said wrong," began Father Cullen, rising up and putting his hands on the table, as if he was going to make a speech, " Whoever said so, said wrong. His father was a Catholic, and his mother was a Catholic, but he never was a Catholic; and how could he, for he never was a Christian,"—and as he sat down he turned round his large obtruding eyes for approval.

"Oh, if you go on that high ground, you'll lose half your flock. We are glad to get them whether they are Christians or not, so long as they are good Protestants; so you see Keegan's good enough for us; and what could he do, poor fellow? if you wouldn't have him, he must come to us."

"Oh then, Father John, he's satisfied to say men become Protestants when they are no longer fit to be Catholics; was that the way yourself become a Protestant, Captain Ussher?"

"If I'm to be d——d for that, you know, it's my father's and mother's fault. I ain't like Keegan. I didn't choose the bad road myself."

"Oh, but isn't it for yourself to choose the good road? didn't you say you knew ours was the ould church as it stood always down from Christ? If you do go wrong, you don't do it from ignorance, but you do it wilfully, and your sowl will howl in hell for it."

Captain Ussher only burst out laughing at this little outbreak, but Father John exclaimed, "Whist! whist! Cullen, none of that here: if you can take any steps towards sending Captain Ussher to heaven, well and good; but don't be sending him the other way while the poor fellow is over his punch."

"Never mind, Father John; I and Father Cullen are very good friends, and I think he'll hear me read my recantation yet; but he can't do it to-night, as here's my mare. I must go by Ballycloran, Thady; will you walk as far as the avenue with me?"

"Thank you, Captain Ussher, I'll not be going out of this just yet."

"Ah, well; I see you're out with me for the tiff we had this morning. He's angry now, Father John, just through my telling him he couldn't count all the money he'd received this week."

Father John observed the different manners of the young men towards each other, and from Thady's silence, was quite sure that matters had gone amiss between them.

"I didn't know it before then, Captain Ussher," said Thady; "but if you must know, I've business to spake to Father John about."

"Oh, well; open confession's good for the soul; I hope he'll absolve you for your bad temper."

"It's I am to get the absolution, if I can, this time; it's the old story, Captain, 'a thrifle of rint that's owing, nothing more.'"

"Well, it's all one to me: good night to you all," and Captain Ussher rode away home to Mohill.

Father Cullen reseated himself by the fire, and again assumed his gaze at the hot turf, just as he was before Ussher came in, and looked hopelessly immovable. Thady shifted about uneasily in his chair, then got up and walked round the room, and then sat down again; but the curate wouldn't move. At last Father John ended the affair by saying,

"Any more punch, Cullen?"

"Thank you, no, Sir."

"Then just go home, there's a good fellow."

Cullen rose up, not the least offended—nothing would offend him—took his hat, and did as he was bid. At last Thady and Father John were left alone.

"Now, my boy," said the priest, as he put on more turf, "we'll be alone for half an hour, or it is odd. Well, you spoke to Feemy?"

"I did spake to her, Father John; but I'd better have left it alone; for when I began she only snubbed me, and she told me she'd manage her own business; but, oh Father John, I fear it will be a bad business! She told me she loved him, and that he had gone so far as asking her to marry him, and all that; but as far as I could learn, it was only just talk, that. But I could say nothing to her, for she got the better of me, and then flew out of the room, saying, it did not matter what I said."

And then Macdermot told the priest exactly what had passed; how headstrong Feemy was, how infatuated she was with her lover, and how regardless of what any one could say to her on the subject; "and now, Father John, what on 'arth shall I do at all, for the heart's broken in me, with all the throubles that's on me."

"I'll tell you what, Thady: don't be falling out with Captain Ussher—any way, not yet—for he may mean honestly, you know, though I own my heart doubts him; but take my advice, and don't be falling out with him yet. I'll see Feemy to-morrow, and if she won't hear or won't heed what her priest says to her, I'll tell you what we'll do. One woman will always listen to another, and I'll ask Mrs. McKeon to speak to Feemy, and tell her the character she'll be giving herself. Mrs. McKeon has daughters of her own, and when I remind her that Feemy has neither mother, nor sister, nor female friend of any kind, she'll not be refusing me this, disagreeable though it may be to her. And now, Thady, do you go home to bed, and pray to God to protect your sister; and, remember, my boy, that though you may have reason to be displeased with her, as I said, she has neither mother nor sister; she has no one to look to but yourself, and if there is much in her to forgive, there are many causes for forgiveness."

Thady silently shook hands with his friend, and went home; and whether or no he obeyed the priest's injunctions to pray for protection for his sister, that good man himself did not go to sleep till he had long been on his knees, imploring aid for her, and the numerous unfortunates of his flock.

CHAPTER VIII.

MISS MACDERMOT AT HOME.

At any rate the priest's admonitions had this effect on Thady, that when he came in to breakfast after his morning avocations, he spoke to Feemy, whom he had not seen since their stormy interview of yesterday, with kindness, and, for him, gentleness. But she seemed only half inclined to accept the proffered olive branch. Thady's morning salutations couldn't go far towards putting a young girl in good humour, for even now that he meant to be gracious it was only—" Well, Feemy, how's yourself this morning; and will you be ready for Mary Brady's wedding?" But her answer—" Oh, in course; will you take your breakfast there?" showed him that she had not forgiven his aspersions against her lover, and the breakfast passed over in silence, with the exception of Larry's usual growls. Thady, therefore, when he had swallowed his potatoes and milk, betook himself again to Pat Brady and the fields. Larry was left alone to sleep, if he could, over the fire, and Feemy betook herself to her own parlour, and proceeded to penetrate farther into the mysteries of the " Mysterious Assassin."

There she sat—a striking contradiction of that proverb which we so often quote with reference to young ladies, and which so seldom can be quoted with truth, " Beauty unadorned, adorned the most."

Ussher would not come till the evening, and her hair was therefore in papers—and the very papers themselves looked soiled and often used. Her back hair had been hastily fastened up with a bit of old black ribbon and a comb boasting only two teeth, and the short hairs round the bottom of her well-turned head were jagged and uneven, as though bristling with anger at the want of that attention which they required. She had no collar on, but a tippet of different material and colour from her frock was thrown over her shoulders. Her dress itself was the very picture of untidiness; it looked as though it had never seen a mangle; the sleeves drooped down, hanging despondingly below her elbows; and the tuck of her frock was all ripped and torn—she had trod on it, or some one else had done it for her, and she had not been at the trouble of mending it. It was also too tight, or else Feemy had not fastened it properly, for a dreadful gap appeared in the back, showing some article beneath which was by no means as white as it should be;—" but then, wasn't it only her morning frock?" In front of it, too, was a streaked mark of grease, the long since deposited remains of some of her culinary labours. Her feet were stuffed into slippers—truth compels me to say they would more properly be called shoes down at heel—her stockings were wofully dirty, and, horror of all horrors, out at the heels! There she sat, with her feet on the fender, her face on her hands, and her elbows on her knees, with her thumb-worn novel lying in her lap between them.

There she sat; how little like the girl that had eclipsed Mary Cassidy at the ball at Mohill! Poor though Feemy was, she could make out a dress, and a handsome dress, for such an occasion as that. Then every hair on her fine head had been in its place; the curls of her rich brown hair were enough to win the heart of any man; the collar round her fair neck had been beautifully washed and ironed, for her own hands had been at work on it half the morning; her white long gloves had been new and well fitting, and her only pair of silk stockings had been scrupulously neat; her dress fitted her fine person as though made by Carson, and she had walked as though she knew she need not be ashamed of herself. But now how great was the contrast!

No girls know better how to dress themselves than Irish girls, or can do it with less assistance or less expense; but they are too much given to morning dishevelment. If they would only remember that the change in a man's opinion and mind respecting a girl will often take place as quick as the change in her appearance, and that the contrast will be quite as striking, they would be more particular. And they never can be sure of themselves, take what precautions they will. Lovers will drop in at most unseasonable hours; they have messages to deliver, plans to propose, or leave to take. They can never be kept out with certainty, and all the good done by a series of brilliant evenings—satin dresses, new flowers for the hair, expensive patterns, and tediously finished toilets—may be, and often is, suddenly counteracted by one untidy head, soiled dress, or dirty stocking.

I will, however, return to my story. There sat Feemy, apparently perfectly contented with her appearance and occupation, till a tap at the door disturbed her, and in walked Mary Brady, the bride elect.

"Well, Miss Feemy, and how's your beautiful self this morning?"

"And how are you, Mary, now the time is coming so near?"

Mary Brady was a very tall woman, being about the same height as her brother, thirty or thirty-three years of age, with a plain, though good-humoured looking face, over which her coarse hair was divided on the left temple. She had long ungainly limbs, and was very awkward in the use of them, and though not absolutely disagreeable in her appearance, she was so nearly so, that she would hardly have got married without the assistance of the "two small pigs, and thrifle of change," which had given her charms in the eyes both of Ginty and Denis McGovery.

"Oh! Miss Feemy, and I'm fretting so these two days, that is, ever since Denis said it was to be this blessed day,—the Lord help me!—and I with it all on my shouldhers, and the divil a one to lend a hand the laste taste in life."

"Why, Mary, what can there be so much to do at all?"

"Och! then, hadn't I my white dress to get made, and the pair of sheets to get hemmed, for Denis said his'n warn't large enough for him and I,"—and here the Amazon gave a grin of modesty,—"and you know it was part of the bargain, I was to have a pair of new sheets" (Denis had kept this back from Father John in his inventory of his bride's fortune); "and isn't there the supper to get ready, and the things, and the house to ready and all!—and then when I'd done that, it war all for nothing, for the wedding isn't to be at Pat's at all."

"The wedding not to be at Brady's, where is it to be then?"

"Oh, jist at Mrs. Mehan's shop below, at the loch."

"Oh, that's better still, Mary; we won't have so far to go in the mud."

"That's jist what the boys war saying, Miss; and there be so much more room, and there be so many to be in it, they couldn't all be in it, at all at all, at home. So you see we is to be married in the room inside, where the two beds is, and they is to come out of it, and the supper is to be there, Miss, you see, and the most of the dhrinking, and then we'll have the big kitchen comfortable to ourselfs for the music and the dancing. And what do you think! Pat has got Shamus na Pe'bria, all the ways out of County Mayo, him that makes all the pipes through the counthry, Miss; and did the music about O'Connell all out of his own head, Miss. Oh, it 'll be the most illigant wedding intirely, Miss, anywhere through the counthry, this long time back! When one is to be married, it's as well to do it dacently as not; arn't it, Miss?"

"Oh! that it is Mary, and yours 'll be quite a dash."

"Yours 'll be the next, you know, Miss Feemy, and that will be the wedding! But there's one thing that bothers me intirely."

"Well, out with it at once, Mary; I suppose you want to borrow the plates, and knives, and forks, and things?"

"Oh, that's in course, Miss Feemy; and it's very good in you to be offering them that way before I axed the loan of them at all; but that ain't all. You see I'm so bothered intirely with them big sheets, and they not half finished, and not a taste in life done to the cap of me yet, and the pratees and vegetables to get ready, and the things to dress, and not a sowl to lend me a hand at all, unless jist Mrs. Mehan's bit of a girl, and she's busy readying the rooms; and so, Miss Feemy, if you'd jist let Biddy slip up for the afthernoon,—you know Katty could be doing for you down here,—and then, Miss, I'd be made intirely."

"Well, Mary, I suppose she must go up then; one thing's certain, you can't be getting married every day."

"Why no, Miss, that is sartain; for even if Denis were to die away like,—as in course he must one day, for he ain't quite so young now,—I would have to be waiting a little, Miss, before I got my second."

Mary Brady had been above thirty years getting one husband; she was, therefore, probably right as to the delay she might experience in obtaining a second.

"Well, Mary, Biddy may go with you."

"Long life to you, Miss; and about the things then you know—the plates, and the knives, and the glasses?"

"Oh! Mary, I'll not have you bringing the glasses down there at all; sure Mrs. Mehan's glasses enough of her own, and she selling whiskey. You may take the knives, and the forks, and the plates; though you must leave us enough for ourselves—and there an't so many of them in it after all."

"Well, Miss Feemy, that's very good of you now. And you'll be bringing your own sweetheart with you, won't you, dear?—and it's I'd be sorry you'd be at my wedding, and no one fit to dance with your father's daughter."

"Oh! if you mean Captain Ussher, he told me Pat asked him himself, and he'd sure be there."

"And who else should I main, alanna; sure isn't he your own beau, and ain't you to be married to him, Miss Feemy?"

"Nonsense, Mary."

"Well, now, but sure you wouldn't be ashamed of telling me —isn't you going to have him, Miss?"

"But musn't I wait to be asked, like another?—Sure, Mary, you didn't go asking Denis McGovery, did you?"

"No, then, indeed I didn't, darling; and glad enough he was to be axing me."

"Well, and musn't I be the same?"

"Oh! in course; but, Miss Feemy, the Captain's been up here coorting at Ballycloran now these six months; sure he axed you before this, Miss Feemy?"

Feemy was rather puzzled; she didn't like to say she was not engaged; she had a presentiment Mary Brady was fishing to find out if the report about the Captain's inconstancy was true, and as matters stood she did not exactly like to say that the affair was arranged.

"Well, Mary, then I'll tell you exactly how it is—but mind, I don't want it talked about yet for rasons; so you won't say anything about it if I tell you?"

"Och then! is it I? Sorrow a word in life shall any one be the better av me, and you know, Miss Feemy, I wouldn't tell you a lie for worlds."

"Well, then, it's jist this way—I and the Captain is engaged, but there's rasons for him why we couldn't be married just immediately; so you see that's why I don't want it talked about."

"Ah! well dear, I knew there was something av that in it, and a nice handsome gentleman like the Captain wouldn't be trating the likes of you that way."

"What way, Mary?"

"Why they do be saying—"

"Who do be saying?"

"Why, jist through the counthry,—people you know, Miss, who must always have their gag; they do be saying—that's only some of them you know, Miss, who don't be quite frindly to Ballycloran —that the Captain don't main to be married at all, and is only playing his tricks with you, and that he's a schamer. But I knew you wouldn't be letting him go on that way, and so I said to Pat."

Feemy didn't quite like all this—it was a corroboration of what her brother had said; for though the Captain had certainly promised to marry her, he had never thought it necessary to ask her. She knew the matter did not rest on a proper footing; and though she was hardly aware of it, she felt the indignity of the probability of being jilted being talked over by such persons as Pat Brady.

"Your brother, Mary, might have saved himself the throuble of telling lies about either the Captain or me; not of course that I care."

"Oh! it warn't Pat, Miss, said it, only he heard it you know, Miss, through the counthry."

"Well, it don't signify who said it, but don't you be repeating what I told you."

"Is it I, Miss? Sorrow a word, Miss, will any one hear from me av it. Would I tell a lie about it? But I'll be glad to see the day you're married, for that'll be the great wedding through the counthry.——Oh laws!"

This exclamation was not a part of the last speech, but was a kind of long-drawn, melancholy sigh, which did not take place for some minute or two after she had done speaking, during which time Feemy had been thinking of her own affairs, quite forgetful of Mary Brady and her wedding.

"My! Mary, what are you sighing about?"

"Well then, Miss Feemy, and isn't it a dreadful thing to be laving one's home, and one's frinds like, and to be going right away into another house intirely, Miss; and altogether the thoughts of what is the married life at all frets me greatly."

"Why, you needn't be married unless you like it, Mary."

"Oh! Miss Feemy, that's in course too; but then a young woman is behove to do something for her family."

"But you haven't a family, you know, Mary, now."

"No, but Miss Feemy alanna, you know the chances is I shall have now I'm to be married; and it's for them, the little innocents, I does it."

The strength of this argument did not exactly strike Feemy, but she thought it was all right, and said nothing.

"And then the throubles of a married life, darling,—supposing them is too many for me, what'll I do at all? I wonder, Miss Feemy, will I get any sleep at all?"

"Indeed, Mary, I was never married; but why shouldn't you sleep?"

"'Deed then, Miss, I don't jist know, but they do be saying that Denis is so noisy at nights, a-shoeing all the cattle over again as he shod in the day, and counting the money; and you see, av he was hammering away the blessed live-long night that way, maybe I'd be hurted."

"It's too late for you to think of that now; but he'll be quieter than that, I should think, when you're with him."

"Maybe he will, Miss; and as you say, I couldn't dacently be off it now. But thin—oh laws!—I'm thinking what will poor Pat be doing without me, and no one in it at all to bile the pratees and feed the pigs—the craturs!"

"That's nonsense, Mary—you and he was always fighting; he'll have more peace in it when you're gone."

"That's thrue for you, Miss, sartanly, and that's what breaks the heart of me intirely. Too much pace isn't good for Pat, no how; he'll never do no good, you'll see, when he comes to have so much of his own way. 'Deed then, the heart's low within me, to be laving Pat this way!" And Miss Brady put the tail of her gown into the corner of her eye.

"But Mary, you'll have to be caring more for your husband

F

now. I suppose you love Denis McGovery, don't you? I'd never marry a man unless I loved him."

"Oh! that's in course—I do love him; why wouldn't I? for he has a nice little room all dacently furnished for any young woman to go into—besides the shop; and he never has the horses at all into the one we sleeps in, as is to be. And he's a handful of money, and can make any woman comfortable; and in course I love him—so I do. But what's the use of loving a man, if he's to be hammering away at a horseshoe all night?"

"Oh, they're making game of you—they are, Mary; depend upon it, when he's tired working all day, he'll sleep sound enough."

"Well, I s'poses he will; but now, Miss Feemy, I wonder is he a quiet sort of man? will he be fighting at all, do you think?"

"Really then, I can't tell; but even if he does, they say you can take your own part pretty well, when it's necessary."

"For the matter of that, so I can; and I don't mind a scrimmage jist now and again—sich as I and Pat have—av it's only to show I won't be put under; but they do say Denis is very sthrong. I don't think I'd ever have had him, av' I'd known afore he'd been so mortial sthrong."

"Well, that's all too late now for you to be talking of; and take my advice, Mary, don't be fighting with him at all if you can help it; for from what people say of him I think your husband, as will be, sticks mostly to his own way, and I don't think he'll let his wife interfere. But he's a hard-working man, and it'll be a great comfort to you that you'll never see your children wanting."

"Oh, the childhren, the little dears! it's of them I'm thinking. God he knows, it's chiefly along of them as makes me do it; but— oh laws! Miss, it's a dreadful thing to come over one all at once. But it's a great comfort anyway your letting Biddy come down to ready the mutton and pratees, and things; and so, Miss, as I've so much to do, you'll excuse my waiting any longer; and you and Mr. Thady and the Captain,—for I'm thinking the Masther won't be coming,—'ll not be down later than sivin, for Father John's to be in it at sivin exact."

"And who's to get the kiss, Mary?"

"Oh, Miss!"

"The Captain says he'll have a try for it anyway."

"Oh that'd be too much honor intirely, Miss. But av here isn't Father John coming up the avenue!"

And Mary hurried off into the realms under ground to secure the willing assistance of Biddy, and Father John's ponderous foot up the hall steps gave Feemy anything but a pleasant sensation.

She was very fond of Father John too, but somehow, just at present she did not feel quite pleased to see him.

The doors were all open, and Father John walked into Feemy's boudoir. However, he was only Father John, and it wasn't her dress therefore that annoyed her; any dress would do for a priest.

After the common greetings were over, and Father John had asked after the family, and Feemy had surmised that it was either her father or her brother that he wished to see, the priest began his task.

"No, Feemy, my dear, it's not your father or your brother I want to see this turn, but just your own self." And Father John sat himself down by the fire. "I'm come just to have a little chat with you, and you musn't be angry with me for meddling with what, perhaps, you'll say was no business of mine."

This exordium made Feemy's heart palpitate, for she knew it must be about Captain Ussher, but she only said,

"Oh! no, Father John, I won't be angry with you."

"That's my darling, for you know it's only out of love for you and Thady that I'm speaking, and a real friend to you can't do you any harm, if after all you shouldn't take his advice."

"Oh! no, Father John, and I'm sure I'm very much obliged to you."

Father John himself hardly knew how to take the sting from the rebuke, which he was aware his mission could not but convey; and he was no less aware, that unless the dose had a little sugar in it, at any rate to hide its unprepossessing appearance even if it did not render it palatable, his patient would never take it.

"Thady, you know, was dining with me yesterday, and we were talking over Ballycloran and old Flannelly's money matters; and I was, you see, just making a bad tenant's excuses to him, and so on from one thing to another, till we got talking about you, Feemy;—in short, he didn't seem quite happy about you."

"I don't know I ever did anything to make him unhappy."

"No, it wasn't anything you had done to make him unhappy, but he is afraid you ain't happy in yourself; and Feemy, my dear, you should always remember, that though Thady is rough in his manners, and perhaps not at all times so gentle in his words as he should be, his heart is in the right place,—at any rate where you are concerned. Though maybe he doesn't say so as often as others might, he's a very fond brother to you."

"And I'm sure I'm always very fond of him—but then he's so queer; but, Father John, if I've offended Thady, I'll beg his pardon, for I'm sure I don't want to be out with him."

"I'm sure you don't, Feemy; but that's not exactly it either.

Thady's not the least in life offended with you; he's not at all easy to take offence, at least not with you; but he doesn't think you are just at ease with yourself; and to come to the truth at once, he was telling me what passed between you yesterday."

Feemy blushed up to her paper curls, but she said nothing.

"Now, I'm thinking Thady didn't go about saying what ne wanted to say yesterday, quite the way he should have done, and I am not sure I shall do it any better myself. But I thought it as well to step up, as I was certain you'd hear whatever your priest had to say to you."

"I don't think the better of Thady, though, for going and talking about me. If he'd only let me alone by myself I'd do well enough; it's all that talking does the harm, Father John."

Father John didn't exactly like to tell Feemy that girls in her situation were just the people that ought not to be left alone by themselves,—which probably means being left alone with some one of their own choosing; and that he was of opinion that she would not do very well if left alone in that way. That, however, was what he wished to convey to her.

"Oh, but, my dear, you must think better of Thady for wishing to protect you as well as he can, and you left alone so much yourself here. So you know,"—and Father John even blushed a little as he said it,—"it's about this fine lover of yours we are speaking. Now, my dear, I've nothing whatever to say against Captain Ussher, for you know he and I are great cronies; indeed, it's only last night he was taking his punch with your brother and Cullen down at the cottage—"

"You weren't saying anything to Captain Ussher about me, Father John?"

"You may take your oath of that, my dear. I respect a lady's secret a great deal too much for that. No; I was only saying that he was down at the cottage last night, to prove that he and I are friends, and it's not out of any prejudice I'm speaking—about his being a Protestant, and all that; not but that I'd sooner be marrying you to a good Catholic, Feemy—but that's neither here nor there. But you've known him now a long time; it's now four months since we all heard for certain it was to be a match; and, to tell you the truth, my dear, people are saying that Captain Ussher doesn't mean anything serious."

"I think they'll dhrive me mad with their talk! And what good will it do for you and Thady to be coming telling me what they say?"

"This good, Feemy; if what they say is false and unfounded, as I am sure I hope it is,—and if you're so fond of Captain Ussher,—

don't you think it would be as well to put an end to the report by telling your father and brother of your being engaged, and settling something about your marriage, and all that?"

"I did tell my brother I was engaged, Father John; what would you have?"

"I'll tell you what I'd have. I'd have Captain Ussher ask your father or brother's consent: there's no doubt, we all know, but he'd get it; but it's customary, and, in my mind, it would only be decent."

"So he will, I dare say; but mayn't there be rasons why he don't wish to have it talked about yet?"

"Then, Feemy, in your situation, do you think a long clandestine engagement is quite the thing for you; is quite prudent?"

"And how can it be clandestine, Father John, when you and Thady, and every one else almost, knows all about it?"

Feemy's sharpness was too much for Father John, so he had to put it on another tack.

"Well, Feemy, now just look at the matter this way, one moment: supposing now—only just for supposition—this lover of yours was not the sort of man we all take him to be, and that he was to turn out false, or inconstant; suppose now it turned out he had another wife somewhere else—"

"Oh, that's nonsense, you know, Father John."

"Yes, but just supposing it,—or that he took some vagary into his head, and changed his mind! You must have heard of men doing such things, and why shouldn't your lover as well as another girl's? We're all likely to be deceived in people, and why mayn't we be as well deceived in Captain Ussher, as others have been in those they loved as well? We'll all hope, and think, and believe it's not so; but isn't it as well to be on the safe side, particularly in so important a thing as your happiness, Feemy? You wouldn't like it to be said through the country that you'd been jilted by the handsome captain, and that you'd been thrown off by your lover as soon as he was tired of you?"

"And that's thrue for you, Father John; but Myles isn't tired of me, else why should he be coming up here to see me oftener than ever?"

"But it's that he never may be tired of you, Feemy; take my word for it, he'll respect you a great deal more if you'll show more respect to yourself."

"Well, Father John, and what is it you'd have me be doing?"

"Why, then, I'd just ask him to speak a word to Thady—just to propose himself in the regular way."

"But Thady hates him so."

"No; Thady don't hate him: he's only jealous lest Captain Ussher isn't treating you quite as he ought to do."

"But Thady is so queer in his manners; and I know Myles wouldn't like to be asking leave and permission to be courting me."

"But, Feemy, he must like it; and you shouldn't like your lover the more for thinking so little of your brother, or, for the matter of that, of yourself either."

"You know, Father John, I can't help what he thinks of Thady. As to his thinking of me, I'm quite satisfied with that, and I suppose that's enough."

Father John was beginning to wax wroth, partly because he was displeased with Feemy himself, and partly because Feemy answered him too knowingly.

"Well, then, Feemy, it'll be one of the two: either Captain Ussher will have to speak to Thady, and settle something about the marriage in a proper and decent way; or else Thady will be speaking to him. And now, which do you think will be the best?"

"It's not like you, Father John, to be making Thady quarrel with Captain Ussher. You know it'd come to a quarrel if Thady was to be spaking to Myles that way; and he would never think of doing so av you didn't be putting him up to it."

"And that's little like you, Feemy, to be saying that to your priest; telling me I put the young men up to be quarrelling: it's to save you many a heart-ache, and many a sting of sorrow and remorse; it's to prevent all the evil of unlawful love—bad blood, and false looks—that I've come here on a most disagreeable and thankless errand; and now you tell me I'd be putting the young men up to fight!"

Feemy had, by this time, become sullen, but she didn't dare go farther with her priest.

"I didn't say you'd be making them fight, Father John. I only said, if you told Thady not to be meddling with Myles, why, in course, they wouldn't be quarrelling."

"And how could I tell a brother not to meddle with his sister's honour, and reputation, and happiness? But now, Feemy, I'll propose another plan to you. If you don't think my advice on such a subject likely to be good—and very likely it isn't, for you see I never had a lover of my own—what do you say to your speaking to your friend, Mrs. McKeon, about it? Or, if you like, I'll speak to her; and then, perhaps, you won't be against taking her advice on the subject. Supposing, now, she was to speak to Captain Ussher—from herself, you know, as your friend—do you think he'd love the girl that's to be his wife worse for having a friend that was willing to stand in the place of a mother to her, when she'd none of her own?"

"Why, I do think it would look odd, Mrs. McKeon meddling with it."

"Well, then, Feemy, what in the blessed name do you mean to do, if you won't let any of your friends act for you? I think you must be very much afraid of this lover of yours, when you won't allow any one speak to him about you. Are you afraid of him, Feemy?"

"Afraid of him?—no, of course I'm not afraid of him; but men don't like to be bothered about such things."

"That's very true; men, when they're false, and try to deceive young girls, and are playing their own wicked game with them, do not like to be bothered about such things. But I never heard of an honest man, who really wanted to marry a young woman, being bothered by getting her friends' consent. And you think, then, things should go on just as they are?"

"Now, Father John, only you've been scolding me so much, I'd have told you before. I mane to spake to Myles myself to-night, just to arrange things; and then I won't have Mrs. McKeon cocking over me that she made up the match."

"There's little danger of that kind, I fear, Feemy, nor would she be doing so; but if you are actually going to speak to Captain Ussher yourself to-night, I'll say no more about it now; but I hope you'll tell Thady to-morrow what passes."

"Oh, Father John, I won't promise that."

"Will you tell me, then, or Mrs. McKeon?"

"Oh, perhaps I'll be telling you, you know, when I come down to confession at Christmas; but indeed I shan't be telling Mrs. McKeon anything about it, to go talking over the counthry."

"Then, Feemy, I may as well tell you at once—if you will not trust to me, to your brother, or any friend who may be able to protect you from insult—nor prevail on your lover to come forward in a decent and respectable way, and avow his purpose—it will become your brother's duty to tell him that his visits can no longer be allowed at Ballycloran."

"Ballycloran doesn't belong to Thady, and he can't tell him not to come."

"That's not well said of you, Feemy; for you know your father is not capable of interfering in this business; but if, as under those circumstances he will do, Thady quietly and firmly desires Captain Ussher to stay away from Ballycloran, I think he'll not venture to come here. If he does, there are those who will still interfere to prevent him."

"And if among you all, that are so set up against him because he's not one of your own set, you dhrive him out of Ballycloran, I can tell you, I'll not remain in it!"

"Then your sins and your sorrows must be on your own head!"

And without saying anything further, Father John took his hat, and walked off. Feemy snatched her novel into her lap, to show how little what was said impressed her, and resumed her attitude over the fire. But she didn't read; her spirit was stubborn and wouldn't bend, but her reason and her conscience were touched by what the priest had said to her, and the bitter thought for the first time came over her, that her lover, perhaps, was not so true to her, as she to him. There she sat, sorrowfully musing; and though she did not repent of what she thought her own firmness, she was bitterly tormented by the doubts with which her brother, Mary Brady, and the priest, had gradually disturbed her happiness.

She loved Ussher as well as ever—yes, almost more than ever, as the idea that she might perhaps lose him came across her—but she began to be discontented with herself, and to think that she had not played her part as well as she might. In fact, she felt herself to be miserable, and, for the time, hated her brother and Father John for having made her so.

Father John walked sorrowfully back to his cottage, thinking Miss Feemy Macdermot the most stiff-necked young lady it had ever been his hard lot to meet.

CHAPTER IX.

MOHILL.

We must now request our reader to accompany us to the little town of Mohill; not that there is anything attractive in the place to repay him for the trouble of going there.

Mohill is a small country town, standing on no high road, nor on any thoroughfare from the metropolis; and therefore it owes to itself whatever importance it may possess—and, in truth, that is not much. It is, or, at any rate, was, at the time of which we are writing, the picture of an impoverished town—the property of a non-resident landlord—destitute of anything to give it interest or prosperity—without business, without trade, and without society. The idea that would strike one on entering it was chiefly this: "Why was it a town at all?—why were there, on that spot, so many houses congregated, called Mohill?—what was the inducement to people to come and live there?—Why didn't they go to Longford, to Cavan, to Carrick, to Dublin,—anywhere rather than there, when they were going to settle themselves?" This is a question which proposes itself at the sight of many Irish towns; they look so poor, so destitute of advantage, so unfriended. Mohill is by no means the only town in the west of Ireland, that strikes one as being there without a cause.

It is built on the side of a steep hill, and one part of the town seems constantly threatening the destruction of the other. Every now and again, down each side of the hill, there is a slated house, but they are few and far between; and the long spaces intervening are filled with the most miserable descriptions of cabins—hovels without chimneys, windows, door, or signs of humanity, except the children playing on the collected filth in front of them. The very scraughs of which the roofs are composed are germinating afresh, and, sickly green with a new growth, look more like the tops of long-neglected dungheaps, than the only protection over Christian beings from the winds of heaven.

Look at that mud hovel on the left, which seems as if it had thrust itself between its neighbours, so narrow is its front! The doorway, all insufficient as it is, takes nearly the whole facing to the street. The roof, looking as if it were only the dirty eaves hanging from its more aspiring neighbour on the right, supports itself against the cabin on the left, about three feet above the ground. Can that be the habitation of any of the human race? Few but such as those whose lot has fallen on such barren places would venture in; but for a moment let us see what is there.

But the dark misery within hides itself in thick obscurity. The unaccustomed eye is at first unable to distinguish any object, and only feels the painful effect of the confined smoke; but when, at length, a faint, struggling light makes its way through the entrance, how wretched is all around!

A sickly woman, the entangled nature of whose insufficient garments would defy description, is sitting on a low stool before the fire, suckling a miserably dirty infant; a boy, whose only covering is a tattered shirt, is putting fresh, but, alas, damp turf beneath the pot in which are put to boil the potatoes—their only food. Two or three dim children—their number is lost in their obscurity—are cowering round the dull, dark fire, atop of one another; and on a miserable pallet beyond—a few rotten boards, propped upon equally infirm supports, and covered over with only one thin black quilt—is sitting the master of the mansion; his grizzly, unshorn beard, his lantern jaws and shaggy hair, are such as his home and family would lead one to expect. And now you have counted all that this man possesses; other furniture has he none—neither table nor chair, except that low stool on which his wife is sitting. Squatting on the ground—from off the ground, like pigs, only much more poorly fed—his children eat the scanty earnings of his continual labour.

And yet for this abode the man pays rent.

The miserable appearance of Irish peasants, when in the very lowest poverty, strikes one more forcibly in the towns than in the open country. The dirt and filth around them seems so much more oppressive on them; they have no escape from it. There is much also in ideas and associations. On a road-side, or on the borders of a bog, the dusty colour of the cabin walls, the potato patch around it, the green scraughs or damp brown straw which form its roof, all the appurtenances, in fact, of the cabin, seem suited to the things around it. But in a town this is not so. It evidently should not be there—its squalidness and filth are all that strike you. Poverty, to be picturesque, should be rural. Suburban misery is as hideous as it is pitiable.

Again, see that big house, with such pretensions to comfort, and even elegance,—with its neat slated roof, brass knocker on the door, verandahs to the large sashed windows, and iron railing before the front. Its very grandeur is much more striking, that from each gable-end hangs another cabin, the same as those we have above described. It is true that an entrance for horses, cars, and carriages has been constructed, as it were through one end of the house itself; otherwise the mansion is but one house in the continuous street.

Here lives Mr. Cassidy, the agent; a fat, good-natured, easy man, with an active grown up son. Every one says that Mr. Cassidy is a good man, as good to the poor as he can be. But he is not the landlord, he is only the agent. What can he do more than he does? Is the landlord then so hard a man? so regardless of those who depend on him in all their wants and miseries? No, indeed; Lord Birmingham is also a kind, good man, a most charitable man! Look at his name on all the lists of gifts for unfortunates of every description. Is he not the presiding genius of the company for relieving the Poles? a vice-presiding genius for relieving destitute authors, destitute actors, destitute clergymen's widows, destitute half-pay officers' widows? Is he not patron of the Mendicity Society, patron of the Lying-in, Small Pox, Lock, and Fever Hospitals? Is his name not down for large amounts in aid of funds of every description for lessening human wants and pangs? How conspicuous and eager a part too he took in giving the poor Blacks their liberty! was not his aid strongly and gratefully felt by the friends of Catholic emancipation? In short, is not every one aware that Lord Birmingham has spent a long and brilliant life in acts of public and private philanthropy? 'Tis true he lives in England, was rarely in his life in Ireland, never in Mohill. Could he be blamed for this? Could he live in two countries at once? or would the world have been benefited had he left the Parliament and the Cabinet, to whitewash Irish cabins, and assist in the distribution of meal?

This would be his own excuse, and does it not seem a valid one? Yet shall no one be blamed for the misery which belonged to him; for the squalid sources of the wealth with which Poles were fed, and literary paupers clothed? Was no one answerable for the grim despair of that half-starved wretch, whom but now we saw, looking down so sadly on the young sufferers to whom he had given life and poverty? That can hardly be. And if we feel the difficulty which, among his numerous philanthropic works, Lord Birmingham must experience in attending to the state of his numerous dependents, it only makes us reflect more often, that from him to whom much is given, much indeed will be required!

But we are getting far from our story. Going a little further down the hill, there is a lane to the right. This always was a dirty, ill-conditioned lane, of bad repute and habits. Father Mathew and the rigour of the police have of late somewhat mended its manners and morals. Here too one now sees, but a short way from the main street, the grand new stirring poor-house, which ten years ago was not in being.

In this lane at the time to which we allude the widow Mulready kept the shebeen shop, of which mention has before been made.

In her business Mrs. Mulready acquired much more profit than respectability, for, whether well or ill-deserved, she had but a bad name in the country; in spite of this, however, to the company assembled here on Wednesday evening,—the same evening that Thady dined with Father John,—we must introduce our readers.

The house, or rather cabin, consisted only of two rooms, both on the ground, and both without flooring or ceiling; the black rafters on which the thatch was lying was above, and the uneven soil below; still this place of entertainment was not like the cabins of the very poor: the rooms were both long, and as they ran lengthways down the street, each was the full breadth of the house: in the first sat the widow Mulready, a strong, red-faced, indomitable-looking woman about fifty. She sat on a large wooden seat with a back, capable of containing two persons; there was an immense blazing fire of turf, on which water was boiling in a great potato pot, should any of her guests be able to treat themselves to the expensive luxury of punch. A remarkably dirty small deal table was beside her, on which were placed a large jar, containing a quantity of the only merchandize in which she dealt, and an old battered pewter measure, in which she gave it out; in a corner of the table away from the fire was cut a hole through the board, in which was stuck a small flickering candle. No further implements appeared necessary to Mrs. Mulready in the business which she conducted. A barefooted girl, with unwashed hands and face, and unbrushed head, crouched in the corner of the fire, ready to obey the behests of Mrs. Mulready, and attend to the numerous calls of her customers. This Hebe rejoiced in the musical name of Kathleen.

The Mohill resort of the wicked, the desperate, and the drunken, was not certainly so grand, nor so conspicuous, as the gas-lighted, mahogany fitted, pilastered gin palaces of London; but the freedom from decent restraint, and the power of inebriety at a cheap rate, were the same in each.

There was a door at the further end of the room, which opened into the one where Mrs. Mulready's more known and regular visitors were accustomed to sit and drink, and here rumour said a Ribon lodge was held; there was a fire also here, at the further end, and a long narrow table ran nearly the whole length of the room under the two windows, with a form on each side of it. Opposite this was Mrs. Mulready's own bed, which proved that whatever improprieties might be perpetrated in the house, the careful widow herself never retired to rest till they were all over.

The assembly on the night in question was not very numerous; there might be about twelve in it, and they all were of the poorer kind; some even had neither shoes or stockings, and there was one poor fellow had neither hat nor coat,—nothing but a tattered shirt and trousers.

The most decent among them all was Pat Brady, who occupied a comfortable seat near the fire, drinking his tumbler of punch and smoking like a gentleman; Joe Reynolds was sitting on the widow's bed, with a spade in his hand; he had only just come in. They were all from Drumleesh, with one or two exceptions; the man without the coat was Jack Byrne, the brother of the man whom Captain Ussher had taken when the malt was found in his brother-in-law's house.

"Kathleen, agra," hallooed Joe Reynolds, "bring me a glass of sperrits, will you?"

"Send out the rint, Joe," hallooed out the wary widow, and Kathleen came in for the money.

"Sorrow to your sowl then, mother Mulready; d'ye think I'm so bad already then, that they haven't left me the price of a glass?" and he put three halfpence into the girl's hand.

"Oh, Joe," said Brady, "don't be taking your sperrits that way; come over here, like a dacent fellow, and we'll be talking over this."

"Oh, that's all right for you, Pat; you've nothing to be dhriving the life out of yer very heart. I am cowld within me, and divil a word I'll spake, till I dhriv it out of me with the sperrits," and he poured the glass of whiskey down his throat, as though he was pouring it into a pitcher. "And now, my boys, you'll see Joe Reynolds 'll talk may be as well as any of you. Give us a draw of the pipe, Pat."

He took the pipe from Pat's hand, and stuck it in his mouth.

"Well, Jack, I see'd your brother in Carrick; and I towld him how you'd done all you could for him, and pawned the clothes off your back to scrape the few shillings together for him; and what d'ye think he'd have me do then? why he towld me to take the money to Hyacinth Keegan, Esq., jist to stand to him and get him off. Why he couldn't do it, not av he was to give his sowl—and that's not his own to give, for the divil has it; and av he could, he wouldn't walk across Carrick to do them a good turn—though, by Jasus, he'd be quick enough pocketing the brads. Begad, Jack, and it's cowld you're looking without the frieze; come and warm your shins, my boy, and take a draw out of Pat's pipe."

"And Joe," said Pat, "what magisthrates war there in it?"

"Why, there war Sir Michael, and Counsellor Webb, and there war that black ruffian Jonas Brown."

"And they jist sent him back to gaol agin, Joe?"

"No, they didn't! Counsellor Webb stuck to the boys hard and fast, while he could; both his own boys and poor Tim; and that he may never sup sorrow; for he proved hisself this day the raal friend to the poor man—"

"But it war all no good in the end?"

"Divil a good. That thief of the world, old Brown, after axing Ussher a sight of questions, was sthrong for sending 'em back; and then Counsellor Webb axed Ussher how he could prove that the boys knew the stuff was in it; and he, the black-hearted viper, said, that warn't necessary, so long as they war in the same house; and then they jawed it out ever so long, and Ussher said as how the whole counthry through war worse than ever with the stills; and Counsellor Webb said that war the fault of the landlords; and Brown said, he hoped they'd take every mother's son of 'em as they could lay hands on in the counthry, and bring 'em there; and so they jawed it out a long while; and then, Sir Michael, who'd niver said a word at all, good, bad, or indifferent, said, as how Paddy Byrne and Smith war to pay each twenty pounds, and Tim ten, or else to go to gaol as long as the bloody owld barrister chose to keep 'em there."

"Jack," said one of the others, "did Paddy, d'y remimber, happen to have an odd twenty pound in his breeches pocket? becase av so, he might jist put it down genteel, and walk out afore thim all."

"Well, then, Corney," answered Jack, with Pat Brady's pipe in his mouth, " av Paddy had sich a thrifle about then, I disremember it entirely; but shure, why wouldn't he? He'd hardly be so far as Carrick, in sich good company too, without a little change in his pocket."

"But to go and put twenty pound on them boys!" observed the more earnest Joe: "the like of them to be getting twenty pounds! mightn't he as well have said twenty thousand? and tin pounds on Tim too! More power to you, Jonas Brown; tin pounds for a poor boy's warming his shins, and gagging over an owld hag's bit of turf!"

"But Joe," said Brady, "is it in Carrick they're to stop?"

"Not at all; they're to go over to the Bridewell in Ballinamore. Captain Greenough was there. A lot of his men is to take them to Ballinamore to-morrow; unless indeed, they all has the thrifle of change in their pockets, Corney was axing about."

"And supposing now, Joe," said Jack, "the boys paid the money, or some of the gentlemen put it down for 'em; who'd be getting it?"

"Sorrow a one of me rightly knows. Who would be getting the brads, Pat, av they war paid?"

"Who'd be getting 'em? why, who would have em but Masther Ussher? D'ye think he'd be so keen afther the stills, av he war not to make something by it? where d'ye think he'd be making out the hunters, and living there better nor the gentlemen themselves, av he didn't be getting the fines, and rewards, and things, for sazing the whiskey?"

"Choke him for fines!" said Jack; "that the gay horse he rides might break the wicked neck of him!"

"Sorrow a good is there in cursing, boys," continued Joe. "Av there war any of you really'd have the heart to be doing anything!"

'What'd we be doing, Joe? kicking our toes agin Carrick Gaol, till the police comed and spiked us? The boys is now in gaol, and there they're like to be, for anything we'll do to get 'em out again."

Joe Reynolds was now puzzled a little, so he fumbled in his pockets, and bringing out another three halfpence, hallooed to Kathleen.

hear, ye young divil's imp! bring me another
rits," and he gave her the halfpence; "and here,
ack too."
int, Joe, my darling," again bawled the widow,
little said in the inner room was lost upon her.
and your rint, you owld hag!" but he paid for
iend; "and may I be d——d if they aint the very
ot."
you, Joe," said the other, as he swallowed the
ay be I'll be able to stand to you, the same way,
s, bad as things is yet. You is all to be up at
to-morrow, with the rints, eh Brady? What'll
he young Masther, Joe?"
mewhat elated by the second glass of whiskey.
saying to him, is it? well I'll tell you what I'll
ıst say this—'I owes two years' rint, Misther
ıe thrifle of bog, and the cabin I holds up at
ere's what I got to pay it!' And I'll show him
ıt in his eye and see none the worse: and
ll say, 'Now, Misther Macdermot, there is the
ere, as I and poor Tim broke the back of us
for last winter; and there is the bit of pratees;
e cutting of the one, nor digging of the other;
e may go and do both; and take them with yer
ıay take the roof off the bit of a cabin I built
uld mother; and ye may turn out the ould hag
d and the bog; and ye may send me off, to get
st gaol as is open to me. That's what you can
lermot: and when you've done all that, there'll
have stood betwixt you and all harum, will then
give you back your own in the hardships you've
And then I'll go on, and I'll say, 'And you
can tell me to go and be d——d, as ye did many a
what bad language ye like; and you can send
ıy or so, jist to tell me to sell the oats, and bring
an; and then, Mr. Thady, there'll be one who'll
ger of that hell-hound Keegan go on Ballycloran:
-and when there's me, my boys, there'll be lots
p you safe and snug in yer own father's house,
eegans and Flannellys in County Leitrim come
' And that's what I'll say to the Masther; and
tells you pretty much all—what'll the Masther
?"
e saying to it, Joe! Faix then I don't know

what he'll be saying to it; it's little mind, I think, he'll have to be saying much comfort to any of you; for he'll be vexed and out with everything, jist at present. He doesn't like the way that Captain Ussher is schaming with his sister."

"Like it! no, I wonder av he did; a black-hearted Protestant like him. What business is it a Macdermot would have taking up with the likes of him?"

"That's not it neither, Joe; but he thinks the Captain don't mane fair by Miss Feemy! and by the blessed Virgin, he ain't far wrong."

"Then why don't he knock the life out of the traitor? or av there is rasons why he shouldn't do it hisself, why don't he get one of the boys as'd be glad of the job to help him. Look here, Pat—" and Reynolds went over to the fire-place, and with his arm against the back wall and leaning down over the seat where Brady was sitting, began whispering earnestly in his ear; and then Brady muttered something dissenting, in a low voice; and Reynolds went on whispering again, with gesticulations, and many signs. This continued for a long time, till Corney exclaimed,

"What the divil, boys, are ye colloquing about there; arn't we all sworn frinds, and what need ye be whispering about? Why can't ye spake what ye've got to say out like a man, instead of huggery muggering there in the corner with Brady, as though any one here wasn't thrue to ye all."

"Whist, Corney, ye born idiot, ye don't know I s'pose what long ears the old hag there has? and ye'd be wanting her to hang two or three of us, I s'pose?"

"Divil a hang, Joe; av no one towld of any but her, we'd be safe enough that way; but what is it ye're saying?"

But instead of answering him Reynolds continued urging something to Pat Brady; at last he exclaimed,

"Tear and ages! and why wouldn't he side with the boys as lives on his own land? av he don't make frinds of them, where will he find frinds? Is it among the great gintlemen of the counthry? By dad, they don't think no more of him nor they do of us. And is it the likes of Captain Ussher as'll be good frinds to him? He's thinking of his own schames, and taking the honest name from his sister. Is that his frind, Pat?"

'Didn't I tell ye, Joe, he hates Ussher a d—d sight worse nor you or I; there's little need to say anything to him about that."

"Why wouldn't he join us then? Who else is there to help him at all? won't he be as bad as we are, if Flannelly dhrives him and the ould man out of Ballycloran; but av he'll stick to us, divil a lawyer of 'em all shall put a keeper on the lands; and I said before, and I say it agin,—and av I prove a liar, may I never see the blessed glory,—av young Macdermot 'll help the boys to right themselves, the first foot Keegan puts on Ballycloran, he shall leave there, by G—d!"

"But, Joe, s'pose now Mr. Thady agreed to join you here, what'd you have him be doing at all?"

"I'd have him lend a hand to punish the murthering ruffian as have got half the counthry dhruv into gaols, and as is playing his tricks now with his own sisther."

"But what could any of you do? You wouldn't dare knock the chap on the head?"

"Who wouldn't dare? by the 'tarnal, I'd dare it myself! Isn't there two of us here, whose brothers is now in gaol along of him? Wouldn't you dare, Jack, av he was up there again in the counthry, to tache him how to be sazing your people?"

"By dad, I'd do anything, Joe; but I don't know jist as to murthering. I'd do as bad to him as he did to Paddy: av they hung him, then I'd murther him, and wilcome; but Paddy'll be out of that some of these days—and I think therefore, Joe, av we stripped his ears, it'd do this go."

Jack Byrne's equal justice pleased the majority of his hearers; but it did not satisfy Joe. As for Pat, he continued smoking, and said nothing.

"Oh, my boys, that's nonsense," said Joe; "either do the job, or let it alone. Av you've a mind to let Captain Ussher walk into your cabins and take any of you off to Carrick, jist as he plazes— why you can; but I'm d—d if I does! I've had enough of him now; and by the 'tarnal powers, though I swing for it, putting Tim in gaol shall cost him his life!"

Joe was very much excited and half tipsy; but he only said what most of them were waiting to hear said, and what each of them expected; not one voice was raised in dissent. Pat said nothing, but smoked and gazed on the fire.

"Masther Thady 'll be in at the wedding to-morrow, Pat?"

"Oh in course he will."

"Will you be axing him, thin?"

"Axing him what? is it to murther Ussher?"

"No, in course not that; but will you be thrying him, will he join wid us to rid the counthry of him?"

"I tell ye, Joe, he's willing enough to be shut of him entirely, av he knew how."

"Oh yes, Pat, I dare say he'd be willing any poor boy'd knock him on the head, and so be rid of him; and av that he who did do it, did be hung for it, what matther in life to him? That may do very well for Masther Thady, but by the powers, it'll not do for me!"

"Well, you can be spaking to him yourself to-morrow."

"Yes, but you must be getting him jist to come out, and spake to us; jist dhraw him out a bit, you know."

"Well then, boys, I've said as much to the Masther already, and he expects to meet you up there."

"That's the sort, Pat! and av he'll but join us, divil a fear at all for Captain Ussher. Come, my boys, we'll dhrink the gentleman's health, as would be only dacent and proper of us, seeing the great throuble he's at with us."

"But where'll ye get the whiskey, Joe?" said Corney; "I don't think mother Mulready'll be too quick giving you thrust."

"That's thrue any way; which of ye's got the rint among yer? come, Pat, fork out for once."

"Is it for all of ye? I'll stand a glass for myself, and one for Joe."

"Well, Jack," said Corney, "you and I'll have a dhrop together; you shan't say I let you go away dhry."

The rest made it up among them; and Kathleen, having duly received the price in advance, brought in a glass of spirits for each. The widow Mulready had only two glasses, and they therefore had to drink one after the other. Joe took his first, saying, "And there's more power and success to you, Captain Ussher; and it's a fine gentleman is the only name for ye; but av you're above the sod this day three months, may none of us that is in it this night ever see the blessed glory!"

And they all drank the toast which their leader gave them.

They now prepared to leave; but not so quickly but that Mrs. Mulready had to give them very forcible hints that she wanted quiet possession of her bed-room; and much animated conversation passed on the occasion.

"And now, an't ye a pretty set of boys, the whole of ye, blackguards that ye are! that ye can't dhrink yer sperrits quietly, in a lone woman's house, but you must be bringing the town on her, by yer d—d ructions; and av I niver saw the foot of any of ye agin, it's little I'd be grieving for ye."

"Quit that, you ould hag of the divil! or I'll give you more to talk about than'll plaze you."

"Is it you, Joe? by the mortial then, if ye don't quit that, you'll soon be having a stone roof over yer head. By the blessed Virgin, I'll be the hanging of you av you don't be keeping yerself to yerself."

"Is it hanging yer talking of? And where'll you be yerself?

Not but hanging's twice too good for you. Come, Corney, is you coming up to Loch Sheen?"

After a few more exchanges of similar civilities between the landlady and her guests, the latter at length took their departure; and the widow having duly put away the apparatus of her trade, that is, having drank what whiskey there remained in the jug, betook herself to her couch in her usual state of intoxication.

Joe Reynolds and Pat Brady had each about three miles to go home, and the greater part of the way they walked together—talking over their plans, and discussing the probability of their success.

The two men were very different. The former was impoverished, desperate, all but houseless; he had been continually at war with the world, and the world with him. Whether, had he been more fortunate, he might have been an honest man is a question difficult to solve; most certainly he had been a hard working man, but his work had never come to good; he had long been a maker of potheen, and from the different rows in which he had been connected, had got a bad name through the country. The effect of all this was, that he was now desperate; ready not only to take part against any form of restrictive authority, but anxious to be a leader in doing so; he had somehow conceived the idea that it would be a grand thing to make a figure through the country; and, as he would have said himself, "av he were hanged, what harum?"

Pat Brady was a very different character. In a very poor country he enjoyed comparative comfort; he had never been rendered desperate by want and oppression. Poor as was the Ballycloran property, he had always, by his driving and ejecting, and by one or another art of rural law which is always sure to be paid for, managed to live decently, and certainly above want: it was difficult to conceive why he should be leagued with so desperate a set of men, sworn together to murder a government officer.

Yet in the conversation they had going home he was by far the most eager of the two; he spoke of the certainty they had of getting young Macdermot to join them the next evening; told Reynolds how he would get him, if possible, to drink, and, when excited, would bring him out to talk to the boys; in short, planned and arranged all those things about which Reynolds had been so anxious—but as to which he could get so little done at the widow's. When there, Pat had been almost silent; at any rate, he had himself proposed nothing. It had never occurred to the other, poor fellow, that Brady was making a tool of him; that though the rent-collector was now so eager in proving how easily young Macdermot might be induced to join their party, he would commit himself to nothing when they were congregated at the widow Mulready's. Had Reynolds not been so completely duped, he would have seen that Brady made him take the part of leader when others were present, who might possibly be called upon as witnesses; but that when they were alone together, he, Brady, was always the most eager to press the necessity of some desperate measure. On the present occasion too Reynolds was half drunk, whereas Brady was quite sober.

"So," said the latter on their way home, "thim boys is fixed in gaol for the next twelve months any way. Tim warn't thinking he'd get lodgings for nothing so long, when he went up to widow Smith's there at Loch Sheen."

"Well, Pat, a year is a dreary long time for a poor boy to be locked up all for nothing; and poor Tim won't bear up well as most might; but he that put him there will soon be sent where he'll be treated even worser than Tim at Ballinamore;—and he won't get out of it that soon. By G—d, I'd sooner be in Tim's shoes this night than in Captain Ussher's, fine gentleman as he thinks hisself!"

"But, Joe, will them boys from Loch Sheen let Tim and the others be taken quietly to Ballinamore? Won't they try a reskey on the road?"

"There arn't that sperrit left in 'em, Pat;—and how should it? what is the like of them with their shilelahs, and may be a few stones, agin them b—— pailers in the daylight? Av it had been at night, we might have tried a reskey; but the sperrit ain't in 'em at all. I axed 'em to go snacks with me in doing the job, but they was afeard—and no wonder."

"Well, you'll be up at Mary's wedding to-morrow, and see what the young masther 'll be saying."

And so the two friends parted to their different homes.

CHAPTER X.

MR. KEEGAN.

It will be remembered that the priest left Feemy after his stormy interview in a somewhat irritable mood; she was still chewing the cud of the bitter thoughts to which the events of the last few hours had given rise, and was trying to make herself believe that her brother and Father John and Pat Brady, and all the rest of them, were wrong in their detestable surmises, and that her own Myles was true to her, when another stranger called at Ballycloran; and a perfect stranger he must have been, for he absolutely raised the lion-headed, rusty knocker, and knocked at the door—a ceremony to which the customary visitors of the house never dreamed of having recourse. So unusual was this proceeding, that it frightened the sole remaining domestic, Katty, out of all her decorum. It will be remembered that Mary Brady had absconded with Biddy. Poor Katty did not well know how to act under the trying emergencies of the case; she could not get to the door of Miss Feemy's parlour, as a strange gentleman was standing in the hall, so she ran round the house, and ascertaining that the intruder was well in the hall, and could not see her, she clambered up to her mistress's window, and exclaimed,

"Hist! Miss Feemy, there's a sthranger gintleman a rapping at the big knocker, and I think it's the fat lawyer from Carrick; what'll I do thin, Miss?"

"Why, you fool!" whispered Feemy through one of the broken panes of glass, "go and ask him who he wants, and tell him Thady an't at home."

So Katty dropped from the window-sill again, and went to receive the gentleman into the house by following him in at the hall door. By the time, however, that she had entered herself, old Larry Macdermot had been aroused out of his lethargy by a third knocking of the stranger; and on opening his own parlour door, was startled to see Mr. Hyacinth Keegan, the attorney from Carrick on Shannon, standing before him.

Mr. Hyacinth Keegan requires some little introduction, as he is one of the principal personages of my tale. As Father Cullen before remarked, his father was a process-server living at a small town called Drumshambo;—that is, he obtained his bread by performing the legal acts to which Irish landlords are so often obliged to have resort in obtaining their rent from their tenants. This process-server was a poor man, and a Roman Catholic, but he had managed to give his son a decent education; he had gotten him a place as an errand boy in an attorney's office, from whence he had risen to the dignity of clerk, and he was now, not only an attorney himself, but a flourishing one, and a Protestant to boot. His great step in the world had been his marriage with Sally Flannelly,—that Sally whom Macdermot had rejected,—for from the time of his wedding he had much prospered in all worldly things. He was a hardworking man, and in that consisted his only good quality; he was plausible, a good flatterer, not deficient in that sort of sharpness which made him a successful attorney in a small provincial town, and he could be a jovial companion, when called on to take that part. Principle had never stood much in his way, and he had completely taught himself to believe that what was legal was right; and he knew how to stretch legalities to the utmost. As a convert, Mr. Keegan was very enthusiastically attached to the Protestant religion and the Tory party, for which he had fought tooth and nail at the last county election.

Mr. Keegan boasted a useful kind of courage; he cared but little for the ill name he had acquired by his practice in the country among the poorer classes, and to do him justice, had shown pluck enough in the dangerous duties which he sometimes had to perform; for he acted as agent to the small properties of some absentee landlords, and for a man of his character such duties in County Leitrim were not at that time without risk. He had been shot at, had once been knocked off his horse, and had received various threatening letters; but it always turned out that he discovered the aggressor, and prosecuted and convicted him. One man he had transported for life; in the last case, the man who had shot at him was hung; and consequently the people began to be afraid of Mr. Keegan.

Our friend was fond of popularity, and was consequently a bit of a sportsman, as most Connaught attorneys are. He had the shooting of two or three bogs, kept a good horse or two, went to all the country races, and made a small book on the events of the Curragh. These accomplishments all had their effect, and as I said before, Mr. Keegan was successful. In appearance he was a large, burly man, gradually growing corpulent, with a soft oily face, on which there was generally a smile; and well for him that there was, for though his smile was not prepossessing, and carried the genuine stamp of deceit, it concealed the malice, treachery, and selfishness which his face so plainly bore without it. His eyes were light, large, and bright, but it was that kind of brightness which belongs to an opaque, and not to a transparent body—they never sparkled; his mouth was very large, and his lip heavy, and he carried a huge pair of brick-coloured whiskers. His dress was somewhat dandified, but it usually had not a few of the characteristics of a horse jockey; in age he was about forty-five. His wife was some years his senior, he had married her when she was rather falling into the yellow leaf; and though Mr. Hyacinth Keegan was always on perfectly good and confidential terms with his respected father-in-law, report in Carrick on Shannon declared, that great battles took place beside the attorney's fireside, as to who was to have dominion in the house. The lady's temper also might be a little roused by the ill-natured reports which reached her ears, that her handsome Hyacinth lavished more of his attentions and gallantry abroad than at home. Such was the visitor who now came to call at Ballycloran.

Mr. Macdermot was very much surprised, for Mr. Keegan's business with Ballycloran was never done by personal visits. If money was received, Thady used to call and pay it at Keegan's office; if other steps were to be taken, he employed one of those messengers, so frequently unwelcome at the houses of the Connaught gentry, and this usually ended in Thady calling at Mr. Keegan's for a fresh bill for his father to sign. Old Macdermot was therefore so surprised that he knew not how to address his visitor. This, together with his hatred of the man, and his customary inability to do or say anything, made him so perplexed that he could not comprehend Mr. Keegan's first words, which were not only conciliatory and civil, but almost affectionate.

"Ah! Mr. Macdermot, how do you do—how d'ye do? I'm glad to see you—very glad to see you—looking so well too. Why, what a time it is since I last had the pleasure—but then I'm so tied by the leg—so much business, Mr. Macdermot; indeed, though I was determined to drop in this morning as a friend, still even now I've just a word to say on business. You see I must join business and pleasure; so if you are not very much engaged, and could spare a minute or two, why I have a little proposal to make to you—acting for Mr. Flannelly you know—which I think you'll not be sorry to hear."

The attorney had been obliged to begin his story thus far in the hall—as the old man had shown no inclination to ask him into the parlour: nor did Larry even now move from the door; and, indeed, he did not look as though he was a fit subject to enter on business with an attorney. He had not shaved, or rather been shaved, since Sunday last; his eyes, though wide open, looked as if they had very lately been asleep, and were not quite awake; his clothes were huddled on him, and hung about him almost in tatters; the slaver was running down from his half open mouth, and his breath smelt very strongly of whiskey.

Keegan, finding that his host did not seem bent on hospitality, was edging himself into the room, when Feemy, who had heard his address to her father, came out to the old man's relief, and told the visitor that he was not just himself that morning—that Thady was out, but that she would desire him to call at Mr. Keegan's office the next day.

"Ah! Miss Feemy, and how's your pretty self this morning?—and is it the fact what we hear down at Carrick, that we are to have a wedding soon at Ballycloran? Ah! well, of course you wouldn't be after telling me, but I was very glad to hear it; that

I was, Miss Feemy. But, Mr. Macdermot—it was your father Miss Feemy, I was wishing to see this morning, not Mr. Thady—if you could allow me ten minutes or so—just a message from our old friend, Flannelly:"—and by this time Keegan had wedged his way into the room, out of which any one who knew him would be very sure he would not stir, until he had said what he had come to say.

Larry, hobbling back after him, sat himself down in his accustomed chair, and Feemy, as if to protect her father in her brother's absence, followed him.

"It's very hard, then, Mr. Keegan, that you should come up here; as if sending your processes, and latitats, and distraining, weren't enough, but now you must—"

"Ah! my dear Sir, it's not about such disagreeable business at all—we're done with all that. It's not about such business at all. When I've disagreeable jobs to do—of course we must have disagreeable jobs sometimes—why, I always send some of my disagreeable fellows to do it; but when I've good news, why I like to bring it myself, and that's why I rode down this morning"

Larry, stupid as he was, couldn't be talked round by the attorney so easily.

"If it's good news you have, why shouldn't Thady hear it then? I am sure, poor fellow, he hears enough of bad news from you one way or another. And I tell you I can't understand business to-day, and Flannelly's bill doesn't come round till next month—I know that; and so, if you plaze, Thady can hear what you have to say, at Carrick, on Saturday or Monday, or any day you plaze. Feemy, my darling, get something for Mr. Keegan to eat. I'll be glad to see you eat a bit, but I can't talk any more." And the old man turned himself away, and began groaning over the fire.

"You see, Mr. Keegan, my father can't go to business this morning. When shall I tell Thady to call down?—But wouldn't you take a glass of—"

Wine, Feemy was going to say, but she knew she had none to offer.

"Not a taste in life of anything, thank you, Miss Feemy; not a drop, I'm very much obliged to you: but I'm sorry to find your good father so bent on not hearing me, as I have something to propose which he couldn't but be glad to hear."

"Well, father, will you listen to what Mr. Keegan has to say?"

"Don't I tell you, Feemy, that the bill doesn't come round before November? and it's very hard he won't lave me in pace till that time comes."

"You see," continued Feemy, "that he won't hear anything; don't you think you'd better wait and see Thady down at Carrick?"

Now this was what Mr. Keegan did not want; in fact, his wish was to talk over Larry Macdermot to agree to something to which he feared Thady would object; but he had had no idea the old man would be so obstinate. He, however, was at a loss how to proceed, when Feemy declared that Thady was seen approaching.

"Well, then, Miss Feemy, as your brother is here, and as your father isn't just himself this morning, I might as well do my business with him; but as it is of some importance, and as Mr. Flannelly wishes to have your father's answer as soon as possible, he will not object, I hope, to giving his opinion, when he shall have heard what I have to say."

By this time Thady was before the door, and on Feemy's calling to him, informing him that Mr. Keegan was in the house, waiting to speak to him, he came up into the parlour.

"How do you do this morning?" said the lawyer, shaking Thady by the hand, "how d'ye do? I've just ridden up here to bring a message to your father from Mr. Flannelly about this mortgage he holds; but your father doesn't seem quite the thing this morning, and therefore it's as well you came in. Of course what I have to say concerns you as well as him."

"Of course, Mr. Keegan; I look after the affairs at Ballycloran mostly, now. Don't you know it's me you look to for the money? —and I'm sorry you should have to bother my father about it. Just step out of the room, Feemy."

And the young lady retreated to her own possessions.

"Why, now, Mr. Thady, how you all put your backs up because an unfortunate attorney comes to call on you. What I'm come to say is what I hope and think you'll both be glad to hear; and I trust you've too much good sense to put your father against it merely because it comes from me."

"You may be sure I shall not put my father against anything which would be good for him or Feemy—"

"Well, Mr. Thady, so far so good; and I'm sure you wouldn't; besides, what I've got to say is greatly to your own advantage."

"Well, Mr. Keegan, out with it."

"Why, you see, Mr. Macdermot,"—and the attorney turned to the father, who sat poring over the fire, as if he was determined not to hear a word that passed,—" you see, Mr. Macdermot, Mr. Flannelly is thinking how much better it would be to settle the affair of this mortgage out and out. He's getting very old, Mr. Macdermot. Why, Thady, he's more than thirty years older than your father; and you see he wants to arrange all his money matters.

Between us and the bedpost, by the by, I wish he didn't think so much of those nephews of his. However, he wishes the matter settled, and I explained to him that after knowing one another so long, it wouldn't be fair—though, for the matter of that, of course it would be fair, but, in fact, the old man doesn't exactly wish it himself—that is, you know, to foreclose at once, and sell the estate—"

Here he paused; while Larry merely fidgeted in his chair, and Thady said, "Well, Mr. Keegan?"

"So, you see, he just wishes the affair to be settled amicably. I fear, Mr. Thady, your father hasn't just got the amount of the principal debt."

"Oh! you know that of yourself, Mr. Keegan; you know he hasn't the interest itself, till I screw it out of them poor devils of tenants."

"Well, Mr. Macdermot, as you haven't the money to pay the principal debt, of course you can't clear the estate. Why, you see, the interest amounts to £198 odd shillings a year; and before that's paid—times is so bad, you see—Mr. Flannelly is obliged—obliged, in his own defence, you see—to run you to great expense. Well, now, perhaps you'd say, if Flannelly wants his money at once, you'd borrow it on another mortgage—that is, sell the mortgage, Mr. Thady; but money's so scarce these days, and the property is so little improved, and the tenants so bad, that you couldn't raise the money on it—you couldn't possibly raise the money on it."

"Why, Mr. Keegan, father pays Mr. Flannelly £5 per cent., and the property is near to £400 a year, even now."

"Well, of course, if you think so, I wouldn't advise you to the contrary; only, if so, Mr. Flannelly must foreclose at once, in which case the property would be sold out and out; but perhaps you could effect a loan in time—"

"Well, Mr. Keegan, what was it you said you had to propose?"

"What Mr. Flannelly proposes, you mean;—of course I'm only his messenger now. What he proposes is this. You see, the property is so unimproved, and bad—why, the house is tumbling down—it's enough to kill your father, now he's getting a little infirm."

"Well, well, Mr. Keegan; what is it Mr. Flannelly wishes to do with us?"

"Wishes to do?—oh, he doesn't wish anything, of course; the law is open to him to get his own; in fact, the law would give him much more than he wishes to take: but he proposes to buy Ballycloran himself."

"Buy Ballycloran!" screamed Larry.

"Well, well, father; let's hear what Mr. Keegan has to say.—Well, Mr. Keegan, does he propose giving anything but what he has got himself already?—or does he propose to take the estate for the mortgage, and cry quits; so that father, and Feemy, and I, can walk out just where we plaze?"

"Of course not, of course not. It's to make your father what he thinks a fair offer that I'm come up; and it's what I'm sure you must think is a generous offer."

"Well, out with it."

"Well then; what he proposes to do is, to settle an annuity on your father for his life; and give you a sum of money down for yourself and your sister."

"Let's hear what he offers," said Thady.

Larry, whose back was nearly turned to the chair where the attorney was sitting, said nothing; but he gave an ominous look round, which showed that he had heard what had passed. But it did not show that he by any means approved of the proposition.

"I'm coming to that. You see the rent is mostly all swallowed up by this mortgage. Now can you say you've £50 a year coming into the house? I'm afraid not, Mr. Thady—I'm afraid not; and then all your time is occupied in collecting it, and scraping it; and if it's true what I hear—to be plain, I fear you'll hardly have the interest money this November; and if you like Mr. Flannelly's proposal, he'll give in that half year; so that you'd have something in hand to begin. And how comfortable Mr. Macdermot would be in lodgings down at Carrick; you've no idea how reasonable he might board there; say at Dargan's for instance, for about ten shillings a week. And I'm very glad, I can assure you, to hear of the very respectable match your sister is making. Ussher is a very steady nice fellow, knows what's what, and won't be less ready to come to the scratch when he knows he'll have to touch a little ready cash."

"You'd better let us know what your offer is, and lave my sisther alone. It doesn't do to bring every old woman's story in, when we're talking business; so, if you plaze, we won't calculate on Feemy's marriage."

"Well, well, I didn't mean anything more than that I just heard that a match was made between them. So, Mr. Macdermot, Mr. Flannelly will settle £50 a year on you, paid as you like; or come, say a pound a week, as you would probably like to pay your lodgings weekly; and he would give £100 each to your son and daughter, ready money down you know, Mr. Thady. What do you say, Mr. Macdermot?" And he got up and walked round so as to stand over the side of Larry's chair.

"Didn't I tell you, then, I wouldn't be bothered with your business? If you must come up here jawing and talking, can't you have it out with Thady there?"

"Well, Thady, what do you say? You see how much your father's comfort would be improved; and as I suppose, after all, your sister is to be married, you couldn't well keep the house up; and I'll tell you what more Mr. Flanelly proposes for yourself."

"I don't want what Mr. Flannelly will do for me; but I'm thinking of the old man, and Feemy there."

"Well, don't you see how much more comfortable he must be?—nothing to bother him, you know; no bills coming due; and as for yourself, you should have a lease, say for five years, of any land you liked; say forty acres or so, and with your ready money you know."

"Sure isn't the land crowded with tenants already?" said Thady.

"Ah yes; those wretched cabin holders with their half acres. Mr. Flannelly would soon get shut of them: he means to have no whiskey making on the land! Let me alone to eject those fellows. By dad! I'll soon clear off most of them."

"What! strip their roofs?"

"Yes, if they wouldn't go quietly; but they most of them know me now; and I give you my word of honour—indeed, Flannelly said as much—you should have any forty acres you please, at a fair rent. Say what the poor devils are paying now, without any capital you know."

"No, Mr. Keegan; I wouldn't have act or part in dhriving off the poor craturs that know me so well; nor would I be safe if I did; nor for the matter of that, could I well bring myself to be one of Mr. Flannelly's tenants at Ballycloran. But I won't say I won't be advising the owld man to take the offer, if you only make it a little fairer. Consider, Mr. Keegan; the whole property—nigh £400 a year, besides the house—and Mr. Flannelly's debt on it only £200."

"Ah! £400 a year and the house is very well," said Keegan; "but did you ever see the £400—and isn't the house half falling down already?"

"Whose fault is that—who built it then, Mr. Keegan?—bad luck to it for a house!"

"Well, I don't know it's much use going into that now; but you can't say but what the proposal is a fair one."

"Ah! Mr. Keegan, £1 a week is too little for the owld man; make it £100 a year for his life, and give Feemy £300, so that she, poor girl, may have some chance of neither begging or starving, if she shouldn't get married, and I'll not go against the bargain. I'd get a bit of land somewhere, though I couldn't be a tenant on Ballycloran. 'Deed for the matter of that, if we must part it, I don't care how long it is before I see a sod of it again."

"Nonsense, Mr. Thady; £100 a year is out of the question; why, your father's hardly to be called an elderly man yet. I couldn't think of advising Mr. Flannelly to give more than he has already proposed.—Don't you think, Mr. Macdermot,"—and he began speaking loudly to the old man;—"£1 a week, regularly paid, you know, would be a nice thing for you, now that your daughter is going to get married, and that Thady here thinks of taking a farm for himself?"

"I towld you before I'd nothing to say about it—and I will say nothing about it; the bill don't come round till November, and it's very hard you should be bothering the life out of me this way."

Keegan turned away, and taking Thady by the collar of his coat, led him to the window; he began to find he could do nothing with Larry.

"You see, Macdermot," he said in a half whisper, "it is impossible to get your father to listen to me; and therefore the responsibility must rest upon you as to advising him what he'd better do. And now let me put it to you this way: you know that you have not the means of raising the money to pay off this debt, and that Flannelly can sell the estate any day he pleases; well,—suppose you drive us to this, and suppose the thing fetches a little over what his claim is, don't you know there are great expenses attached to such a sale? All would have to come out of the property; and your father's other creditors would come on the little remainder, and where would you be then? You see, my boy, it's quite impossible the estate should ever come to you. Now, by what I propose, your father would sell the estate while still he had the power; he would get comfortably settled—and I'd take care to manage the annuity so that the other creditors couldn't touch it; and you'd get a handful of money to set you up something more decently than the way you're going on here with your tenants."

"But my sisther, Mr. Keegan; when the home came to be taken from over her head, what would become of Feemy? She and the owld man could hardly live on a pound a week. And when the owld man should die—"

"Why, nonsense, man! Isn't your sister as good as married? or if not, a strapping girl like her is sure of a husband. Besides, when she's a hundred pounds in her pocket, she won't have to go far to look for a lover. There's plenty in Carrick would be glad to take her."

"Take her, Mr. Keegan! Do you think I'd be offering her that way to any huckster in Carrick that wanted a hundred pound;—or that she would put up with the like of that?—Bad as we are, we an't come to that yet."

"There you go with your family pride, Thady; but family pride won't feed you, and the offer I've made will; so you'd better bring the old man round to accept it."

"Make it £80 a year for my father, and £250 for Feemy, and I'll do the best I can."

"Not a penny more than I offered. Indeed, Mr. Flannelly would get the property cheaper if he sold it the regular way under the mortgage, so that he doesn't care about it: only he'd sooner you got the difference than strangers.—Well, you won't get the old man to take the offer—eh?"

"I can't advise him to sell his property, and his house, and everything, so for nothing."

"Then you know we must sell it for him."

"Will you give me till Monday," said Thady, "till I ask some friend what I ought to do?"

"Some friend;—what friend do you want to be asking—some attorney? Dolan, I suppose, who of course would tell you not to part with the property, that he might make a penny of it. No, Master Thady, that won't do; either yes or no—no or yes; I don't care which; but an answer, if you please, as Flannelly is determined he will do something."

"It's no lawyer I want to spake to, Mr. Keegan; I've had too much of lawyers; but it's my friend, Father John."

"What, the priest! thank ye for nothing; I'll have no d—d priest meddling; and to tell you the truth at once, it's either now or never. And think where your father 'll be if the house is sold over his head, before he has a place to stretch himself in."

"Oh! you know, and I know, you can't sell it out of hand, in that way,—all at once."

"'Deed but we can though; and, by G—d, if you mean to be stiff about it, you shall be out of the place before the May rents become due."

"Would you want me to go and sell all that's left in the family, without giving me a day to consider?—without asking my friends what's best to do for the old man, and for poor Feemy? Surely, Mr. Keegan—"

"Surely, nonsense. You see how it is; I want to give Flannelly an answer; he's not asking anything of you—he's offering a provision to you all, which you might go far to look for if the law takes its course,—as of course it will do if you oppose his offer. But perhaps you're thinking we can't sell the estate; and from the old man's state, because he's not *compos*, you can get Ballycloran into your own hands. If that's the game you're playing, you'll soon find yourself in the wrong box, my lad."

"It's not of myself I'm thinking; and it's only you, and such as you, would be saying so of me. But supposing now, the owld man consinted to this bargain,—how would he be sure of his money?"

"Sure of his money! why, wouldn't it be settled on him?—wouldn't it be named as one of the conditions of the sale? He'd be a deal surer of that, than he is now of his daily dinner; for that I believe he's not very sure of as things are going at Ballycloran."

Thady looked at the attorney as though he longed to answer him in the same strain; but he said nothing of the sort; he remained looking out of the window for a short time, considering what he should do.

"Well, Macdermot, I can't be waiting here all day you know; what do you say to it?"

"I'll spake to my father; it's he must decide you know, at last, and not me. Larry, you heard what Mr. Keegan said, didn't you?" and he explained to his father the nature of the offer; and tried to make him understand that at any rate Ballycloran must go; and that it would be better to go at once, with some provision to look to, than to stay there, and be driven out, without any; and that Mr. Flannelly would not be content any longer with getting the interest for his money, but that he was determined to get the principal, either by having the property sold, or by taking possession of it himself. It was long before he could make the old man precisely understand what it was that was required of him; during which time Keegan remained at the window, as if he was not hearing a word that passed between the father and son.

"And does he want us to go clane out of it, Thady?"

"Root and branch, father, for iver and iver; and there'll be the finish of the Macdermots of Ballycloran; but Larry,"—and he put his hand, with more tenderness than seemed to belong to his rough nature, on his father's arm;—"but Larry, you know you'll never want for anything then; you'll be snug enough jist wherever you plaze; and your money coming due and paid every week—you'd be better than in this wretched place; eh Larry?"

"And what's to become of Feemy?"

"Why, we must get Feemy a husband; till then she'll stay with you; she'll have a thrifle of money herself, you know; she'll be poor enough, though, God knows!—It's the thought of her that throubles me most."

"And yourself, Thady, where would you go, till you got Ballycloran again?"

"Got Ballycloran again! why Larry, you're to sell it outright; clane away altogether. As for me, I must get a bit of land, I suppose, or 'list, or do something; go to America, perhaps."

"And was it Keegan wanted to buy Ballycloran?"

"Oh, it's between them, I suppose; but what does it matter—Keegan or Flannelly?"

"And what did you say, Thady?"

"What did I say! Oh, I could say nothing, you know; it's for you to do it. But, Larry, I think it's the best for you, and you may be sure I'll not be complaining afther; or saying ill of you for what you did, when you could do no other."

"And you didn't tell the blackguard ruffian robber to be gone out of that, when he asked you to dhrive your own family out of your own house?"

"Whist, father, whist!"

When Keegan heard old Macdermot break out in this way, he was obliged to turn round; so he walked up to the fire, and said, "Mr. Macdermot, may I ask who you are speaking of?"

Larry was again commencing, when Thady held him down gently, and said,

"It's not so asy, Mr. Keegan, for an old man to hear for the first time, that he's to lave his house and his home for iver; where he and his father and his grandfather have lived. You'd better let me talk to him a while."

"Oh! for the matter of that, I don't care for his passion; but if he means to come to reason, let him do so at once, for as I said before, I won't wait here all day."

"Nobody wants you to wait—nobody wants you to wait!" said the father.

"Whist, Larry, whist! be asy a while."

"I won't whist, and I won't be asy: so, Mr. Keegan, if you want to have my answer, take it, and carry it down to that old bricklayer in Carrick, whose daughter has the divil's bargain in you; and for the like of that you're not bad matched. Tell him from me, Larry Macdermot—tell him from me, that I'm not so owld yet, nor so poor, nor so silly, that he can swindle me out of my lands and house that way. So clever as you think yourself, Mr. Keegan, you may walk back to Carrick again, and don't think to call yourself masther of Ballycloran yet awhile."

"Very well, Mr. Macdermot; very well, my fine fellow; look to yourself, and mind, I tell you I'll have a cheaper bargain of the place by this day six months, than I should have now by the terms I'm offering myself."

"You dirthy mane ruffian—if it was only myself you was wanting to turn out of it—but to be robbing the boy there of his property, that has been working his sowl out these six years for that dirthy owld bricklayer!—And you want the place all to yourself, do you, Mr. Keegan? Faix, and a fine estated gintleman you'd make, any how!"

"Well now; you'll repent the day you made yourself such a fool. However, good morning, Mr. Macdermot—good morning; I'll tell them down at Carrick, to keep a warm corner for you in the lane there, where them old beggars sleep at night!"

"Kick him out, Thady; kick him out, will ye?—Have ye none of the owld blood left round your heart, that you'll not kick him out of the house, for a pettifogging schaming blackguard!" and Larry got up as though he meant to have a kick at the attorney himself.

"Be asy, father, and let him go of himself; he'll go fast enough now. Sit down awhile; sit down till I come back," and Thady followed the attorney down the steps on to the gravel road.

"You'll see, my boy," said Keegan—and now the benevolent attorney had altogether lost his smile,—"you'll see, my boy, whether I won't make the two of you pay for this; ay! and the whole family too, for a set of proud, beggarly, starved-out paupers. By G—, I'll sell every rotten stick of old furniture left in the house, on the 6th of next month; and the three of you shall be tramping in the roads before the winter's over!"

"You're worse than the old man with your passion, Mr. Keegan," said Thady; "ten times worse; you know I did what I could to advise him; and even now, if you'll lave him to me, I'll bring him round."

"Be d—d to you with your bringing round! I'll have no more to do with the pack of you."

"Would you go to remember the passionate words of an owld man that's lost his senses, Mr. Keegan? for shame on you. If you'll stick to the offer you made before, I'll bring the old man round yet."

"I tell you I'll do no such thing, Master Thady; but root and branch I'll have you out of that, and that right soon; a pack of beggars like you! What right have you to be keeping a respectable man out of his money?"

"Respictable indeed! very respictable!—Look at the house, Mr. Keegan, for which you want to take the whole property,—tumbling down already; and you call that respictable! And to be threatening to be dhriving an owld man, past his senses, out of his house for a few foolish words; and a poor innocent defenceless girl too!" Thady himself was beginning to get in a passion now,—"And since you will have it, the owld man was not far wrong, for it is robbers you are, both of you, and that's your respectability!"

"Robbers are we? and what are you and your innocent sister? You know, Thady, she can go to Ussher; he says he'll keep her. She won't be a huckster's wife, you say? better that than a captain's misthress, as all agree she is now."

As Keegan said this, he seemed to expect that he would be answered by some personal violence. The two were together, standing at the end of the avenue, all but on the public road. Keegan had a stout walking-stick in his hand, and he walked out into the road as he said the last words, turning round as he did so, so as to face Thady.

The young man stood still for a second or two, as if the meaning of the words had hardly reached him, and then rushed at the attorney with his clenched fist; but the man of law was too quick for him, for striking out with his stick, he cried,

"By the Lord of heaven, if you come nearer I'll brain you!" and, as the young man endeavoured to get within the sweep of the stick, he received a blow on the arm and elbow, which, for the moment, disabled him; and the pain was so sharp, as to prevent him from any further immediate attack.

"Mr. Keegan, by the living Lord, this day's work shall cost you dear!" and then, indulging that ready profuseness of threats in which the less educated of his countrymen are so prone to indulge, he returned within the gateway of the avenue, and proceeded a short way towards the house. Here he reached a felled tree, lying somewhat across the path, on which he sat down; for he felt that he could not go to the house before he had considered, in his sad heart, what he would say there, and how he would say it.

Keegan, when he found that his antagonist, like a dog cowed by a blow, was not inclined to come again to the fight, turned on his heel, and walked back to the place where he had left his horse.

For some time Thady did not recover from the immediate sharp pain arising from the blow, and during these minutes firm determinations of signal vengeance filled his imagination, damped by no thought of the punishment to which he might thereby be subjecting himself. But the luxury of these resolves—for they had a certain luxury—was soon banished by the thoughts that crowded on his mind, when pain gave him liberty to think. Firstly, his own impotence with regard to retaliating on Keegan; secondly, the horrid charge brought against Feemy, and the conviction that the scurrility of it would not have occurred to Keegan had it not previously been rumoured or suggested by others; and the dreadful doubt—for it was dreadful to Thady—whether there could be any grounds for it: then the recollection of their defenceless state —the certainty that Flannelly would take every legal step against them, and that Keegan's threat, that they should be turned out to wander through the roads, would be realized:—all these things forced themselves on his recollection, and he could not go up to the house. He could not meet his father, and tell him that, between them, they had destroyed all hopes of conciliation; that they must wander forth as beggars, to starve. He could not ask counsel from Feemy; his inability to protect her made him averse to see her.

In his misery, and half broken-hearted as he was, he all but made up his mind to join the boys, who, he knew, were meeting with some secret plans for proposed deliverance from their superiors. Better, at any rate, join them now, thought he, than be driven to do it when he was no better than them—as would soon be the case; and, if he was to perish, better first strike a blow at those who had pressed him so low! And then it occurred to him that, at any rate, he would first go to his only good counsellor; and he accordingly retraced his steps to the bottom of the avenue, resolved, if he could find him, to tell all his new sorrow to Father John.

CHAPTER XI.

PAT BRADY.

When Thady reached the end of the avenue, where the fracas had taken place between himself and Keegan, he met Pat Brady.

As I fear that this talented young man must by this time be subject to heavy suspicions; that his faith and honesty must be greatly doubted; and as, even with those who may still look upon him as a trusty servant, it would be impossible to keep up the delusion much longer, I may as well now make his character no longer doubtful, by explaining some passages which had occurred in his life during the last few months.

In the first place, however, we must return for a short time to Mr. Keegan.

It will be remembered that this gentleman was the son-in-law of Larry Macdermot's creditor, Mr. Flannelly; and it had been arranged between the two worthy relations that if, by some law-craft or other means, Keegan could obtain possession of the estate of Ballycloran in payment of the debt due by the proprietor, it should become his, Keegan's, property.

Now, this gentleman had long looked forward to the day when he should be able to describe himself as Hyacinth Keegan, Esq., of Ballycloran—having been aware that, after his father-in-law's death, all right in the property would become his own; but since he had induced the old man to make a gift instead of a legacy of the debt, his passion to become an estated gentleman had hourly increased. An ambitious man in his own way was Hyacinth Keegan: he had first longed to obtain admission into the more decent society of Carrick-on-Shannon—that he had some time since achieved; he then sought to mix among the second-rate country gentlemen; and by making himself useful to them, by plausibility, by some degree of talent, and by great effrontery, he had become sufficiently intimate with many of them to shake hands with them at race-courses and ordinaries, and to talk of them to others as "Blake," "Brown," and "Jones." To some few, who now usually called him "Hyacinth," and occasionally invited him to drinking parties at their houses, he had lent small sums of money on good security; and now he was looking to obtain the sub-shrievalty of the county, and to be Hyacinth Keegan, Esq., of Ballycloran.

Since the immediate probability of realizing this brilliant vision had occurred to him, he had left nothing undone which could, as he thought, lead to its completion. From the constant business which he had with Thady, he pretty well knew all the difficulties of the Macdermots, and the great poverty of their house; and he had observed how completely Pat Brady was in young Macdermot's confidence. He also knew that if any direct legal steps were necessary in selling the estate under the mortgage, or if any underhand scheming should be required to drive the Macdermots into further difficulties, Pat Brady could, and probably would—for a consideration—give him his zealous co-operation. There were also other reasons why he desired the assistance of our friend Pat. It was a part of Mr. Keegan's daily practice to obtain what information he could of the habits of those with whom he was likely to form any connection; and it was generally believed through the county, that he could usually tell those who were, and who were not, guilty of the common crimes of the times—illicit distillation, and secret conspiracies among the poor to injure their superiors, or to redress their fancied wrongs. It was from his accurate information on these points that he was usually employed in their defence when they were brought to trial, and that he had been able to detect and punish those by whom he had himself been attacked. This, moreover, as his character became known, had materially led to his own safety; for the boys knew that he knew everything through the county, and thus had learnt to become afraid of him.

He felt, therefore, that as it was probable that Ballycloran would become his own, Pat Brady's assured services might be of great utility; and he found but little difficulty in obtaining them. Pat was clever enough to foresee that the days of the Macdermots were over, and that it was necessary for him to ingratiate himself with the probable future "masther;" and though he, of course, made a sufficiently good market of his treachery, he felt that in all ways he consulted his own interest best in making himself useful to Keegan. He had dim prospects, too, of great worldly advantages which might accrue from being chief informer to so conspicuous a man as Mr. Keegan was likely to prove himself, and, with no false self-vanity, he felt himself qualified for such a situation. There was considerable danger in being always among people of a wild and savage nature, to entrap and ensnare whom would be his duty, and he felt that he had the requisite courage. Moreover, there was a certain cunning and prudence necessary, and in that also he, with some truth, fancied himself not deficient; and as Mr. Keegan's scheme opened upon him, the idea of entrapping his young master into the difficulties which lay around, offered not a bad opportunity for the display of his talents.

That such a man as Brady is described to be, should exist and find employment in a country, is a fact which must shock and disgust; but that it is a fact in great parts of Ireland, those who are most conversant with the country will not pretend to deny. It is true, that by paid spies and informers, real criminals may not unfrequently be brought to justice; but those who have observed the working of the system must admit that the treachery which it creates—the feeling of suspicion which it generates—but, above all, the villanies to which it gives and has given rise, in allowing informers, by the prospect of blood-money, to give false informations, and to entrap the unwary into crimes—are by no means atoned for by the occasional detection and punishment of a criminal.

Let the police use such open means as they have—and, God knows, in Ireland they should be effective enough; but I cannot but think the system of secret informers—to which those in positions of inferior authority too often have recourse—has greatly increased crime in many districts of Ireland. I by no means intend to assert that this system is patronised or even recognised by Government. I believe the contrary most fully; but those to whom the execution of the criminal laws in detail are committed, and who look to obtain advancement and character by their activity, do very frequently employ what I must call a most iniquitous system of espionage.

A very few years since I was walking down the street of a small town with a gentleman who was at that time in the immediate employment of the Government. It was a fair day, and we were strolling through the crowd, which was moving slowly hither and thither, as though in absolute idleness. The dusk was fast commencing, and he pointed out to me two or three men, who had come in from the country like the others, telling me that they were waiting till it was dark to speak to him; that they did not dare to speak to him during the light; that they were in his pay; and that they had information to give him respecting illegal societies, and hidden arms. He ridiculed me when I questioned the propriety of his system; in fact he was so accustomed to it that he could not conceive the possibility of going on without it. In the same way I have had men pointed out to me by the officer leading a party of revenue police in quest of illicit stills, who were dressed as policemen though not belonging to the force, and who were brought in that disguise that they might not be known by their neighbours whose haunts they were going to disclose.

The momentary success no doubt reconciles this usage to the officer employing it; but the result must be to create suspicion of each other among the poor, and fearfully to increase instead of diminishing crime.

Now that our friend Brady's character is perfectly understood, we will return to our story; first, however, explaining that he had witnessed the scene between the attorney and his master, and had determined to make the most of it.

Thady had turned on the road towards the priest's house without taking any notice of his dependant, but this Pat could not allow.

"Well, Mr. Thady, you'll live to be even with him yet—the born ruffian! faix and a good sight more nor even; else it'll be no one's fault but yer own."

"Even with who?"

"With who now? why didn't I see it with my own eyes?—the born thief of the world! Didn't he knock flashes out of yer shoulther with the shilaleh he had—Mr. Keegan, I main? And if it worn't that you hadn't—bad cess to the luck of it!—your own bit of a stick in your hand, wouldn't you have knocked the life out of him for the name he put on your sisther, Miss Feemy?—the blackguard!"

"And did you hear him, Pat?"

"Shure I did, yer honer."

"And did you see him?"

"See him, yes, shure; I seed him riz his big stick, and I thought it was nigh kilt you were."

"And you heard him call your misthress the name he called; and you saw him sthrike at me the way he did, and I having nothing but my fist to help me; and were you so afraid of a man like Keegan, you wouldn't step forward to strike a blow for me?"

"Afraid of Keegan! No, Masther Thady, I arn't afraid of him; but you wouldn't have had me come up, jist to witness that you war the first to strike at him."

"Nonsense! wasn't he the first to call my sisther the name he did?"

"Ah! but that warn't a braich of the pace. You see, Mr. Thady, thim divils of lawyers is so cute; and av I had come to help you, or sthrike a blow, or riz my stick, he'd have had both before old Jonas Brown to-morrow morning; and where'd we've been then? But, Mr. Thady, as I said before, you'll be more nor even with Mr. Keegan yet, any way."

"How'll I be even with him, Pat?"

"But where are you going, Mr. Thady? shure an't it your dinner time at the house? and remimber you've to be at the wedding to-night."

"Oh! d—n the wedding. Do you think I'd be playing the fool at weddings to-night, afther what just took place? I want to see Father John; and I'll go and catch him before he goes down to your sisther."

"What, Mr. Thady! to tell about the blow, and the dishonour the ruffian put on you and Miss Feemy?—shurely you wouldn't be doing that."

"And why not?—won't all Carrick have it before long?"

"That's no rule why you should be going and telling Father John about it yourself. And won't he be putting you against revenging yourself; and you wouldn't, Mr. Thady, with the owld blood in your veins, and in Miss Feemy's—may the divil's curse blacken him for the name he give her!—you wouldn't be putting up quiet and aisy with what he's done?—and the like of him too!"

By this time Thady had stopped, and was beginning to waver in his determination of going to the priest. He felt that what Brady said was true—that the priest would implore him not to avenge himself, in the manner in which his heart strongly prompted him to do. He felt he could not forego the impulse to inflict personal punishment on Keegan. And after all, what could Father John do for him?

"Besides, Mr. Thady, now I think of it, Father John an't in

it at all, for he was to be at Drumsna before the wedding; and I know he's to dine with Mrs. McKeon; he does mostly when he's in Drumsna this time of day, so I'm sure he arn't in it."

Satisfied by this, Thady allowed himself to be led back again; and they walked together in silence a little way.

"You've only to say the word," continued Pat, in a low voice, "you've only to say the word to them boys as 'll be there to-night, and they'll see you righted with Keegan."

"What boys—and how righted?"

"How righted! why how should you be righted afther what he's afther doing?—and I tell you them's the boys as will not see your father's son put upon that way."

"Which them d'ye main, Pat?"

"Oh! there's a lot of them up to anything. There's Jack Byrne and Joe Reynolds is mad to be having a fling at Ussher; you know their brothers is in gaol about the malt they found away at Loch Sheen; and there's Corney Dolan, and McKeon, and a lot more of them; I knows them all, and it'll be jist as good to them to be making a job of Keegan, as the other."

"I wouldn't have the ruffian murthered, Pat; you don't think I want to have him murthered?"

"Whist, Mr. Thady; may be the children about in the trees there would hear you. Who says anything of murdher? No, but just give him a bating that would go nigh taching him the taste of being murdhered,—and the same for Master Ussher; for I tell ye—may the tongue of the cowardly ruffian be blisthered for putting the name he did on your sisther!—but he was only repating what Ussher has said hisself, and that more nor once nor twice."

Thady made no reply, but walked on slowly; he gave no assent, but he showed no indignation at the kind of revenge which was proposed to him.

"And what was he saying about the estate,—Keegan, I main, Mr. Thady,—before you came to be quarrelling that way?"

"He was saying what 'll be thrue enough,—that Ballycloran 'll be sold, right away, before next May; and that he himself will be the purchaser—and that we'll be wandering the road like any other set of beggars."

"And did he say he'd buy Ballycloran?"

"He did."

"And turn you all out, Mr. Thady?"

"And he'll do it too," said Thady.

"Tunder and ages! man, and would you be letting him come over ye that way? If any blackguard of a lawyer could be selling an estate that way, because money may be a little scarce or so, would there be so many gintlemen in the counthry, enjoying themselves in their own houses, just keeping the right side of the door? Only take care the owld man don't be showing hisself that way he does be doing on the big steps there; and take care the door is kept shut, instead of right open; and make Biddy understand she an't to open it for any one at all, at all—except yerself jist, and Father John, or the like, who wouldn't mind going round to the back door. I tell ye that all the Flannellys and Keegans in Ireland can't sell Ballycloran, unless they first get hould of the owld man."

"But can't they put resavers on every acre of the land, and wouldn't that be all one as selling it?"

"Oh! let the boys alone for that; stick to them, and they'll not let a resaver do much among them; faix, I'm thinking I for one wouldn't like to go resaving rents up to Drumleesh for any one but the Masther hisself. But any way you'll be coming down to the boys and spaking to them yerself this night—you wouldn't go, Mr. Thady, not to be at Mary's wedding?"

"You know that ruffian Ussher'll be there; and I don't want to be meeting him."

"But that's jist it; don't let him be there playing what tricks he plazes with Miss Feemy, and you not there to purtect her—and there's all them boys expect you. You won't let Keegan run off with land and house, and all without a blow sthrick?"

"They'll all be up at Ballycloran to-morrow, and I'll hear what they have to say then."

"But I tell you, they won't be there at all to-morrow, unless you come down to them to-night," answered Pat.

"Do they main to say they refuse out and out to pay the rint?"

"Not at all; but they'll be getting stiff if they think you're so thick with him as is their inimy—and isn't that natural too? It's only to come down and say a kind word or so to 'em yourself, and you'll find them all right—and ready to stand by you and yours to the last, Mr. Thady."

"Well, Pat, I'll be down there. Father John would think it odd if I weren't there."

By this time they had got round to the back of the house, where the outhouse stood; and the young man told Brady to go into the kitchen and get him a coal for his pipe, and to tell the girl to say he wouldn't be in to dinner.

"And won't you be wanting your dinner, Mr. Thady?"

"No, Pat; I'll jist sit and have a smoke in the stable, till it's time to go down to you. I couldn't face the owld man and Feemy, afther what jist happened."

So we will for the present leave him smoking in the stable, and return to the inmates of the house.

It will be remembered that when Father John left Feemy after his morning visit, she remained alone till Mr. Keegan came: and that she was dismissed from the dining-room when they began to talk on business. She then betook herself to dress for the evening amusement; that is, to make herself something decent before she met Ussher; to brush her hair, and to dismiss all the traces of that disenchanting dishabille which I have attempted to describe. Whilst at her toilet Feemy turned over in her mind all that her brother and Father John had said, and firmly resolved not to let the evening pass without telling her lover the comfort it would be to have some decided steps taken as to their engagement: and yet she almost shuddered at the thoughts of doing so; there was a frown which occasionally came over Ussher's face, which made her dread him; and she couldn't but feel that if he wished to take any such steps, he would do so without her asking him; in fact, that it would be much better that he should do so unasked. And then, if he got angry,—if he should tell her that as she could not wait and trust him, they must part; how could she bear the idea of losing him? What could she say or do, if he answered her sternly?—if he scolded her, or perhaps worse, absolutely quarrelled with her? Poor Feemy began to wish the evening over to which she had looked forward as the source of so much pleasure; she feared to neglect the warnings she had received, and she felt that things could not go on always as they were; but she trembled at the idea of telling this to Ussher.

Her silent dinner was soon over; she made her father's punch, and sat down to wait for her lover. Larry kept up a continual growl about Thady's absence, suggesting that Keegan had cozened him off to Carrick, to sign the estate away; accusing him of conspiracy with the attorney, to rob him, his father; wondering why he wouldn't come to dinner, &c.: to all which Feemy made no reply; she never noticed his grumblings; she sat absorbed in her own thoughts, meditating what she would say to Ussher, till she heard his horse's feet at the head of the avenue, and then she jumped up to meet him at the hall-door.

"How are you, Myles?" and "Well, Feemy, how's yourself?" and then, having reached the hall door, he took the fond girl in his arms and kissed her. "Ah; don't then, Myles; there's Katty on the stairs; come in then, and take your punch;" and they entered the room where Larry was sitting over the fire.

"How are you this evening, Sir?" said Ussher, "this fine night."

The old man always brightened up a little when Ussher came in.
"How d'ye do, Captain?—I'm glad to see you. Did the Captain get his dinner then, Feemy?—you don't ask Captain Ussher whether he got his dinner."

"Feemy knows she needn't ask about that; that's one of the things I always take care of. But where's Thady, Mr. Macdermot? I wanted to speak to him about Keegan, that sworn friend of his:" and Ussher began to make himself comfortable with the hot water, sugar, &c.

"Thady is it you're axing afther? 'Deed then, I don't know where he is. And as for Keegan—but you don't make your punch, Captain—as for Keegan, the ruffian, he was here this blessed morning,—wanting me, and Feemy, and Thady too, to walk clane out of the place! but I walked him off. The like of him to be buying Ballycloran; and his father a process-server, and his wife's father that d—d bricklayer Flannelly!"

"Holloa! Mr. Macdermot; so you've had a breeze with the attorney, have you? And was Thady here at the time?"

"He was in it all the time; and divil a word he'd say for himself, or Feemy, or his father, or the owld place either; but just wanted me, Captain, to give it all up to them at once, the ruffians! and when I wouldn't, he went off with Keegan to Carrick. There's my own son joined with 'em agin me; and he'll help to dhrive me out, he will,—and Feemy too, poor girl!"

In vain Ussher endeavoured to make him believe that his son had not conspired against him, to deprive him of his property. The old man had taken it into his head that Thady had gone off to Carrick with Keegan, and was determined to make the most of this new grievance, and would not be comforted. He seemed cunning enough in his determination to thwart the attorney in his plan of buying the estate, and explained to Ussher that he had made up his mind not to be taken personally; assuring him, that from that time nothing should induce him to leave his own fireside, or so much as show himself at the hall-door; that he would have the hall-door barricadoed; and, in short, that he would himself take all those precautions which Brady had enumerated to his son, as proper to be put in practice on such an occasion. And from that time, with one sad exception, it was many months before Larry Macdermot was seen to cross his threshold; he strictly adhered to his resolution; and although during that time many attempts to arrest him were made, he eluded them all. He could not, however, be brought to understand that, for the present, this was useless—that no one could arrest him till after Christmas. The dread of losing his property had come upon him, and he would not allow himself even to be seen by any one but those of his own household, and by Ussher.

After listening to his grievances as long as he thought necessary, Ussher followed Feemy into her own room, and here we will leave them, till we meet them again at Denis McGovery's wedding; merely remarking, that poor Feemy, though more than once she prepared to make her dreaded speech to her lover, each time hesitated and stopped, and at last made up her mind that it would be just as well to put off the evil hour till her pleasure was over; and finally determined to have the conversation on the return home, for she well knew that Ussher would walk back with her to Ballycloran, where his horse would be left.

CHAPTER XII.

THE WEDDING.

When Ussher first came into the parlour at Ballycloran, he asked after Thady, and it will be necessary to explain why he did so; the terms on which the two men stood towards each other not being such as to render it probable that either should be very anxious for the presence of the other.

It had come to the knowledge of Denis McGovery that Brady had asked to the wedding a lot of men from Drumleesh, and some also from Mohill—characters with whom Denis was not apt to consort himself, and whom he looked on as paupers and rapparees. He had also made out, it is presumed with the aid of his affianced, that some other motive was probably ensuring their attendance than merely that of doing honour to his, Denis's, nuptials. Pat Brady was not likely to have made a confidant of his sister or of Denis on the occasion, but nevertheless, the bridegroom had discovered that the meeting was, to some extent, to be a political one, and moreover, that Thady Macdermot was expected to be there.

Now McGovery, although it must be presumed that, in common with all Irishmen of the lower order, he conceived that he was to a certain degree injured and oppressed by the operation of the existing laws, nevertheless had always thought it the wiser course to be with the laws, bad as they might be, than against them. When, therefore, he learnt that the brothers of the men whom Ussher had put into prison were to be of the party, and that many of their more immediate neighbours would be there, and remembered also that Captain Ussher himself had promised to come to the "divarsion," mighty fears suggested themselves to him, and he began to dread that the occasion would be taken for offering some personal injury to the latter! In which case, might not all be implicated?—and among the number that dear person for whom Denis felt the tenderest regard—viz., himself?

Actuated by these apprehensions, Denis, on the morning of the wedding, had gone to Ussher to unfold his budget of dreadful news,—to assure the Captain that his only object "was to get himself married," and to see that the "pigs and the thrifle of change were all right,"—and strongly to advise the Captain to stay away; "not that it wouldn't be a great honer for a poor boy like him to see his honer down there, for he had the greatest rispect in life for him, and all that wore the King's sword; but there war no knowing what them boys might be afther when they got the dhrink in them."

Ussher thanked Denis for his communication, but at the same time begged him not to disquiet himself—told him that there was no danger in life; and declared that he felt so confident of the good feeling of the men through the country towards him, particularly those at Drumleesh and Mohill, that he should always feel perfectly safe in their company—in fact, that he looked on their presence as a protection. Poor Denis stared hard at him; but as he soon perceived that the Captain was laughing at him for his solicitude, he retreated with a grin on his face, remarking that he had meant all for the best.

Though Captain Ussher affected to set no value on McGovery's tale, he nevertheless thought that there might be something in it. He determined, however, not to be deterred from going to the wedding. Though in many respects a bad man, Ussher was very vigilant in the performance of his official duties, and, as has been before said, was possessed of sufficient courage. It had been part of McGovery's disclosure that Thady Macdermot was to be at the wedding, and it occurred to Ussher, that at any rate no personal violence would be offered as long as young Macdermot was with him; he therefore determined to see him first, and tell him what he had heard. It is true he had no great love for the poor fellow; still he would have been sorry to see him, from any cause of uneasiness or distress, throw himself into the hands of men who might probably induce him to join in acts which would render him subject to the severest penalties of the law. Ussher understood Thady's character tolerably well; and though he had no real sympathy for his sufferings, still he had manly feeling enough to wish to save him, as Feemy's brother, from the danger into which he believed him so likely to fall.

It was for the purpose of talking on this subject that he asked for Thady; but when he found he was not in the house, nor expected home to dinner, he was obliged to postpone what he had to say till he met him at Mary Brady's wedding.

About seven o'clock, Feemy and her lover arrived at Mrs. Mehan's little whiskey shop, where the marriage was to take place. The whole party were already there: Father John was standing with his back to a huge turf fire, in the outer room—the usual drinking room of the establishment—amusing the bystanders with jokes, apparently at the expense of the bridegroom. Mary Brady was dressed in a white muslin gown, which, though it was quite clean, seemed to have been neither mangled nor ironed, so multitudinous had been the efforts to make it fit her ungainly person. She had a large white cap on her head, extending widely over her ears; and her hair, parted on her left brow, was smeared flat over her forehead with oil: her arms were bare, and quite red, and her hands were thrust into huge white cotton gloves, which seemed to make them so ashamed of themselves as utterly to unfit them for their ordinary uses. Every one that entered, said, "Well, Mary," or, " Well, alanna, how's yourself?" or some greeting of the kind, to which she answered only with a grin. She and her future husband seemed totally unacquainted with each other, for since he came in he hadn't spoken to her. In fact, poor Mary, as she expressed herself to Feemy, " Couldn't get her sperrits up at all, and felt quite cowed like."

Biddy, from Ballycloran, was her bridesmaid, and she, though she did not emulate the bride in her white dress, had also thrust her head into a huge cap, which, if it did not much add to her beauty, at any rate made her sufficiently remarkable to show that she was one of the principal characters of the evening.

Denis had procured himself a second-hand light brown coat, with metal buttons; this was the only attempt at wedding finery which he had made; but even this seemed to make him somewhat beside himself, and gave him a strong resemblance to that well-known martyr to unaccustomed grandeur—a hog in armour. Pat seemed to scorn the party altogether, though he was to officiate in giving away the bride; he was talking apart to Reynolds and one or two others, and seeing to the proper arrangement and distribution of the good things which were to follow the wedding. Thady was not in the place; he had not yet arrived.

"Ah! Feemy," began Father John, as she walked in, followed by Ussher, " how are you? and this is kind of you, Captain."

"Long life to you, Miss Feemy! and you, too, Captain dear," said Mary, at last excited to speak by the greatness of the occasion.

"Your honers are welcome, Miss; your honers are welcome, Captain Ussher," said Denis, forgetting that, for the present, he was only a guest himself; and then Brady, and then Shamuth na Pibu'a, the blind piper from County Mayo, "who had made the music out of his own head, all about O'Connell"—and then Biddy, and Mrs. Mehan, and all the boys and girls one after another, got up, and ducked their heads down in token of kindly welcome to the "young misthress and her lover;" and though most of those present, at other times, would have said that it was a pity their own Miss Feemy should be marrying "a born inimey of the counthry, like a Revenue officer, and a black Prothestant too," it wasn't now, when she had come to honour the wedding of one of themselves, that they would be remembering anything against her or her lover.

"Well, Mary, so the time's nearly come," said Feemy, as she sat down on the bench by the fire, that Mary, regardless of all bridal propriety, wiped down for her with the tail of her white dress; saying, as she did so, "What harum? sure won't the dust make it worse, when the dancing comes on, and—"

"Whisper, Mary."

"What is it, Miss?"

"Whisper, then."

"Ah, now! you'll be at me like the rest of 'em;" and she put her big face down over Feemy's.

"Are the sheets done, Mary?"

"Ah now! Miss, you're worse than 'em all!" and Mary put her big hand with the big cotton glove, with the fingers widely extended, before her face to hide the virgin blush.

"What's that, Feemy?" said Father John; "what's that I heard?"

"Go asy, now, Father John, do;" and Mary gave the priest a playful push, which nearly put him into the fire; "for God's sake, Miss, don't be telling him, now; you won't, darlint?"

"What was it, Feemy? all's fair now, you know."

"Only just something Mary was to get ready for her husband, then, Father John—nothing particular. You'll never be married yourself, you know, so you needn't ask."

"Oh! part of the fortune, was it? Trust Denis, he'll look to that; is it the pigs, eh, Denis?"

"No, Father John, it jist a'nt the pigs," said Mary.

"Come, what is it?—out with it Denis."

"Scrrow a one of me knows what you're talking about," said Denis.

"It a'nt the calf at last, Denis, is it?"

"Bad luck to it for a calf!" exclaimed McGovery; and then, sidling up to the priest, "you wouldn't be setting all the boys laughing at me, Father John, and thim sthrangers, too."

"Well, well, Denis, but why didn't you tell me the whole?"

When Ussher had first entered, Brady had come up, expressly to welcome him; and there was something in his extreme servility which made Ussher fear all was not quite right. But Ussher had become habituated to treat the servility of the poor as the only means they had of deprecating the injuries so frequently in his power to inflict; he had, too, from his necessity of not attending to their supplications, acquired a habit of treating them with constant derision, which they well understood and appreciated; and the contempt which he always showed for them was one of the reasons why he was so particularly hated through the country. Though now a guest of Brady's, he could not help showing the same feeling. Moreover, Ussher, who as far as the conduct of man to man is concerned had nothing of treachery about him, strongly suspected Pat's true character, and was therefore less likely to treat him with respect.

"Thank you, Brady, I'll do very well; don't you expect Mr. Thady here?"

"Is it the young masthur, Captain? In course we do. Mary wouldn't be married av he warn't to the fore."

"Indeed! I didn't know you'd so much respect for Mr. Macdermot as that."

"Is it for the masthur, Captain?"

"For the matter of that, Brady, you wouldn't much mind how many masters you had if they all paid you, I'm thinking."

"And that's thrue for you, Captain," said Pat, grinning in his perplexity, for he didn't know whether to take what Ussher said for a joke or not.

"Keegan, now, wouldn't be a bad master," said Ussher.

"And what puts him in your head, Captain Ussher?"

"Only they say he pays well to a sharp fellow like you."

"'Deed I don't know who he pays. They do be saying you pay a few of the boys too an odd time or two yourself."

"Is it I? What should I be paying them for?"

"Jist for a sight of a whiskey still, or a little white smoke in the mountains on a fine night or so. They say that same would be worth a brace of guineas to a boy I could name."

"You're very sharp, Mr. Brady; but should I want such assistance, I don't know any I'd sooner ask than yourself."

"Don't go for to throuble yourself, for I don't want to be holed of a night yet; and that's what'll happen them that's at that work, I'm thinking; and that afore long—not that I'm blaming you, for, in course, every one knows it's only your dooty."

"You're very kind; but when will Mr. Thady be here?"

"'Deed I wonder he a'nt here, Captain; but war you wanting him?"

"Not in particular. Is it true the brothers of those poor fellows I took up at Loch Sheen are here to-night?"

"They is, both of 'em; there's Joe Reynolds, sitting behind there—in the corner where I was when you and Miss Feemy come in."

"It's lucky he wasn't with his brother, that's all: and he'd better look sharp himself, or he'll go next."

"Oh, he's a poor harmless boy, Captain. He never does nothing that way: though, in course, I knows nothing of what they do be doing; how should I?"

"How should you, indeed! though you seem to be ready enough to answer for your friend Reynolds. However, I don't want to be taking any more of the boys at Drumleesh; so if he is a friend of yours, you'd better warn him, that's all:" and he walked away.

"And it's warning you want yourself, Captain, dear," said Pat to himself; "how clever you think yourself, with your Mr. Keegan and your spies, and your fine lady Miss, there; but if you a'nt quiet enough before Christmas, it's odd, that's all."

They were called into the inner room now, as Father John was going to perform the ceremony; and such marshalling and arranging as he had!—trying to put people into their proper places who would be somewhere else—shoving down the forms out of the way—moving the tables—removing the dishes and plates; for the supper was to be eaten off the table at which the couple were to be married. And though all the company had probably been at weddings before, and that often, they seemed new to the proceedings.

"Denis, you born fool, will you come here, where I told you? and don't keep the mutton spoiling all night;" and he shoved McGovery round the table.

"Mary Brady, if you wish to change the ugly name that's on you this night, will you come here?" and he seized hold of the young woman's arm and dragged her round; "and who's wanting you, Biddy?" as the girl followed close behind her principal.

"Shure, Father John, a'nt I to be bridesmaid then?"

"You, bridesmaid, and Miss Feemy to the fore! stay where you are. Come, Feemy."

"Oh! Father John, I a'nt bridesmaid."

I

"Oh! but you will be; and, as Thady a'nt here, Captain Ussher 'll be best man; come round, Captain,"—and Ussher came round. "And mind, Captain," he added, whispering, "when I come to '*salute nostrá*'—those are the last words—you're to kiss the bride; you are to kiss her first, and then you'll be married yourself before the year's out."

"But I am not all ambitious that way."

"Never mind, do as I tell you; and don't forget to have a half-crown in your hand, or so, when I bring the plate round. Come, Pat, where are you? you've to give her away."

"She'll jist give herself away, then, Father John; by dad, she's ready and willing enough!"

"Do as I tell you, and don't stand bothering. You want to keep those shiners in your pocket—I know you;" and Brady, shamed into compliance, also went into his place.

"Now, Denis, the other side of her, boy; why, you're as awkward to marry as shoeing a colt."

"Why then, Father John, that's thrue; for I shod many a colt, and never was married."

"You'll not be so long, avick; and may be you'll know more about it this time next week. But here's the plate; what do you mean to give the bride? you must put something handsome here for Mary."

"Faix then I forgot about that;" and he put his hand into his pocket and forked out half-a-crown, which, with a sheepish look, he put in the plate.

"Half-a-crown, indeed, for a tradesman like you! There's Corney Dolan there, who don't seem to have a coat that fits him too well, would do more for his wife, if it was God's pleasure he was to have one this night."

"Well, there;" and Denis put down another half-crown. This money, which is always put down just before the marriage, is a bridal present to the bride, and becomes her exclusive property.

"Well, Mary, you must be getting the rest of it from him another time."

"Let her alone for that, yer riverence," said Corney Dolan—who considered that Father John's allusion to his coat privileged him to put in his joke—"let her alone for that; she knows how to be getting the halfpence, and to hoult them too."

"It's a great deal you're knowing about it, I'm thinking, Mr. Dolan," retorted Denis; "it's a pity you couldn't keep the hoult of any yerself."

"Wisht, boys! how am I to marry you at all, if you go on this way? Come, Mary, off with that glove of yours; now for the ring

Denis:" and Mary hauled away at the glove, which the heat of her hand prevented her from pulling off.

"Drat it for a glove, then!"

"Ah, alanna, gloves come so nathural to your purty hand, they don't like to lave it at all."

At last, however, Mary got her hands ready for action; the ring was in the plate with the two half-crowns; Father John was standing between the two matrimonial aspirants; Ussher and Feemy were close behind Mary, and Brady was sitting down on the right hand of Denis; and the priest opened his book and began.

The marriage ceremony took about five minutes; but during this time Father John found occasion to whisper Ussher to come up close to the bride; and then, after hurrying over a great part of the service almost under his breath, he pronounced the final words—*salute nostrâ*—in a loud voice, adding at the same time to Ussher, "Now, my boy!"

Ussher, in obedience to the priest's injunction, seized hold of the bride at one side, to kiss her; while McGovery, determined to vindicate his own right, pounced on her on the other; justly thinking that the first kiss she should have after her wedding ought to be given to her by her lawful married husband.

But, alas! both aspirants were foiled, and Mary got no kiss at all. She, in her dismay at the energy of the two aspirants, ducked her head down nearly to the level of the table, and Denis, in his zeal and his hurry, struck Ussher in the face with his own forehead with no slight force. The Captain retreated, half-stunned, and not very well pleased with the salute he had received; and Denis was so shocked at what he had done, that he forgot his wife—and, apparently even the pigs and the money—in his regrets and apologies.

"Egad, Captain," said Father John, "that's more of a kiss than I meant to get you; why, you're as awkward, McGovery, as a bullcalf. Who'd have thought to see you butting at the Captain, like an old goat on his hind legs!"

"Faix then, yer riverence, I didn't intend to be trating the Captain in that way; but any way the Captain's head is 'most as hard as my own, for the flashes isn't out of my eyes yet."

"Never mind," said Ussher; "and if you always take care of your wife the same way, my good fellow, you'll be sure she'll not come to any harm, for want of looking after."

In the meantime Mary had escaped from the salute intended for her, and was, with the aid of Biddy, Mrs. Mehan, and sundry others of her visitors, engaged in extricating two legs of mutton, a ham, and large quantities of green cabbages from the pots in which they had been boiling in the outer room.

"God bless you, Sally dear, and will you drain them pratees? they'll be biled to starch. And Mrs. Mehan, darling, my heart's broke with the big pot here, will you lend me a hand? good luck to you then. There's Denis and Pat, bad manners to them, they'd see me kilt with all the bother, and stand there doing nothing under the sun."

And poor Mary McGovery, as we must now call her, toiled and groaned under the labours of her wedding day till the perspiration ran from under her wedding cap; and her wedding-dress gave manifold signs of her zeal in preparing the wedding-supper.

Whilst Mary was dishing the mutton, &c., Father John was employed in the not less important business of collecting his dues.

Between McGovery and Pat Brady he had succeeded in getting two thirty-shilling notes, which lay in the bottom of the plate, and formed a respectable base for the little heap of silver which he would collect; and if he did not get as much as the occasion would seem to warrant, the deficiency arose from no delicacy in asking, or want of perseverance in urging.

"Now, Captain, you're the only Protestant among us; show these Catholics of mine a liberal example—show them what they ought to do for their priest,"—here Captain Ussher put a couple of half-crowns in the plate. "There, boys, see what a Protestant does for me. Well, Feemy, I never ask the ladies, you know, but I shan't let Thady off; though he ain't here, I shall settle that in the rent."

"Oh, yes, Father John; make Thady pay for himself and me; Mrs. Brennan has got all my money."

"But where's Thady, Feemy dear? I hope you and he are good friends now."

"Oh yes, Father John; that is, I didn't see him since morning."

"But will he be here to-night?"

"He said he would; but you'd best ask Pat, he knows most about him."

This conversation took place in an under tone, and the priest walked on with his plate.

"Come, Mr. Tierney, how's yourself? I see you're waiting there, quite impatient, with your hands in your pocket. It's nothing less than a crown piece, I'll go bail."

"'Deed then, crown pieces a'nt that plenty in the counthry, these days, Father John; the likes of them"—and he put half-a-crown in the plate—"are scarce enough."

The speaker was an old man, rather decently dressed in knee-breeches and gaiters; he was one of those who, even in bad times, manage by thrift and industry to get, among the poor, the reputation of comparative wealth.

"And that's true for you, Mr. Tierney, and thank you kindly; they do however say, that however scarce they are in the country, you've your share of them."

"Go on, Father John, go on, you do be saying more than you know."

And by degrees the priest went through them all. From most of them he got something; from some a shilling, from some only sixpence; some few gave nothing at all: these in general endeavoured to escape observation behind the backs of the donors, but Father John let none of them off; and those who were unprepared, and who alleged their poverty, and their inability, he reproved for their idleness, and hinted rather strongly that their visits to Mrs. Mulready's, or similar establishments, were the cause of their not being able to do what he called their duty by their priest.

Standing in a corner, at the further end of the room, and resting against a wall, was Joe Reynolds: as Father John had a bad opinion of this man, and as he was not a parishioner of his, he was returning without speaking to him, when Joe said,

"You're in the right of it, Father John, not to be axing such a poor divil as me; you know, betwixt them all, they've not left me the sign of a copper harp."

"I know, Reynolds, you're too fond of Mrs. Mulready's to have much for your own priest, let alone another."

"Faix then, Father John, you shouldn't spake agin mother Mulready, for she's something like your riverence; and a poor boy with an empty pocket will get neither comfort nor good words from either of ye."

Father John did not think it to be consistent with his dignity to answer this sally; so he returned to the other end of the room, carefully counting as he went, and pocketing the money which he had collected. In the meantime the bride, with such assistance as she could get, had succeeded in putting the supper on the table: a leg of mutton at the top, reclining on a vast bed of cabbage; a similar dish at the bottom; and a ham, with the same garniture, in the middle. The rest of the table was elegantly sprinkled with plates of smoking potatoes; and what knives and forks and spoons and plates could be spared from the head of the table, where a few were laid out with some little order for the more aristocratic of the guests, were collected together in a heap. At first, no one seemed inclined to sit down; every one was struck with a sudden bashfulness, till Father John, taking up the knife and fork at the top of the table, called McGovery to bring his wife to supper.

"Now, Denis, my man, don't be thinking of those two pigs, but bring your better half with you, and let's see how you can behave as a married man."

"Come, Miss Feemy," said Mary, "if you and the Captain now would jist sit down, and begin—there's a dear, Miss, do."

"Oh, Mary, nobody must sit down before you, to-night."

"Never mind me, Miss,—if I could only get you and the Captain seated; yer honer," and she turned round with a curtsey to Ussher, "there's Denis and Pat there will do nothing in life to help me!" and the poor woman seemed at her wit's end to know how to arrange her guests.

At last, however, Ussher and Feemy sat down at one side of the priest, Denis and his wife at the other, and by degrees the table got quite full; so much so, that when the boys saw one another taking their seats, they were as eager as before they had been slow; and they hustled each other at the bottom of the table, till they were so crowded that they hadn't room to use their arms. Pat sat at the bottom, and he and the priest emulated each other in the zeal and celerity with which they cut up and distributed the joints before them.

At Pat's end of the table plates were scarce, and the boys round him took the huge lumps of blood-red mutton in their fists, and seemed perfectly independent of such conventional wants as knives and forks, in the ease and enjoyment with which they dispatched their repast. At last Brady had done all to the joint that carving could do, and having kept a tolerably sufficient lion's share for himself, he passed the bone down the table, which was speedily divided into as many portions as nature had intended that it should be.

Matters were conducted in a rather more decorous manner among the aristocrats at Father John's end of the table—though even here they were carried on in a somewhat rapid and voracious fashion. The priest helped Feemy and Ussher, Mary and her husband; and then remarking that he had done all the hard work of the evening, and that he thought it was time to get a bit himself, he filled a moderate plate for his own consumption, and passed the joint down to be treated after the same manner as its fellow.

As long as the eating continued there was not much said; but when the viands had disappeared, and the various bottles came into requisition, the clatter of tongues became loud and joyous; and though the first part of the entertainment had to all appearance come to a rather too speedy termination for want of material to carry it on, there seemed, from the quantity of whiskey produced, little chance of any similar disappointment in what the greater portion of the guests considered the more agreeable part of the entertainment.

"Well, Denis," said Father John, "I believe I've done all I can this time; and as I know you'll want to be looking after the cow that's in calf—no, not the cow, but the pigs—I'll be off."

"Folly on, Father John, folly on; it's always the way with yer riverence—to be making yer game of a poor boy like me! But you're not going out of this till you've dhrunk Mary's health here, and heard a tune on the pipes, any way."

"Not a drop, Denis, thank ye," and Father John got up; "and now, boys and girls, good night, and God bless you—and behave yourselves."

"Faix, then, yer riverence," said Joe Reynolds from the bottom of the table, "you may tell by the way the boys take to the bottle, that they'll behave themselves dacently and discreatly, like Christians."

"Indeed, then, Reynolds, where you are, and the whiskey with you, I believe there's likely to be little discretion but the discretion of drunkenness,—and not much of that."

"Thank ye, Father John, and it's you have always the kind word for me."

"But, Father John," began Mary, "you're not really going to go without so much as a tumbler of punch?"

"Not a drop, Mary, my dear; I took my punch after dinner—and I can't stand too much. Good night, Feemy—you'll stay and have a dance I suppose; good night, Captain Ussher."

And Father John got up from table, and went out of the room. As soon, however, as Denis saw that he was really going, he rose and followed him out of the door.

"Sit down, Denis, sit down—don't be laving your company such a night as this."

"But I want to have jist a word with yer riverence."

"Well, what is it?"

"Jist step outside then, Father John."

"Well, Denis; is it anything about Betsy Cane? or has Ginty come home, and is he wanting the pigs?"

"No, but would you just step outside here, Mr. McGrath; where those long-eared ruffians won't be hearing me?" and he and the priest walked a little distance from the door of Mrs. Mehan's house.

"I'm afeard, Father John, them born divils from Drumleesh and Mohill, as Pat brought here to-night, are maning more than good to Captain Ussher."

"And what makes you think that, Denis?"

"Why, Father John, Mary was saying that Pat towld her a lot of his own frinds would be up with him, and that if they war talking together, she and those as are with her dancing and the like, warn't to be disturbing them; and then I knows them boys is very mad with the Captain about that whiskey business up at Loch Sheen; and then Joe Reynolds and Jack Byrne are in it, and their brothers are two of them as war sazed and are now in Ballinamore Bridewell;—and I know there is something of the sort going on through the counthry; and faix, Father John, I wouldn't for money that anything happened, and I in it the while; for a poor boy is always made to be mixed up in them affairs, if by bad luck he is anywhere near at the time."

"But what do you think they'd do to the Captain to-night, Denis?"

"Faix then, yer riverence, I don't know what they'd be doing, —murther him, maybe."

"God forbid! But, Denis, those men from Drumleesh could hardly know Captain Ussher was going to be at the wedding to-night."

"Oh! yer riverence, they'd know it well enough from Pat Brady."

"But you don't think your wife's brother would join a party to murder Ussher?"

"Why then, Father John—I think it's just he that would be putting the others up to it."

"Good gracious, Denis! and what would he get by such deeds as that? Isn't he comfortable enough."

"It isn't them as is poorest, is always the worst. But any how, Father John, if you'd come back, and yer riverence wouldn't mind for the onst jist sitting it out—jist dhrinking a dhrop at an odd time, or colloguing a bit with owld Mr. Tierney, till we get the Captain out of that, shure they'd never be doing anything out of the way as long as yer riverence is in it."

"It isn't here—in the house, where there are so many together— they'd attack him, even if they meant to do so; and I don't think they mean it to-night; but it's on his way home—and my going back would not in any way prevent that. But why don't you at once tell Captain Ussher, and warn him that you fear he is not safe among those fellows at night."

"That's jist what I did then; but he's so foolish, and so bowld, there's no making him mind what one would say. I did tell him, Father John, that I was afeared that there would be some lads in it wouldn't be his well-wishers. But he laughed at me, and towld me there were none of the boys through the counthry war so fond of him as those Reynoldses and Byrnes, and all them others down at Drumleesh."

"Well, Denis, and what can I do more; if he laughs at you, why wouldn't he also laugh at me?"

"Why, yer riverence, you and he are frinds like; besides, he wouldn't trate the like of you as he would such a one as I; why I believe he don't think the poor are Christians at all."

"It's true enough for some of them; but what would you have me do? I couldn't walk back to Mohill by his horse's side;—and I tell you if they attack him at all, it will not be at the house there, but on his way home."

"'Deed then, Father John, any way I wish he was well out of that."

"It seems, Denis, it's yourself you're thinking of, more than the Captain."

"Shure, and why wouldn't I—and I just married? A purty thing for me just now, to be took up among a lot of blackguard ruffians for murthering a king's officer."

"Well, Denis, I won't go back now,—it would look odd and do no good; so do you go back and drink a tumbler of punch with the men, and dance a turn or two with the girls, as you should on your wedding night; and by and by I'll come down again as if to see what was going on—and to walk home with Miss Feemy. The Captain must go back to Ballycloran for his horse; and if he can be persuaded that there is any danger, he can go up and sleep at the cottage; for I tell you, if they mean to hurt him at all, it's on the road home to Mohill they'd make the attempt. Do you go in and say nothing about it, and I'll be down by and by."

Father John walked away towards his house, and Denis McGovery went back with a heavy heart to dance at his own wedding; for though his solicitude for the "king's officer" would not have been of the most intense kind, had he thought that he was to be murdered anywhere else, he had a great horror at the idea of any evil happening to that important personage, when it could in any way affect his own comfort.

When Denis returned into Mrs. Mehan's big kitchen, the amusements of the evening—dancing and drinking—were on the point of commencing. Shamuth of the pipes, the celebrated composer and musician, was sitting in the corner of the huge fireplace, with a tumbler of punch within reach of his hand, preparing his instrument,—squeaking, and puffing, and blowing in the most approved preparatory style. Mary was working and toiling again for the benefit of her guests—carrying kettles of boiling water into the inner room—emptying pounds of brown sugar into slop-basins and mugs—telling the boys to take their punch—taking a drop herself now and again, with some one who was wishing her health and happiness, and comfort with the man she'd got—inciting the girls to go and dance—and scolding her brother and husband, because, "bad manners to them, divil a hand they'd lend to help her, and she with so much to do, and so many to mind."

"And now, Miss Feemy, if you'd only get up and begin, dear, the others would soon folly; come, Captain Ussher—would yer honer jist stand up with Miss Feemy?"

"Oh, no, Mary,—you're the bride you know; Captain Ussher must dance with you first."

"Oh! laws, Miss, but that'd be too much honour intirely."

"No, Mrs. McGovery, but it's I that'll be honoured; so if you will be good enough to stand up with me, I shall be glad to shake a foot with you:" and the gallant Captain led Mary into the middle of the floor.

"But, Captain, dear, sorrow a sup of dhrink did I see you take this blessed evening; shure then you'll let me get you a glass of wine before we all begin, jist to prevent your being smothered with the dust like; shure, yer honour hasn't taken a dhrop yet."

"I won't be so long, Mary; but I won't have the wine yet, I'll wash the dust out with a tumbler of punch just now. Here's your husband, you must make him dance with the bridesmaid."

"I'm afraid then he ain't much good at dancing."

"Oh! but he must try.—Come, McGovery, there's Biddy waiting for you to take her out; and here's Shamuth waiting— you don't think, man, he'd begin till you're ready."

"Come, Denis," said his gentle spouse, "I never see sich a man; can't ye stand up and be dancing, and not keeping every one waiting that way?"

"Mind yourself, Mary, and you'll have enough to mind. Come, Biddy, alanna, let us have a shake together, all for luck;" and the happy husband led forth Biddy of Ballycloran—she with the big cap—who was only now beginning to regain the serene looks, which had been dispelled by Father John's not permitting her to act as bridesmaid.

And now Shamuth—his preparatory puffs having been accomplished—struck up "Paddy Carey" with full force and energy. As this was the first dance, no one stood up but the two couple above named; there were therefore the more left to admire the performance, and better room left for the performers to show their activity.

"Faix then, Mary," said one, "it's yerself that dances illigant—the Lord be praised!—only look to her feet."

"Well, dear—Denis, shure no one thought you were that good at a jig; give him a turn, Biddy—don't spare him—he's able for you and more."

"Ah! but see the Captain, Kathleen; it's he that could give the time to the music; a'nt he and Mary well met?—you must put more wind into the pipes, Shamuth, before they're down."

"But if you want to see the dancing, wait till Miss Feemy stands up—it's she that can dance; you'll stand up with the Captain, Miss Feemy, won't you?"

"Indeed I will, Corney, if he asks me."

"Axes you! ah, there's little doubt of that; it's he that's ready and willing to ax you, now and always."

"Ah! Mr. McGovery, shure man, you're not bait yet! you wouldn't give in to Biddy that soon?"

Poor Denis was giving signs of having had enough of the amusement. There was a tolerably large fire on the hearth, near which he had been destined to perform his gyrations—which, if not very graceful, had, at any rate, been sufficiently active; and the exertion, heat, and dust were showing plainly on his shining countenance.

"Ah! Mr. McGovery," panted Biddy, "shure you're not down yet, and I only jist begun!"

"Indeed, then, Biddy, I am, and quite enough I've had, too, for one while. Here, Corney, come and take my place;" and Denis deposited a penny in a little wooden dish by the piper's side.

"By dad, Denis," said Corney, "you'll sleep to-night, any ways—to look at you."

"That's jist what he won't, then; for it'll be morning before he's in bed, and Mary'll have too much to say to him, when he is there, to let him sleep."

"Never mind, boys; do you dance, and I'll get myself a dhrink, for I'm choked with the dust;—and here's Mr. Thady. Why, Mr. Thady, why didn't you come in time for the supper, then?"

Just as Denis McGovery gave over dancing, Thady entered the house, having anything but a wedding countenance. He had been, since the time we parted from him after his interview with Keegan, lying in the stable, smoking. He had eaten nothing, but had remained meditating over the different things which conspired to make his heart sad.

His father's state—the impossibility of carrying on the war any longer against the enmity of Flannelly and Keegan—his own forlorn prospects—the insult and blow he had just received from the overbearing, heartless lawyer—but, above all, Feemy's condition, and his fears respecting her, were too much for him to bear. After his sister and Captain Ussher had left Ballycloran, he had gone up to the house and had swallowed a couple of glasses of raw whiskey, to drive, as he said to himself, the sorrow out of his heart; and he had now come down to seek the friends whom Brady had recommended to him, and determined, at whatever cost, to revenge himself, by their aid, against Keegan, for the insults he had heaped upon him, and against Ussher for the name which, he believed, he had put upon his sister.

It was with these feelings and determinations that Thady had come down to McGovery's wedding; and, as he entered the room, Ussher and Feemy were just standing up to dance.

CHAPTER XIII.

HOW THE WEDDING PARTY WAS CONCLUDED.

When Thady entered the room where the party was dancing, the welcomes with which he was greeted by McGovery and his wife prevented him from immediately seeking Pat Brady, as he had intended; for he was obliged to stop to refuse the invitations and offers which he received, that supper should be got for him. And it was well for those that made the offers that he did refuse them; for every vestige of what was eatable in the house had been devoured, and had he acceded to Mary's reiterated wishes that he would "take jist the laste bit in the world," it would have puzzled her to make good her offer in the most literal sense of the words.

Luckily, however, Thady declined her hospitality, and was passing through to the inner room when he was stopped by Ussher, who, as we have before said, was standing up to dance with Feemy. The last time the two young men had met was at the priest's house, when, it will be remembered, Thady had shown a resolution not to be on good terms with the Captain, and subsequent events had not at all mollified his temper; so when Ussher good-humoredly asked him how he was, and told him he wanted to speak to him a word or two as soon as he should have tired Feemy dancing, or, what was more probable, Feemy should have tired him, Thady answered him surlily enough, saying that if Captain Ussher had anything to say to him, he should be within, but that he didn't mean to stay there all night, and that perhaps Captain Ussher had better say it at once.

"Well, Macdermot, perhaps I had; so, if your sister 'll excuse me, I won't be a minute.—Just step to the door a moment, will you?" and Thady followed him out.

"Well, Captain Ussher, what is it?"

"I don't know why it is, Macdermot, but for the last two or three days you seem to want to quarrel with me; if it is so, why don't you speak out like a man?"

"Is that what you were wanting to say to me?"

"Indeed it was not; for it's little I care whether you choose to quarrel or let it alone; but I heard something to-night, which, though I don't wholly believe it, may like enough be partly true; and if you choose to listen, I will tell you what it was; perhaps you can tell me whether it was all false; and if you cannot, what I tell you may keep yourself out of a scrape."

"Well."

"McGovery tells me that he thinks some of the boys that are here to-night are come to hold some secret meeting; and that, from the brothers of the two men I arrested the other day being in it, he thinks their purpose is to revenge themselves on me."

"And if it war so, Captain Ussher, what have I to do with it?"

Ussher looked very hard at Thady's face, but it was much too dark for him to see anything that was there.

"Probably not much yourself; but I thought that as these men were your father's tenants, you might feel unwilling that they should turn murderers; and as I am your father's friend, you might, for his sake, wish to prevent them murdering me."

"And is it from what such a gaping fool as McGovery says, you have become afraid that men would murder you, who never so much as raised their hand agin any of those who are from day to day crushing and ruining them?"

"If I had been afraid, I should not have come here. Indeed, it was to show them that I am not afraid of coming among them without my own men at my back that I came here. But though I am not afraid, and though it is not what McGovery says I mind —and he is not such a fool as some others—nevertheless I do think, in fact, from different sources, I know, that there is something going on through the country, which will bring the poor into worse troubles than they've suffered yet; and if, as I much think, they've come here to talk of their plans to-night, and if you know that it is so, you're foolish to be among them."

"Is that all you've to say to me, Captain Ussher?"

"Not quite; I wanted to ask you, on your honour, as a man and an Irishman, do you know whether there is any conspiracy among them to murder or do any injury to me?" Ussher paused for a moment; and as Thady did not answer him, he went on—" and I wanted to warn you against one who is, I know, trying his best to ruin you and your father."

"Who is that, Captain Ussher? I believe I know my own friends and my own inimies," said Thady, who thought the revenue officer alluded to Keegan.

"Answer my question first."

"And suppose I don't choose to answer it?"

"Why, if you won't answer it, I cannot but think you are aware of such a conspiracy, and that you approve of it."

"Do you mean to say, Captain Ussher, that I have conspired to murdher you?"

"No, I say no such thing; but surely, if you heard of such a scheme, or thought there was such an intention in the country, wouldn't you tell me, or any one else that was so doomed, that they might be on their guard?"

"You're very much frightened on a sudden, Captain."

"That's not true, Macdermot; you know I'm not frightened; but will you answer the question?"

Thady was puzzled; he did not know what to say exactly. He had not absolutely heard that the men whom he was going to meet that night, and whom he knew he meant to join, intended to murder Ussher; but Brady had told him that they were determined to have a fling at him, and it was by their promise to treat the attorney in the same way, that Thady had been induced to come down to them. It had never struck him that he was going to join a body of men pledged to commit murder—that he was to become a murderer, and that he was to become so that very night. His feeling had been confined to the desire of revenging himself for the gross and palpable injuries with which he had been afflicted, whilst endeavouring to do the best he could for his father, his sister, and his house. But now—confronted with Ussher—asked by him as to the plots of the men whom he was on the point of joining, and directly questioned as to their intentions by the ver man he knew they were determined to destroy, Thady felt awe abashed, and confused.

Then it occurred to him that he had not, at any rate as yet pledged himself to any such deed, or even in his mind conceived the idea of such a deed; that there was no cause why he should give his surmises respecting what he believed might be the intentions of others to the man whom, of all others—perhaps, not excepting the lawyer—he disliked and hated; and that there could be no reason why he should warn Captain Ussher against danger. Though these things passed through Thady's mind very quickly, still he paused some time, leaning against the corner of an outhouse, till Ussher said,

"Well, Macdermot, surely you'll not refuse to answer me such a question as that. Though—God knows why—we mayn't be friends, you would not wish to have such ill as that happen to me."

"I don't know why you should come to me, Captain Ussher, to ask such questions. If you were to ask your own frinds that you consort with, in course they would feel more concerned in answering you than I can. Not that I want to have art or part in your blood, or to have you murdhered—or any one else. But to tell you God's holy truth, if you were out of the counthry intirely, I would be better plased, as would be many others. And since you are axing me, I'll tell you, Captain Ussher, that I do think the way you do be going on with the poor in the counthry—dhriving and sazing them, and having spies over them—isn't such as is likely to make you frinds in the counthry, except with such as Jonas Brown and the like. And though, mind you, I know nothing of plots and conspiracies among the boys, I don't think you're over safe whilst staying among thim you have been trating that way; and if they were to shoot you some night, it's no more than many would expect. To tell you the truth, then, Captain Ussher, I think you'd be safer anywhere than at Mohill."

Thady considered that he thus made a just compromise between the faith he thought he owed to the men with whom he was going to league himself, and the duty, which he could not but feel he ought to perform, of warning Ussher of the danger in which he was placed.

Ussher felt quite satisfied with what Thady had said. He was not at all surprised at his expressions of personal dislike, and he felt confident, from the manner in which young Macdermot had spoken of his perilous situation, that even if any conspiracy had been formed, of which he was the object, there was no intention to put it into immediate operation, and that, at any rate in Macdermot's opinion, no concerted plan had yet been made to attack him. A good many reasons also induced Ussher to think that he stood in no danger of any personal assault. In the first place, though the country was in a lawless state—though illicit distillation was carried to a great extent—though many of the tenants refused to pay either rent, tithes, or county cesses till compelled to do so—the disturbances arising from these causes had not lately 'ed to murder or bloodshed. He had carried on his official duties in the same manner for a considerable time without molestation, and custom had begotten the feeling of security. Moreover, he thought the poor were cowed and frightened. He despised them too much to think they would have the spirit to rise up against him. In fact, he made up his mind that Thady's intention was to frighten him out of the country, if possible, and he resolved that he would not allow anything he had heard on the subject either to disturb his comfort, or actuate his conduct.

"Well, Macdermot, that's fair and above board—and what I expected, though it's neither friendly nor flattering; and I am not vexed with you for that; for if you don't feel friendly to me you shouldn't speak as if you did, and therefore I'm obliged to you. And I will say that if I am to be shot down, like a dog, whilst performing my duty to the best of my ability, at any rate, I won't let the fear of such a thing frighten me out of my comfort before it happens. And now if you'll let me say a word or two to you about yourself—"

"I'm much obliged to you, Captain Ussher, but if you can take care of yourself, so can I of myself."

"Why how cranky you are, man! If you hate me, hate me in God's name, but don't be so absurd as to forget you're a man, and to act like a child. I listened to you—and why can't you listen to me?"

"Well, spake on, I'll listen."

"Mind, I don't pretend to know more of your affairs than you would wish me; but, as I am intimate with your father, I cannot but see that you, in managing your father's concerns, put great confidence in the man within there."

"What! Pat Brady?"

"Yes, Brady! Now if you only employed him as any other farm servant, he would not, probably, have much power to injure you; but I believe he does more than that—that he collects your rents, and knows the affairs of all your tenants."

"Well?"

"I have very strong reason to think that he is also in the employment, or at any rate in the pay, of Mr. Keegan, the attorney at Carrick."

"What makes you think that, Captain Ussher?"

"I could hardly explain the different things which make me think so; but I'm sure of it; and it is for you to judge whether, if such be the case, your confidence will not enable him, under the present state of affairs at Ballycloran, to do you and your father much injury. He is also, to my certain knowledge, joined in whatever societies—all of them illegal—are being formed in the country; and he is a man, therefore, not to be trusted. I may add also that if you listen too much to his advice and counsels, you will be likely to find yourself in worse troubles than even those which your father's property brings on you."

"Don't alarm yourself about me; I don't be in the habit of taking a servant's advice about things, Captain Ussher."

"There's your back up again; I don't mean to offend you, I tell you; however, if you remember what I have said to you, it may prevent much trouble to you:"—and Ussher walked into the house.

"Prevent throubles," soliloquised Thady; "there is no way with me to prevent all manner of throuble—I believe I'll go in and get a tumbler of punch;"—and determined to adopt this mode of quieting troubles, if he could not prevent them, he followed Ussher.

Ussher was now dancing with Feemy, and the fun had become universal and incessant; there were ten or twelve couple dancing on the earthen floor of Mrs. Mehan's shop. The piper was playing those provocative Irish tunes, which, like the fiddle in the German tale, compel the hearers to dance whether they wish it or no; and they did dance with a rapidity and energy which showed itself in the streams of perspiration running down from the performers' faces. Not much to their immediate comfort a huge fire was kept up on the hearth; but the unnecessary heat thus produced was atoned for by the numerous glasses of punch with which they were thereby enabled to regale themselves, when for a moment they relaxed their labours.

This pleasant recreation began also to show its agreeable effects in the increased intimacy of the partners and the spirit of the party. All diffidence in standing up had ceased—and now the only difficulty was for the aspirants to get room on which to make their complicated steps; and oh, the precision, regularity, and energy of those motions! Although the piper played with a rapidity which would have convinced the uninitiated of the impossibility of dancing to the time, every foot in the room fell to the notes of the music as surely as though the movements of the whole set had been regulated by a steam machine. And such movements as they were! Not only did the feet keep time, but every limb and every muscle had each its own work, and twisted shook and twirled itself in perfect unison and measure, the arms performed their figure with as much accuracy as the legs.

"Take a sup of punch now, Miss Tierney; shure you're fainting away entirely for the want of a dhrop." The lady addressed was wiping, with the tail of her gown, a face which showed the labour that had been necessary to perform the feat of dancing down the whole company to the tune of the " wind that shakes

K

the barley," and was now leaning against the wall, whilst her last partner was offering her punch made on the half and half system: "Take a sup, Miss Tierney, then; shure you're wanting it."

"Thank ye, Mr. Kelly, but I am afther taking a little jist now, and the head's not sthrong with me afther dancing;" she took the tumbler, however. "Faix, Mr. Kelly, but it's yourself can make a tumbler of punch with any man."

"'Deed then there's no sperrits in it at all—only a thrifle to take the wakeness off the water. Come, Miss Tierney, you didn't take what'd baptize a babby."

"It'd be a big babby then; one like yerself may be."

"Here's long life to the first you have yerself, any way, Miss Tierney!" and he finished the glass, of which the blushing beauty had drunk half. "Might a boy make a guess who'd be the father of it?"

"Go asy now, masther Morty," the swain rejoiced in the name of Mortimer Kelley. "It'll be some quiet, dacent fellow, that an't given to chaffing nor too fond of sperrits."

"By dad, my darling, and an't that me to a hair's breadth?"

"Is it you a dacent, asy boy?"

"Shure if it an't me, where's sich a one in the counthry at all? And it's I'd be fond of the child—and the child's mother more especial," and he gave her a loving squeeze, which in a less energetic society might have formed good ground for an action for violent assault.

"Ah don't! Go asy I tell you, Morty. But come, an't you going to dance instead of wasting your time here all night?" and the pair, re-invigorated by their intellectual and animal refreshment, again commenced their dancing.

Whilst the fun was going on fast and furious among the dancers, those in the inner room were not less busily engaged. Brady was still sitting in the chair which he had occupied during the supper, at the bottom of the table, though he had turned round a little towards the fire. At the further end of it Thady was seated, with a lighted pipe in his mouth, and a tumbler of punch on the shelf over the fireplace. Joe Reynolds was seated a little behind, but between Thady and Pat Brady; and a lot of others were standing around, or squatting on the end of the table—leaning against the fireplace, or sitting two on a chair, wherever two had been lucky enough to secure one between them. They were all drinking, most of them raw spirits—and all of them smoking. At the other end of the room, three or four boys and girls were standing in the door-way, looking at the dancing, and getting cool after their own performances; and Denis McGovery was sitting in the chair which Father John had occupied, with his head on the table, apparently asleep, but more probably intent on listening to what was going on among them at the other end of the room, whom he so strongly suspected of some proposed iniquity. The noise, however, of the music and the dancing, the low tones in which the suspected parties spoke, and the distance at which they sat, must have made Denis's occupation of eaves-dropping difficult, if not impracticable.

Thady had just been speaking, and it was evident from the thickness of his voice that the whiskey he had drunk was beginning to have its effects on him. Instead of eating his dinner, he had been drinking raw spirits in the morning, to which he was not accustomed; for though when cold, or when pressed by others, he could swallow a glass of raw whiskey with that facility which seems to indicate an iron throttle, he had been too little accustomed to give way to any temptation to become habitually a drunkard. Now, however, he was certainly becoming tipsy, and, therefore, more likely to agree to whatever those around him might propose."

"Asy, Mr. Thady!" said Pat; "there's that long-eared ruffian, McGovery, listening to every word he can catch. Be spaking now as if you war axing the boys about the rint."

"And isn't it about that he is axing?" said Joe. "But how can he get the rint, or we be paying it, unless he gives us his hand to rid the counthry of thim as robs us of our manes, and desthroys him and us, and all thim as should be frinds to him and the owld Masther, and to Ballycloran?"

"You know, all of ye, that I never was hard on you," continued Thady, "when, God knows, the money was wanted bad enough at Ballycloran. You know I've waited longer for what was owed than many a one has done who has never felt what it was to want a pound. Did I ever pull the roof off any of you? And though queer tenants you've most of you been, an't the same set on the land now mostly that there was four years ago? There's none of you can call me a hard man, I think; and when I've stuck to you so long, it isn't now I'll break away from you."

"Long life to you, Mr. Thady!" "Long life to yer honer— and may ye live to see the esthate your own yet, and not owe a shilling!" "It's thrue for the masther what he says; why should he turn agin his own now? God bless him!" Such were the exclamations with which Thady's last speech was received.

"And I'll tell you what it is," and he now spoke in a low thick whisper, "I'll tell you what's on my mind. Those that you hate,

I don't love a bit too well. You all know Hyacinth Keegan, I think?"

"'Deed we do—may the big devil fetch him home!"

"Well, then, would you like him for your landlord, out and out? such a fine gentleman as he is!"

"Blast him for a gintleman!" said Joe; "I'd sooner have his father; he war an honest man, more by token he war no Protestant; he sarved processes for Richard Peyton, up by Loch Allen."

"Well then," continued Thady, "if you don't like him, boys, I can tell you he don't like you a bit better; and if he can contrive to call himself masther at Ballycloran, as I can tell you he manes to try, it's not one of you he'll lave on the land."

"Did he tell you that himself, Mr. Thady?" whispered Brady. Now though young Macdermot was nearly drunk—quite drunk enough to have lost what little good sense was left to him, after being fool enough to come at all among those with whom he was at present drinking—still what Ussher had said about his follower was not forgotten, and though he did not absolutely believe that Brady was a creature of Keegan's, what he had heard prevented his having the same inclination to listen to Pat, or the same confidence in what he said.

"Faith then, he told me so with his own mouth; and it isn't only the others 'd be going, but you'd have to walk yourself, masther Pat."

"And why wouldn't I? D'ye think I'd be staying at Ballycloran afther you war gone, Mr. Thady?"

"Don't be making any vows, Pat; maybe you wouldn't be axed, and maybe, av you war, you wouldn't refuse to ate yer bread, though it war Keegan paid for it."

"That the first mouthful may choke me that I ever ate of his paying for!"

"Well, however, boys, Hyacinth Keegan will sthrip the roof off every mother's son of you if he ever conthrives to put his foot in Ballycloran; but, by God, he never shall! Mind, boys, he can never do that till he can lay his hands on the owld man; and where'll you all be, I wonder, to let him or any one he sends do that, or take a sod of turf, or a grain of oats off the land either?"

"By dad, you're right, Mr. Thady," said one of them. "Shure wouldn't we have him in a bog-hole, or as many as he'd send; and then they might take away what they could carry in their mouths."

"I'll tell you what, Sir." said Joe Reynolds, and he laid his hand on Thady's knee, and leant forward till his mouth was near the young man's ear—so near, that not only could not McGovery overhear his words, but of the whole party round the fire, only Brady and Byrne, besides Thady himself, could catch what he said; "I'll tell you what, Sir, Keegan shall never harum you or yours, if you'll be one of us—one of us heart and sowl; and I know you will, and I know it's not in you to put up with what they're putting on you; an' dearly he'll pay for the blow he strik you, an' the word he said—surely, Mr. Thady!" And he whispered still lower into his ear, "Let alone the esthate, an' the house, an' all that, you'd niver put up with what he has been about this day, paceable an' in quiet?"

"You're thrue in that, Joe, by G—d!"

"Well then, won't we see you righted? Let the bloody ruffian come to Ballycloran, an' then see the way he'll go back again to Carrick. Will you say the word, Mr. Thady? Will you join us agin thim that is as much, an' a deal more, agin you than they are agin us?"

"But what is it you main to do?"

"That's what you'll know when you've joined us; but you know it isn't now or here we'd be telling you that which, maybe, would put our necks in your hand. But when you've taken the oath we've all taken, we'll be ready then not only to tell you all, but follow you anywhere."

The young man paused.

"Isn't it enough for you to know that our inimies is your inimies —that thim you wishes ill to, we wishes ill to? Isn't Keegan the man you've most cause to hate, an' won't we right you with him? Don't we hate that bloody Captain that is this moment playing his villain's tricks with your own sisther in the next room there? and shure you can't feel very frindly to him. By the holy Virgin, when you're one of us, it's not much longer he shall throuble you. If you can put up with what the likes of them is doing to you—if you can bear all that—why, Mr. Thady, you're not the man I took you for. But mind, divil a penny of rint 'll ever go to Ballycloran agin from Drumleesh; for the matter's up now;—you're either our frind or our inimy. But if, Mr. Thady, you've the pluck they all says you have—an' which I iver see in you, God bless you!—it's not only one of us you'll be, but the head of us all; for there isn't one but 'll go to hell's gate for your word; an' then the first tinant on the place that pays as much as a tinpenny to Keegan, or to any but jist yourself—by the cross! he may dig his own grave."

What Thady immediately said does not much signify; before long he had promised to come over to Mrs. Mulready's at Mohill with Pat Brady, on an appointed night, there to take the oath of the party to whom he now belonged.

Though it was agreed that the secret determinations of the party were not to be divulged to him until he had joined them there, it nevertheless was pretty clearly declared that their immediate and chief object was the destruction of Ussher, and, if possible, the liberation of the three men who had lately been confined in Ballinamore Bridewell, for the malt that had been seized in the cabin by Loch Sheen. However, to prevent the evil arising from this carelessness in the performance of their duties as conspirators, Thady was requested to swear on a cross made with the handles of two knives, that he would not divulge anything that had occurred or been said in that room that night—with which request he complied.

By the time this was done most of them were drunk, but none were so drunk as poor Macdermot. His intoxication, moreover, was unfortunately not of that sort which was likely to end in quiescence and incapability. It was a sign of the great degradation to which Macdermot had submitted, in joining these men, that in talking over the injuries which Ussher had inflicted on them all, he had quietly heard them canvass Ussher's conduct to his sister, and that in no measured terms. This had gone much against the grain with him at first, because he could not but strongly feel that, in abusing Ussher, they were equally reproaching Feemy. But the fall of high and fine feelings, when once commenced, is soon accomplished, even when the fall is from a higher dignity than those of Thady's had ever reached; and though, a few hours since, he would have allowed no one but Father John, even to connect his sister's name with Ussher, he had soon accustomed himself to hear the poorest tenant on his father's property speak familiarly on the subject, when urging him to join them in common cause against his enemy. But though he had so far sacrificed his sister's dignity in his drunken conversation with these men, he was not the less indignant with the man whose name they had so unceremoniously joined with hers; and he got up with the resolution to inform Ussher that the intercourse between him and Feemy must immediately cease. The spirits he had taken gave him a false feeling of confidence that he should find means to carry his resolution into effect without delay.

When he got into the outer room, Ussher and Feemy were not there. The dancing and drinking were going on as fast as ever; Shamuth, the piper, was in the same seat, with probably not the same tumbler of punch beside him, and was fingering away at his pipes as if the feeling of fatigue was unknown to him; and Mary, the bride, was still dancing as though her heart had not been broken all the morning with the work she had had to do. Biddy also, the Ballycloran housemaid, was in the seventh heaven of happiness—for hadn't she music and punch galore? and though the glory of her once well-starched cap was dimmed, if not totally extinguished by the dust and heat, her heart was now too warm with the fun to grieve for that, especially when such a neat made boy as Barney Egan was dancing foranenst her. It did not, however, add to her happiness, when, after being addressed once or twice in vain, she heard her young master's voice.

"Biddy—d'ye hear, and be d—d to you!—is your misthress gone home?"

"'Deed, Mr. Thady, I think she be."

"And why the divil, then, a'nt you gone with her? d'you mane to be dancing here all night?"

Now Thady was in general so very unobservant—so little inclined to interfere with, if he could not promote, the amusements of his dependants—moreover, so unaccustomed to scold—that Biddy and the others round her soon saw that something was the matter.

"What are you staring at, you born fool? If Miss Feemy's gone up to Ballycloran, do you follow her."

Thady's thick voice, red face, and sparkling eyes showed that he was intoxicated, and Biddy, if not preparing to obey him—for the temptation to stay was too strong—was preparing to pretend to do so, when Mary McGovery, by way of allaying Macdermot's wrath, said,

"I don't believe then, Mr. Thady, that Miss Feemy's gone home, at all at all. I think she and the Captain is only walked down the lane a bit, jist to cool themselves, for sure it's hot work dancing—"

Thady did not stop to ask any more questions, but hurried out of the door, and turning away from Ballycloran, walked as fast as his unsteady legs would carry him towards Mohill; and, unfortunately, Ussher and Feemy were strolling down the lane in that direction.

When Pat Brady saw Macdermot hurry out of the house, he said to his sister, "Begad! Mary, you'd better hurry down the lane—if Captain Ussher and Miss Feemy is in it—jist to take care of her; for he and the masther 'll have a great fight of it this night. The masther's blood's up, and the two'll be slating one another afore they're parted."

"Goodness gracious!" exclaimed Mary, "why don't you go yourself, Pat? Mr. Thady's taken a dhrop, and maybe he'll be hurting Miss Feemy or the Captain. Denis, dear,"—her husband came in the room just then,—"there's a ruction between the Captain and Mr. Thady; in God's name go and bring away Miss Feemy!"

Ussher and Feemy had not been out of the house many minutes; it was a beautiful mild moonlight night in October, and as the girl had said, they had come out to cool themselves after the heat and noise and dirt of the room in which they had been dancing. Myles was in one of his best humours; he had persuaded himself that he had no real danger to fear from the men who, as he was told, were so hostile to him. Feemy, too, had looked very pretty and nice, and had not contradicted him; and whereas what Thady had drunk had made him cross, Ussher had only just had enough to make him good-humoured. Feemy too was very happy; she had contrived to forget her brother's croaking and Father John's warning, or at least the misery which they had occasioned her, and was very happy in Ussher's good-humour. It were bootless to repeat their conversation, or to tell how often it was interrupted by some unchided caress on the part of Ussher. Feemy, however, had not forgotten her resolution, and was bringing up all her courage to make some gentle hint to Myles on the subject on which she had promised Father John to speak to him, when her heart sunk within her, on hearing her brother's voice calling to her from behind.

"Good heaven, Myles, there's Thady! what can he be wanting here?"

Ussher's arm fell from the fair girl's waist as he answered, "Never fear, dear, don't you speak to him; leave him to me." By this time, Thady had nearly joined them.

"Is that you, Feemy, here at this hour? What the d— are you doing there, this time of night? Here, take my arm, and come home; it's time you had some one to mind you, I'm thinking."

Feemy saw that her brother was intoxicated, and was frightened; she turned, though she did not take his arm, and Ussher turned too.

"Your sister's not alone, Macdermot; as I'm with her, I don't think you have much cause to fear, because she is about a mile from Ballycloran."

"May be, Captain Ussher, you're being with her mayn't make her much safer; at any rate you'll let me manage my own affairs. I suppose I can take my sisther to her own home without your interference," and he took hold of his sister's arm, as if to drag it within his own.

"Good heavens, Thady, what are you afther? shure an't I walking with you; don't be dragging me!"

"It appears to me, Macdermot," said Ussher, "that though your sister was in want of no protector before you came, she is in great want of one now."

"She wanted it thin, and she wants it now, and will do as long as she's fool enough to put herself in the way of such as you; but, by G—d, as long as I'm with her, she shall have it!" and he dragged her along by the arm.

"But, Thady," said the poor girl, afraid both of her brother and her lover, and hardly knowing to which to address herself; "but, Thady, you're hurting me, and I'll walk with you quiet enough. I was only getting a little cool afther the dancing, and what's the great harm in that?"

"Well—there," and he let her go, "I'm not hurting you now; it's very tender you've got of a sudden, when I touch you. Captain Ussher, if you'll plaze to go on, or stay behind, I'll be obliged, for I want to spake to Feemy; and there's no occasion in life for my throubling you to hear what I've to say."

"You can say what you like, Macdermot, but I shan't leave you; for though Feemy's your sister, you're not fit to guide her, or yourself either, for you're drunk."

"And there you lie, Captain Ussher! you lie—that's what you're used to! but it's the last of your lies she'll hear."

"Ah! you're drunk," replied Ussher, "besides, you know I'd not notice what you'd say before your sister; if, however, you're not so very drunk as to forget what you've called me to-morrow morning, and would then like to repeat it, I'll thrash you as you deserve."

"Then, by Jasus, you'll have your wish! you asked me to-night if I had a mind to quarrel with you, and now I'll tell you, if I find you at Ballycloran schaming agin, you'll find me ready and willing enough."

"That's where you'll find me to-morrow morning then, for I'll certainly come to ask your sister how she is, after the brutal manner you've frightened her this night; and then perhaps you'll have the goodness to tell me what you mean by what you call 'schaming.'"

"I'll tell you now, then; it's schaming to be coming with your lies and your blarney afther a girl like Feemy, only maning to desave her—it's schaming to go about humbugging a poor silly owld man like my father,—and it's the higth of schaming and blackguardness to pretend to be so frindly to a family, when you know you're maning them all the harum in your power to do. But you'll find, my fine Captain, it an't quite so asy to play your thricks at Ballycloran as you think, though we are so poor."

Feemy, when the young men had begun to use hard words to one another, had commenced crying, and was now sobbing away at a desperate rate.

"Don't distress yourself, Feemy," said Ussher, "your brother 'll be more himself to-morrow morning; he'll be sorry for what he has said then—and if he is so, I am not the man to remember what any one says when they've taken a little too much punch."

They had now come near enough to Mrs. Mehan's to see that there were a number of people outside the door. As soon after Thady's departure as Denis McGovery and the rest had been able to make up their minds what it would be the best to do in the emergency of the case, Denis and his wife sallied forth; the former to carry home whichever of the combatants might be slaughtered in the battle, and Mary to give to Feemy what comfort and assistance might be in her power. Pat Brady prudently thought that under all circumstances it would be safest for himself to remain where he was. The married pair, however, bent on peace if possible, and if not, on assuaging the horrors of war, had barely got into the road, when they encountered Father John returning to the wedding party.

"Oh, and it's yer riverence is welcome agin this blessed evening. God be praised that sent you, for it's yerself 'll be wanted, I'm afeard, and that immediately."

It was some time before the priest could learn what was the matter. At last he discovered that Ussher and Feemy had gone out walking,—that Thady had got drunk, and had gone after them; and he was inquiring whether he had gone towards Mohill, or towards Ballycloran, which none of them knew, when the three came in sight.

Father John instantly walked up to them, and if he had learnt it from nothing else, soon discovered from Feemy's tears, that something was the matter.

"How are you, Thady?" he said, putting out his hand to take the young man's, which was given with apparent reluctance; "how are you? is there anything wrong, that Feemy is crying so?"

"Oh, you know, Father John, there is a d—d deal wrong, and I've jist told the Captain what it is, that's all. I'll not have the girl humbugged any longer, that's all."

"There must be a great deal wrong, Thady, when you'd curse that way before me."

"I can't be picking my words now, for priest or parson."

They were now surrounded by the whole crowd out of the house, who were staring and gaping, and absolutely shocked at Thady's impudence to his friend and priest. Feemy was sobbing, and on Ussher offering her his arm to take her from the crowd, took it.

"By G—d!" exclaimed Thady, "if you touch that ruffian's arm

again, I'll niver call you sisther, or shall you iver call me brother; so now choose betwixt us."

Feemy dropped her hand from Ussher's arm, but turning to the priest, she said, "For heaven's sake take him away, Father John, he's drunk!"

"Drunk or sober, you may choose now; it's either me or him; but if you disgrace yourself, you shall not disgrace me!"

Father John took Feemy's arm on his, and telling the people to go back to their dancing, laid his hand on Thady's shoulder, and said,

"At any rate, Thady, come a little out of this; if you must speak to your sister in that way, you don't wish all the parish to hear what you're saying."

"What matthers, Father John; what matthers? Shure they've all heard too much already;—don't they all say she's the blackguard's misthress?"

"Oh, Thady, how can you repeat that word of me?" sobbed the poor girl.

"Why did you let them say it? Why don't you tell the man that's blackening your name while he's desaving you, to be laving you now, and not following you through the country like a curse?"

By this time the whole party, consisting of Father John, the two young men, and Feemy, were walking on rapidly towards Ballycloran. Feemy was crying, but saying nothing. Ussher was silent, although Thady was heaping on him every term of abuse he could think of;—and Father John was in vain attempting to moderate his wrath. Thus they continued until they came to the avenue leading up to the house, and on Ussher's proceeding with them through the gate, Thady put himself in the way, stopping him.

"You'll not come a step in here, Captain, if I know it; you might follow us along the road, for I couldn't help it,—but, by G—d, you don't come in here!"

"Nonsense, man; do you think I'll stop out for a drunken man's riot? let me pass."

"Set a foot in here, you blackguard, and I'll stretch you!"

Thady had an alpine in his hand, and was preparing to strike a blow at the Captain, exactly on the spot where Keegan had struck him, when the priest pushed his burly body in between them. "I'll have no blows, boys, at any rate while I'm with you; put your stick down, Thady," and he forced the young man's stick down; "run up to the house, Feemy, and get to bed; I'll see you in the morning." Feemy, however, did not move. "Now, Captain Ussher, I am not saying a word on the matter, one way or other, for I don't well know how the quarrel began,—but do you think it's well to be forcing your way in here, when the master desires you not?"

"But, Mr. McGrath, I've yet to learn that this drunken fellow is master here; besides, I suppose it is not a part of his project to rob me of my horse, which is in his father's stable."

Thady was at length persuaded to allow Ussher to go to the stables for his horse, and the Captain, after what had passed, did not now wish to go into the house. He was, however, going up to Feemy to shake hands with her, when the priest caught him by the arm, saying,—

"Why would you anger a drunken man, and that too, when the feeling in his heart is right? I'll tell you what, Captain, if what that young man fears is true, you're almost as much worse than him as vice is than virtue."

"Spare me your sermon now, Father John; if I see you to-morrow I'll hear it in patience," and he galloped down the avenue.

Thady and Feemy went into the house, and we hope each got to bed without further words; and Father John walked slowly home, thinking of all the misery he saw in store for his parishioners at Ballycloran.

CHAPTER XIV

DENIS M'GOVERY'S TIDINGS.

As soon as he had finished his breakfast on the morning after the night's events just recorded, Father John took his hat and stick, and walked down to Drumsna, still charitably intent on finding some means to soften, if he could not avert, the storm which he saw must follow the scenes he had witnessed on the previous evening. Ussher would have considered it want of pluck to stay away because Thady had told him to do so; Feemy also would encourage his visits, and would lean more to her lover than her brother—especially as her father, if it were attempted to make him aware of the state of the case, would be sure to take Feemy's part. Father John felt it would be impossible to induce the old man to desire Ussher to discontinue his visits, and he was confident that unless he did so, the Captain would take advantage of the unfortunate state of affairs at Ballycloran, and consider himself as an invited guest, in spite of the efforts Thady might make to induce him to leave it. But what the priest most feared was, that the unfortunate girl would be induced to go off with her lover, who he knew under such circumstances would never marry her; and his present object was to take her out of the way of such temptation. Father John gave Feemy credit for principles and feelings sufficiently high to prevent her from falling immediately into vice, but he at the same time feared, that with the strong influence Ussher had over her, he might easily persuade her to leave her home, partly by promising at some early time to marry her, and partly by threatening her with desertion. He thought that if were she at present domiciled at Mrs. McKeon's, Ussher might then be brought to hear reason, and be made to understand that if he was not contented to propose for and marry Feemy, in a proper decent manner, he must altogether drop her acquaintance.

He was not far wrong in the estimate he formed of both their characters. Though Ussher loved Feemy, perhaps as well as he was ever likely to love any woman, circumstances might easily have induced him to give her up. It was the impediments in the way, and the opposition he now met with, which would give the affair a fresh interest in his eyes. He certainly did not intend to marry the poor girl; had she had sufficient tact, she might, perhaps, have persuaded him to do so; but her fervent love and perfect confidence, though very gratifying to his vanity, did not inspire him with that feeling of respect which any man would wish to have for the girl he was going to marry. I do not say that his premeditated object had been to persuade her to leave her home, but Father John was not far wrong in fearing, that unless steps were taken to prevent it, it would be the most probable termination to the whole affair.

With regard to Feemy, he was quite right in thinking that her love of Ussher was strong enough to induce her to take almost any step that he might desire; and that that love, joined to her own obstinacy and determined resistance to the advice of those to whom she should have listened, was such as to render it most unlikely that she should be induced to give him up; but though he so well understood the weakness of her character, he was not aware of, for he had had no opportunity of trying, its strength.

As long as Feemy had her own way, as at the present time she had, she would, as we have seen, yield entirely to her strong love; but this was not all; had circumstances enabled her friends to remove her entirely out of Ussher's way, and had they done so, her love would have remained the same; her passion was so strong, that it could not be weakened or strengthened by absence or opposition. When Father John calculated that by good management Ussher might be brought to relinquish Feemy, he was right, but he was far from right, when he thought that Feemy could be taught to forget him. She literally cared for no one but him; her life had been so dull before she knew him, and so full of interest since—he so nearly came up to her *beau idéal* of what a man should be, for she had seen, or at any rate had known, no better—he so greatly excelled her brother and father, and was so much better looking than young Cassidy, and so much more spirited than Frank McKeon, that to her young heart he was all perfection.

She had lately been vexed, tormented, and even frightened; but her fear was merely that Ussher did not love her as she did him—that he might be made to leave her; and she was learning to hate her brother for opposing, as she would have said, the only source of her happiness. As to being induced by prudence or propriety to be cool to her lover—as to taking the first step herself towards making a breach between them—nothing that her brother or the priest had said, nothing that they could ever say, could either make her think of doing so, or think that it could be advisable, or in any way proper, that she should do so. For this strong feeling Father John did not give our heroine credit; but he still felt that she was headstrong enough to make it a very difficult task for him to manage her in any way. But as his charity was unbounded, so were his zeal and courage great.

His present plan was to induce his friend, Mrs. McKeon, to ask Feemy to come over and spend some time with her and her daughters at Drumsna. There were difficulties in this; for, in the first place, although Feemy and the Miss McKeons had been very good friends, still the reports which had lately been afloat, both about her and the affairs of her family, might make Mrs. McKeon, a prudent woman, unwilling to comply with the priest's wishes—though indeed it was not often that she contradicted him in anything; then, after he had talked Mrs. McKeon over, when he had aroused her charitable feelings and excited the good nature, which, to tell the truth, was never very dormant in her bosom, he had the more difficult task of persuading Feemy to accept the invitation. Not that under ordinary circumstances she would not be willing enough to go to Mrs. McKeon's, but at present she would be likely to suspect a double meaning in everything. Father John had already mentioned Mrs. McKeon's name to her, in reference to her attachment to Ussher; and it was more than probable that if he now brought her an invitation from that lady, she would perceive that the object was to separate her from her lover, and that she would obstinately persist in remaining at Ballycloran.

As Father John was entering Drumsna, he met his curate, Cullen, and McGovery, who, considering that he had only been married the evening before, and that if he had not been dancing himself, he had been kept up by his guests' doing so till four or five in the morning, had left his bride rather early; for, according to custom, he had slept the first night after his wedding at his wife's house, and, though it was only ten o'clock, he had been on a visit to Father Cullen, with whom he was now eagerly talking.

On the previous evening, when feigning to be asleep, he had managed to overhear a small portion of what had passed between Thady, Joe Reynolds, and the rest; but what he had overheard had reference solely to Keegan; for when they began to speak of Ussher, everything had been said in so low a voice, that he had been unable to comprehend a word. He had contrived, however, to pick up something, in which Ballycloran, rents, Keegan, and a bog-hole were introduced in marvellous close connection, and he was not slow in coming to the determination that he had been wrong when he fancied that Ussher was the object against whom plots were being formed, and that Keegan was the doomed man; but what was worse still, he was led to imagine that the perpetrators of Mr. Keegan's future watery grave were instigated by young Macdermot! He was well aware that Flannelly and Keegan, for they were all one, had the greater portion of the rents out of Ballycloran, and he now plainly saw that the more active of this firm was to be made away with, while collecting, or attempting to collect, the rent.

Denis was puzzled as to what he should do; his conscience would not allow the man to be murdered without his interference; he had no great love for Mr. Keegan, and his sympathies were not more strongly excited than they had been when he thought Ussher was to be the victim. Should he tell Mr. Keegan? that would be setting the devil in arms against his wife's brother—against his wife's brother's master—and against his wife's brother's master's tenants; this was too near cutting his own throat, to be a line of action agreeable to Denis. Then it occurred to him to have recourse again to Father John: but Father John had made light of his former warning. Besides, the fact of his having been wrong in his last surmises, would have thrown stronger doubts on those he now entertained. Father John too was always quizzing him, and Denis did not like to be quizzed. After much consideration, McGovery resolved to go to Father Cullen, and disclose his secret to him; Father Cullen was a modest, steady man, who would neither make light of, or ridicule what he heard; and if after that Keegan was drowned in a bog-hole, it would be entirely off Denis's conscience.

When Father John met the pair, they had just been discussing the subject; Cullen was far from making light of it; for, in the first place, he believed every word McGovery told him, and in the next, he was shocked, and greatly grieved, that one of his own parishioners, and one also of the most respectable of them, should be concerned in such a business: he felt towards Keegan all the abhorrence which a very bigoted and ignorant Roman Catholic could feel towards a Protestant convert, but he would have done anything to prevent his meeting his death by the hands, or with the connivance, of Thady Macdermot.

As soon as Cullen had heard McGovery's statement—which, by the by, had been made without any reference to his previous statement to Father John, or his warning to Captain Ussher—he determined to tell it all to the parish priest, and to take McGovery with him. This plan did not, however, suit Denis at all, and he used all his eloquence to persuade Father Cullen, that if he told Mr. McGrath at all, he, Denis, had better not make one of the party; and he was at the moment considering what excuse he could give for refusing to go into the priest's cottage, when they met Father John on the road coming into Drumsna.

Denis was greatly disconcerted,—but Cullen, full of his news, and as eager to communicate it as if it had been arranged definitely that Keegan was to be put into the bog-hole at noon precisely, was very glad to see him, and instantly opened his budget.

"I'm very glad to meet you this morning, Mr. McGrath," he began, "and it's well since you're out so early, that it's not the other way you went,—for I'd been greatly bothered if I hadn't found you."

"But here I am, you see,—and if it was only after me you were going, I suppose you can turn, for I'm going to Drumsna."

"Oh to be sure I can; don't you be going, Denis McGovery." Denis had taken off his hat, and muttering something about his wife, and "good morning, yer riverence," was decamping towards Ballycloran.

"Why, man," said Father John, "what business have you so far from your wife at this hour of the morning, after your wedding? Have you been to take the two pigs home?"

"He, he, Father John, you'll niver have done with them pigs!—But the wife'll be waiting for me, and, as yer riverence says, I mustn't be baulking her the first morning."

"Stay a while,—as you've come so far without her, you can stop a moment."

"Oh yes," said Cullen, "wait till you've told Mr. McGrath what you told me."

Denis was unwillingly obliged to remain, and repeat to Father John the whole story he had told Cullen. Though he could hardly tell why himself, he softened down a little the strong assurance he had given Cullen that Thady himself had been urging the boys to make away with Keegan. Father John listened to all in silence, till Denis ended by wishing "that the two young men got home safe last night, and that there war nothing worse nor harder than words betwixt them."

"Get home safe, you fool!" answered Father John, "and why wouldn't they?—don't you know the difference yet, between a few foolish words, said half in fun, and a quarrel? To be sure they got home safe;—and let me tell you, Denis, for a sensible fellow as you pretend to be, you'd be a deal better employed minding your business, than thinking of other people's quarrels, or trying to pick up stories of murders, and heaven knows what —filling your own mind and other people's too with foolish fears, for which there are no grounds. And now, if you'd take my advice, you'll go home, and leave your betters to take care of themselves, for you'll find it quite enough to take care of yourself; —and mind, McGovery, if I find this cock and bull story of yours gets through the country, so as to reach Mr. Keegan's ears, or to annoy Mr. Macdermot, I shall know where it came from; and perhaps you're not aware, that a person inventing such a story as you've been telling Mr. Cullen, might soon find himself in Carrick Gaol."

It would be impossible to say whether Cullen was most astonished, or McGovery disconcerted, by Father John's address.

"But," began Cullen, "if the man really heard the plan proposed, Mr. McGrath, and if Mr. Thady was one of them—"

"Ah, nonsense, Cullen."

"But I haven't invented a word, Father John," said McGovery; "I heard it every word; and shure, afther hearing it all with my own ears, was I to let the man be shot into a bog-hole, without saying a word to no one about it, Father John?"

"Ah, you're a nice boy, Denis,—and why did you pass my gate to come all the way down to Father Cullen, to tell him the dreadful tale? why didn't you come to me, eh—when you knew, not only that I was nearer you than Mr. Cullen, but also nearer to the place where all this was to happen?"

"Why then, Father John, not to tell you a lie, it is because you do be going on with your gagging at me so."

"Nonsense, man;—how can you say you are not going to lie, when you know you've a lie in your mouth at the moment."

"Sorrow a lie is there in it at all, Father John,—I wish the tongue of me had been blistered this morning, before I said a word of it."

L

"I wish it had been. Why, Cullen, it was only last night that he wanted to persuade me that a lot of boys were to meet at the place where he was married, to agree to murder Ussher; and to hear the man, you'd think it was all arranged, who was to strike the blow and all; and now here he is with you, with a similar story about Keegan! He was afraid to come to me, because he knew he'd half humbugged me with his other story last night."

"But I tell you, Father John, I heard it all with my own ears this time."

"And I tell you, you were dreaming. Do you think you'd make me believe that such a young gentleman as Mr. Thady would turn murderer all of a sudden? Now go home, and take my advice; if you don't want to find yourself in a worse scrape than Captain Ussher, or Mr. Keegan, don't repeat such a tale as that to any one."

McGovery sneaked off with his tail, allegorically speaking, between his legs. He didn't exactly know what to make of it; for though, as has been before said, he did not wish on this occasion to make Father John the depositary of his fears, he did not expect even from him to meet with such total discomfiture. He consoled himself, however, with the recollection that if anything did happen now, either to the revenue officer or the attorney,—and he almost hoped there would,—he could fairly say that he had given warning and premonitory tidings of it to the parish priests, which, if attended to, might have prevented all harm. With this comfortable feeling, to atone for Father John's displeasure, and now not quite sure whether he had overheard any allusion last night to Keegan and a bog-hole or not, he returned to his wife.

As soon as he was gone, Cullen, as much surprised as McGovery at the manner in which Father John had received the story, asked him if he thought it was all a lie.

"Perhaps not all a lie," answered the priest; "perhaps he heard something about Keegan—not very flattering to the attorney; no doubt Thady was asking the boys about the rent, and threatening them with Keegan as a receiver over the property, or something of that sort; and very likely one of those boys from Drumleesh said something about a bog-hole, which may be Thady didn't reprove as he ought to have done. I've no doubt it all came about in that way,—but that fellow with his tales and his stories, will get his ears cut off some of these days, and serve him right. Why he wanted yesterday, to make me believe that these fellows who are to drown Keegan this morning, were to shoot Ussher last night! He's just the fellow to do more harm in the country than all the stills, if he were listened to.—Well, Cullen, good day, I'm going into Mr. McKeon's here;"—and Cullen went away quite satisfied with Father John's view of the affair.

Not so, Father John. For Thady's sake—to screen his character, and because he did not think there was any immediate danger—he had given the affair the turn which it had just taken; but he himself feared—more than feared—felt sure that there was too much truth in what the man had said. Thady's unusual intoxication last night—his brutal conduct to his sister—to Ussher, and to himself—the men with whom he had been drinking—his own knowledge of the feeling the young man entertained towards Keegan, and the hatred the tenants felt for the attorney—all these things conspired to convince Father John that McGovery had too surely overheard a conversation, which, if repeated to Keegan, might probably, considering how many had been present at it, give him a desperate hold over young Macdermot, which he would not fail to use, either by frightening him into measures destructive to the property, or by proceeding criminally against him. Father John was not only greatly grieved that such a meeting should have been held, with reference to its immediate consequences, but he was shocked that Thady should so far have forgotten himself and his duty as to have attended it. But with the unceasing charity which made the great beauty of Father John's character, he, in his heart, instantly made allowances for him; he remembered all his distress and misery—his want of friends—his grief for his sister—his continued attempts and continued inability to relieve his father from his difficulties; and he determined to endeavour to screen him.

His success with McGovery, whom he had made to disbelieve his own senses, and with Cullen, who was ready enough to take his superior's views in any secular affair, had been complete; and he did not think that either would now be likely to repeat the story in a manner that would do any injury. We shall, in a short time, see what steps he took in the matter with Thady himself. In the meanwhile, we will follow him into Mrs. McKeon's house, at whose door he had now arrived.

CHAPTER XV.

THE M'KEONS.

When Father John opened the wicket gate leading into the small garden which separated Mrs. McKeon's house from the street, he saw her husband standing in the open door-way, ruminating. Mr. McKeon was said to be a comfortable man, and he looked to be so; he was something between forty-five and fifty, about six feet two high, with a good-humoured red face. He was inclined to be corpulent, and would no doubt have followed his inclination had he not accustomed himself to continual bodily activity. He was a great eater, and a very great drinker; it is said he could put any man in Connaught under the table, and carry himself to bed sober. At any rate he was never seen drunk, and it was known that he had often taken fifteen tumblers of punch after dinner, and rumour told of certain times when he had made up and exceeded the score.

He was comfortable in means as well as in appearance. Though Mr. McKeon had no property of his own, he was much better off than many around him that had. He had a large farm on a profitable lease; he underlet a good deal of land by con-acre, or cornacre;—few of my English readers will understand the complicated misery to the poorest of the Irish which this accursed word embraces;—he took contracts for making and repairing roads and bridges; and, altogether, he contrived to live very well on his ways and means. Although a very hard-working man he was a bit of a sportsman, and usually kept one or two well-trained horses, which, as he was too heavy to ride them himself, he was always willing, and usually able, to sell at remunerating prices. He was considered a very good hand at a handicap, and understood well—no one better—the dangerous mysteries of "knocking." He was sure to have some animal to run at the different steeple-chases in the neighbourhood, and it was generally supposed, that even when not winning his race, Tony McKeon seldom lost much by attending the meeting. There was now going to be a steeple-chase at Carrick-on-Shannon in a few days, and McKeon was much intent on bringing his mare, Playful,—a wicked devil within twenty yards of whom no one but himself and groom could come,—into the field in fine order and condition. In addition to this, Mr. McKeon was a very hospitable man, his only failing in that respect being his firm determination and usual practice to make every man that dined with him drunk. He was honest in everything, barring horse-flesh; was a good Catholic, and very fond of his daughters—Louey and Lydia. His wife was a kind, good, easy creature, fond of the world and the world's goods, and yet not selfish or niggardly with those with which she was blessed. She was sufficiently contented with her husband, whose friends never came out of the dining-room after dinner, and therefore did not annoy her; she looked on his foibles with a lenient eye, for she had been accustomed to such all her life; and when she heard he had parted with her car in a handicap, or had lost her two fat pigs in a knock, she bore it with great good-humour. She was always willing to procure amusement for her daughters, and was beginning to feel anxious to get them husbands; she was a good neighbour, and if she had a strong feeling at all, it was her partiality for Father John. Her daughters had nothing very remarkable about them to recommend them to our attention: they were both rather pretty, tolerably well educated, to the extent of a two years' sojourn in a convent in Sligo; were both very fond of novels, dancing, ribbons and potato cakes; and both thought that to dance at a race-ball with an officer in his regimentals was the most supreme terrestrial blessing of which their lot was susceptible.

We have, however, kept the father too long standing at his own door, while we have been describing his family.

"Well, Father John," said McKeon, "how are you this morning?"

"Why then, as luckily I didn't dine with you, Mr. McKeon, I'm pretty much as I usually am,—and, thank God, that's well. I'm told you had those poor fellows that were with you last night, laid on a mattress, and that you sent them home that way to Carrick on a country car, and that they couldn't move, leaving this at six this morning."

"Oh, nonsense, Father John! who was telling you them lies?"

"But wasn't it true? Didn't they go home on one of the cars off the farm, and young Michael driving them, and they on a mattress?"

"And sure, Father John, you wouldn't have had me let them walk home to Carrick after dinner?"

"They were little fit for walking, I believe; why they couldn't so much as sit up in the car. Will you never have done, Mr. McKeon; don't you know the sin of drunkenness?"

"The sin of drunkenness! me know it! Indeed I don't then. When did you ever see me drunk? Come, which was a case last, Father John—you or I?"

"God forgive me, but I believe some boys did make me rather

tipsy the first day I ever was in France; and my head should have been full of other things; and I believe if you were to swim in punch it wouldn't hurt you; but you know as well as I can tell you, it's worse for you to be making others drink so much who can't bear it as you can, than if you were hurting yourself."

"And you know, as well as I can tell you, that yourself would be the last man to take the whiskey off the table, as long as .he lads that were with you chose to be drinking it; and I think when I sent them boys off to Carrick as comfortably asleep as if they were in bed, so that they wouldn't be too late at business this morning, I acted by them as I'd wish anybody to act by me if I had an accident; and if that an't being a good Christian, I don't know what is. So lave off preaching, Father John, and come round to the stables, till I show you the mare that'll win at Carrick; at least, it 'll be a very good nag that 'll take the shine out of her."

"I hope you'll win, Mr. McKeon, in spite of your villany in making those young fellows drunk. But I'll not look at the mare just at present; more by token I'm told she's not very civil to morning visitors."

"Arrah, nonsense, man! she's as quiet a mare as ever went over a fence, when she's well handled."

"But you see I can't handle her well; and as I want to see the good woman that owns you, if you please, I'll go into the house instead of into the stable."

"Well, every man to his choice; and I'll see Playful get her gallop. But I tell you what, Father John, if you don't mind what you're after with Mrs. McKeon, I'll treat you a deal worse than I did those two fellows I sent home to Carrick on a mattress."

So Mr. McKeon walked off to superintend the training of his mare; and the priest, in spite of the marital caution he had received, walked into the dining-room, where he knew that at that hour he should probably find the mother and daughters surrounded by their household cares.

When the usual greetings were over, and the two girls had asked all the particulars of Mary Brady's wedding, and Mrs. McKeon had got through her usual gossip, Father John warily began the subject respecting which he was so anxious to rouse his friend's soft sympathies.

Mrs. McKeon had gone so far herself as to ask him whether anything had been settled yet at Ballycloran, about Ussher, and whether he thought that the young man really intended to marry the girl.

The way this question was asked, was a great damper to Father

John's hopes. If there had been any kindly feelings towards poor Feemy at the moment in her breast, she would have called her by her name, and not spoken of her as "the girl;" it showed that Mrs. McKeon was losing, or had lost, whatever good opinion she might ever have had of Feemy: and when Louey ill-naturedly added, "Oh laws!—not he—the man never thought of her," Father John felt sure that there was a slight feeling of triumph among the female McKeons at the idea of Feemy's losing the lover of whom, perhaps, she had been somewhat too proud.

Still, however, he did not despair; he knew that if they spoke with ill-nature, it arose from thoughtlessness—and that it was, at any rate with the mother, only necessary to point out to her the benefit she could confer, to arouse a kindly feeling within her.

"I think you're wrong there, Miss Louey," said Father John; "I think he not only did think of her—but does think of her; and I'll tell you what I know, that if Feemy Macdermot had the great blessing which you have, and that is a kind, good, careful mother to the fore, she'd have been married to him before this."

"But, Father John," said the kind, good, careful mother, "what is there to prevent them marrying, if he's ready? I always pitied Feemy being left alone there with her father and brother; but if Captain Ussher is in earnest, I don't see how twenty mothers would make it a bit easier for her."

"Don't you, Mrs. McKeon!—then it's little you know the advantage your own girls have in yourself. Don't you think a man would prefer taking a girl from a house where a good mother gave signs that the daughter would make a good wife, than from one where there was no one to mind her but a silly old man, and a young one like Thady?—a very good young man in his way, but not very fit, Mrs. McKeon, to act a mother's part to a girl like Feemy."

"That's true enough; but then why did she make all the world believe he was engaged to her, if he wasn't?—And if he wasn't, why did she let him go on as though he was, being at all hours, I'm told, with her at Ballycloran?—and if they are not to be married, why does her brother let him be coming there at all? I know you're fond of them, Father John, and I'd be sorry to think ill of your friends; but I must say it begins to look odd."

"You're right any how, in saying I'm very fond of them; indeed I am, and so is yourself, Mrs. McKeon; and I know, though you speak in that way to me, you wouldn't say anything that could hurt the poor girl, any where but just among ourselves. If it wasn't in a kind mother, with such a heart as your own,—especially in one she'd known so long,—in whom could a poor motherless, friendless girl, like Feemy, expect to find a friend?"

"God forbid I should hurt her, Father John! And indeed I'd befriend her if I knew how; but don't you think, yourself now, she's played a foolish game with that young man?"

"Why, as I never was a young lady in love, I can't exactly say how a young lady in love should behave; but, my dear woman, look at it this way; I suppose there's no harm in Feemy wishing to get herself married, more than anyother young lady?"

"Oh! dear no, Father John; quite right she should."

"And every one seems to think this Captain Ussher would be a proper match for her."

"Why, barring that he's a Protestant, of course he's a very good match for her."

"Oh! as to his being a Protestant, we won't mind that now. Well then, Mrs. McKeon, under these circumstances, what could Feemy do better than encourage this Captain?"

"I never blamed her for encouraging him; only she should not have gone the length she has, unless he downright proposed for her."

"But he has downright proposed for her."

"No! Father John," said Louey.

"Has he though, really!" exclaimed Lyddy.

"Then, why, in the name of the blessed Virgin, don't he marry her?" said the mother.

"That's poor Feemy's difficulty, you see, Mrs. McKeon. Now if any man you approved of were to make off with Miss Lyddy's heart—and I'm sure she'll never give it to any one you don't approve of—why of course he'd naturally come to you or her father, and the matter would be settled; but Feemy has no mother for him to go to, and her father, you know, can't mind such things now."

"But she has a brother; in short, if he meant to marry her, it would soon be done. Where there's a will, there's a way."

"But that's where it is; you know young men, and what they are, a deal better than I do; and you can understand that a young man may propose to a girl, and be accepted, and afterwards shilly shally about it, and perhaps at last change his mind altogether—merely because the girl's friends don't take care that the affair is regularly and properly carried on; now isn't that so, Mrs. McKeon?"

"Indeed, Father John, it's all true."

"Well, that's just Feemy's case; may be, after, as you say, having given the young man so much encouragement, she'll lose him because she has no mother to keep him steady as it were, and fix him; and no blame to her in the matter either, is there, Mrs. McKeon?"

"Why, if you look at it in that way, of course, she's not so much to blame."

"Of course not," said Father John, obliged to be satisfied with this modicum of applause; "of course not; but it's a pity for the poor girl."

"You think he'll jilt her altogether, then?"

"I don't think he means it yet; but I think he will mean it soon,—unless, indeed, Mrs. McKeon, you'd befriend her now."

"Me, Father John!"

"If you'd take a mother's part with her for a week or so, it would all be right; and I don't know a greater charity one Christian could do another this side the grave, than you could do her."

"What could I do, Father John?" said the good woman,—rather frightened, for she would now be called on to take some active part in the matter, which perhaps she might not altogether relish;—"what could I do? You see Ballycloran is three miles out of this, and I couldn't always be up there when Ussher was coming. And though I believe I'd be bold enough where one of my own girls was concerned, I'd be shy of speaking to a man like Captain Ussher, when it was no business of my own."

"As for that, I believe you'd never want wit or spirit either, to say what you'd wish to say to any man, and that in the very best manner. It's true enough, though, you couldn't be always up at Ballycloran; but why couldn't Feemy be down at Drumsna?"—Father John paused a minute, and Mrs. McKeon said nothing, but looked very grave.—"Now be a good woman, Mrs. McKeon, and ask the poor girl down here for a fortnight or so; I know Lyddy and Louey are very fond of their friend, and Feemy 'd be nice company for them; and then as you are acquainted with Captain Ussher, of course he'd be coming after his sweetheart; and then, when Feemy is under your protection, of course you'd speak to him in your own quiet lady-like way; and then, take my word for it, I'd be marrying them in this very room before Christmas. Wouldn't we have dancing up stairs, eh, Miss Louey?"—Mrs. McKeon still said nothing.—"And even supposing Ussher did not come down here, and nothing was done, why it would be evident the match was not to take place, and that Ussher was a blackguard; then of course Feemy must give up all thoughts of him. And though, maybe, she'd grieve awhile, it would be better so than going on as she is now up at the old place, with no one to give her any advice, or tell her what she ought to do or say to the man. Any way, you see, it would be doing her a kind service. Come, Mrs. McKeon, make up your mind to be a kind, good neighbour to the poor girl; and do you and the two young ladies go up to Ballycloran, and ask her to come down and spend a week or two with you here."

"But perhaps," said Louey, "Feemy won't like to leave Ballycloran, and come so far from her beau; because she couldn't see him here as she does there, you know, Father John."

"Why, Miss Louey, I don't think you know how she sees him. I believe he goes and calls there, much as you'd like your beau to come and call here, if you had one."

"Indeed, Father John, when I do have one, I hope I shall manage better than to be talked about as much as she is, any way. I hardly think it would do to ask her at present, mother. You know Mr. Gayner is to be here the night of the race-ball, and we've only the one bed."

"Come, come, Miss Louey, I didn't expect to hear you say a word against your old friend; why should you be less good-natured than your mother? You see she's thinking how she can best do what I'm asking."

"As for old friends," said Louey, "I and Miss Macdermot were never so very intimate; and as for being ill-natured, I never was told before that I was more ill-natured than mother. But of course mamma will do as she likes, only she can't very well turn Mr. Gayner out of the house after having asked him to come for the races, that's all:" and Miss Louey flounced out of the room.

"Come, Mrs. McKeon," continued Father John, "think of the benefit this would be to Feemy; and you can't have any real objection; the race-ball is only for one night, and the girls will be too tired after that, to think very much of sleeping together."

"But you seem to forget—very likely Mr. McKeon wouldn't like my asking her; you know I couldn't think of doing it without asking him."

"Oh! Mrs. McKeon, that's a good joke! You'll make me believe, won't you, that you're not as much mistress of your own house as any woman in Ireland? As if Mr. McKeon would interfere with your asking any one you pleased to your own house."

"But you see the girls are against it."

"I hope they are not against anything that would be charitable and kind in their mother; but if they were, I'm quite sure their mother shouldn't give way to them. Wouldn't you be glad to have Miss Feemy here a short time, Miss Lyddy?"

"Indeed, I'd have no objection, if mamma pleases, Father John."

"There, you see, Mrs. McKeon;—I am afraid I said something rude which set Miss Louey's back up, but I am sure in her heart she'd be glad of anything that would be of service to Feemy. Come, Mrs. McKeon, will you drive over to Ballycloran this fine morning, and ask her?"

"But suppose she won't come?"

"Then it won't be your fault;—you can tell her it's just for the races and the ball you're asking her—that she may see Mr. McKeon's horse win the race, and dance with Ussher at the ball afterwards. Oh! if you mean her to come, she'll come fast enough;—let you alone for carrying your point when you're in earnest. I know your way of asking, when you don't mean to take a refusal;—and to give you your due this day, I never heard you give an invitation you didn't mean to be accepted."

"Well, Father John, as you think it will be of so much service to Feemy, and as, as you say, she has no mother, poor girl, of her own, and no female friend that she can look to, I'll ask her over here. But it mustn't be for a week or a fortnight, but till the affair of Captain Ussher is finally settled. And if the girl behaves herself as she ought, when once she is here, Tony won't see her wronged by any man."

"That's my own friend!" said Father John with tears in his eyes. "What could any poor priest like me do in a parish, if it wasn't that there were such women as yourself to help him?"

"But, Father John—whisper here," and she took him aside into the window, and spoke in a low voice; "you can't have helped hearing the stories people have been talking about Feemy. As I have heard them, of course you must."

"Heard them! of course I have—but you know what lies get talked abroad."

"But they say she walks with him after dark; and goes in and out there at Ballycloran, at all hours, just as she pleases. Of course I can have none of those doings here."

"Of course not; it is because she has no one there to tell her what is right or wrong that I wish her to be here. Of course you have regular hours here, and you'll find you'll have no difficulty with her that way."

"Well, Father John, I've only one more thing to say, and you'll answer me that as a priest and a Christian. God knows, I wouldn't believe any ill-natured story against any poor girl situated as Feemy is; but you know, such things will get about: —people say Ussher speaks of her as his mistress, instead of as his wife. Now, Father John, if this unfortunate girl, whom I'm ready and willing to help, has done anything really wrong, you would not be the means of bringing her into the house with my own dear girls! Have you, Father John, told me all you know about her attachment to this man?"

"Indeed then if she was unfit to associate with your girls, Mrs. McKeon, I'd be the last man on earth to ask you to invite her here. If Feemy has been imprudent in going out too much alone with Ussher, it's the most that with truth can be said against her; and as you ask me to tell you all, I'll tell you one thing I didn't wish to mention before the girls." And Father John told her how Thady had got drunk, and insulted Ussher, telling him not to come to Ballycloran again, and all that: but he did not tell her how strongly he suspected that Thady was right in his fears for his sister, and that his chief object in getting Feemy away from Ballycloran was to remove her as far as possible from Ussher's influence.

"Well, Father John, I'll go to Ballycloran, and ask her here; I suppose she'll hardly be ready to come to-day, but if she pleases, I'll drive over again for her after to-morrow. I'll go now and talk Louey over, for you and she seem to have quarrelled somehow."

"And God bless you, Mrs. McKeon; it's yourself is a good woman; and you never did a kinder action than the one you're going to do this morning!" and Father John took his leave.

The breakfast party at Ballycloran the morning after the wedding was not a very lively one; indeed the meals at Ballycloran seldom were very gay, but this was more than usually sombre.

Larry was brooding over Keegan's threats, his fears that Thady meant to betray him into the attorney's hands, and his determination never from that day forth to stir from his fireside, lest the horrid myrmidons of the law should pounce upon him.

Feemy was intent on the insults which had been offered to her lover, and her temper was somewhat soured by the remembrance that she had not effected her purpose of questioning Ussher about his intentions. Thady, however, was the blackest looking of the family. Everything was dark within his breast. He thought of the ruffians with whom he had leagued himself; and though previously he had only considered them as poor, hard used, somewhat lawless characters, they now appeared to him everything that was iniquitous and bad. Secret murder was their object—black, foul, midnight murder—and he was sworn, or soon would be sworn, not only to help them, but to lead them on. What he had already done might hang him. He felt his life to be in the power of each of those blackguards, with whom, in wretched equality, he had been drinking on the previous evening. And what had led him to this? If he had been wronged and injured, why could not he redress himself like other injured men? If revenge were necessary to him, why could he not avenge himself like a man, instead of leaguing with others to commit murder in the dark, like a coward and a felon? And then he thought of his position with Keegan and Ussher. There was something manly in his original disposition; he would have given anything for a stand up fight with the attorney with equal weapons; if it had been sure death to both, he would have fought him to the death; but he had no such opportunity; the dastardly brute had trampled on him when he could not turn against him. And then with rancorous hatred he thought of the blow that Keegan had struck him,—of the manner in which he had insulted his father, and worse than all, of the name he had applied to his sister; and, remembering all this, he almost reconciled himself to the only means he had of punishing the wretch that had inflicted all these injuries on him. Then he thought of Ussher, and the scene which had passed between them last night; he knew he had been drunk, and had but a very confused recollection of what he had done or said. He remembered, however, that he had insulted Ussher; this did not annoy him; but he had a faint recollection of having committed his sister's name, by talking of her in his drunken brawl, and of having done, or said something, he knew not what, to Father John.

Though Thady had never known the refinements of a gentleman, or the comforts of good society, still he felt that the fall, even from his present station to that in which he was going to place himself, would be dreadful. But it was not the privations which he might suffer, but the disgrace, the additional disgrace which he would bring on his family, which afflicted him. How could he now presume to prescribe to Feemy what her conduct should be, or to his father in what way he should act respecting the property? He already felt as though he was unworthy of either of them, and was afraid to look them in the face. After breakfast he wandered forth, striving to attend to his usual work, but the incentives to industry were all gone; he had no longer any hope that industry would be of service to him; he walked along the hedges and ditches, unconsciously planning in his mind the different ways of committing the crimes which he really so abhorred, but in which he was about to pledge himself to join. He thought, if it should be his lot to murder Keegan, how he would accomplish it. Should it be at night?—or in the day? —would he shoot him?—and if he did, would not the powder or the gun be traced home to him?—would not his footsteps in the bog be tracked and known?—if he struck him down on the road, would not the blood be found on his coat, or his shirt be torn in the struggle?—and, above all, would not his own comrades betray him? He had, some short time since, heard the whole of a trial for murder at Carrick assizes, and though he had not then paid particular attention to it, all the horrid detail and circumstances of the case now came vividly before his mind's eye. He planned and plotted how, had he in that case been the murderer, he would have foreseen and provided against the different things, the untoward accidents, which then came in evidence against the prisoner; he thought how much more wary he would be than the poor wretch who was then tried, and of what benefit the experience he had gained would be to him. Then he remembered that the principal witness in the case was an ill-featured, sullen-looking fellow, who had been called king's evidence—one who, in answering the tormenting questions put to him, had appeared almost more miserable than the prisoner himself;—that this man had been the friend and assistant of the murderer—the sharer and promoter of all his plans—the man who had led him on to the murder—his sworn friend. He remembered how it had come out on the trial, that the two had for months shared the same bed—tilled in the same field—eat from the same mess—and had sinned together in the same great sin. Yet this man had come forward to hang his friend!—and Thady shuddered coldly as he thought how likely it might be that his associates would betray him. He had not slept, eat, and worked with them—he was not leagued to them by equal rank, equal wants, and equal sufferings. If that wretched witness had been induced to give evidence against the man so strongly bound to him, how much more likely that Byrne or Reynolds should hang him! or Pat Brady! And as Brady's name occurred to him, he remembered Ussher's caution respecting that man, and his assurance that he was in Keegan's pay. If this were true, he had already committed the oversight to guard against which he had calculated that his superior cunning would be sufficient; and then the cold perspiration trickled from his brow, and he abruptly stopped, leaning against a bank, to meditate again on the position in which he stood.

It was not that during this time Thady had been absolutely planning murder. He had not been making any definite scheme, to be carried into immediate execution against any individual. He was not a murderer, even in mind or wish; he would have given anything to have driven the idea from his mind, but he could not; he could not avoid thinking what he would do, if he had resolved to do the deed—how the crime would be most safely perpetrated—how the laws most cunningly evaded. Then he half resolved to have nothing more to do with Reynolds and his followers, and to quiet his conscience while yet he possibly could; but the insolence of Keegan, the injuries of Ussher, and the sure enmity of those whom he had sworn to join, and now scarcely dared to desert, stifled his remorse, and destroyed the resolution before it was half made. He thought of enlisting—but he could not desert his sister; of going to Father John, and confessing all; but would Father John befriend him after his late conduct to him? Thus he wandered on, through the whole long morning. Twice he returned to the house, and creeping in through the back door, got himself a glass of spirits, which he swallowed, and again sallied forth, to find if movement would give him comfort, or his thoughts suggest anything to him in mitigation of his sorrows.

As he was returning, the third time, for the same bad purpose, —for the short stimulus of the dram was the only relief he could find to the depression which seemed to weigh him down and make his heart feel like a cold lump within him,—and just as he was turning from the avenue to the back of the house, he met Ussher walking down. He did not know what to do; he remembered that the evening before he had defied this man; he even recollected that he had arrogantly declared that he should not again set his foot on Ballycloran; he had forbad him the house, as if he had been the master; and at the present moment he felt as though he did not dare address him, for it seemed to him as if every one now would look down on him, as he looked down on himself,—as if every one could see what was in his breast, as plainly as he saw it himself.

This annoyance, however, was of short duration, for Ussher passed him with a slight unembarrassed nod, as if nothing had passed between them on the previous evening—as if they were still good friends, and had met and been talking together but a short time before. Ussher had walked by quickly, and there was a look of satisfaction or rather gratified vanity in his face; he seemed, also, absorbed with the subject of his thoughts; Thady, however, as soon as he had passed, took but little notice of him, but walked on into the kitchen, at the rear of the house.

Here, on a small settle by the fireside, where he had been placed out of the way by Biddy or Katty, sat a ragged bare-legged little boy, known as Patsy, the priest's gossoon; he was the only assistant Judy had in the management of Father John's *ménage*. He ran on errands to Drumsna, and occasionally to Carrick-on-Shannon— fetched the priest's letters—dug his potatoes—planted his cabbages, and cleaned his horse Paul. He had now come up to Ballycloran with a message to Thady, and having been desired to stay there till he could see him himself, he had been quietly sitting in the kitchen since a little after Thady had first left the house; he now jumped up to give his message.

"Misther Thady, yer honer, Father John says as how he'll be glad av yer honer'll come down to dinner with him at six; and he says as how you must come, Mr. Thady, because divil a bit he'll ate himself, he says, till you're in it."

"For shame, Patsy!" interposed Biddy, "putting those words into his riverence's mouth. I'm sure thin Father John wasn't cursing that way."

"Faix thin, ma'am, thim wor his very words—'Tell Mr. Thady, av he don't come down to the cottage to his dinner this day, divil a bit will I ate till he does.'"

"Well, to hear the brat!" continued Biddy, shocked at the indecorous language which was put into her priest's mouth.

"And who's to be at Father John's else?" said Thady.

"Sorrow a one av me rightly knows thin, for I wasn't hearing; all I wor told wor, I warn't to come out of this widout yer honer."

"But I can't go to-night, Patsy."

"But Father John says you must, Mr. Thady."

"Tell Father John, Patsy, that I am very much obliged to him, but that I'm not just well enough to come out to-night. I couldn't go to-night, do you hear; go down and tell him so, or he'll be waiting dinner."

"But, Mr. Thady," said the boy, half sobbing, "Father John said as how I warn't to come at all widout you."

"Do as I tell you, you fool; but mind you tell Father John I'm very much obliged to him, only I'm ill."

"Well," muttered the boy, at length taking his departure, "I know Father John 'll be very mad, but any way it ain't my fault."

Thady was gratified with the priest's invitation, for it showed that he at least had forgiven him; but he did not dare to face him by accepting it.

He got himself another glass of whiskey, and lighting his pipe, sat down to smoke by the kitchen fire; after he had been some time sitting there, Pat Brady came into the kitchen. Thady, however, took no notice, except muttering something in answer to Pat's usual salutation. They remained both some time silent, till at last Brady observed that, "They'd all of them had ilegant diversion last night—most of them stayed a power later nor you, Mr. Thady."

This allusion to last night was not at present the subject most likely to make Thady talk freely, so he still continued silent. At last Pat said,

"Could I spake to you a moment, Mr. Thady?"

"Spake out—what is it?"

"Oh, it's business, yer honer; it's something about money—wouldn't you step out to the rint-office?"

"Don't you see I'm just going to dinner; besides, I ain't well—it'll keep till to-morrow, I suppose?"

"But it won't keep, Mr. Thady."

At this moment, Biddy, who had been taking some smoking

viands out of a big black pot and transferring them to a dish, went out of the kitchen with them on her road to the dining-room, and Pat took the opportunity of whispering to his master that, "the boys wor to meet at Mulready's on the next evening."

"What of that?" answered Thady; "I suppose some of them meet there mostly every night?"

"But to-morrow's the night, Mr. Thady, when yer honer's to be inisheated among us sworn brothers."

"I shan't be in it at all to-morrow, then."

"Not be in it! why you promised; and the boys is all noticed now. Didn't you take the oath, Mr. Thady?" and he whispered down close to his ear.

"I took no oath about any day. I suppose I needn't come before I choose?"

Biddy now returned, and Thady got up to go to his dinner; Pat followed him, and renewed the conversation in the passage. Thady, however, would give no definite promise to come to-morrow, or the next day, but said he meant to come some day. Pat observed that the boys would be furious—that they would think themselves deceived and betrayed—then urged the necessity of taking steps to prevent their paying the rent to Keegan—hinted that Ussher had been with Miss Feemy that morning—and at last departed when he found that his master was not in a proper mood to be persuaded, remarking that "he would come up again in the morning, when perhaps his honer would be thinking better of it, and not break his promised word to the boys, as there would be a great ruction among them, av he didn't go down jist to spake a word to them afther what had passed; besides, Mr. Thady," he added, "av you wor to go back now, some of thim boys as wor in it last night, would be going to Jonas Brown's, thinking to get the first word agin you—thinking, you know, as how you would 'peach agin thim, may be."

After this threat, Pat took his leave, and Thady, with a sad heart, and low spirits, which even three glasses of whiskey had not raised, went in to dinner. After swallowing a few hasty morsels, without speaking either to his father or his sister, he returned to the kitchen and again sat there smoking, till one of the girls came in, telling him that Father John was on the steps of the hall-door waiting for him—that he couldn't come in, but that he said he had important business to speak of, and must see Mr. Thady.

"Confound you," muttered Thady, in a low voice, "why didn't you say I was out?"

"Shure, you niver told me, Mr. Thady."

Thady considered a moment, whether he should escape through the back door; at last, however, he plucked up his courage, and went out to meet the priest.

CHAPTER XVI.

PROMOTION.

As soon as Father John had gone, Mrs. McKeon prepared to persuade her refractory daughter to agree to the propriety of what she was going to do with respect to Feemy, and to inform her husband of the visitor she intended to ask to her house; she had not much difficulty with either, for though Louey was indignant when Father John hinted at her want of a beau, she was not really ill-natured, and when her mother told her that Father John had said that this invitation would be the performance of a Christian duty, she soon reconciled herself to the prospect of Feemy's company, in spite of Mr. Gayner and his bed. And as for Mr. McKeon, he seldom interfered with the internal management of his house, and when his spouse informed him that Feemy was coming to Drumsna, he merely remarked that "no wonder the poor girl was dull at that old ramshackle place up there, and that though Drumsna was dull enough itself, it was a little better than Ballycloran, especially now the Carrick races were coming on;" and so the three ladies put on their best bonnets and set off on their journey of charity.

Feemy was in her own sitting-room, and was somewhat more neat in her appearance than the last time we saw her there, for Ussher had said he would call early in the morning; but she was employed in the same manner as then—sitting over the fire with a novel in her hand, when she heard the sound of the car wheels, and on going to the window, saw Mrs. McKeon and her daughters.

That lady managed her business with all the tact and sincerity for which Father John had given her credit; she made no particular allusion to Ussher, but merely said that they should have a party to the race-course, as Mr. McKeon had a horse to run, and that afterwards they should all go to the ball at Carrick; and Mrs. McKeon added, "You know, Feemy, you'll meet your old friend Captain Ussher there."

She then assured Feemy how glad she would be if she would stay a short time at Drumsna, after the races were over, as her two daughters were now at home, and that if she would, she would try to make the house as pleasant as possible for her.

This was all said and done so pleasantly, that Feemy did not detect any other motive in her friend's civility than the one which was apparent, and after a little pressing, agreed to accept the invitation. It was agreed that Mrs. McKeon was to call for her on the Monday following, when, if her father made no objection, she would accompany her home to Drumsna.

As soon as they were gone, Feemy made her father understand who had been there, and obtained his consent to her proposed visit, which he gave, saying at the time, "God knows, my dear, whether you'll ever come back, for your brother's determined to part with the owld place if he can, in spite of all your poor father can say to the contrary."

She then returned to her room, resuming her novel, and waiting with what patience she could for Ussher's coming. About two o'clock he made his appearance, and she was beginning gently to upbraid him for being so late, when he stopped her, by saying,

"Well, Feemy, I have strange news for you this morning."

"Strange news, Myles! what is it? I hope it's good news."

Ussher had not quite his usual confidence and ease about him; he seemed as if he had something to say which he almost feared to disclose at once, and he did not give Feemy a direct answer.

"Why, as to that, it is, and it isn't. I suppose it's good news to me,—at least I ought to think so; but I don't know what you'll think of it."

Poor Feemy's face fell, and she sat down on the chair from which she had risen, as if she had not strength to stand. Myles stood still, with his back to the fire, trying to look as if he were not disconcerted.

"Well, Myles, what is it? won't you tell me?" And then, when he smiled, she said, "Why did you try and frighten me?"

"Frighten you! why you frightened yourself."

"But what is it, Myles?" and she walked up to him, and put her two hands on his shoulders, and looked up in his face—"what is your strange news?"

"In the first place, I am promoted to the next rank. I'm in the highest now, next to a County Inspector."

"Oh! Myles, I'm so glad! but you couldn't but know that would be good news to me;—but what else?"

"Why, they've sent me a letter from Dublin, with a lot of blarney about praiseworthy energy and activity, and all that—"

"That's why they've promoted you: but you don't tell me all."

"No, that's not all: then they say they think there's reason why I'd better not stay in this immediate neighbourhood."

"Ah! I thought so!" exclaimed the poor girl; "you're to go away out of this!"

"And they say I'm to commence in the new rank at Cashel, in County Tipperary."

Feemy for a time remained quiet. She was endeavouring to realize to herself the idea that her lover was going away, and then trying in her mind to comprehend whether it must follow naturally, as a consequence from this, that he was going away from her, as well as from Ballycloran. Ussher still stood up by the fireplace, with the same smile on his face. What he had told Feemy was all true; he had unexpectedly received an official letter that morning from the Dublin office, complimenting him on his services, informing him that he was to be moved to a higher grade, and that on his promotion he was to leave Mohill, and take charge of the men stationed at Cashel. All this in itself was very agreeable; promotion and increased pay were of course desirable; Mohill was by no means a residence which it would cause such a man as Ussher much regret to leave; and though he had made up his mind not to fear any injury from those among whom he was situated, he could not but feel that he should be more assured of safety at any other place than that at which he now resided. All this was so far gratifying, but still he was perplexed to think what he should do about Feemy. It was true he could leave her, and let her, if she chose, break her heart; or he might promise to come back and marry her, when he was settled, with the intention of taking no further notice of her after he had left the place;—and so let her break her heart that way. But he was too fond of her for this; he could not decide what he would do; and when he came up to see her at the present time, the only conclusion to which he could bring himself with certainty was this—that nothing should induce him to marry her; but still he did not like to leave her.

He was, however, rather perplexed to know what to say to her, and therefore preferred waiting to see what turn she herself would give to the conversation. At length Feemy said,

"And when do you leave this?"

"Oh! they've given me a month's leave of absence. I'm to be in Cashel in a month."

Even this seemed a reprieve to Feemy, who at first thought that he would have to start immediately,—perhaps that evening; a good deal might be done in a month; now, however, she regretted that she had promised to go to Mrs. M'Keon's.

"Then, Myles, you'll not leave this for a month?"

"I don't know about that; that depends on circumstances. I've to run up to Dublin, and a deal to do."

"But when do you mean to be out of this?"

"Why, I tell you, I haven't settled yet—perhaps immediately after the races."

Again they were silent for some time; Feemy longed for Ussher to say something that might sound at any rate kind; he had never met her before without an affectionate word—and now, on the eve of his departure, he stood at the fire and merely answered her questions coldly and harshly. At length she felt that this must be the time, if ever, for saying to him what she had made up her mind to say on the previous evening, when her courage failed her. So, plucking up all the heart she could, and blushing at the time to the top of her forehead, she said,

"An't I to go with you, Myles, when you go?"

Ussher still remained silent; he did not know how to answer to this question. "Come, Myles, speak to me. I know you came down to tell me your plans. What am I to do? You know you must settle now, if you're going so soon. What are your plans?"

"Why, Feemy, it's not two hours or more since I've received the letter; of course I couldn't think of everything at once. Tell me; what do you think best yourself?"

"Me! what do I think?—you know I'd do anything you bid me. Won't you step in and tell father about it?"

"Oh, you can tell him. I couldn't make him understand it at all, he's so foolish."

Feemy bore the slur on her father without indignation.

"But, Myles, if you go so soon, am I to go with you?" and when after a few minutes he did not answer,—"Speak, Myles, an't we to be married before you go?" When she said this, she sat down on the old sofa, looking up into his face, as if she would read there what was passing in his mind. That which was passing in his mind must be the arbitrament of her fate.

"Why, Feemy, how can you be so foolish?—How can we be married in eight days' time? I must go, I tell you, in eight days from this."

"But you won't go to this new place then. You'll be back here, won't you, before you go to Cashel?"

"How can I be back again?—No, I could not be back again then; besides, Feemy, I wouldn't be married in this place after what your brother and Father John said to me last night. If we are to be married at all, it can't be here."

"If we are to be married!" exclaimed Feemy, rising up—"if

we are! Why, Myles, what do you mean?" and rushing to him she threw her arms round his neck, and hiding her face on his bosom, she continued, "Oh, Myles! you don't mean to desert me! Myles—dear Myles—my own Myles—don't you love me?—you won't leave me now—say you won't leave me!" and she sobbed and cried as though her heart was breaking.

Ussher put his arm round her waist and kissed her; he seated her on the sofa—sat down by her—and tried to comfort her by caresses: but he still said nothing.

"Why don't you speak, Myles? I shall die if you don't speak! Only tell me what you mean to do; I'll do anything you bid me, if you'll only say you don't mean to desert me."

"Desert you, Feemy! who spoke of deserting you, dearest?"

"Then you won't leave me, my own Myles? You won't leave me here with those I hate! I love no one—I care for no one but you; only say you won't leave me here when you're gone!" and again she clung to him as though she could have detained him there for ever by holding him.

"But, Feemy, what can I do?—you see I've told you after what passed I couldn't be married here."

"Why not, Miles? why not?—never mind what Thady said—or Father John. What does it signify?—you'll be soon away from them. I'll never treat you that way, my own Myles—I'd put up with more than that for you—I wouldn't mind what the world might say to me—I'd bear anything for you!"

"I tell you, Feemy, there are reasons why I couldn't be married before I get to Cashel. There,—to tell you the whole, they wouldn't let a man take his rise from one rank to another if he's married. They can't prevent the officers in the force marrying, but they don't like it; and it's a rule that they won't promote a married man. You see I couldn't marry till after I was settled at Cashel."

Feemy received the lie with which Ussher's brain had at the moment furnished him, without a doubt; she believed it all, and then went on.

"But when you've got your rank, you'll come back, Myles, won't you?"

"Why that's the difficulty—I couldn't well again get leave of absence."

"Then, Myles, what will you do?"

And by degrees he proposed to her to leave her home and her friends, and trust herself to him, and go off with him unmarried, without her father's blessing, or the priest's—to go with him in a manner which she knew would disgrace herself, her name, and her family, and to trust to him afterwards to give her what reparation a tardy marriage could afford. She, poor girl, at first received the offer with sobs and tears. She proposed a clandestine marriage, but he swore that when afterwards detected, it would cause his dismissal;—then that she would come to him at Cashel, when he was settled; but no,—he told her other lies equally false, to prove that this could not be done. She prayed and begged, and lay upon his bosom imploring him to spare her this utter degradation; but now that the proposal had been fairly made, that he had got her to discuss the plan, his usual sternness returned; and at last he told her, somewhat roughly, that if she would not come with him in the manner he proposed, he would leave her now and for ever.

Poor Feemy fell with her knees on the ground and her face on the sofa, and there she lay sobbing for many minutes, while he again stood silent with his back against the fireplace. During this time, old feelings, principles, religious scruples, the love of honour and fair fame, and the fear of the world's harsh word, were sorely fighting in her bosom; they were striving to enable her to conquer the strong love she felt for Ussher, and make her reject the disgrace to which he was alluring her. Then he stooped to lift her up, and as he kissed the tears from her face, passion prevailed, and she whispered in his ear that she would go.

He stayed there for a considerable time after that; at first Feemy was so agitated and so miserable, that she was unable to converse with him, or listen to his plans for her removal. She sat there sobbing and crying, and all he could say—all his protestations of love—all his declarations that it was his firm intention to marry her at Cashel—all his promises of kind and good treatment, were unable to console her. He tried to animate her by describing to her the pleasure she would have in seeing Dublin— the delight it would be to her to leave so dull a place as Ballycloran, and see something of the world, from which she had hitherto been excluded. But for a long time it was in vain; she was thinking—though she rarely thought of them—of her father and her brother; of what the old man would feel, when she, his only joy, had gone from him in such a manner; of what Thady would do and say, when he found that the suspicions, which she knew he already entertained, were too true. She could not bring her heart to give up Ussher; but the struggles within her breast at length made her hysterical, and Ussher was greatly frightened lest he should have to call in assistance to bring her to herself. She did not, however, lose her senses, and after a time she became more tranquil, and was able to listen to his plans. She first of all told him that she had promised Mrs. McKeon to go to her house for a short time, during the races, and suggested that she should now send some excuse for declining the visit; but this he negatived. He desired her to go there—to go to the races and the ball—and, above all, to keep up her spirits, and at any rate seem to enjoy herself there as if nothing particular had happened. This she promised to do, but with a voice and face which gave but little sign of her being able to keep her promise.

He told her that he would occasionally call at Mrs. McKeon's, so that no remark might be made about his not coming to see her; he desired her to tell no one that he was going permanently to leave the country, and that he should not himself let it be known at Mohill till the day or so before he went; and he added that even when it was known that he was going, there would be less suspicion arising respecting her, if she was at Drumsna, than if she remained at Ballycloran.

To all this she quietly submitted. He was to meet her at the ball at Carrick-on-Shannon, and then tell her what his definite plan of carrying her off would be; but he added that the ball night would be the last she would spend in the country, for that they would leave the next evening.

About five o'clock Ussher took his leave; she begged of him to come and see her the next day—every day till they went; but this he refused; she said that unless she saw him every day to comfort her, she would not be able to keep up her strength —that she was sure she would fall ill. It was now Friday, and she was to go to Mrs. McKeon's on Monday; on Tuesday he said he would call on her there; the races and ball were to be on the Tuesday week. In vain she asked him how she was to bear the long days till she saw him again; Ussher had no true sympathy for such feelings as were racking Feemy's heart and brain; he merely bid her keep up her spirits, and not be foolish;—that he would see her on Tuesday, and that after Tuesday week she would have nothing more to make her unhappy. And then, kissing her, he went away,—and as we have seen, Thady met him in the avenue, so satisfied in appearance, so contented, so triumphant, that he was able to forget the words which had been applied to him on the previous evening, and to nod to Feemy's brother with as pleasant an air as though there were no grounds for ill-feeling between them.

Poor Feemy! those vain words that "after Tuesday week she would have nothing more to make her unhappy," sounded strangely in her ears. Nothing more to make her unhappy! Could she have anything more, then or ever, to make her happy? Could she ever be happy again? All that had happened during the last few days passed through her mind, and added to her torment. How indignant had she been when her brother had hinted to her that Ussher did not intend honestly by her; into what a passion had she flown with Father John, when he had cautioned her that she should be circumspect in her conduct with her lover; what an insult she had felt it when Mary Brady alluded to the chance of Ussher's deserting her! And now so soon after all this—but a few hours after this strong feeling—after the indignation she had then shown, she had herself submitted to worse than they had even dared to suspect; she had herself agreed to leave her father's house as the mistress of the man, of whom she had then confidently boasted as her future husband! And it was not only for her own degradation, dreadful as that was, that she grieved, but Ussher himself—he of whom she had felt so fond—whom she had so loved—was this his truth, his love?—was this the protection he had sworn to give her against her father's folly, and her brother's violence?—and, as he had basely added, against Father John's bigotry? Was this the protection—roughly to swear he'd leave her, desert her for ever, unless she agreed to give up her family, her home, her principles, and follow him, a base low creature, without a name? And was it likely that after she had agreed to this—after she had so debased herself, that he who had already deceived her so grossly would at last keep his word by marrying her?

She was lying down with her face buried in her hands, tormenting herself with such thoughts, when Biddy came to tell her that dinner was on the table. Feemy did not dare to refuse to go in lest something should be suspected; so she rubbed her red eyes till they were still redder, and went into the parlour, where she alleged that she had a racking headache, which would give her no peace; and having sat there for a miserable half hour till her father and Thady had finished their dinner, she went up stairs to her bed-room, and after laying awake half the night, at last succeeded in crying herself to sleep.

When Thady came from the kitchen, on being told that Father John was waiting for him at the hall-door, he left his pipe behind him, swallowed a draught of water to take off the smell of the spirits, and prepared to listen to the priest's lecture, as he expected, with sullenness and patience; but he was surprised out of his determined demeanour by the kindness of the priest's address. He came forward, and taking his hand, said,

"What, Thady, are you ill? What ails you?"

"Not much, then, Father John; only a headache."

"Are you too bad, my boy, to take a turn with me? I've a

word or two I want to say; but if you're really sick, Thady, and are going to bed, I'll come down early to-morrow morning. Would you sooner I did so?"

Father John said this because he thought that Thady really looked ill. And so he did; his face was yellow, his hair unbrushed, his eyes sunken, and the expression of his countenance sad and painful; but he was overcome by the kindness of the priest's manner, and replied,

"Oh no! I'm not going to bed. I believe, Father John, I did not come up to you because I was ashamed to see you afther last night."

"So I thought, my boy; and that's why I came down. I'm not sorry for your shame, though there was not much cause for it. If it was a usual thing with you to be drinking too much, you wouldn't be thinking so much of it yourself the next day."

"But I believe I said something to yourself, Father John.'

"Something to me! Egad, I forget what you said to me, or whether you said anything. Oh no! you weren't so bad as that; but you were going to eat Ussher about something. But never mind that now; don't get tipsy again, if you can help it, and that's all about it. It's not the drinking I'm come to talk to you about; for you're no drunkard, Thady; and indeed it's not as your priest I want to talk to you at all, but as one friend to another. And now, my dear boy, will you take what I've to say in good part?"

These gentle words were the first comfort that had reached Thady's heart that day, and tears were in his eyes as he answered,

"Indeed I will, Father John, for you're the only friend I have now."

It was a fine moonlight evening, and they were on the road leading to the Cottage.

"Walk up this way, Thady; we'll be less likely to be interrupted in the little parlour than here;" and they walked on to the priest's house, Father John discoursing the while on the brightness of the moon and the beauty of the night, and Thady alternately thinking with pleasure of his kindness, and with dread of the questions he was about to be called upon to answer.

When they were in the parlour, and Thady had refused his host's offers of punch, tea, or supper, and the door was close shut, Father John at once struck into the subject at his heart.

"I told you, Thady, that I thought but little of your having been drinking yesterday evening; not but that I think it very foolish for a man to make himself a beast; but what I did think of was the company you were drinking in. Now I heard—and I know you won't contradict me unless it's untrue—that the party consisted of you, and Brady, and Joe Reynolds, and Byrne, and Corney Dolan, and one or two others from Drumleesh, your own or your father's tenants, and the very lowest of them—all of them infamous characters—men never, or seldom, seen at mass—makers of potheen—fellows who are known to be meeting nightly at that house of Mrs. Mulready, at Mohill, and who are strongly suspected to be Ribbonmen, or Terryalts, or to call themselves by some infernal name and sect, by belonging to which they have all become liable to death or transportation."

The priest paused; but Thady sat quite still, listening, with his eyes fixed on the fender.

"Now, Thady, if this is so, what could you gain by mixing with them? You weren't drunk when you went among them, or I should think nothing about it—for a drunken man doesn't know what he does; and it wasn't from chance—for a man never seeks society so much beneath himself from chance; and it wasn't from habit—for I know your habits well enough, and that's not one of them; but I fear you were there by agreement. If so, what could you get by a secret meeting with such men as those? You know their characters and vices; are you fool enough to think that you will find comfort in their society, or assistance in their advice?"

"I didn't think so, Father John."

"Then why were you with them? I know the most of your sorrows, Thady, and the most of your cares; and I also know and appreciate the courage with which you have tried to bear them; and if you would make me your friend, your assistant, and your counsellor, though I mightn't do much for you, I think I could do more, or show you how to do more, than you are likely to learn from the men you were with yesterday; and at any rate, I shall not lead you into the danger which will beset you if you listen to them, and which, you may be sure, would soon end in your disgrace and destruction. Can you tell me, Thady, why you were with them, or they were with you?"

"I was only just talking to them about—" Thady began; but he felt that he was going to tell his friend a falsehood, and again held his tongue.

"If you'll not tell me why you were there, I'll tell you; at least, I'll tell you what my fears are. You went to them to talk over your father's affairs respecting Keegan and Flannelly; you went to induce those poor misguided men not to pay their rent to him; and oh! Thady, if what I've heard is true, you went there to consult with them respecting a greater crime than I'll now name, and to instigate them to do that which would lead to their and your eternal shame and punishment."

Thady now shook in his chair, as though he could hardly keep his seat; he felt the perspiration stand upon his brow, and he wiped it off with his sleeve; he did not dare to deny that he had done this, of which Father John was accusing him, though he felt that he had been far from instigating them to any crime like murder. Father John continued:

"If you have joined these men,—if you have bound yourself to these men by any oath,—if there is any league between you and them, let me implore you to disregard it; nothing can be binding, that is only to bind you to greater wickedness. I do not ask you to tell me any of their secrets or plans, though, God knows, what you tell me now would be as sacred as if I heard it in the confessional; but if you have such secrets, if you know their signs, whatever may be the consequence, at once renounce them."

"I know no secrets or signs, Father John, and I don't belong to any society."

"Then, if you don't, you can have nothing to bind you. Is it true that you were rash enough, mad enough, to speak to these men about murdering Keegan? Tell me; have you a plan made to murder Keegan? Have you had such a crime in your thoughts?"

It had been in his thoughts all day: what answer should he make? should he lie, and deny it all? or should he confess it all, just as it was?

"If you'll not tell me, I must, for Mr. Keegan's sake, take some step to secure his safety. Come, Thady, come; you know it's not by threats I wish to guide you; you know I love you. I know well enough your patient industry—your want of selfishness. I know, if you have for a moment thought of this crime, you have now repented it: tell me how far you have gone, and if you are in danger; —if you have done that which was very, very wicked. I will still try and screen you from the effects of a sin, which I am sure was not premeditated. Is there any plot to murder Keegan?"

"There is not."

"As you are a living man, there's none?"

"There is not."

"What were you saying about Keegan, then, to those men yesterday?"

"I don't know what I said—I don't know I said anything; they were threatening him, if he came on Drumleesh for rent; if they have a plot, I don't know it."

"But, Thady, are you to join them again? do you mean again

to renew your revellings of last night? have you agreed to see them again?"

"I have."

"And where?"

"At Mulready's in Mohill."

"And when?"

"They sent to-day to say it was to-morrow night, but I have refused to go."

"You have refused?"

"Yes, Father John. I got the message from them just before dinner, and I said I'd not go to-morrow."

"But have you said you'd never join them again? have you sent to them to say you'd never put your foot in that hole of sin? did you say you were mad when you promised it, and that you would never keep that promise? did you say, Thady, that you would not come? or are you still, in their opinion, one of their accursed set?"

"I'll niver go there, Father John. I've not had one moment's ase since I said I would; it's been on my heart like lead all the morning; indeed, indeed, Father John, I'll niver go there."

"I will not doubt you, Thady; but still, that you may feel how solemnly you are bound not to peril your life and soul by joining them who can only wish to lead you into crime, give me your honour, on the sacred word of God, that you will never go to that place;—or join those men in any lawless plans or secret meetings."

And Thady swore most solemnly, on the sacred volume, that he would do as the priest directed him respecting these men.

Father John then gradually drew from him in conversation what had really taken place. He told him what he had heard from McGovery—how he had quieted that man and Cullen—and advised him by his own demeanour to his tenants, to pass over what had been said, as though it had been a drunken frolic. He asked him, however, whether he considered that Mr. Keegan or Ussher were in any real danger; and Thady assured him that he did not think they were—that there was no plot laid—that the men were angry and violent, but that, unless further instigated, he did not think they would commit any act of absolute violence. These opinions were not given spontaneously, but in answer to various questions from the priest, who at last satisfied himself that in confirming the horror with which Thady evidently regarded what he had already done, and in preventing him from following any further the course he was about to pursue, he had done all that was possible in the case to prevent crime.

Whether he thought that either of those who had been named as the object of hatred to these unruly men might ultimately fall a victim to the feeling to which their actions had given rise in the country, is another question. If he did, he could not prevent it— nor was it his especial business to attend to it; but he felt tolerably sure that to whatever bad feelings hardships and cruelty might have given rise in Thady's breast, he would not now gratify them by such atrocious means as those which McGovery's statement had induced him to apprehend.

Under this impression he bade him good night, with another kind shake of the hand; telling him that though, at present, there might be much to sadden and distress him, if he confronted his difficulties with manly courage and honest purposes, he would be sure sooner or later to overcome them.

Thady returned home more comfortable than he had been in the morning, but he could not bring himself to that state of mind in which Father John had hoped to dismiss him. He felt, that though he was determined not to go to Mrs. Mulready's, the affair could not rest there. He felt himself to be, in some horrible manner, in the power of Brady and Joe Reynolds—as though he could not escape from them. A general despondency respecting all his prospects weighed him down, and when he reached Bally-cloran, he was nearly as unhappy as he had been in leaving it.

CHAPTER XVII.

SPORT IN THE WEST.

CARRICK-ON-SHANNON, the assize town of County Leitrim, though an assize town, is a very poor place. It consists of one long narrow, irregular street, lying along the Shannon, in which slated houses and thatched cabins delightfully relieve each other, and prevent the eye from being annoyed with sameness or monotony. The houses are mostly all shops, and even the cabins profess to afford "lodging and entherthainment;" so that it is to be presumed that the poverty of the place is attributable to circumstances and misfortune, and not to the idleness of the inhabitants. The prevailing feeling, however, arising in any human mind, on entering the place, would be that of compassion for the judges, barristers, attorneys, crown clerks, grand jury, long panel, witnesses, &c., who have to be crammed into this little place, and lodged and fed for five or six days, twice a year during the assizes.

There is, however, a tolerably good hotel in the place, and we at present beg to take our reader with us into the largest room therein, which was usually dignified by the name of the Ball Room. It was not, however, by any means dedicated solely to the worship of Terpsichore : all the public dinners eaten in Carrick were eaten here ; all the public meetings held in Carrick were held here ; all the public speeches were spoken here. Here committees harangued ; Gallagher ventriloquised ; itinerant actors acted ; itinerant concert-givers held their concerts ; itinerant Lancashire bell-ringers rang their bells. Here also were carried on the mysteries of the Carrick-on-Shannon masonic lodge, with all due zeal and secrecy.

On the present occasion the room was, or rather had been, devoted to the purpose of feeding; an ordinary had been held here previous to the races ; and most of those who were in any way interested in the coming event were there. The cloth had been just taken away, decanters of whiskey and jugs of boiling water alternated each other down the table, and large basins of white sugar were scattered about unsparingly. The party were evidently about to enjoy themselves. There were about thirty of them there, some of them owners of horses, some of them riders, some of them backers ; the rest were eaters, drinkers, and spectators.

The chair was filled by Major McDonnell, one of the stewards —a little man, who had probably never crossed a horse himself, and had nothing of the sportsman about him. He had, however, lately inherited an estate in the neighbourhood, and having some idea of standing for the county on the Tory interest at the next election, was desirous of obtaining popularity, and had consequently given forty pounds to be run for—had agreed to wear a red coat at the races, and call himself a steward—sit at the top of the table and carve for thirty hungry sportsmen to-day, with each of whom he had to drink wine—and get partners for all the ugly girls, if there be any in County Leitrim, on the morrow. This was certainly hard work; in reward for which he was probably destined to have his head broken at the next election, if he should have sufficient courage to show himself as a Tory candidate for the county.

There, however, he sat on this day, very unfit to take the chief part among the spirits by whom he was surrounded.

Opposite to him, at the other end of the room, sat our big and burly friend, McKeon, a very different character. Whenever six or eight were talking aloud together, his voice might always be heard the loudest. Whenever a shout of laughter arose—and that was incessantly—his shout was always the longest. It seemed that every bet that was offered was taken by him, and that every bet taken by any one else had been offered by him. He was always scribbling something in that well-worn book of his, and yet he never had his hand away from his tumbler—except when it was on the decanter. All the waiters came to him for orders, and he seemed perfectly competent to attend to them. If any man finished his punch and did not fill again, McKeon reminded him of his duty—and that not only by preaching, but by continual practice. In fact, he was just in his element, and enjoying himself.

There was an empty chair next Mr. McKeon, where his friend Mr. Gayner had been sitting—I won't say during his dinner, for he had not swallowed a mouthful. He was now standing up against the fireplace, sucking a lemon. He had a large great coat on, buttoned up to the neck, and a huge choker round his throat. He was McKeon's jockey, and was to ride Playful for the forty pounds on the morrow.

Bob Gayner, as he was usually called, was one of the best gentlemen riders in the country. He came from County Roscommon,—the county, by the by, which can probably boast the best riders in Ireland,—where he had a small property of his own, near Athlone; but the chief part of his time was spent in riding races and training for them. He had been at it all his life—and certainly, if there be any merit in the perfection of such an art, Bob was entitled to it, for he rode beautifully. It was not only that he could put his horse at a fence without fear, and sit him whilst he was going over it—any man with practice could do that; but Bob had a sympathy with the animal he was riding, which enabled him not only to know what he could do himself, but also what the horse could do. He knew exactly where a horse wanted assistance from his rider. And he had another knack too, not unfrequently made use of in steeple-chases—Bob seldom let his own horse baulk, but he very generally made those that others were riding do so. And then, at a finish, how admirable was Bob! In leap races the finish is seldom so near a thing as in flat races; but when it did come to be neck and neck at the post, there was no man in Ireland could give a horse a stretch and land him in a winner like Bob. He had also an exquisite genius for tumbling. Horses will occasionally fall, and when they do, riders must follow them; but no one fell so safely, recovered so actively, and was again so instantly in the saddle as our friend; and, consequently, wherever there was a steeple-chase to be run, where pluck, science, and practice were wanting, there Bob was in requisition, and there he usually was found. It was a great thing to secure his services; and knowing this, Tony McKeon had, in his own way, long since, made Gayner his fast friend; how, I cannot say, for Bob was much above being bought, and though, no doubt, he made money by his races, he would have thought little of shooting any one who was bold enough to offer to pay him for riding. When in his cap, jacket, boots, and breeches, he would, if he thought occasion required or his interests demanded it, wrangle like a devil. Though its back were turned to him, he could see a horse go on the wrong side of a post; and woe betide the man who came to the scales as a winner an ounce below the weight. Bob, from long practice, knew all these dodges, and he made the most of them. But when once his cap was off, and his coat was on, he was a quiet, easy, unassuming fellow—liked and petted by all he knew; for he never spoke little of others nor bragged of himself.

He was now talking to another member of the same confraternity, but of a very different character. He also had been sitting dinnerless,—for both these gentlemen, in the pursuit of their amusement, were obliged to starve and sweat themselves down to a certain standard, about twenty pounds below their ordinary weight,—and he was now also sucking a lemon. George Brown was the second son of Jonas Brown, of Brown Hall, the magistrate by whom Tim Reynolds and the others had been committed to Ballinamore, and, like his father, was most unpopular in his own country. He was arrogant, overbearing, conceited, and passionate—without any rank which could excuse pride, or any acquirement that could justify conceit. It is, however, as a gentleman jockey that we are at present to make his acquaintance, and in that capacity he was about as much inferior to the grooms by whom the horses were trained as Bob was superior to them. He had courage enough, however, and would ride at anything; and as his own relations and friends, for whom he rode, were tolerably wealthy, and he was therefore generally well mounted, he sometimes won; but he had killed more horses under him than any man in Ireland—and no wonder, for he had a coarse hand and a loose seat; and it was no uncommon thing to see George coming the first of the two over a fence headlong into the next field as if he had been flung there by a petard, leaving the unfortunate brute he had been riding panting behind him, with his breast cut open, or his knees destroyed by the fence, over which his rider had had neither skill nor patience to land him. He was now going to ride his own horse, Conqueror, and had talked himself, and had been talked, into the belief that it was impossible that anything could beat him.

These two were standing talking at the fireplace, and as they also had their little books in their hands, it is to be presumed that they were mixing business with amusement.

There were others there, sitting at the table, who were to ride to-morrow, but whose usual weight allowed them to do so, without the annoyance to which Gayner and Brown had to subject themselves. There was little Larry Kelly, from Roscommon, who could ride something under eight stone; Nicholas Blake, from the land of the Blakes, Burkes, and Bodkins; Pat Conner, with one eye, from Strokestown, who had brought his garron over under the speculation that if the weather should come wet, and the horses should fall at the heavy banks, she would be sure to crawl over,—knowing, too, that as the priest was his second cousin, he could not refuse him the loan of a stable gratis.

There was Ussher there also, sitting next to George Brown, who was a friend of his—much more intent, however, on his own business than that which had brought the others here; and Greenough, the sub-inspector of police, from Ballinamore; and young Fitzpatrick, of Streamstown, who kept the subscription pack of harriers; and a couple of officers from Boyle, one of whom owned a horse, for which he was endeavouring to get a rider, but which none of those present seemed to fancy; and there was Peter Dillon, from beyond Castlebar, who had brought up a strong-looking, long-legged colt, which he had bred in County Mayo, with the hope that he might part with it advantageously in a handicap, to some of those Roscommon lads, who were said to have money in their pockets; and there were many others apparently happy, joyous fellows, who seemed not to have a care in the world; and last, but not least, there was Hyacinth Keegan, attorney at law, and gent.

There he was, smiling and chatting, oily and amiable; getting a word in with any one he could; creeping into intimacy with those who were not sharp enough to see what he was after; jabbering of horses,—of which he considered himself a complete judge,—and of shooting, hunting, and racing, as if the sports of a gentleman had been his occupation from his youth upwards.

"Well, boys!" said McKeon; "I suppose we're to have an auction. What's it to be? the owld thing—half-a-crown each, I suppose?"

"An auction, Mr. McKeon!" said the chairman. "What's an auction?"

"We'll show you, Major. All you've to do is to give me half-a-crown."

Now, as many may be as ignorant as Major McDonnell respecting an auction in sporting phraseology, I will, if I can, explain what it is.

It has but little reference or similitude to those auctions from which Sir Robert Peel has removed the duty.

Supposing there may be twenty members, each having half-a-crown; and six horses to run. Twenty bits of paper are placed in a hat, on six of which are written the names of the running horses—the others are blanks—and they are then drawn, as lots, out of the hat. The tickets bearing the horses' names are sold by the auctioneer; the last bidder has to pay twice the sum he bids —one moiety to the man who drew the horse, the other is added to the fund composed of the twenty half-crowns. After the race, the happy man holding the ticket bearing the name of the winning horse receives the whole. There are, therefore, different winners in this transaction; the man drawing the name of the favourite horse of course wins what is bid for the ticket; any one drawing the name of any horse would probably win something, as his chance, if the beast have more than three legs, must be worth at least five shillings. Such, however, is an auction, and on the present occasion it was a very animated one.

The thirty half-crowns were now collected and handed over to McKeon; the names of the eight horses expected to start scrawled in pencil on the backs of fragments of race-bills; and those, together with the blanks, deposited in the hat, which was carried round by one of the party.

"Ah! now, Pat, come to me last," said Gayner; "I've never any luck with the first haul; never mind, I'll take it," and he drew a lot, "and, by the Virgin, Tony, I've got my own mare!"

"Have you got Playful, Gayner?" said a dozen at once. This made their chance less, for Playful was second favourite.

Brown was next, and he got a blank; and the next, and the next.

"I've drawn Brickbat," said Fitzpatrick, "a d—d good horse; he won the hunters' plate at Tuam last year."

"Oh! I wish you joy," said Gayner, "for he won't start to-morrow, my boy: he's at Tuam now."

"Begad! he'll start as soon as yourself, Bob," said little Larry; "he came to Castleknock last night, and he's at Frenchpark now: Murphy from Frenchpark is to ride him."

These details brought Brickbat up in the market.

"They might have left him at Tuam then, and saved themselves money," said Gayner. "Why, he hadn't had a gallop last Tuesday week; I was in his stable myself. If Burke's cattle had been as fat at Ballinasloe, he'd have got better prices."

"I say, McKeon," said Fitzpatrick, "what odds will you bet Bob doesn't buy Brickbat himself?"

The hat went round, and others got blanks. Ussher got Miss Fidget, Larry Kelly's mare, and was advised in a whisper by that cunning little gentleman—who meant to buy Conqueror by way of a hedge, and who therefore wanted to swell the stakes—to be sure and buy the mare himself, for she didn't know how to fall; "and," he added, "you know she's no weight on her;" and when Ussher looked at Larry Kelly, who was to ride her himself, he couldn't but think the latter part was true.

Then Nicholas Blake drew Kickie-wickie, the officer's mare, whereupon the gallant Captain, who knew Blake was a sporting fellow, thought this was a good opportunity to sound that gentleman about getting him a rider, and began whispering to him all the qualities of the mare; how she could do everything a mare should do; how high she was bred and how well she was trained, and how she was like the poacher, and could "leap on anywhere;" for all which, and Kickie-wickie herself, with her owner into the bargain, Blake did not care a straw;—for he was confident of winning himself with the Galway horse, Thunderer.

Then some one else drew Thunderer; and Peter Dillon got Conqueror, greatly to his joy, for he reckoned that his expenses from Castlebar would thus be mostly paid, even if he couldn't sell the long-legged colt. The Major drew Crom-a-boo, a Carrick horse, who had once been a decent hunter, and whose owner had entered it at the instigation of his fellow townsmen, and by the assurance that these sort of races were often won by your steady old horses; and Mr. Stark, the owner, since he had first made up his mind to pay the £5 stake, had gradually deceived himself into the idea that he should probably win; and having never before even owned a horse—for this was a late purchase, or rather the beast had been taken in lieu of a debt—had now, for the last three weeks, talked of nothing but sweats, gallops, physics, training, running, and leaping: and having secured the services of a groom for the day, who was capable of riding his horse, had entirely given himself up to the delights of horse-racing. Lucky was it for Mr. Stark that Crom-a-boo was sure to lose; for had he won, Stark would have been a ruined man; nothing would have kept him from the Curragh and a conviction that the turf was his proper vocation.

The Major was delighted at his prize; he had not drawn a blank, and that was sufficient for him.

Then, at last, Keegan got Pat Conner's mare from Strokestown. She was called Diana, and his was the last paper drawn.

"Faith, Keegan, you're in luck," said McKeon, "for the mare can't but run well. Pat's been training her since May last. I was over there going to Castlereagh, and I saw Pat at her then."

"'Deed, then, Mr. McKeon," said Conner, "maybe she'll beat your own mare, much as you think of her."

"Oh! I'm sure she will; there's so much running about her. Was she at plough after last winter, Pat?"

"She had other work to do, then, for she had to carry me twice a week through the season; and that she did—and that's not light work, I think."

"Carry you, Pat!" said Gayner; "why, you don't mean to say you hunt that old garron you call Diana? Faith, man, you're too bold; your friends ought to look to you; what would the country do if you broke your neck?"

"It's your own is in most danger, I'm thinking," replied Pat; "faith, I wouldn't take all the pick up to-morrow, to ride that devil you're to ride over the course."

"And I'll take devilish good care you're not asked," said McKeon: "but now, boys, as I fear the Major's hardly up to it, I'll dispose of the prizes. Come, which shall I put up first? which was drawn first?"

"Your own mare, Tony; Gayner got Playful at the first start."

"Well, gentlemen, here's the mare Playful. I believe I'm to say all the good I can about her, and upon my word she doesn't want spirit." Here he whispered Gayner, whom he told to bid for themselves conjointly. "Come, gentlemen, what do you offer? people say she's wicked, but she'll not kick you if you don't come in her reach. She can go if she likes, and she can, I suppose, if she likes, stand still; but upon my soul, I never saw her to do so in the field."

"I'll say thirty shillings, Tony," said Bob.

"Five and thirty," said young Brown.

"Two pounds," said Bob.

"I'll not go beyond that," said Brown.

"Two pounds—who'll give more than two pounds for Playful? Gentlemen, the horses are all favourites, and the pool will consequently be a large one. Who'll give more than two pound? Bob, you've got the mare; hand me two pound, and hand yourself two more."

Then Brickbat and Miss Fidget were sold, both at good prices; for the horse had won the last race at Tuam, and that put him up in the market, in spite of Bob's vile comparison between him and his owner's bullocks; and the mare was a favourite among the Roscommon gentry, who knew little Larry could ride when he meant it.

Kickie-wickie was the next put up, but in spite of all that had been said about her by her gallant owner, she was in very little request, and was purchased cheap.

Thunderer fetched a good price; Galway horses always do; and it was easy to see that Nicholas Blake was in earnest, and Nick was a man that wouldn't come from Loughrea to Carrick-on-Shannon, and lose a day with the Galway dogs for nothing; George Brown made the purchase, for if anything could beat Conqueror it was Thunderer.

Then came Conqueror, and bidding began in earnest. George offered two pound to frighten the field; but both Larry Kelly and McKeon wanted to hedge, and they raised the price against each other by half crowns, till at last little Larry Kelly got the winner, that was to be, for three pound ten, much to Gayner's satisfaction, who felt no such confidence in George Brown's invincibility, and was very glad to see the pool increased by those who did.

When Crom-a-boo was put up—his owner rashly offered five shillings—for which sum he was allowed to retain him. He could not, however, comprehend that, because he had bid five, he was to pay ten—however, he had to do it, and began to find that the pleasures of the turf were not entirely unalloyed.

The Strokestown garron did not create much emulation, but Peter Dillon, knowing that though Pat had only one eye, that one was a good one, and that he wouldn't lose the race for want of hard work and patience, and having little Larry's three pound ten in his pocket to back him, at length doubled Keegan's offer of half-a-crown which he made to keep his own ticket, and Diana was knocked down to him at the same price that Crom-a-boo had fetched.

Then the fun grew fast and furious, and calls for hot water and spirits were loud and incessant.

"By the holy poker, boys, I'm thirsty after that," said McKeon; "you should stand me a bottle of champagne among ye, no less—just to take the dryness out of my throat, before I begin drinking."

"Champagne, indeed, Tony; wouldn't a bucket of brandy and water serve you?"

"Indeed, Fitz, if you're to pay for it yourself, a mouthful of brandy and water wouldn't be a bad thing—for I want something more than ordinary afther that work. Ah! Conner, it was the bidding afther that mare of your's that broke my heart entirely—why, man, you see, every one wanted her."

"Niver mind, Mr. McKeon, niver mind!" said Pat, with his one eye fixed on his punch. "She's a nice, good, easy creature, anyway. I don't have to be sending a boy down through the rack to be cleaning her, as they say you do with the one you're going to start to-morrow—pray God she don't kill any of us, that's all."

"Pray God she don't, Pat, and especially you. Well, Fitz, where's this brandy and water you're talking about?"

"To hear Tony talking," said little Larry, "one would think

he didn't drink this week; when he got a sup at every bid that was made, and finished a tumbler as every horse was knocked down; why that was eight tumblers of punch!"

"Water, Larry, all water to clear my throat—ask the waiter else."

"It's little of that cure you take, I'm thinking—waiter, bring some tobacco here."

And now the party began smoking as well as drinking; and an atmosphere was formed, which soon drove the Major out of the room—not, however, before McKeon implored him to stay just for one handicap, as he wanted to challenge the bay gelding he drove under his gig; and as the Major was waiting for his hat, Tony threw a shilling on the table.

"Come, Major, cover that, just for luck; I must have a shy at that gig horse; I want him for Mrs. McKeon's car. Come, I'll tell you every beast I've got, and you may choose from them all, from the mare that's to win to-morrow, down to the flock of turkeys that's in the yard at Drumsna."

But the Major was inexorable; he thought the £40 and the red coat which he had had to buy for to-morrow's use, together with the hard work he had to do, was enough for popularity; and may be he had heard of Tony's celebrity in a knock, and he did not wish to sacrifice his own nag, for a chance selection out of those in McKeon's yard, nor yet for a flock of turkeys.

However, though the Major wouldn't join in a handicap, others would—and McKeon wasn't baulked of his amusement. Men soon had their hands in their pockets, waiting the awards of the arbiter, which were speedily pronounced; and various and detailed were the descriptions given of the brutes which were intended to change hands; but not in general such as made those who got them satisfied with their bargains, when they afterwards became acquainted with their real merits.

Peter Dillon threw away sundry shillings in endeavouring to part with the Mayo colt, but either he had been there before with the same kind of cattle, or he priced him too high; he couldn't get his money for him, either from little Larry Kelly, or his elder brother who was there.

Tony, before the evening was over, gave the Boyle officers two or three most desperate bargains. First, he got the celebrated mare Kickie-wickie for a pair of broken down gig horses, to run tandem: engaged to go quiet and not kick in harness. They couldn't be warranted sound: but then, as Tony said, what horse could? and he was so particular—he would never say a horse was sound, unless he knew it; in fact he never warranted a horse sound; which was true enough, for Tony knew no one would take his warrant; and then when the Captain was in the first fit of grief for Kickie-wickie, some good-natured friend having told him that the two gig horses weren't worth a feed of oats, Tony gave her back again for a good hack hunter, and a sum of money to boot, about the real value of the mare. Again, late in the evening—when the punch had made further inroads upon the poor warrior's brain—he gave him back his own hunter for the two gig horses and a further sum of money: from all which it will be seen by those who understand the art, that the officer from Boyle could not have made a great deal, and that Tony McKeon could not be much out of pocket.

This fun continued till about two, when half the party were too drunk to care about winning and losing—and the other half, mostly consisting of the married men, too wary to attempt business with those as knowing as themselves. Gayner and Brown had gone home to bed, as they had to be up and walk ten miles before breakfast, with their great coats on; after which, as Gayner had told Mrs. McKeon, he would trouble her for the loan of two feather beds, and three or four buckets of turf; as he thought that after laying between them for an hour or so before a roaring fire, and then being rubbed down with flannels by Tony and his two men, there was little doubt but he'd be able to ride 11 stone 4; and he was to be up at that weight on the next day.

Keegan had become very drunk and talkative, had offered to sing two or three songs, to make two or three speeches, and had ultimately fallen backwards, on his chair being drawn away, from which position he was unable to get up, and little Larry's brother was now amiably engaged painting his face with lampblack. Mrs. Keegan the while was sitting in her cold, dark, little back parlour, meditating the awful punishment to be visited on the delinquent when he did return home.

Vain woman, there she sat till four, while Hyacinth lay happy beneath the table; nor did he return home, till brought on the waiter's back, at eight the next morning.

Pat was winking with his one eye, and nodding on his chair, with his pipe still stuck in his mouth. Little Larry was laughing till he cried at his brother's performance. Peter Dillon and young Fitzpatrick, each with a whiskey bottle in his hand, were guarding the door, at which Stark, the unfortunate owner of Crom-a-boo, was vainly endeavouring to make his exit, which he was assured he should not be allowed to do till he had sung a song standing on the sideboard. And the younger son of Mars, conquered by tobacco and whiskey, was leaning his unfortunate head on the table, and deluging Keegan's feet with the shower which he was unable to restrain.

Ussher was detailing in half drunken glee to his friend Fred Brown, George's brother, his plan for carrying off poor Feemy; and Brown, always as he said, ready to help a friend in necessity, was offering him the loan of his gig to take her as far as Longford, at which place he could arrive in time to catch the mail, if he could manage to take Feemy away from Ballycloran immediately after sunset. "And I'll send a boy to bring the gig back from Longford," added Fred, "so you'll have no trouble at all; and I'll tell you what it is, you're taking the prettiest girl out of County Leitrim with you—so here's her health."

Tony, Nicholas Blake, and Greenough were the only three left who were still able to drink steadily, and they kept at it till about four, when they all agreed, that if they meant to do any good at all to-morrow, they'd better be getting to bed; they consequently took one tumbler more, because it was to be the last, and made towards the door, out of which Stark had at length escaped, after having a bottle of whiskey poured over his head. As they passed the Captain, who was snoring against the wall, McKeon slightly touched his foot with his toe, and said to Blake, "Well; if I was as soft as that fellow, I'd have my head boiled in a pudding-bag. By gad, the Colonel oughtn't to let him out without his nurse."

"You oughtn't to talk then, Tony, for you didn't make a bad thing of him to-night."

"Oh, d—n his money," said McKeon; "I'd much sooner be without such a fellow. I'd sooner by half have a bargain with a man that knew how to take care of himself, than a greenhorn, who'd let you rob him of his eyes without seeing you."

By this time they'd got to the front door, at which was now standing Tony's buggy and servant; Greenough was going to walk to his lodgings, and Blake had come to the door to see his friend off; when they heard a loud shrieking down the street, and they saw the unfortunate Stark running towards the hotel, still followed by Fitzpatrick and Dillon, each with an empty bottle in his hand.

When he had escaped from the inn, his persecutors had followed him, still swearing that he should sing. Stark had run towards his home, but before he got there his pursuers headed him in the street and turned him back, and now as he rushed along, half blinded by the spirits in his eyes, they followed him, whooping and yelling like two insane devils, and were just catching him near the door of the hotel, when poor Stark, striking his foot against the curb stone, fell violently on his face, and Dillon, who was just behind him, stumbled and fell upon him.

"Halloo, Fitzpatrick, is that you?" said Tony, "what in G—d's name are you doing with that poor devil? I believe you and Dillon have killed him."

By this time Dillon had got up; and McKeon and Blake together helped the other man to his feet; his wrath was by this time thoroughly kindled, and he was swearing all manner of vengeance against Fitzpatrick—the other man's name he did not know. They, contented with their sport, carried the decanters, wonderful to relate, unbroken in triumph into the hotel,—and McKeon, bidding the boy to bring the gig after him, helped Stark, whose face was dreadfully bleeding, to his home, trying to console him, and assuring him that the mischief was all owing to Dillon, and that Fitzpatrick, who was a neighbour and friend of Tony's, had had little or nothing to do with it; and having left him at his hall-door, he drove quietly home to his own house, and went soberly to bed.

CHAPTER XVIII.

HOW PAT BRADY AND JOE REYNOLDS WERE ELOQUENT IN VAIN.

The day after Ussher had obtained Feemy's consent to go off with him, she passed in the same manner as she had that afternoon—sometimes sitting quiet with her eyes fixed on vacancy—sometimes sobbing and crying, as though she must have fallen into an hysterical fit. Once or twice she attempted to make some slight preparation for her visit to Mrs. McKeon's, such as looking through her clothes, mending them, &c., but in fact she did nothing. The next day, Sunday, she spent in the same manner; she omitted going to mass, a thing she had not done for years, unless kept at home by very bad weather, or real illness; she never took up a book, nor spoke a word, except such as she could not possibly avoid, to the servant or her father. Of Thady she saw nothing, except at her meals, and then they took no notice of each other. They had not spoken since the night when Thady had upbraided her whilst walking in the lane with Ussher.

On the Monday morning she was obliged to exert herself, for she had to pack the little trunk that was to carry her ball-room finery to Mrs. McKeon's, and prepare everything that was necessary for her visit.

Biddy, the favourite of the two girls, had once or twice asked her mistress what ailed her, and whether she was ill; but Feemy only answered her crossly that she was bothered with that horrid headache, and the girl could only believe that either this was actually the case, or else that she had quarrelled with her lover; and as it was now three days since he had been at Ballycloran, she at last determined that this was the case.

During these three days, Feemy had frequently made up her mind, or rather she fancied she had made up her mind to give Ussher up,—to go and confess it all to Father John, or to tell it to Mrs. McKeon; and if it had not been for the false pride within her, which would not allow her to own that she had been deceived, and that her lover was unworthy, she would have done so. His present coolness, and his cruelty in not coming to see her, though they did not destroy her love, greatly shook it; and had she had one kind word to assist her in the struggle within herself, she might still have prevented much of the misery which her folly was fated to produce.

When Mrs. McKeon and her daughters came for her about one o'clock on Monday, the small exertion necessary for putting up her clothes, had made her somewhat better—something more able to talk than she had been before, and they did not then observe anything particular about her; but she had been but a very short time at Drumsna, before it was evident to Mrs. McKeon, that something was the matter with her. When she questioned her, Feemy gave the same answer—that she had a racking headache; and though this did very well for a time, before the evening was over, the good lady was certain that something more than a headache afflicted her guest.

The next day, according to his promise, Ussher called, but of course at Mrs. McKeon's house he could not see her alone; that lady and her daughters were present all the time. When he came in, Ussher shook hands with Feemy as he would with anybody else, and began talking gaily to the two other girls. He had regained his presence of mind completely, and however deficient Feemy might be in that respect, he now proved himself a perfect master of hypocrisy. He did not stay long, and as he got up to go away, he merely remarked that he hoped he should meet the ladies that day week on the race-course, and at the ball; and the only thing he said especially to Feemy was, that he should call at Ballycloran on his way to the races, and that when he saw her on the course, he would tell her how her father and brother were; and he remarked that he should not go home that night, as he had been asked to dine and sleep at Brown Hall.

The week passed on, and Feemy remained in the same melancholy desponding way; saying nothing to Mrs. McKeon, and little to the two girls, who, in spite of Feemy's sin in having a lover, did everything in their power to cheer and enliven her.

Father John usually dined at Mrs. McKeon's on Sunday, and

she came to the determination of having another talk with him about Feemy. So before dinner on that day, she opened her mind to him, telling him the state in which Feemy had been the whole of the week, and that she thought the sooner she could be made to understand that she must give up all thoughts of Ussher, the better.

Feemy had been at mass with the family, and when she met Father John afterwards, she exerted herself to appear before him as she usually did, and to a certain extent she succeeded. Father John was himself usually cheerful, and he spoke to her good humouredly, and she made an effort to answer him in the same strain; this deceived the priest, and when Mrs. McKeon spoke to him about Feemy's deep melancholy, and suggested the propriety of speaking to her on the subject which they supposed was nearest her heart, he said,

"Better let her alone, Mrs. McKeon; I think you'd better let her alone, and time will cure her. You see Feemy is proud, and perhaps a little too headstrong, and I don't think she'd bear just as quietly as she ought, any one speaking to her about the man now. It isn't only the losing him that vexes her; it isn't only that she has been deceived: but that everyone knows that she has lost him, and has been deceived. It's this that hurts her pride, and talking to her about it will only make her more fretful. If you'll take my advice, you'll just leave her to herself, take no especial notice of her, and let her go to this ball; and when she sees the man paying attention to others,—dancing and philandering with them, and neglecting her—her pride will make her feel that she must at any rate appear to be indifferent; and when she has once enabled herself to appear so, she will soon become really so. Just let her go to the races, and the ball; and your kindness and the girls' society will soon bring her round."

All Monday Feemy spent in bed, but Mrs. McKeon and her girls took no notice of it, except carefully tending her—offering to read to her, and bring her what she wanted. They soon, however, found that she preferred being left alone; and they consequently allowed her to think over her own gloomy prospects in solitude and silence.

Feemy had, however, declared her intention of going both to the races and to the ball. Ussher had desired her to do so, and she feared to disobey him; besides, at one of these places he had to give her final instructions as to their departure. She was, therefore, dressed for starting on the Tuesday morning, when the other girls were ready; and though her eyes and nose were somewhat red, and her cheeks somewhat pale, and though she did not now deserve the compliment that Fred Brown had paid her, when he told Ussher that he was going to carry off the prettiest girl in County Leitrim, still she did not look unwell, and Mrs. McKeon kindly comforted herself by the reflection, that as she was both able and willing to dress herself for amusement, there could not be much really the matter with her.

In the meantime Thady had been honestly firm to the promise he had made to Father John, not to join the Mulreadyites. His sister's absence from Ballycloran at the present time had been a relief to him; and on the morning after his visit to the priest he had returned to his work, not certainly with much happiness or satisfaction, but still with his mind made up to struggle on in the best way he could—to do nothing which he knew to be wrong, and come what come might, to leave Reynolds and his associates to their own schemes and villanies. He felt determined, if he could not protect himself and his family from his enemies by honest means, to leave it to circumstances to protect him; and though he could not shake off a deep desponding as to the future, still there was a kind of contentment in the feeling that he knew he had to suffer, and that he had made up his mind to do so firmly and bravely.

On the Saturday morning, Pat Brady had again come to his master, informing him that all the boys were to be on that evening at the whiskey shop, and using all his powers of oratory to induce him to come down; but Thady was firm, and he not only refused to come then, but plainly told Pat that he had entirely altered his mind, and that he did not intend to go down to them at all. He advised Pat also to give them up, hinting that if he did not, they two, viz., Pat Brady and Thady Macdermot, would probably soon have to part company.

This was a threat, however, for which Pat did not much care; for he knew that there was little more to be made by his old master; and, like a wise man, he had already provided himself with a new one, and a more prosperous and wealthy one than him he was going to leave. Rats always leave a falling house, and Brady was a real rat.

Still, however, though he did not expect to get much more from his service with Thady, he was, for his own reasons, anxious that his present master should not be quit of the companions with whom he had been so anxious to join him: and therefore when he found that he could no longer work on his master's mind by the arguments he had hitherto used, he began to threaten him—telling him of the different perils from the law which he would have to encounter by having joined the party, and various dangers to which he would subject himself by deserting it. But in vain—Thady was firm; and when Pat got violent and inclined to be impertinent on the subject, he told him that he would knock him down with the alpine in his hand if he said another word about it.

On Sunday, Thady went to mass, and afterwards took a walk with his friend the priest, who said everything he could to raise his spirits, and to a certain degree he did so. On the next morning, as he was going to his work, a messenger brought a letter from Keegan to his father. This was a legal notice on Flannelly's part, that on some day in November, which was named, he—Flannelly—would require not only the payment of the interest money which would then be due, but also the principal; and in this notice was set forth the exact sum to be paid for principal, for interest, for costs; and it further stated that if the sum was not paid on or before that day, writs would be issued for his body—that is the body of poor Larry Macdermot—and latitats, and sheriff's warrants, and Heaven knows what besides, for selling the property at Ballycloran; and that the mortgage would be immediately foreclosed, and the property itself disposed of for the final settlement of the debt.

This agreeable document was very legibly addressed to Lawrence Macdermot, Esq., &c. &c. &c., Ballycloran; and its unusual dimensions and appearance made Thady at once feel that it was some infernal missile come still further to harass him, and leave him, if possible, more miserable than it found him. However, such as it was, it was necessary that it should be read; so he took it to his father, and having broken the seal, said,—

"Here's a letter from Keegan, Larry; shall I read it you?"

"D—n Keegan," was the father's consolatory reply, "I don't want his letters. I tell you he can't call for his money before November, and this is October yet."

"That's thrue," said Thady, when he had spelt through the epistle; "that's thrue, father; but this is to say that he manes to come in 'arnest, when that time comes."

"And don't he always come in 'arnest? is it in joke he comes, when he axes for a hundred pound every half year? come in 'arnest! why, d—n him, he's always in 'arnest!"

"But, father, it's not only the hundred pound now, but the whole debt he demands;" and, at last, Thady succeeded in reading the letter to his father.

Larry at first got into a violent passion, swearing fearfully at Keegan, and hinting that he, Larry, knew well enough how to take care of his own body; and that he, Keegan, might get more than he bargained for, if he came to meddle with it. After that he began to whimper piteously and cry, complaining that it was a most grievous thing that his own son should bring such a letter to him; and he ended by accusing Thady of leaguing with the attorney to turn him out of his own house, and even asked him whether, when they had effected their purpose, he and Keegan intended to live at Ballycloran together.

All this was not comfortable. Thady, however, quietly folded up the letter, put it in the old bureau, left his father to his pipe and his fireside, and went out again to his occupations.

Nothing new occurred at Ballycloran for a few days, and he began to flatter himself that Mrs. Mulready's boys and their threats would annoy him no more, and he was even thinking of sending Pat down to Drumleesh to notice the tenants again to come up with the rents, if it were only to see what steps they would then take. As he was returning home, however, on Friday evening, across the fields, a little after dusk, he saw the figure of a man standing in a gap through which he had to pass, and when he came close to him, he perceived it was Joe Reynolds.

Thady had been rather surprised that he had not seen Joe before, and had been inclined to think that that worthy gentleman had been intimidated, when he heard of his own defection; but Joe was not a character so easily frightened. The truth was that he had for the last few days left his own cabin at Drumleesh, and had been engaged with others in the mountains which lay between Loch Sheen and Ballinamore, in making potheen in large quantities, and drinking no small portion of what they made. The morning after the wedding, he had been boasting to his comrades there of the success he had had in bringing over his landlord to their ranks; and he had brought down a large party of them from that quarter, all sworn friends, to be present at his proposed initiation—and great was their wrath and loud were their threatenings when they found that Thady would not come. Joe had, however, been obliged to join them again at their business, and though he had heard the ill success of Brady's second attempt, he had not been able till now to try the effects of his own eloquence.

He had now come down for that purpose, and had been for the greater portion of the evening watching Thady, till he could get a good opportunity of talking to him undisturbed; and he was now determined not to leave him, till he had used every means in his power of inducing him to change the resolution to which he had so suddenly come.

When Thady came close to him he respectfully raised his old battered hat, and said—

"Long life to ye, Mr. Thady; I hope yer honer i self well this evening."

"Quite well thank you, Joe," and Joe walked o: few steps.

"Have you the rint ready for me yet?" continued

"Rint is it? faix then I have not—not a penny; rint I was wanting to talk to your honer about j but what the rint 'll be coming, and that right soo1 and plenty too—if you'll only listen to me."

"Those'd be glorious times, Joe, when the rint ca and Thady walked on faster, for he didn't want t(conversation beyond what he could help.

"Stop, Mr. Thady; what are ye in sich a hurr come a long way to spake to you—and we'll both t av' you'd go a little aisier."

"Well, Joe, what is it then? I'm in a hurry."

"In a hurry is it? but why wor ye in sich a l the promise you made us all, at Mrs. Mehan's, T week past. Ah! Mr. Thady, you worn't in a hu1 said you'd come down and be one of us at Mohill—i it too on the blessed cross; you worn't in sich a hu what hurries you now so fast?"

"Now, Reynolds, it's no use you're saying mor sent you word by Pat that I wouldn't come, and I wo an end of it."

"But that an't an end of it; no, nor nigh the end pose, Mr. Thady,"—and he paused, and, resuming tone, said, "and didn't you say you niver had de niver would, and that you'd always stick to us that so long? Shure, Mr. Thady, you'll not change you And Reynolds paused in the little path they were w Thady was obliged to stand too, for Reynolds had g and he couldn't pass unless he pushed the man ¿ shure—do you mane to let Keegan off, and Ussl ruffians, that way; do you intend to put up with ev the likes of them? Come, Mr. Thady, say the w(the word you swore before, and by the holy cross before next week is over Keegan shall be put whe spake another bad word, or do another bad deed."

"Come, Reynolds, out of this, and let me pass,' perceiving that he must now absolutely make the m that he was not to be talked over, "out of that, and And I'll tell you what, I'll not have my neck in dar hear you threatening murdher, I'll have you befo thrates," and he pushed by the man, who, however, still walked close behind him.

"And is that the way with you now? Have me before the magisthrates will you? and where'd you be all the time? Why there's not one of them that was in it, at Mrs. Mehan's that night, but could have you before the magisthrates, and I'm thinking thim folk would make a deal more of you than they would of me. Av you talk of magisthrates, Mr. Thady, may be you'll find there's too many of them in the counthry for yerself."

Thady walked on fast, but did not answer him, and Reynolds continued—"Come, Mr. Thady, I don't intend to anger you, or affront you; and av I've said anything that way, I axes your pardon; but just answer me—will you come down there only for once, av it wor only becase you swore it afore them all on the holy cross?"

"No, Joe, I will not; av I took any oath at all, I was dhrunk: besides, I said I wouldn't, and I won't; so now good night."

"But, Mr. Thady, av you'd only come there to tell the boys so themselves, it would be all right. Shure you're not afeard to trust yerself among them."

"Not a foot, Joe."

"Well, then, I tell you, you'll be sorry; not that I'd say a word agin you myself, becase though you've ill-trated me now, you wor always a kind landlord, and becase it's not in your heart to hurt a poor man; but I tell you, and you'll find it comes thrue enough, there were them there that night at Mrs. Mehan's as will turn agin you, unless you do as I'm axing you now."

"Well, Joe, I cant help it if they do, so good night."

They had now come to a lane, and as Thady was going to jump on the bank to get over, Joe put his hand on his coat.

"One more word, yer honer, may be yet you'll change your mind."

"Indeed, I shall not then."

"May be you will, and I'm thinking when you find Keegan too hard on you it'll come to that. Well, av you do, let me know, and I'll make it all right for you. Just tell Corney Dolan, and he's still at Drumleesh, that you're wanting me, and I won't be far off."

Thady did not answer him, but merely saying, "Good night, Joe," jumped into the road, and Joe by some devious path, through bogs and bottoms, betook himself to Mrs. Mulready's, and drowned the feeling of his ill success in whiskey.

Thady went home to his dinner or supper—rather glad that he had had the in view, for the man's manner was not so insolent as he had expected it would be; and he now felt tolerably confident

o

that he should not again be solicited to keep the unfortunate promise which he had made.

His father, however, was still muttering over the misfortunes which he was doomed to bear from the hands of his own son. Thady took all the pains he could, and all the patience he could muster, to prove to the old man that he was only desirous to do the best he could for him and Feemy. He had even told him that he had absolutely quarrelled and come to blows with the attorney, on the day of his visit; but it was all in vain, and when he got himself to bed he was puzzled to think whether Keegan and Ussher, or his father and Feemy, caused him most trouble and unhappiness.

CHAPTER XIX.

THE RACES.

ALTHOUGH we have hitherto only seen Ussher as a guest at Ballycloran, or figuring as a lion at Mary Brady's wedding, he was, nevertheless, in the habit of frequenting much better society, and was not unfrequently a guest at the houses of certain gentlemen in the neighbourhood of Carrick-on-Shannon.

For Ussher could assume the manners of a gentleman when he chose, and moreover, be a lively and agreeable companion; and this, perhaps, quite as much as the attribute, made him somewhat of a favourite among many of the surrounding gentry. He was, however, more intimate at Brown Hall than at any other house; and he had now been asked over there, to spend the few days previous to his final departure from County Leitrim.

The establishment at Brown Hall consisted of Jonas Brown, the father—an irritable, overbearing magistrate, a greedy landlord, and an unprincipled father—and his two sons, who had both been brought up to consider sport their only business; horses and dogs their only care; grooms and trainers the only persons worthy of attention, and the mysteries of the field and the stable the only pursuits which were fit to be cultivated with industry or learnt with precision. They could read, as was sufficiently testified by their intimate knowledge of the information contained in "Nimrod upon Horses," and the Veterinary Magazine; and the Clerk of the Course at the Curragh could prove that they could write, by the many scrawls he had received from them—entering horses, and giving their particulars as to age, colour, breeding, qualifications, &c., but beyond this they had no acquirements. For the elder son, who was only intended to be a landlord and a magistrate, and to spend about a thousand a year, this did not signify; but for the younger it afforded but a melancholy prospect, had his eyes been open to see it.

For the estate, which was all set at a rack rent, was strictly entailed; and as Jonas had always lived beyond his income, there would be little to leave to a younger son. When their mother died the two young men, together with a sister, had been left to the father's care. She also had learnt to ride, and ride hard—to go to the stable and see that her own horse was made up—and to rate her groom in no gentle terms, if things in that department were not as they should be. She also could be eloquent on thrush, sandcracks, and overreaches—could detect a splint or a spavin at a glance—knew all the parts and portions and joints of a horse much more accurately than she did of a sheep, and was a thorough judge of condition. Rumour also not unfrequently hinted, among the tabbies of Carrick-on-Shannon, that Miss Julia could not only ride with her brothers in the morning, but that she was also occasionally not ill inclined to drink with them of an evening.

Things were in this state, when it occurred to Jonas and his favourite son Fred, that it were well for all parties if they could get Miss Julia off from Brown Hall, as there was reason to fear she was coming out a little too fast; and that if they did not get rid of her now, she might in a short time become a card somewhat hard to play. They consequently invited a squireen of three or four hundred a year to the house, who had rather unequivocally expressed his admiration for Di Vernon; and under the fostering auspices of father and brother, the two soon made up matters together, though the lady was unable to follow her prototype's example, by wooing her lover over the pages of Dante. However, though Dante was wanting, opportunity was not, which for one so well inclined as Miss Julia was sufficient; and before the young gentleman had been three weeks in the house, Fred was enabled to hint to him one day, as he was pulling off his boots before dinner, that of course he presumed his intentions to his sister were honourable and explicit, now that things had gone so far. Toby Armstrong—for such was the name of Di Vernon's admirer—not relishing pistols and coffee, made no objection to the young lady; but he absolutely refused to take her empty handed, and, in consequence, Jonas and Fred had to hand him over their joint bond for two thousand pounds, before he would be induced to make her mistress of Castle Armstrong. There she now reigned supreme, and it is to be hoped, for the sake of the future generation, that she had by this time learnt to transfer her attention from the stable to the nursery.

The Browns were at any rate quit of the young lady, and had Brown Hall now wholly to themselves; and this was a satisfaction. Still the hundred a year which they had to pay their dear brother-in-law, Toby, was a great loss to them, and made it more improbable that when the old man should be gathered to his fathers, George should have anything to subsist on except his brother's affection and bounty.

As Fred inherited all his father's love of money, joined to an irresistible passion for everything that he called pleasure; and as he was already continually quarrelling with his younger brother, who was as continually impertinent to him, George's prospect in life was not particularly bright. As to turning his mind to any useful pursuit—studying for any profession, or endeavouring in any way to earn his own bread honestly—he would have been as angered and felt as insulted by such a proposition, as though any one had asked him to turn cobbler, and sit cross-legged at the window of one of the little shops at Carrick-on-Shannon.

As, however, he at present had food to eat, wine to drink, horses to ride, and usually cash to bet with, he concerned himself but little for the future; and we, therefore, may fairly be equally apathetic respecting it. It would not, however, be difficult to foretell his fate. Should he not break his neck before his father's death, he will quarrel with and slander his brother; he will ride for those who are young and green enough to trust their horses to him, and pay him for mounting them; he will spunge upon all his acquaintance till he is turned out of their houses; he will be a hanger on at the Curragh and all race-courses; he will finally become a blackleg and swindler; and will die in the Marshalsea, if he does not, as he most probably will, break his neck by a fall from the saddle; for, to the last, George will preserve his pluck—the only quality on which he could ever pride himself.

On the morning of the races the two brothers and Ussher were sitting over a very late breakfast at Brown Hall. The father had long since been out; careful to see that he got the full twelve hours' work from the unfortunate men whom he hired at five pence a day, and who had out of that to feed themselves and families, and pay their rent; we will not talk about clothing them, it would be a mockery to call the rags with which the labouring poor in that part of the country are partially covered, clothes, or to attach value to them, though I suppose they must once have cost something.

"Why, what nonsense, Ussher," said Fred, "to be sending that mare of yours down to Munster; she'd never be fast enough for that country—not the thing at all for Tipperary fences—all gaps and breaks; besides the expense of sending her, and the chances that she's lamed on the road. You'd better let me have her; she's only fit for this country. I'll tell you what I'll do: I'll give you the horse and gig you're to take that girl of yours to Longford in to-morrow for her."

"Hush, man, for G—d's sake! If the servants hear you talking that way, I'm dished. If it once got abroad about my taking her off, I'd have the devil to pay before I got out of the country."

"I believe Ussher thinks," said George, "no one ran away with a girl before himself. Why if you were going to seize a dozen stills, you couldn't make more row about it."

"I shouldn't make any about that, for it would come natural to me; and I'd a deal sooner be doing that, than what I have to do to-morrow night. I'm d—d, but I'd sooner take a score of frieze-coats, with only five or six of my own men to back me, than drive twenty miles in a gig with a squalling girl."

"If you're sick of the job, I'll take her off your hands," said the good-natured Fred.

"Thank ye, no; as I've got so far with it, I believe I'll go on now."

"Well, if you won't take a kind offer about the girl, will you take the one I made about the mare? To tell the truth, I'd sooner have the mare than the girl myself."

"Thank ye, no; I believe I'll keep both."

"I'll tell you what I'll do," said Fred, getting anxious in his hankering after the mare, "I'll throw the harness into the bargain—spick and span new from Hamilton's. I paid eight pound ten for it not a month since. All the new fashion—brass fittings and brass haines. You could have the crests taken out, and new ones put in, for a few shillings; only send me down the old ones."

"What would I do with a gig and horse? Besides, the gig's shook, the shafts are all loose, and the boxes are battered; and the horse was saying his prayers lately, by the look of his knees."

"Never down in his life, by G—d," said George, willing to help his brother in a matter of horseflesh; "it's only a knock he got when I was trying to put him over the little wall beyond the lawn there; but I couldn't make the brute jump, though he's the sweetest horse in harness I ever sat behind."

Ussher was not to be done; and Fred consoled himself by assuring him that he'd be sorry for it, when he found the mare was not the least use in life down in Munster, and that no one would give him a twenty-pound note for her.

A drag now came round to the door. George was making his toilet before the fire, having eaten about half an ounce of dry toast after his morning exercise under the three great-coats. He was adjusting his boots and breeches—and George was not a little proud of his appearance in his riding costume; the jacket and cap were carried loose; and after many exclamations from Fred, that they would be late, and that as he had backed Conqueror, it was a shame for his brother to give the stewards the chance of starting the horses without him, which were answered by rejoinders from George that they wouldn't dare to do so—showing that he didn't care how much all the rest might be inconvenienced by his delay, so long as he didn't suffer himself, the three got into the conveyance at the door, about an hour after the time at which the horses were advertised to start punctually; and Fred drove them to the course, which was not above a mile distant.

I cannot say that the ground displayed much that was elegant in the way of equipages, or anything very refined in the countenances belonging to the race-course.

The weighing stand consisted of the scales in which potatoes and oats were usually weighed in the market-place in Carrick, and were borrowed from the municipality for the occasion. The judge's chair was formed of a somewhat more than ordinary high stool, with a kind of handle sticking up at one corner, by holding on to which he was barely able to keep his place, so constantly were the mob pressing round him.

There was a stand, from which a tolerable view of the race could be obtained, admission one shilling; but few ascended it, and long before the start, the price had fallen to sixpence.

There were two or three carriages; one containing Counsellor Webb's family. He himself was one of the stewards, and, consequently appeared on horseback in a red coat. Another belonged to Sir Michael Gipson, who owned the greater part of the town, and who drawing about six thousand a year from this county and the next, had given ten pounds, to be run for by farmers' horses, contriving thereby to show them that he thought they ought to indulge in expensive amusements, and to stimulate them to idleness and gambling. As, however, the land in the country was chiefly let in patches under twenty acres each, and to men who were unable to feed the sorry beast necessary to keep them in tillage, Sir Michael's generosity had not the effect which it might be presumed to cause; and his ten pound was annually won by some large tenant, who might call himself a farmer, but who would make a desperate noise if another man presumed to call him anything but a gentleman. Of cars there were plenty, crowded with pretty faces, all evidently intending to be pleased; not invariably, however, for there was Mrs. Keegan in one of those altogether abominable affairs called inside cars, not because you had any of the comforts of an inside place in case of rain, for they have no covering, but because the inmates, sitting on each side, have full power to kick each other's shins, and no liberty to stretch their legs. There she sat alone, as sour as at the moment when she had first seen her Hyacinth as he was deposited by the hotel waiter on the mat inside her hall-door.

She looked little as if she was there for amusement, and, in truth, she was not. After a time, Hyacinth had come to himself; and by dint of continual scolding, much soda-water, and various lavations, he had enabled himself to make a very sickly appearance on horseback; but the wife of his bosom was determined that he should not escape from thence to another ordinary, or even to any hospitable table where he might get drunk for nothing; and, consequently, she was there to watch him.

There was but one other there that did not seem bent on enjoyment, and this was poor Feemy. There she was, sitting on the same side of the car with Lyddy McKeon; and the good-natured mother had taken care that this should be the side facing the horses; but Feemy took no interest in them. She had given over crying and sobbing; but she was silent, and apparently sullen, and would much have preferred her own little room at Ballycloran.

There were to be three races. Had there been a prospect of thirty, and among them a trial of speed between all the favourites of the Derby, there could not have been a greater crowd, or more anxiety; every ragged, bare-footed boy there knew the names of each horse, and to whom he belonged, and believed in the invincibility of some favourite beast,—probably from attachment to its owner,—and were as anxious as if the animals were their own. Among this set, McKeon or little Larry Kelly were booked to win; —they were kind, friendly masters, and these judges thought that kind men ought to have winning horses.

"Shure thin," said one half-naked urchin, stuck up in a small tree, growing just out of one of the banks over which the horses were to pass; "shure thin, Playful's an illigant swate baste entirely. I'll go bail there's nothin 'll come nigh her this day!"

"That Tony may win the day thin!" said another. "It's he is the fine sportsman."

"Bedad, ye're both out," said a third, squatting as close on the bank as the men would let him; "it's Mr. Larry 'll win, God bless him!—and none but him—and he the weight all wid him, and why not? There's none of 'em in the counthry so good as the Kellys. Hoorroo for the Kellys! them's the boys."

"They do say," said the second speaker, who was only half way up the tree, "that Conqueror 'll win. By Jasus, av he do, won't young Brown be going it!"

"Is it Conqueror?" said the higher, and more sanguine votary of McKeon. "Is it the Brown Hall horse? He can't win, I tell ye! I saw him as Paddy Cane was leading him down, and he didn't look like winning; he hasn't got it in him. That he may fall at the first lep, and never stir again! Tony 'll win, boys! Hurroo for Tony McKeon."

The weighing was now accomplished, and jockeys mounted. Major McDonnell had to look after this part of the business, of which he knew as much as he did of Arabic. However, he was shoved about unmercifully for half an hour—had his toes awfully trodden on, for he was told he should dismount to see the weighing —narrowly escaped a half-hundredweight, which was dropped within three inches of his foot, and did, I daresay, as much good as stewards usually do on such occasions.

Counsellor Webb was to start them, and, though a counsellor, he was an old hand at the work. He always started the horses at the Carrick races, and usually one of his own among the lot. The Counsellor, by the by, was a great favourite with all parties, and what was more, he was a good man and a gentleman.

Major Longsword from Boyle was the third steward, and he, like his military colleague, was rather out of his element. He was desired to keep the populace back and preserve the course; but it seemed to Major Longsword that the populace didn't care a button for him and his red coat, and though he valiantly attempted to ride in among men, women, and children, he couldn't move them; they merely pushed the horse back with their hands, and the brute, frightened by their numbers, wouldn't go on. They screamed, "Arrah, sir! go asy; shure you're on my foot; musha thin, can't you be quiet with the big horse? faix I'm murdhered with you, sir,—is you going to ride over us? shure, yer honer, won't you go over there? look how the boys is pressing in there." The Major soon saw he could do no good, so he rode out of the crowd, mentally determining that the jockeys might, if they could, clear the course for themselves.

And now they were off—at least seven of them; for when the important morning came, the Captain had in vain used every exertion to get a rider for Kickie-wickie. His ambition had at first soared so high that he had determined to let no one but a gentleman jockey mount her; but gradually his hopes declined, and at the ordinary he was making fruitless inquiries respecting some proper person; but in vain, and now he had been from twelve to one searching for any groom in possession of the necessary toggery. He would have let the veriest tailor in Carrick get on his mare if he had merely been legitimately dressed. Really, his exertions and his misery were distressing, for at last he was obliged to send her back to Boyle, after having paid the stakes and the stable charges for her, and console himself by telling his friends that the gentleman from Galway, who was to ride for him, had deceived him, and that he could not possibly have put any one he did not know upon Kickie-wickie.

But the seven are off. There they go, gently cantering, looking so pretty, and so clean—the riders so steady—the horses so eager. How different they will look when three or four, or more probably only two, are returning to the post! The horses jaded, the men heated, with whip speedily raised, and sharply falling—spurs bloody—and jackets soiled, by perhaps more than one violent fall; and yet in ten minutes this will be their appearance.

"There they go—Hurroo! they're off. Faix, there's Playful at her tricks already—by dad she'll be over the ropes! steady, Bob—steady, or she'll back on you—give it her, Gayner, my boy, give it her, never spare her—laws! did you see that? Well if he gets her over the course, he'd ride the very divil. Well done, Bob, now you've got her—Hurroo, Tony, my boy, you're all right now:"—and the mare, after a dozen preliminary plunges, joined the other horses. "Faix, they're all over that—did you see that big brown horse? He's Thunderer—he's a good horse intirely; did you see the lep he took at the wall?"—and now they had come to a big drain; all the horses being well together as far as this, excepting Crom-a-boo, who having been forced through a breach made by some other of the horses in the first wall, had baulked at a bank which came next, and never went any further. Some one told poor Stark on the course that the horse didn't run to-day nearly so well as his owner did last night; and it was true enough.

"There goes Conqueror—he's over! Faith then, George is leading.—Brown Hall against the field!"

"Never mind," said some knowing fellow, "he's a deal too fond of leading—he's a deal oftener seen leading than winning."

"There's little Larry—my! how sweet the mare went over the water. There's Brickbat in it;—no, he's out. He's an awkward beast. That's Thunderer—Holy Virgin, what a leap! He goes at everything as if there were twenty foot to cross, and a six foot wall in the middle."

"There's Playful at it again—he'll never get her round. Bad cess to you, you vixen—what made me bet on you? There, she's over—no she's not;—there's Diana—did you see Pat walk her through? Faith, she'd crawl up a steeple, and down the other side. There's Playful over—no, she's not;—right in the middle, by heavens!"

"And Bob under her—come away. My God, he'll be drowned!"

"Gracious glory! did you see that? He's up again;—d—n it but he dived under her; well, I never saw the like of that; she's out."

"And look, look! Bob's in the seat—you'll win your money now. Well, Bob Gayner, afther that you'll never live till you're drowned! Come away to the double ditch; that's where they'll show what they're made of—the mare'll be cooled now, and she'll run as easy as a coach-horse."

And the two rode away to the big fence mentioned, which consisted of a broad flat-topped bank between two wide dry ditches; while the horses went the round of the course over four or five intermediate banks.

"Here they come! there's Blake leading. What a stride that horse has! but you'll see he'll die away now. Larry's second—no, George is second, but Larry's well up."

"Faith, and he's been down too—he and the mare. There's Playful, how she pulls—where's Brickbat? now then!"

And the Galway horse came at the big fence—Blake pulling him off a little as he came to it, then stuck his spurs into his horse's flank—gave a lift at his head, and threw his left hand to the tree of the saddle. The horse gave a terrific leap on the bank—paused for a moment—and clearing the second ditch, came down safe on his legs with a shock that seemed to shake the field.

"Hurroo! well done! beat that George—now for Brown Hall; no, by Jasus, little Larry's next,—now, Larry, the Virgin send you safe over!" The mare with the light weight on her back made nothing of what seemed in the horse so tremendous a jump, and without losing her running, skimmed on to the bank and off it, and collared the horse before he had regained his stride.

"Good luck to you, masther Larry, it's you that can ride. Hurroo for the Kellys!—Oh, by the holy, they're both dead!" This last exclamation referred to Conqueror, who had come up to the fence much heated, but at a great pace. George, never attempting to pull him off, or give him a moment of breath, using his whip and riding forward over his horse's neck, hurried him on. The gallant brute leapt with all his force, but not being able to master the height, breasted it violently, sending his rider a dozen feet into the next field, and falling himself into the ditch, his head on to the field, with a broken heart, and dead! George, however, was soon on his feet, for his head was hard and he was used to tumbling.

Before he was on his legs, however, up came Playful, awfully rushing, her neck out—her nose forward—her nostrils open—her eye eager—covered with foam, but showing no sign of fatigue, nor any further inclination to baulk. Gayner was sitting her beautifully, not attempting to hold her, for he knew that if he stopped her, whipcord wouldn't make her run again; but with a firm, steady pull on her mouth—his hands low, and both on the reins, and his legs well tucked in. There she came, on at the leap without easing her pace for a moment, and going over the carcass of the dying animal, cleared it all, bank and ditches at one leap—two and thirty feet at one stride! There are the marks to this day, for Tony McKeon, in his pride, measured the ground, and put in stakes to point out the spot where his mare showed herself so worthy of all his trouble.

Brickbat had quarrelled with some of his namesakes at a wall, and was now nowhere; Diana still persevered, and got well over the big fence, but her chance was out, unless some unaccountable accident happened to the three other horses that were still running. On they went; there were only three more fences, two small banks, and a five foot wall. Thunderer and Miss Fidget neck and neck took the two banks, the big horse making awfully high leaps at them, Playful nearing them at every stride, galloping over the banks as though they were but a part of the level field. Now for the wall. "Now, Nicholas Blake, now, show them how little they think of a five foot wall in Galway. Faith though, Larry's first—bravo, Roscommon!" He's over, and a couple of bricks only falling show how lightly Miss Fidget touched it with her hind feet; not so Thunderer; again the horse made an awful leap, but the pace had been too much for him, he struck the wall violently with his knees, and, bursting through, gave Blake a fall over his shoulders. Galway, however, was soon in his saddle again, but not before Bob was over, and had long passed him.

And now there was a beautiful race in between the two mares; and oh! how charmingly both were ridden! But though Miss Fidget was so favoured in weight, and had begun with the lead, her elder rival collared her, and beat her at the post by a head. "And why shouldn't she win?" as Tony said in triumph to his friends, "for hadn't she the dhrop in her? wasn't she by Coriander, out of Pink, by Highflyer? Of course she'd win—hadn't he known it all the time?"

"That's all very well," said Larry, as he stood with his saddle in his hand, waiting till Bob got out of the scales, "it was only her d—d long nose and neck that won after all, for I'll swear my head was past the post before Bob's."

"Well then, Larry, we'll make a case for the stewards, whether it's your head or the horse's the judge should go by."

"There's two of 'em," whispered Gayner, "wouldn't know if you were to ask 'em."

Thunderer came in third, and a couple of minutes afterwards, Diana;—and Pat Conner, when he was laughed at as to his place, truly boasted that at any rate he was the only one that had been able to ride round the course without a fall.

The chief and most exciting race of the day being over, the more aristocratic of the multitude seemed with one accord to turn their attention to luncheon. The ladies began to unpack the treasures with which the wells of their cars had been loaded—cold hams—shoulders of mutton—pigeon pies—bottles of sherry—and dozens of porter soon made their appearance; and pretty girls putting cork-screws and carving knives into the hands of their admirers, bid them work for their food before they ate. Woe betide the young man there who had no female friends on the course—no one to relieve the pangs of his hunger, or to alleviate that intolerable delay which seems always necessary between races.

Then were made engagements for the ball; quadrilles and waltzes were given in exchange for sandwiches and ale—Lieutenants were to be had for sherry—a glass of champagne would secure a Captain.

Great was the crowd round Mrs. McKeon's car, and plentiful the partners who solicited the honour of dancing with Lyddy, Louey, and Feemy. McKeon was there in all his glory, shaking hands with every one—praising his mare with his mouth full of ham, and uttering vehement eulogiums on Gayner between the different tumblers of porter, which in his joy he seemed to swallow unconsciously. Then Bob came up himself, glowing with triumph, for he knew that he had acquitted himself more than ordinarily well. He had changed all his clothes, for he had been completely drenched by his fall in the brook; and now, having nearly altogether fasted for the last forty-eight hours, was not at all disinclined to assist at Mrs. McKeon's banquet.

He shook hands with her, and all the three girls round, and with Tony—although he had already done that three times before; and he began a full history of the race, which we needn't repeat.

"I knew Brickbat was as fat as a bullock; he couldn't keep the pace up; but I'll tell you what, Tony, if any horse there could beat Playful, it was Conqueror. But George can't wait—I win fifteen pound from him—he's made a bad thing of it—lost his horse and all."

"Did you see the horse, Bob, when you came to the big ditch?"

"By my honour, then, I didn't see anything from the time I got out of the brook. I'd enough to do to sit where I was, and keep the mare's head straight. When she made the great leap, I hardly felt her feet come to the ground, she came down so lightly."

While he was speaking, Ussher came up to the car, and began congratulating them. He had now openly stated that he was to leave the country altogether, and that he had been ordered to Cashel. Mrs. McKeon was therefore no longer at a loss to account for Feemy's melancholy; and whilst she felt a cordial dislike to the man, who she thought had so basely deceived Feemy and was now going to desert her, she was heartily glad for her sake he was going, and reflected that as he was to be off to-morrow, it was useless for her now to begin to be uncivil to him.

"I'm glad to congratulate you, Mr. McKeon—I'm glad you won, as my friend Brown didn't; a bad thing his losing his horse, isn't it?"

"Thank ye, Captain; and I'm to congratulate you too. I hear you're promoted, and going away from us—very glad for one, sorry for t'other. Take a bit of cold pie; d—n it, I forgot—the pie's all gone, but there's cold mutton and plenty of sherry. Liddy, give Captain Ussher a glass of sherry."

And Ussher went round to the side of the car where Feemy was sitting, and shook hands with her and the other girls. It was the first time through the whole long morning he had come near her; indeed, it was the first time he had seen her since his short visit at Mrs. McKeon's, and very cruel poor Feemy had thought such conduct. Yet now, when he merely came to speak a few words, it was a relief to her, and she took it actually for a kindness. She felt herself so fallen in the world—so utterly degraded—she was so sure that soon every one else would shun her, that she shuddered at the idea of his ill-treating or deserting her. He soon left her, having got an opportunity of desiring her in a whisper to dance the first quadrille with him, as he didn't think he should remain late at the ball.

As for Ussher himself, he would now have been glad if he had been able to have got rid of Feemy altogether. As I said before, when he started for Ballycloran on the day that he heard he had to remove his quarters, he had by no means made up his mind as to what he would do: it was not at that time at all his purpose to induce Feemy to leave her home, or go with him in the scandalous manner he had at last proposed. It was the warmth of her own affection, and the vanity which this had inspired, or rather strengthened in his breast, that had at the moment induced him to do so; and now he could not avoid it. He had told his sporting friends of his intention, and if even he could have brought himself to endure their ridicule by leaving her behind him, he had gone so far that he could not well break off with Feemy herself.

He was considerably bothered, however, by his position; he felt that she would be a dreadful chain round his neck at the place he was going to, and he began already to dislike her. Poor Feemy! she had already lost that for which she had agreed to sacrifice her pride, her family, her happiness, and herself.

Ussher now returned to his two friends, whose tempers were by no means improved by the calamity which had occurred. Fred declared it was all George's fault—that he had ridden his horse too fast or too slow—that he had been too forward, or not forward enough. His temper was by far too much soured by the loss of his own bets, to allow him to console his brother for the more serious injury he had suffered.

At length, however, the three got into the drag, and returned to Brown Hall. After dinner, each endeavoured to solace himself by no stinted application to the bottle. George declared, that as he had been able to drink nothing for the last three days, he'd make up for it now, and that he wouldn't allow himself to be disturbed to dress for the best ball that could be given in Ireland. Fred, however, was not so insatiable, and at about eleven he and Ussher dressed and again drove into Carrick.

The ball at Carrick passed off as such balls always do. There was but little brilliancy, but a great deal of good humour. The dresses were not the most costly, nor possibly the most fashionable, but the faces were as pretty, and the figures as good, as any that could be adorned for Almack's by a Parisian head-dresser or milliner. The band was neither numerous nor artistic, but it played in good time, and never got tired. The tallow candles, fixed in sconces round the walls of the room, in which a short time since we saw some of our friends celebrating the orgies of Bacchus, gave quite sufficient light for the votaries of the nimble-footed muse to see their partners, mind their steps, and not come in too rude collision with one another. Quadrilles succeeded waltzes, and waltzes quadrilles, with most unceasing energy; and no one dreamt of giving way to fatigue, or supposed that it was at all desirable to sit down for a single dance. From ten to two they kept it up without five minutes' pause, and then went joyfully to supper—not to drink half a glass of wine, and eat a mouthful of jelly or *blanc-manger* standing—but to sit down with well-prepared appetite to hot joints—ham and chicken, veal pies, potatoes, and bottled porter. And then the songs that were sung! It would have done your heart good to hear young Fitzpatrick sing the "Widow Machree;" and then all the punch that was mixed! and the eloquence that was used, not in vain, to induce the fairer portion of the company to taste it!

This state of things was not, however, allowed to remain long. It was not at all the thing that men—at any rate unmarried men —should waste their time in drinking when they had come there to dance; and after the ladies had left them about ten minutes, messages came hot and thick from the ball-room, desiring their immediate presence; nor were they so bold as to neglect these summonses, excepting some few inveterate sinners, who, having whiskey and hot water in their possession, and looking forward to a game at loo, neglected the commands which were brought to them.

Soon again the fiddles sounded, and quick feet flew round the floor with more rapidity than before. The tedium of the quadrille was found to be too slow, and from three till six a succession of waltzes, reels, and country dances, kept the room in one whirl of confusion, and at last sent the performers home, not from a feeling of satiety at the amusement, but because, from very weariness, they were no longer able to use their feet.

Feemy, early in the evening, had danced with Ussher, and received his final instructions respecting their departure on the morrow. He was to leave Brown Hall early for Mohill, and Fred's gig and horse were to be sent over to him there. He was to send his heavy luggage on by the car, and leaving Mohill about seven, when it would be dusk, drive by the avenue at Ballycloran and pick Feemy up as he passed, and they would then reach Longford in time for the mail-coach during the night.

Ussher calculated that Feemy would not be missed till he had had two hours' start, and that then it would be impossible to catch him before he reached Dublin.

"But, Myles," said Feemy, "how am I to get home? You know I am at Mrs. McKeon's now."

"Why how helpless you are," replied he; "can't you easily make some excuse to get home? say you are ill—and sick—and want to be at home. Or if it must come to that, say you will go home; who's to stop you?"

"But I wouldn't like to quarrel with them, Myles; just now, too, when they've been so kind to me."

"Well, dearest, you needn't quarrel with them; say you're ill, and wish to be at home; but don't make difficulties, love; don't look so unhappy; you'll be as happy as the day is long, when we're once away—that is, if you still love me, Feemy. I hope, after all I'm doing for you, you'll not be sullen and cold to me because you're leaving such a hole as Ballycloran. If you don't love me, Feemy, say so, and you may stay where you are."

"Oh! Myles, how can you say such words now! you know I love you—how much I love you—else I wouldn't be leaving my home for you this way! And though Ballycloran is—"

Here the poor girl could say no more; for she was using all her energies to prevent herself from sobbing in the ball-room.

"Good G—d! you're not going to cry here; come out of the room, Feemy;" and he led her into the passage, where, under the pretence of looking at the moon, they could turn their faces to the window. "What are you crying for now?"

"Don't you know I love you? why else would I be going with you?"

"Well, don't cry then; but mind, I shan't see you again before the time, for I'm going out of this at once now. I shall be at the avenue at a quarter before eight; don't keep me waiting. If you are there first, as you will be, walk a few steps along the Mohill road, so as to meet me; no one will know you, if you should meet any one, for it will be nearly if not quite dark; the moon won't rise till past ten; do you understand, Feemy?"

"Oh, yes, I understand!"

"Well, good night then, my own love, for I must be off."

"But, Myles, I want to say one thing."

"Hurry then, dear, what is it?"

"What 'll I do about my things?"

"What things?"

"Why, Myles, I must bring some things with me; clothes, you know, and things of that sort."

This puzzled Ussher rather; he had considered that he should have enough trouble with Feemy herself; he had quite forgotten the concomitant evils of the bandboxes, bundles, and draperies which it would be necessary for Feemy to take with her.

"Ah! you can get clothes in Dublin; you can't want to take much with you; you can bring a bundle in your hand just that distance. Can't you, eh, Feemy?"

Feemy could not but think that a week since he would not have asked her to carry all her travelling wardrobe in a bundle, in her hand. However, she only said,

"Why, not well, Myles; I shall have so many things to think

of; but I shan't have much, and if you'll let me, I'll send **Biddy** to meet you with what I must take. She'll meet you on the road, and put it into the gig."

"Good heavens! what do you mean! would you tell the girl what you're going to do? Why she'll tell your father, and Thady, and raise the whole country on me."

"No, she wouldn't, Myles; she wouldn't tell anybody a word, when I told her not. You don't know those sort of people; she'd not say a word; so if you'll let me, I'll send her on to meet you with my things."

With a good deal of reluctance Ussher agreed to this; and then, again enjoining Feemy not to keep him and the gig waiting in the road, he took his leave, and departed, with his friend Fred, for Brown Hall; first of all taking Feemy into the refreshment-room, and making her drink a glass of sherry. This did her much good, and when she got back into the ball-room, she was able to dance with tolerable spirit; and Mrs. McKeon, who had been watching her, and had seen her dance with Ussher, was glad to think that her *proteyée* had made up her mind to part with her lover in good spirits, and before the evening was over she assured Louey, with great glee, that, in spite of all that had been said, she foresaw that as soon as that horrid man had been gone three or four days, Feemy would be as well and as cheerful as ever.

Feemy was, nevertheless, very glad when she was told to get her cloak on, and found herself on the car going to Drumsna. She then told her friend that she wanted to be home with her father on the morrow,—that she had promised to be home the day after the ball. She even pretended that she had received a message that evening from her father, begging her return. Mrs. McKeon did not think much about it, supposing that Feemy's presence might be necessary for household purposes at Ballycloran, and she readily promised her the loan of the car, at four in the afternoon, on condition that she would return to Drumsna at least in a day or two. This Feemy promised, rejoicing that her expected difficulties as to getting to Ballycloran were so easily overcome, and going to bed, she slept more soundly than she had yet done since she had given her fatal consent to Ussher's proposal.

CHAPTER XX.

HOW CAPTAIN USSHER SUCCEEDED.

Late the next morning, Feemy and the other girls got up; they had slept together to make room in the house for the victorious Bob, but as Father John had prophesied, they were all too tired to be much inconvenienced by this. Immediately after breakfast the car came round, and Feemy, afraid to wish her friends good bye too affectionately lest suspicion should be raised, and promising to come back again in a day or two, returned to Ballycloran.

Thady was out when she got there, but he was expected in to dinner. Her father was glad to see her, and began assuring her that he would do all in his power to protect her from the evil machinations of her brother, and then again took his grog and his pipe. She went into the kitchen, and summoning Biddy, desired her to follow her up to her bedroom. When there, she carefully closed the door, and sitting down on the bed, looked in her attendant's face and said,

"Biddy, if I told you a secret, you'd never betray me, would you?"

"Is it I, Miss Feemy, that's known you so long? in course I wouldn't," and the girl pricked up her ears, and looked all anxiety. "What is it, Miss?—Shure you know av you tould me to hould my tongue, never a word I'd spake to any mortial about anything."

"I know you wouldn't, Biddy; that's why I'm going to tell you; but you mustn't whisper it to Katty, for I think she'd be telling Thady."

"Niver fear, Miss; sorrow a word I'll whisper it to any one, at all at all."

"Well, Biddy, did you hear Captain Ussher's going away from this intirely?"

"What! away from Ballycloran?"

"No, but from Mohill, and from County Leitrim altogether. He's going a long way off, to a place called Cashel."

"And what for is he going there, and you living here, Miss Feemy?"

"That's the secret, Biddy; I'm going with him."

"My! and is you married in sacret, Miss?" said the girl, coming nearer to her mistress, and opening her eyes as wide as she could.

Feemy blushed up to the roots of her hair, and said, "No, we're not married yet; we're to be married in Dublin; we couldn't be married here you know, because Captain Ussher is a Protestant."

"Holy Mary! Miss, you're not a going to lave the ould religion; you're not a going to turn Prothesthant, is you, Miss Feemy?"

"No, Biddy; why should I turn Protestant? but you see there's rasons why we couldn't be married here; we're to be married in Dublin, to-morrow."

"To-morrow!" ejaculated Biddy; "what, is you going to-night?"

"This very evening; and now I want you to help me, and when we're settled, Biddy, if you like to lave this ould place, I mane you to come and live with us."

"To be shure, Miss; and wouldn't I go the world round wid you? and why not? for it's you was always the kind misthress to me. But what'll I be doing to help you?"

And then Feemy explained to her her plans, and began to pack up the few treasures she could take with her, in a box small enough for Biddy to carry; and the two kneeled down together to the work.

Feemy's tears dropped quickly on the little things she was packing, and the poor girl soon followed the example her mistress gave her.

"Ochone! ochone! Miss Feemy, alanna, what'll we be doing widout you?" and she came round and began kissing her mistress's dress, and hands, and face, "What shall we do widout you at all then? what will the ould man be doing, when you're not to the fore to mix his punch?"

"Don't talk that way," said Feemy. "Shure, won't I be coming back to see him when I'm married?"

"In course you will; but it'll be a great miss, when he and Mr. Thady finds you're gone. What'll I say at all, when I come back from seeing you off—and they finds that you are gone?"

"But you mustn't stay to see me off at all. When you've put the box in the gig you must go on to Mrs. Mehan's, and when you come back you can say you'd been down to look for something that was left the day of Mary's wedding; but mind, Biddy, don't say a word about it at Mrs. Mehan's, and above all, don't mention it to Katty."

"Not a word, Miss; niver fear: but what'll I be doing when you're gone? But I suppose it's all for the best; may sorrow seize him thin av he don't make you the good husband."

It was then settled that Feemy's bonnet and shawl were to be brought down into the sitting-room opposite the dining-room—that dinner was to be put off as late as possible—that when Larry and Thady were at their punch, Feemy was to escape unobserved. Biddy was enjoined, when she slipped out with the box, to leave the front door ajar, so that her mistress could follow her without making any noise. The girl was also to carry down her mistress' cloak—so that she might the easier run down the avenue.

When these things were all settled, Biddy returned to the kitchen, big with the secret; but she was too prudent to say or hint anything which could create a suspicion in her colleague's breast.

Thady came in about the usual dinner-hour, and Feemy spoke good-humouredly to her brother—more so than she had done since the day he had desired her not to walk with Captain Ussher. Thady himself was less gloomy than usual, for he had been rejoiced by hearing that the revenue officer was immediately going to leave the country. He had only been told it that morning at Mohill, as a secret, and he therefore presumed that Feemy did not know it. He thought that he would not distress her by telling her of it now—that he had better leave her to find it out herself after he was gone; but the reflection of the misery it would occasion her when she did know it, gave rise to a feeling of pity for her in his heart, which made him more inclined to be gentle and tender to her than he had felt for a long time.

After sitting over the fire with their father for some time, Thady said,

"Well, Feemy, these are fashionable hours you've brought with you from Drumsna. Does Mrs. McKeon always dine as late as this? Why it's half past six!"

"The stupid girl forgot the potatoes, Thady. You could have them now; but you know, you wouldn't eat them as hard as stones. I'll go and hurry her."

"'Deed and I'm starving," said the father. "Why can't we have dinner then, Feemy dear? Why won't they bring dinner in?"

And Feemy went out, not to hurry them, but to cause grounds for fresh delay. At last, a little after seven, she allowed dinner to go in, and following it herself, she sat down and made as good a meal as she could, and endeavoured to answer Thady's questions about the races and the ball with some appearance of having taken interest, at any rate in the latter. If she did not altogether succeed, the attempt was not so futile as to betray her; and the dinner passed over, and the hot water came in, without anything arising especially to excite her alarm. At last she heard the front door open, and she listened with apprehension to every creak the rusty hinges made as Biddy vainly endeavoured to close it without a noise; but the sounds, which, in her fear, seemed so loud and remarkable to her, attracted no notice from her father or brother. Then she mixed their punch. Had Thady been looking at her he might have seen a tear drop into the tumbler as she handed it to him; but his eyes were on the fireplace, and she slipped out of the room without her tell-tale face having been observed.

It was now, as she calculated, about the time that she should start; and with trembling hands she tied on her bonnet. Having thrown her shawl over her shivering shoulders, she opened her book upon the table with a handkerchief upon it—placed her chair by the fire, and leaving the candle alight, slowly crept through the hall-door, down the front steps, and into the avenue leading to the road. She shuddered when she found herself alone in the cold dark air; but soon plucking up her courage, she ran down as quickly as she could to the spot where the old gate always stood open, and leaning against the post, listened intently for the sound of the gig wheels. She stood there, listening for three or four minutes, which seemed to her to be an hour, and then getting cold, she thought she'd walk on to meet Ussher as he had directed her; but before she had gone a dozen yards the darkness frightened her, and she returned. As soon as she had again reached the gateway she heard a man's footstep on the road a little above; and still more frightened at this, she ran back the avenue towards the house till the footsteps had passed the gate. She did not, however, dare again to stand in sight of the road, though it was so dark, that no one passing could have seen her if she were a few yards up the avenue; so she sat down on the stump of a tree that had been lately felled, and determined to wait till she heard the sound of the gig.

There she remained for what seemed to her a cruelly long time; she became so cold that she could hardly feel the ground beneath her feet; and her teeth shook in her head as she sat there alone in the cold night air of an October night, with no warmer wrapping than a slight shawl thrown over her shoulders. There she sat, listening for every sound—longing to catch the rattle of the wheels that were to carry her away—fancying every moment that she heard footsteps approaching, and dreading lest the awful creak of the house-door opening should reach her ears.

She could not conceive why Ussher did not come—she had absolutely been there half an hour, and she thought it must be past ten—she had long been crying, and was now really suffering with bodily pain from cold and fright; and then the whole of Ussher's conduct to her since that horrid morning passed through her mind—she saw things now in their true light, which had never struck her so before. What would she not have given to have been safe again at Mrs. McKeon's; to have been in her own room, of which she could still see the light through the window; in fact, to be anywhere but where she was? She did not dare, however, to return to the house, or even again to walk down the road. Poor, unhappy Feemy! she already felt the wretched fruits of her obstinacy and her pride.

At last she absolutely heard the front-door pushed open, and could plainly see a man's figure standing on the threshold. It must be Thady! They had discovered her departure, and he was already coming to drag her back! She heard his feet descending the hall steps; but they were as slow and as deliberate as usual; and she could perceive that, instead of coming down the avenue, he turned towards the stables. This was a slight relief to her—it was evident she was not yet missed; but she was dreadfully cold, and what was she to do if Thady heard the noise of the gig, and perceived that it had stopped at their gate?

Ussher had driven over to Mohill early in the morning, and had gotten everything ready for his departure in the manner he had proposed; but when the time for starting came, he had been detained by business connected with his official duties, and it was eight o'clock before he was able to bid adieu to the interesting town of Mohill. He had then, at the risk of his own neck, driven off as fast as Fred Brown's broken-knee'd horse could take him, and was proceeding at a gallop towards Ballycloran, when he was stopped near Mrs. Mehan's well-known shop by Biddy, who was standing by the road-side opposite.

He stopped the horse as quick as he could, and Biddy came running to him with Feemy's bundle.

"Is that yer honer, at last? Glory be to God! but I thought you wor niver coming. The misthress 'll be perished with the could."

"Never mind—hurry—give me what you've got!"

And Biddy handed in the bundle and cloak, and Ussher again drove on.

"Musha then, but he's a niggardly baste!" soliloquised Biddy, "not to give me the sign of a bit of money, after waiting there for him these two hours by the road-side, and me with his sacret and all, that could ruin him if I chose to spake the word, only I wouldn't for Miss Feemy's sake. But maybe it was the hurry and all that made him be forgitting, for he was niver the man for a mane action. I wish he may trate her well, that's all; for he's a hard man, and it's bad for her to be leaving the ould place without the priest's blessing."

Ussher was at the gateway; but when he got there, he could not see Feemy. He waited about a minute, and then whistled—a minute more, and he whistled again. What should he do? It would be so foolish now for him to go without her! He knew the horse was steady and would stand; so he got out and walked up the avenue till he saw the figure of Feemy, still sitting on the root of the tree where we left her. There was a light colour in her shawl, and the little white collar round her neck enabled him to see her at some distance; and she saw, or at any rate heard him, but she neither moved to or from him.

She had caught, some time since, the sound of the gig wheels, but just as she did so, she again saw the figure of Thady as he came round from the stables; and he evidently had heard it also, for he stood still on the open space before the house. He was smoking, for she caught the smell of the tobacco, and she plainly heard the stones on the pathway rattle as he now and then struck them with the stick in his hand. He didn't move towards her; but there he stood, as if determined to ascertain whether the vehicle which he must have heard, would pass along the road by the gate.

Then the sound ceased. It was when Biddy was putting in it the cloak and bundle, and again it continued closer and closer. The road came round the little shrubbery through which the avenue passed; the gig was therefore at one time even nearer to Feemy than it would be when it stopped at the avenue gate; and when it passed this place, she fancied she could hear Ussher moving in his seat. She did not dare to stir, however, for there still stood Thady, listening like herself to the sounds within forty yards of her; and had she risen he must have seen her.

And now the gig stopped at the avenue gate. Feemy was all but fainting; what with the cold and her former fear, and the dreadful position in which she found herself, she could not have moved if she had tried; she just preserved her senses sufficiently to torture her, and that was all. Plainly she heard her lover whistle; and plainly Thady heard it too, for he kept his stick completely still, and took the pipe from his mouth: then the second whistle—then she heard Ussher's foot on the ground— heard him approaching, and saw his figure draw nearer; in vain she endeavoured to make signs to him, in vain she thought she whispered, "keep back;" for when she tried to speak, the words would not come. On he came till he was close to her, and in a low voice he said,

"Feemy, is that you? why don't you come? what are you here for?" and he put down his hand to raise her. Feemy tried to rise and whisper something, but she was unable, and when Ussher stooped and absolutely lifted her from her seat, she had really fainted. "Come, Feemy,' said he, still unaware of Thady being near, "come; this is nonsense—hurry, there's a love. Come, Feemy, stand, can't you?"

When Thady had first come out of the house, it had merely been for the purpose of going into the stable, as was his practice, to see the two farm horses fed; as he returned, he caught the sound of Ussher's gig; but it was more for the purpose of smoking his pipe in the open air than from any curiosity that he lingered out of doors. When, however, the vehicle stopped at Ballycloran gate, and he heard the whistle twice repeated, his interest was excited, and he thought that something was not right. He then heard Ussher's footsteps up the avenue, and he fancied he could hear him speak; but he had no idea who he was; nor had he the slightest suspicion that his sister was so near him.

But when Ussher stopped, Thady gently came down the avenue unperceived; he saw him stoop, and lift something in his arms, but still up to this time he had not recognised the voice. It was Thady's idea that something had been stolen from the yard, which the thief was now removing, under cover of the darkness. By degrees, as he got nearer, he perceived it was a woman's form that the man was half dragging, half carrying, and then he heard Ussher's voice say loudly, and somewhat angrily, "This is d—d nonsense, Feemy! you know you must come now."

These were the last words he ever uttered. Thady was soon close to him, and with the heavy stick he always carried in his hand, he struck him violently upon the head. Ussher, when he had heard the footsteps immediately behind him, dropped Feemy, who was still insensible, upon the path; but he could not do so quick enough to prevent the stunning blow which brought him on his knees. His hat partially saved him, and he was on the point of rising, when Thady again struck him with all his power; this time the heavy bludgeon came down on his bare temple, and the young man fell, never to rise again. He neither moved nor groaned; the force of the blow, and the great weight of the stick falling on his uncovered head as he was rising, had shattered his brains, and he lay as dead as though he had been struck down by a thunder-bolt from heaven.

Though it was so dark that Thady could not see the blood he had shed, or watch how immovable was the body of the man he had attacked, still he knew that Ussher was no more. He had felt the skull give way beneath the stroke; he had heard the body fall heavily on the earth, and he was sure his enemy was dead.

At first he felt completely paralysed, and unable to do anything; but he was soon aroused by a long sigh from poor Feemy. The cold had revived her, and she now regained her senses. Thady threw his stick upon the ground, and stooping to lift her up, said,

"Oh! Feemy, Feemy, what have you brought upon me!"

When she recognised her brother's voice, and found that she was in his arms, she said,

"Where am I, Thady? What have you done with him? Where is he?"

"Never mind now. He's gone—come to the house."

"Gone!—he's not gone; don't I know he would not go without me?" and then escaping from her brother's arms, she screamed, "Myles, Myles!—what have you done with him? I'll not stir with you till you tell me where he is!" and then the poor girl shuddered, and added, "Oh! I'm cold, so miserably cold!"

"Come to the house with me, Feemy;—this is no place for you now."

"I'll not go with you, Thady. It's no use, for you shan't make me; tell me what you've done with him—I'll go nowhere without him."

Thady paused a minute, thinking what he'd say, and then replied: "You'll never go with him now, Feemy, for Captain Ussher is dead!"

Feemy only repeated the last word after her brother, and again fell insensible on the ground.

Thady at length succeeded in getting her to the house; and pushing open the front door, which was still unlatched, with his foot, took her into her own room on the left hand side of the passage, and deposited her still insensible on the sofa. He then went into the kitchen, and sent Katty to her assistance.

Pat Brady was sitting over the kitchen fire, smoking. Though this man was still hanging about the place, and had not come to an actual rupture with his master, still there had been no cordiality or confidence between them since Brady had failed to induce Thady to keep his appointment at the widow Mulready's; and for the last two days not even a single word had passed between them. Now, however, there was no one else but Pat about the place, and Thady felt that he must tell some one of the deed that he had done. It would be useless to consult his father; his sister was already insensible; the two girls would be worse than useless; besides, he could not now conceal the deed; he could not leave the body to lie there on the road.

"Brady," said he, "come out; I want to spake to you. Is there a lanthern in the place at all?"

"No, Mr. Thady, there is not," said he, without moving; "what is it you want to-night?"

"Come out, and bring a lighted candle, if you can."

Brady now saw from his master's pale face, and fear-struck expression, that something extraordinary had happened, and he followed him with a candle under his hat; but the precaution was useless, the wind blew it out at once.

"Pat," said Thady, as soon as the two were out before the front door; "Pat," and he didn't know how to pronounce the thing he wished to tell.

"Good God! Mr. Thady, what's the matther? has anything happened the owld man?"

"What owld man?"

"Your father."

"No, nothing's happened him; but—but Captain Ussher is dead!"

"Gracious glory—no! why he was laving this for good and all this night. And how did he die?"—and he whispered in his master's ear—"did the boys do for him?"

"I killed him by myself," answered Thady, in a whisper.

"You killed him, Mr. Thady! ah! now, you're joking."

"Stop!" said Thady—for they were now in the avenue—"joking or not, his body is somewhere here;—and he had Feemy here, dragging her along the road, and I struck him with my stick across the head, and now they'll say I've murdhered him."

Brady soon touched the body with his foot; and the two raised it together, and put it off the path on the grass, and then held a council together, as to what steps had better be taken.

Brady, after his first surprise and awe at hearing of Ussher's death was over, spoke of it very unconcernedly, and rather as a good thing done than otherwise. He recommended his master to get out of the way; he advised him at once to go down to Drumleesh and find out Joe Reynolds; he assured Thady that the man would even now be willing to befriend him and get him out of harm's way. He told him that Reynolds and others had places up in the mountains where he might lie concealed, and where the police would never be able to find him; and that if he only got out of the way for a time, it might probably not be found murder by the Coroner, and that in that case he could return quietly to Ballycloran.

Thady listened sadly to Brady's advice, but he did not know what better to propose to himself. He remembered the last words which Reynolds had said to him, and he made up his mind to go down at once to Corney Dolan's, who was a tenant of his own, and from him find out where Reynolds was.

"But, Pat," said Thady, when he had made up his mind to the

line of conduct he meant to pursue, "what shall we do with the man's body? We can't let it lie here. As I trust in God, I had no thoughts to kill him! and I would not run away, and lave the body here, as though I'd murdhered him."

"Jist lay him asy among the trees, Mr. Thady, till you're out of the counthry; and then I'll find it,—by accident in course, and get the police to carry it off. Thim fellows is paid for sich work."

"No, Pat; that wouldn't do at all. I won't have them say I hid the body; every one 'll know 'twas I did it; mind, I don't ask you to tell a lie about it; and I'll not have it left here, as though I'd run away the moment afther I struck him. We must take him into the house, Brady."

"Into the house, yer honer! not a foot of it! why, you'd have Miss Feemy in fits; and the owld man'd be worse still, wid all thim fellows coming from Carrick and sitting on the body, discoursing whether it wor to be murdher or not."

"Well, then; we'll take it to Mrs. Mehan's."

"Av you do, Mr. Thady, the country 'll have it all in no time. Howsomever, they must take it there if you choose, as it's a public; but you'd better lave it where it is, and let me send it down by and by—jist to give you an hour's start or so."

This Thady absolutely refused, stating that he would not leave the body till he had seen it deposited in some decent and proper place; and the two men took it up between them and carried it away, meaning to take it to Mrs. Mehan's. But at the avenue gate they found Fred Brown's horse and gig, exactly where Ussher had left it, excepting that the horse was leisurely employed in browsing the grass from the ditch side.

Brady soon recognised both the horse and gig as belonging to Brown Hall; and he then proposed putting the body of its former occupant in it, and driving it to the station of the police at Carrick-on-Shannon, and restoring at the same time the horse and gig to its proper owner at Brown Hall. To this scheme Thady at last agreed; but he made the man promise him, that when he got to the police at Carrick he would tell them that he, Thady, had desired him to do so; and that, instead of running away, he had not left the body till he had seen it put into the vehicle, to be carried into Carrick-on-Shannon. And with these injunctions Brady departed with his charge.

CHAPTER XXI.

THE CORONER'S INQUEST.

During the short time that elapsed between the heavy blow which had occasioned Ussher's death, and the departure of Pat Brady with the gig, a great many thoughts had passed through Thady's mind, although he had been in action the whole time. His first idea had certainly been that Ussher was carrying off Feemy against her will; the last words which Ussher had spoken before his death, and which were the only words of his that Thady had heard,—"This is d—d nonsense; you know you must come now,"—certainly were calculated to make him think so. But he soon reflected that had this been so, Feemy could not have been sitting alone in the place where Ussher found her; besides, her own conduct when she came to herself disproved it. Feemy had therefore evidently been a consenting party. Still, however, he thought that he could not but be justified in doing what he had done in his sister's defence, even though his interference was in opposition to her wishes. Then he thought of the man himself, whom he had known so long, seen so frequently, and hated so bitterly. There he was now—dead—a cold corpse—entirely harmless, and unable to injure him or his more. But Thady already felt his enemy's blood heavy on his conscience, and he would have died himself to see him rise on his feet. Thoughts as to his own safety crowded on his mind; he felt that if he intended boldly to justify the deed, he should himself declare what he had done—see that the body was properly taken care of—and give himself up at once to the police. As to the fact of his having killed the man, that he had declared to his sister before he had at all thought what his conduct ought to be, and he had done the same to Brady; it was useless for him therefore to attempt to conceal it, even if he had wished to do so. But he felt afraid to give himself up to the police; he abhorred the idea of what he thought would be the disgrace of being in confinement; and instead of going, as he at first thought to have done, at once to Father John, and telling him all that had happened, he listened to Brady's traitorous advice, and determined to take himself, at any rate for a time, to the fancied security of Joe Reynolds and his haunts.

After Brady had departed he stood on the road, till he could hear no longer the sound of the retreating wheels, and while standing there determined he would not leave the place, for the last time perhaps, till he had told his father what had happened, and ascertained whether Feemy had recovered. He reflected that it would be a dreadful thing for her to tell her father and the servants, and to be called on to explain why her brother was away; having made this resolution he walked again up to the house.

He pushed the door open, and at once went into his sister's room. Here she was still lying on the sofa, and Katty was sitting beside her—begging her mistress to tell her what was the matter. But Feemy had not spoken since she had been there; she had recovered her senses, for she held her hands before her eyes, and the tears were falling fast beneath them: but she had not spoken a word to Katty since her brother had placed her on the sofa.

When he entered the room she uncovered her eyes for a moment; but as soon as she saw him she buried her face in the pillow, and it was plain from her sobbing that she was crying more violently than before.

Thady walked up to the sofa, and as he did so the girl got up.

"Go out, Katty," said he, "I want to spake a word to your misthress, but be in the kitchen; I'll call you when I've done."

She retreated,—not, however, farther than the door, which she closed, and left the brother and sister together. The last time they had been so in that room—the last time the two had conversed alone together before, was when Thady cautioned his sister against the man he just now killed; he thought of this, but he was too generous to let the reflection dwell on his mind at such a moment.

"Feemy," he said, as he attempted to take his sister's hand— which, however, she violently drew back from him—"Feemy, I'm going to lave you a long time, and I must spake to you first,— perhaps the last words I'll ever be able to say to you at all. Feemy darling, won't you listen to me then?—eh, Feemy?"

Feemy, however, only buried her head further in the sofa, and did not answer him a word.

"I must spake a word to you," continued Thady, "about him that is now—him that was with you on the avenue. I told you, Feemy, he was dead, and what I told you then was only too true. God knows when I struck him I did not wish for that; but how was I to see him with you in his arms—carrying you off through the dark night, and from your own house, without raising my stick to strike him? I don't say this to be blaming you now, and I don't ask you to tell me why you were there; but you must know, dearest, that it was for your sake I raised my hand; and though the blow I struck has killed him you loved, you shouldn't now at such a moment turn from your brother, who has brought all this upon himself only to protect your honer and your name."

Still Feemy did not turn her face towards him, or answer him.

"Well! I know what's on your heart, and may be it's as heavy as that which is weighing on my own. I must say a word or two to the owld man, that he may not larn from sthrangers what it is his son has done; and then I must wish good-bye to Ballycloran—I trust for iver! But there's one thing I'll ask you, Feemy, before I go. There'll be men from Carrick here before the night is over, looking for me; and when they come, they'll be asking you all manner of questions about this deed; tell them it was I that did it—but tell them how, and why I did it; tell them that it was not my purpose to kill the man, but that I could not see him dragging my sister from her house before my eyes, without raising my stick against the man that was doing it; that, Feemy, is all I want of you,"—and he turned to go, but when he reached the door, he returned, and putting his hand on his sister's shoulder, said—"Sister, my own sister, will you kiss me before I lave you for so long?"

Feemy shuddered horribly as she felt his hand upon her. Thady quickly withdrew it, for he saw it was all covered with blood; Feemy, however, had seen it, for she screamed loudly—she had raised her head to answer, and at last she said—"Kiss you! no; I hate you—you're a murdherer; you've murdhered him because you knew I loved him; go away—go out of that; you'll kill me too if you stand there with his blood upon your hand!"

Thady, who had fallen on his knees to kiss his sister, now hastily jumped upon his feet, and a dark frown came upon his brow. It was just upon his lips to tell his sister to whose folly it was owing that Myles Ussher was now a corpse; but before the words had left his mouth he checked himself. Even then, at that saddest moment of all, when the horrid word he so dreaded, had been applied to him by the only person whom he really loved, he was able to restrain his passion, and was too high-minded to add to the suffering of his sister, though she was so unjust and cruel to him.

"God forgive you, Feemy," he said; "but that's a cruel word to come from you!"—and he left the room. He met the two girls in the passage, for Biddy had returned from Mrs. Mehan's, whither she had gone after Ussher had passed, and she was now horrified to find that her mistress's plans had been, as she thought, defeated by her brother, and her departure prevented.

"Good God! Mr. Thady," said she, with pretended astonishment, "what ails the misthress then?"

"Go in to her, Biddy, she'll want you; Captain Ussher is dead," and he went into his father's room.

Here a still more distressing scene awaited him. He felt that if he meant to escape he should not lose much time, but he could not leave his father in ignorance of what had taken place. Larry was sitting, as usual, over the fire with his pipe in his mouth, and was nearly asleep, when Thady came in. The noise of the closing door roused him, however; but he only put his empty glass to his lips, and when he found there was nothing in it he turned round again dissatisfied to the fire.

"Larry," said his son, "I've bad news for you."

"You've always bad news. I niver knew you have anything else."

"I'm going to lave you, father, altogether."

"Faix, then, that's no such bad news," said the cross old man. "The door's open, and you've my lave; may be we'll do as well without you, as we're like to do with you."

Thady made no answer to this piece of silly ill-nature, but continued—"Larry, you'll be sorry to hear what I've to tell you, but I'd sooner you should hear it from me than from another. Myles Ussher is dead; it was I, father, that killed him."

At the first declaration the old man had turned round in his chair, and he sat staring at his son; but when he heard the second and more dreadful part of the story, his jaw dropped, and he sat for some time the picture of an idiot.

"He was bringing disgrace on you, Larry, and on your name; he was disgracing your family and your daughter, and myself; he was dragging Feemy away with him by night. I saw him with her, speechless and fainting in his arms, and I struck him down as he was doing it with my stick. I didn't think, father, to strike so hard, but his skull was broken, and he died without a struggle."—The old man still stared at him, and Thady continued,

"And now, father, I am going to lave you; for av I'm found here, when they come to look for me, they'll take me to prison, and may be when they come to hear the truth of it all,—and I suppose they will,—they'll see I didn't mane to kill him; but if they call it murdher, why then I trust you'll niver see me agin."

"Murdher," at last said the old man, laughing; "who doubts but that it was murdher? in course they'll call it murdher. Well, he was the only frind you'd left me, and now that you've murdhered him, you may go now; you may go now—but mind I tell you, they'll be sure to hang you."

This was old Macdermot's last address to his son. It was very evident that the poor old man had gradually become more and more imbecile during the last few days, and the suddenness of the melancholy news he now heard utterly destroyed his mind. Each, however, of the dreadful words he uttered fell with an awful appearance of intention and sane purpose on the ears of his son. He had hitherto restrained his feeling powerfully, and had shown no outward signs of strong emotion; but when his father said that there was no doubt the deed he'd done was murder, he burst into a flood of tears, and left the room without being able to articulate a word.

When the police came, which they did before the night was over, in search of Thady, they were unable to make anything of the old man; at first he took them for emissaries of Keegan's, and swore that they should not have admittance into the house, and when they were in it he endeavoured to hide himself, declaring at the same time, that he understood the law; that the money was not due till November, and that Keegan had no right to send the men there, harassing him, yet. When, however, he was made to understand that it was not about Keegan and the rents, but about the death of Ussher that they had come, he whimpered and whined, declaring that he had not murdered him; that he loved Ussher better than any one in the world—yes, better than his own children—and that for the world he would not hurt him. When at length the men explained to him that they were only there to look for Thady, he was worse than ever; for he began cursing his son dreadfully, swearing that if he had committed the murder, he would neither hide nor screen him, and finally declaring that he hoped they might catch him and hang him.

The next morning he was taken away to give evidence before the Coroner at Carrick-on-Shannon. It was the first day since the summer that he had been above a few yards from his own hall-door, and though the day was fine, he suffered much from the cold. When he got to his destination he could hardly speak; the room was greatly crowded, for the whole neighbourhood had by that time heard of the event; and when the poor old man had warmed himself by the fire, near which a seat had been procured for him, he smiled and nodded to those around, perfectly unconscious of the cause which had brought him there, but evidently thinking it must be holiday occasion.

Brady had stated to the Coroner pretty accurately what he knew, for there was nothing which it could have benefited him to falsify. The two girls proved that after Brady had started with the body, Thady had had interviews with his sister and his father, and it was necessary that both of them should be examined.

When the book, on which he was to be sworn, was handed to Larry Macdermot, he at first refused it, and when it was again tendered to him, he put it in his pocket, and made the man who gave it to him a bow. The Coroner, seeing he was in such a state of mind as rendered him unable to give evidence and unfit to be sworn, asked him some questions on the subject, but Larry instantly began to cry, and protest his own innocence, swearing, as he had done before, that he had loved Ussher better even than his own family.

It was a most melancholy sight—that poor, weak old man, whom so many of those now present had known so long, and who so very few years before had been in the full strength of manhood and health, for even now he was hardly more than fifty.

But sad as all this was, the examination of Feemy was still worse. As she had been actually present at the moment when Ussher had been killed, it was absolutely necessary that her evidence should be taken by the Coroner; and the sergeant of police, who came with a car from Carrick for them in the morning, insisted, in spite of all that she and the maids could say to the contrary, that she must accompany him back. She had got on the same car with her father; Biddy and the other girl were on the same seat with her, one on each side; but before they reached Drumsna, she was in such a state, that they could hardly keep her on the seat.

When they reached that village, the car was stopped by Father John. He had heard of the sad occurrence late on the previous evening, for Pat Brady had spared no exertions in disseminating the news of the catastrophe far and wide as he returned from Carrick. He had stopped at the priest's gate, and finding Father John absent on a sick visit, had nearly frightened Judy out of her life, by telling her what had happened. Father John had not returned home till two in the morning, and he then heard some garbled version of the story, from which he was led to believe that Thady was in custody at Carrick, for the murder of Ussher.

Early on the morning of the inquest, he went into Carrick, and there learnt from the police the truth, and ascertained the fact that an inquest was held on the body that day, and that both old Macdermot and his daughter were to be examined at it.

Up to this time Father John did not know that Feemy had left Drumsna; and though the police informed him that she had been absolutely present when the fatal blow was struck, he could not believe it, and hurried off to Mrs. McKeon's, to tell her all that he knew, and learn from her all that she could tell him.

The kind-hearted man hardly knew what he was doing, so shocked was he, and surprised by what he had heard. He could hardly believe that after what Thady had said to him, after the promises he had made, he would deliberately, and with premeditation, plan and execute Ussher's murder. Such an idea was incompatible with the knowledge that he had of Thady's disposition, and he concluded that

Q

there must have been some quarrel between the two men, in which Ussher had fallen the victim. He little dreamt when he started for Mrs. McKeon's, how much more justly the blood which had been shed was to be attributed to the sister than to the brother, or he would hardly dared again to solicit her kind offices for his *protegée*.

When he got to Drumsna, the McKeons were only just rising from breakfast, but Father John saw, on entering the room, from their grave and anxious faces, that they had all heard the news. Tony had been out to his fields before breakfast, and had there been told by one of the men that Ussher's body had on the previous night been taken through Drumsna to the police station at Carrick, and that it was said that Thady Macdermot, the murderer, had already escaped out of the country.

This tale Tony had communicated in a whisper to his wife, and she had afterwards told the girls. What was the good of keeping it secret? before the evening it would be known to the whole country. When Father John came in, they all crowded round him, to learn what really might be relied on as the truth of the case; but he could only tell them that it was too sure that Ussher had died by Thady's hand,—that that young man was not in custody,—and that he had been informed that Feemy herself was present when the blow had been struck.

"Feemy and their poor father," added Father John, "are to be examined to-day before the Coroner; it will be a dreadful thing for her, poor girl! to be forced to tell all her secrets, to declare all that she would most wish to conceal before the mob that will be in the room at Carrick."

"Yes," added Tony, "and to stand there without any one to support her, and to be asked questions, which if they're answered correctly, may be will hang her brother."

"I'll never believe," said Father John, "that he killed him in cold blood. Yourself, Mrs. McKeon hasn't a kinder heart within you than that young man; he never would have committed a wilful, premeditated murder; I don't think yet it will come to be so bad as what McKeon says. But when did Feemy leave this? I thought she was here, and was to stay here for some time to come."

Mrs. McKeon then explained how Feemy had insisted on returning home the morning after the ball, with the promise of returning again. After talking over the various unaccountable circumstances of the case, without once suspecting that Feemy had consented to and had actually been in the act of going off with Ussher, Mrs. McKeon agreed, at the instigation of her husband and the priest, to accompany Feemy to the inquest, and after it was over to bring her to her own house, and to allow her to remain there till something should be definitely arranged as to her future residence.

"For," said Tony, "Ballycloran will be no place for her again, nor the county either for the matter of that; but now that she's unhappy she shan't want a roof over her head; we were glad enough to see her when she held her head high, and I wouldn't advise any one to say much against her now she's in throuble—unless he wished to quarrel with me." And Tony McKeon closed his fist as much as to show that if any one did entertain so preposterous a wish he could be little better than a born idiot.

Tony then sent a message into Carrick for a postchaise, that Feemy might not be exposed to the curiosity of every one in the street by sitting on an outside vehicle; and when she arrived in Drumsna from Ballycloran, she was taken off the car on which her father was sitting, and brought into Mrs. McKeon's house. She would not, however, speak to any one, and could hardly sit on a chair without being supported. She squeezed, however, her kind friend's hand, when she promised to go to the inquest with her, and seemed grateful when she was told that she should not return to Ballycloran, but should again occupy her old quarters at Drumsna.

At length they got into the hack chaise, and were driven into the yard of the hotel where the inquest was to be held. This was the same house in which McKeon and his party had dined on the evening before the races, and there the cold stiff body of the man was lying on the same table round which he and so many others were carousing but a few hours since. There he lay, at least all that mortal remained of him, who was then so joyous, so reckless, and so triumphant, in the very room in which he had boasted, in his wilful wickedness, of the sad tragedy he was intending to inflict on those who had been so friendly to him at Ballycloran, and of which he was now himself the first victim.

The table on which he was laid out had been hastily removed for the dance, and it had now been as hastily replaced for its present purpose. The laurel wreaths with which the walls had been decorated were yet remaining, and when the Coroner entered the room his foot slipped on a faded flower, which some wearied beauty had dropped when leaving it on the previous morning. Little more than four and twenty hours had elapsed since the fiddles were playing there, and some of those who were now summoned upon their oaths to decide in what manner Ussher had met his death, had on that morning been nearly the last to leave the room in which they were now to exercise so different a vocation.

Biddy and Katty were first examined, and it was from the evidence of the former that Father John first heard that Feemy had agreed to elope with Ussher; and it appeared from what the girl said that her mistress was to have left the house some time previous to the time at which the other girl proved that she had been brought back by her brother. This added greatly to his sorrow; but at the same time, he now instantly perceived under what provocation Thady had struck the fatal blow. Brady proved that his master had confessed to him that it was he who had killed Ussher and that he had said that when he did so his sister was in Ussher's arms. The stick was then brought forward, which was proved to be the one usually carried by Thady; and the blood upon the stick, and the nature of the wound upon the dead man's head, left no doubt that this was the weapon with which he had been killed.

The father was then brought in, and we have already seen the manner in which he conducted himself. It was now necessary to examine Feemy, and at last she came in, almost carried in Mrs. McKeon's arms, with a thick veil over her face, which, however well it hid her countenance, by no means rendered her sobs inaudible. Two chairs were placed for them by the table, and when they were both seated the book was handed to Feemy; then she had to take her glove from her right hand, and this was so wetted with her tears, and she herself was so weak, that it was long before she could get it off; and when she had taken the oath,—when she had sworn to tell not only the truth, but the whole truth,—she found it impossible to speak a word, and the Coroner was obliged to ask her questions, to which Mrs. McKeon was allowed to get the answers, spoken below her breath, and in whispers.

"Did she know Captain Ussher was dead?"

"She did."

"Did she know that it was her brother who had killed him? Was it her brother Thady?"

"Yes, it was."

"How did she know it was he who had done it? Did she see him do it?"

"No, she didn't see him."

"How then did she know it?"

"He had told her so afterwards."

"Could she say how he killed him?"

"No, she could not."

"Or why?"

To this question even Mrs. McKeon could get no answer.

"Where was she when Captain Ussher was killed?"

No answer.

"Was she with Captain Ussher?"

"She believed she was."

"Why, or for what purpose, was she with him?"

To this question, although pressed for some time, she would not answer; and Mrs. McKeon, who was up to this time totally ignorant of the locality in which Ussher had been killed, and was really unaware how it had come to pass that Feemy was present at the time, was quite unable to suggest to her what answer she ought to make; and finding that it was with difficulty she could keep Feemy from falling from her chair, she told the Coroner she was really afraid Miss Macdermot was so ill, that she would be quite incapable of answering any more questions; and she added, that considering all the circumstances of the case,—that the young lady had been engaged to the unfortunate man who was dead, and was the sister of the man who had killed him, it was not to be wondered at, if she found her dreadful position too much for her.

The Coroner answered that he was quite prepared to give Miss Macdermot every indulgence in his power, as he felt as strongly as any one could do the distressing situation in which the young lady was placed, but that it was absolutely imperative that the last question he had asked should be answered. And that he was sure when he stated that the result of the inquest very probably depended on what the answer to the question might be,—as from that the jurors would probably have to decide whether her brother was to be accused of murder, or merely homicide,—he was quite sure, he said, under these circumstances, Miss Macdermot would make an effort to answer it fully and firmly. He was willing, he added, to put the question in a form which might render it more simple for her to answer, though it would oblige him to say that which he feared would be still further distressing to her feelings.

He then told her and Mrs. McKeon, that from the evidence of the servants it had appeared that she, Feemy, had agreed to elope with Captain Ussher; and that, as far as could be judged from circumstantial evidence, she was in fact eloping with him when Thady had killed him; now, it was necessary for her to state whether she was there of her own good will, going away with him; or if not, what she was doing at the moment of the tragical occurrence.

After many fruitless attempts made by Mrs. McKeon to get an answer to this, Feemy said, through her friend, that she was sitting down.

"Does she mean that she was sitting down when the blow was struck?"

"She doesn't know where she was."

"When was she sitting down?"

"She was sitting down till Captain Ussher lifted her up."

"When Captain Ussher lifted her up, was she going away willingly with him?"

"Yes, she was."

"Did she struggle with him at all?"

"No."

"Did any of her friends know she was going with him?"

Before, however, the poor girl could be got to answer this question, she had fainted, and it was found impossible to restore her for a long time; and when she had recovered, it was only to give way to the most distressing cries and hysterical shrieks; she threw herself on the floor of the bedroom to which she had been taken, and Mrs. McKeon was afraid that she would have broken a blood-vessel in the violence of her emotions. As it was, she was for a long time spitting blood, and fell from one fit into another, until the medical man who was now with her was afraid that she would become entirely delirious.

It had long been found impossible to proceed with her examination any further. She had, however, unwittingly, and hardly knowing at the time what she was saying, given evidence against ner brother which the facts of the case did not warrant.

For when Thady had first seen her, she was not going willingly with Ussher; she had then fainted, and Ussher was dragging her, apparently with violence, along the road.

When it was found in the inquest room that Feemy Macdermot could not possibly attend again, the coroner gave the jury the substance of the evidence on the case. He pointed out to them that though there could be no doubt that young Macdermot was the man by whom Captain Ussher had been killed, still if they thought there was sufficient ground for them to believe that Ussher was ill-treating his sister, and that the brother had interfered on her behalf, they should not come to the decision that murder had been committed.

The jury, after consulting for a short time, brought in a verdict of wilful murder against Thaddeus Macdermot; and, accordingly, a coroner's warrant was issued for his apprehension and trial, and was handed over to the police, that they might lose no time in endeavouring to take him prisoner.

CHAPTER XXII.

THE ESCAPE

THADY left the house immediately after the last cruel speech his father made to him, with the tears running fast down his face. He leapt down the steps, hurried across the lawn, through the little shrubbery, and over the wall into the road. He did not dare to go alone down the avenue, and by the spot where Ussher's body had lain, and where the ground would still be moist with his blood.

His father's words still rang dreadfully in his ears—" Murdered! of course they'll call it murder! of course they'll be sure to hang you!" And then he thought of all the bearings of the case, and it seemed to him that his father must be right; that there could be no doubt but that all men would call it by that horrid name which sounded so hideously in his ears. If that which he had done was not murder, what manner in which one man could kill another would be thought so? It was now evident to him that Feemy had been with Ussher willingly—that she was there of her own consent and by appointment; and merely because she had fainted in his arms, he had struck him down and killed him. Of course his father was right; of course they would call it murder. And then again, even if he could justify the deed to himself—even if he could make himself believe that the man was at the time using violence to his sister—how could he get that proved? whereas proofs of her having consented to go off with him would no doubt not be wanting. And then again, Thady remembered—and as he did so the cold sweat stood upon his brow—how lately he had sat in company where the murder of this very man whom now he had killed had been coolly canvassed and decided on, and he had been one of those who were to be banded together for its execution. Would all this be forgotten at his trial? Would there not certainly be some one to come forward at that horrid hour, and swear these things against him—ay, and truly swear them? And then he fancied the precision with which he knew each damning word he had lightly uttered would be brought against him. Would not these things surely condemn him? Would they not surely hang him? It would be useless for him, then, to open his bosom and to declare to them how hateful—even during the feverish hours of that detested evening—the idea of murder had been to his soul. It would be useless for him to tell them that even then, at that same time, he had cautioned Ussher to avoid the danger with which he was threatened. It would be vain for him to declare how soon and how entirely he had since repented of the folly of which he had on that occasion been guilty. The stern faces by whom he would be surrounded at his trial—when he should stand in that disgraceful spot, with his head leaning on that bar so often pressed by murderers, miscreants, and thieves—would receive his protestations very differently from that benign friend who had previously comforted him in his misery. They would neither listen to nor believe his assurances; and he said involuntarily to himself—"Murder! of course they'll call it murder! of course they'll hang me!"

The oftener he thought of this, the more he hurried, for he felt that the police would be soon in search of him, and that at most he had but that night to escape from them. As these ideas crossed his mind he hastened along the lane leading to Drumleesh, sometimes running and sometimes walking, till the perspiration stood upon his brow. If it was murder that he had done—if the world should consider it as murder—then he would most probably soon be in the same condition as that criminal whose trial had so vividly occurred to his recollection a few days ago. At that time the idea had only haunted him; he had only then dreamt of the possibility of his situation being the same as that man's, and the very horror he had then felt at the bare thought had made him determined to avoid those who could even talk of the crime which would lead to that situation. But now he had of his own accord committed that crime; and how had he done it? In such a manner that he could by no possibility escape detection. Then again he tried to comfort himself by reflecting that it was not murder—that his intention had not been to murder the man; but his father's horrid words again rang through his ears, and he felt that there was no hope for him but in flight.

The moon got up when he was about half-way to his destination, and he left the road lest by chance there might be any one out at that hour who would recognise him. He crept on by the hedges and ditches, sometimes running along the bits of grass between the tillage and fences—sometimes having almost to wade through the wet bottoms which he crossed, often falling, in his hurry and in the imperfect light of the cloudy moon, till at last, tired, hot, and covered with dirt, pale with fear, and nearly overcome by the misery of his own reflections, he reached Corney Dolan's cabin. It was now about eleven o'clock; it had been past ten when he left Ballycloran, and in the interval he had traversed above five Irish miles. There was no light in the cabin, which was a solitary one, standing on the edge of a bog. Now he was there he feared to knock, as he did not know what to say to Corney when he should come to the door. Besides, he was aware that his hands and coat were soiled with blood, and he was unwilling that the inmates of the cabin should see him in that plight.

He had, however, no time to spare, and as it was necessary that he should do something, after pausing a few minutes, he knocked at the door. No one answered, and he had to knock two or three times before he was asked in a woman's voice who he was, and what he wanted there at that hour of the night. He stated that he wanted to see Corney Dolan. The woman told him that Corney Dolan wasn't at home, and that he couldn't see him. Thady knew that he lived alone with his mother, an aged woman, nearly eighty years old, and that it was she who was speaking to him now.

"Nonsense, mother," said he; "he's at home I know, and I must see him. Don't you know me?"

"Faix, then, I don't—and I don't want," said the old hag. "At any rate, Corney's not here; so you may jist go back agin, whoever you call yerself."

"But where is he, then? Can you tell me where I'll find him?"

"I can't tell you thin. What should I know myself? So now you know as much about it as I do."

"Well, then, get up and let me in. Don't you know me? I'm Corney's landlord, Thady Macdermot. I'll wait here till he comes; so get up and let me in."

There was a silence for some time; then he heard the old woman say to some one else,

"The Lord be praised! It can't be him—it can't be Mr. Thady coming here at this time of night. Don't stir I tell ye—don't stir, avick!"

"Oh! but it wor him, mother. Shure, don't I know his voice?" answered the child that the old woman had spoken to.

"I tell you it is me," shouted Thady. "Open the door, will you! and not keep me here all night!"

The child now got up and opened the door, and let him into the single room which the cabin contained. There were still a few embers of turf alight on the hearth, but not sufficient to have enabled Thady to see anything had not the moon shone brightly in through the door. There was but one bed in the place,—at the end of the cabin farthest from the door, standing between the hearth and the wall, and in this the old woman was lying. The child, about eight years, had jumped out of bed, stark naked, and now in this condition was endeavouring with a bit of stick to poke the hot embers together, so as to give out a better heat and light.

But Thady was in want of neither, and he therefore desired the boy to get into bed, and upsetting with his foot the little heap which the urchin had so industriously collected together for his benefit, so as to extinguish the few flickering flames which it afforded, he sat down to try and think what it would now be best for him to do.

"Where's Corney, then," he said, "at this hour? Will he be long before he's here?"

"Not a one of me rightly knows, yer honer; maybe it'll not be long afore he's here, and maybe it'll not be afore the morning," said the child.

"And, maybe, not then," added his grandmother. "There's no knowing when he'll be here; maybe not for days. I don't know what's come to them at all now—being out night skirring through the counthry; it can't come to no good, any ways."

"When Corney's at home, where does he sleep?" said Thady, looking round the cabin for a second bed, but seeing none.

"He mostly takes a stretch then down there afore the fire; but Corney's not over partickler where he sleeps. For the matter of that, I b'lieve he sleeps most out in the bog at day time."

Thady now sat down on one of the two rude stools with which the place was furnished, either to wait for Corney, or to make up his mind what other steps he would take. He had closed and bolted the door, and was just in the act of asking the old woman whether Joe Reynolds was at present living on his bit of land, or if not, where he was, when he heard footsteps coming up to the little path to the door, and the woman, sitting up in bed, said,

"There's both on 'em thin; get up, Terry, and open the door."

One of the men outside rattled the latch quietly, to let the inmates know who it was that desired admittance; and the naked boy again jumped out of bed, and opening the door, ran back and jumped in again.

Two men now entered, whom Thady, as they appeared in the moonlight through the open door, at once recognised as Joe Reynolds and Corney Dolan. He was seated close to the fire, and in the darkness and obscurity of the cabin, they did not at first perceive him.

A few moments since he had been longing for these two men who now stood before him, as the only persons on whom he could depend for security and concealment, and now that they were there he almost wished them back again, so difficult did he find it to tell them what he had to say, and to beg of them the assistance he required.

"Who the divil are you?" said Corney; "who's this you've got here, mother?—and what made you let him in here this time of night?"

"Shure it's the young masther, Corney, and he axing afther you; you wouldn't have me keeping him out in the cowld, and he waiting there to see you that ought to have been at home and asleep two hours since."

"Faix, Mr. Thady, and is that yerself?" said Corney; "well, anyway you're welcome here."

"I'm glad to see you here, Mr. Thady," said Joe; "didn't I tell you you'd be coming? though it's a quare time you've chosen. Didn't I tell you you'd be changing your mind?"

"But was yer honer wanting me, Mr. Thady," said Corney; "'deed but this is a bad place for you to come to; sorrow a light for ye or the laste thing in life; what for did you not get a light, you ould hag, when the masther came in?"

"A light is it, Corney; and how was I to be getting a light, when there's not been a sighth of a bit of candle in the place since last winter, nor likely to be the way you're going on now."

"Whisht there now," said Joe; "we'll be doing very well without a light; but why wasn't you down here earlier, Mr. Thady?—We two have just come from mother Mulready's, an' by rights, as you've come round agin, you should have been there with us."

"Never mind that, Joe, but come out; I want to spake to you."

"Did you hear the news about Ussher?" continued Joe without moving, and in a whisper which the old woman could not hear. "That blackguard Ussher has escaped out of the counthry afther all, without paying any of us the debt that he owed us, for all the evils he's done. He went away out of Mohill this night, an' he's not to be back agin; av I'd known it afore he started I'd have stopped him in the road, an' by G—d he should niver have got alive out of the barony."

"But did you hear he was gone?" said Corney.

"I did," replied Thady: "but Joe I want to spake to you, and there's no time to spare; come here," and Joe followed him to the door. "Come further; I don't want him to hear what I've to say to you;" and he walked on some little way before he continued,— "you were wishing just now that you had shed Ussher's blood?"

"Well—I wor; I suppose, Mr. Thady, you're not going to threaten me with the magisthrate again. I wor wishing it—an' I do wish it; he was the hardest man on the poor—an' the cruelest ruffian I iver knew. Isn't there my brother, that niver even acted agin the laws in the laste thing in life,—the quietest boy, as you know, Mr Thady, anywhere in the counthry, an' who knew no more about stilling than the babe that's unborn; isn't he lying in gaol this night all along of him? an' it an't only him; isn't there more? many more in the same way, in gaol all through the counthry; an' who but him put 'em there? I do wish he was for-a-nens't me this moment, an' that I might lave him here as cowld a corpse as iver wor stretched upon the ground!"

"I tell you, Joe, av you had your wish—av you struck the blow, and the man you so hate was dead beneath your feet, you'd give all you had—you'd give your own life to see him agin, standing alive upon the ground, and to feel for one moment that you'd not his blood to answer for."

"By G—d! no, Mr. Thady; I'm not so wake; and as for answering for his blood, by the blessed Virgin, but I'd think it war a good deed to rid the counthry of such a tyrant."

"He'll niver act the tyrant again, Joe, for he is dead. I struck him down with my stick in the avenue at Ballycloran, this night, and he niver moved agin afther I hit him."

"The holy Virgin save us! But are you in arnest, Mr. Thady? D'ye main to say he's dead—that you killed him?" And after walking on a little, he said,—"By the holy Virgin, I'd sooner it had been myself; for I could have borne the thoughts of having done it better than you are like to do. An' what did you do with the body?"

"Brady took it into Carrick."

"And does Brady know it war you did it?"

"Yes, they all know it—father and all; what was the use of telling a lie about? Feemy was with him when I struck him."

"And war she going off with him? Niver mind, Mr. Thady, niver mind; it's a comfort to think you've saved your sisther from him, an' you know what a ruffian he was. By all the powers of glory there's a weight off my mind now I know he's not escaped from the counthry, where he caused so much misery, and did so much ill. But I'd a deal sooner it had been I that done it than yourself."

"I wish it war not done at all—I wish he were alive this day. What will I do now, Joe?"

"Faix, that's the question; any way, this is not the place for you any longer; they'd have you in Carrick Gaol before to-morrow night, av you were not out of this, an' far out of this too."

"Where is it you have the stills, Joe? Av I were there, couldn't I be safe, for a little time at laste, till I got some plan of getting entirely out of the counthry? Or may be when they hear the case, and how it all happened, they mightn't think it murder at all,—the Coroner I main; and then I could go home agin, or at any rate go away where I choose without hindrance; it's little I care where I was, so long as it's not in prison."

"I'm afraid, Mr. Thady, there's no hopes for you in that way. The magisthrates, with Jonas Brown at the head of them, will be a dail too willing to make a bad case of it, the divil mend them, to let you off; an' the only thing for you is, to keep out of their hands."

"Would they find me there, Joe, up in the mountains, where you have the stills?"

"They might, and they mightn't; but if you war there, an' they did find you, they'd be finding the stills too, an' the boys wouldn't like that."

"Where shall I go then? I thought you'd be able to help me. In heaven's name, what shall I do? the night's half over now: can't you think of any place where I might be, for to-morrow at any rate? I depended on you, Joe, and now you won't help me."

"There you're wrong. I'm thinking now, where is the best place for you: and by G—d as long as I can stick to you, I will; both becase you were always a kind masther to the poor, an' becase the man you killed war him I hated worse than all the world besides; but it's no asy thing to say where you'd be safest. D'you know Aughacashel, Mr. Thady?"

"I niver was there, but I know that's the name of the big mountain over Loch Allen, to the north of Cash."

"Well, that's where the stills are mostly at work now, an' that's where I was to be myself, to-morrow evening; but now we must both be there before the sun's up, for no one must see us on the road. But, Mr. Thady, how'll I do about taking you there, when you wouldn't come to Mulready's to take the oath, which all must do afore they'll be allowed among the boys that is together, or as will be together there to-morrow evening?"

Thady then promised him, that when he reached their destination, he would take any or every oath that might be proposed to him; that he would join their society in every respect, whatever might be its laws, and that if they would assist him in his present condition by affording him whatever security might be in their power, he would faithfully conform to all their rules and regulations. So far did his fears and the agitated state of his mind overcome the great repugnance which still he felt to break the solemn promise he had given Father John, and which he had so faithfully intended to keep.

Reynolds reflected that though it was contrary to their regulations to bring a stranger to the haunts where his companions carried on their illegal trade, they could hardly be unwilling to give shelter to the man who had killed the enemy whom they all so cordially hated, and to murder whom they were all sworn; particularly when his present necessity of concealment arose from the fact of his having done so. Reynolds had an idea of justice in his composition: he knew that had he murdered Ussher, his companions would have used every effort to conceal him, and to baffle his pursuers; and he was determined that they should do as much for Thady.

He went back to the cabin for Corney Dolan, and told him the story which he had just heard; and at about midnight the party started for the mountains.

Aughacashel is a mountain on the eastern side of Loch Allen, near the borders of the County Cavan—uncultivated and rocky at the top, but nevertheless inhabited, and studded with many miserably poor cabins, till within about a quarter of a mile of the summit. The owners of these cabins, with great labour, have contrived to obtain wretchedly poor crops of potatoes from the barren soil immediately round their cabins. To their agricultural pursuits many joined the more profitable but hazardous business of making potheen, and they were generally speaking, a lawless, reckless set of people—paying, some little, and others no rent, and living without the common blessings or restraints of civilization: no road, or sign of a road, came within some miles of them; Drumshambo, the nearest village, was seven or eight miles distant from them; and although they knew that neither the barrenness of their locality, nor the want of means of approach would altogether secure them from the unwelcome visits of the Revenue police or the Constabulary, still they felt sure that neither of these inimical forces could come into their immediate neighbourhood, without their making themselves aware of their approach, in time to guard against any injury which they might do them, either by removing all vestiges of their trade, or by sending those who were in fear of being taken up, into the more inaccessible portions of the mountain. On the western side of Aughacashel, immediately over Loch Allen, and about half way between the lowlands and the summit, a kind of rude limekiln had been made, apparently for the purpose of burning lime for the neighbouring land; but the very poor state of the rocky ground about, which gave signs of but little industry, afforded evidence that the limekiln had not added much to the agricultural wealth of the country. It was now at any rate made use of for other purposes, for it was in here that Joe Reynolds at present usually worked his still. There were only two cabins immediately close to it; one of which was occupied by a very old man and his daughter, but in which Corney Dolan and Reynolds resided, when they were away from Drumleesh; and the other belonged to another partner in the business, who considered himself the owner of the limekiln, and the head of the party concerned in it. This man's name was Daniel Kennedy, and to the reckless, desperate contempt of authority and hatred of those who exercised it, which characterized Reynolds, he added a cruelty of disposition, and a love of wickedness, from which the other was much more free.

This was the place to which his two guides were now conducting Thady, and where it was proposed that he should, at any rate for some time, conceal himself from those, who, it was presumed, would soon be scouring the country in search of him. It was now a bright moonlight night, and the three men hurried across the country with all the haste they could make. Little was said between them as they went, excepting observations made between Joe and his comrade, as to the characters and occupations of the residents in the various cabins by which they passed. After going for some considerable way across fields and bogs and bottom lands, they came out on a lane, running close round a small lake lying in the bed of the low hills which rose on the other side of it. The water was beautifully calm, and the moon shining immediately down upon it, gave it the appearance of a large surface of polished silver. At this spot the fields came close down to the road, and also to the water, and in the corner thus formed stood a very small poor cabin.

This lake was Loch Sheen, and it was in that cabin that Ussher had apprehended Tim Reynolds and the two other men, little more than a fortnight ago.

Joe stopped a moment when he reached the spot, till Thady, who was following the other man, had come up, and then, pointing to the low door, close to which he stood, said,

"The last deed as that ruffian did as now lies so low was in that cabin. It war there he sazed Tim, an' dragged him off with ropes round his arms, an' sent him to Ballinamore Bridewell, an' all for spaking a few words of comfort to an owld woman he'd known since he war a little child. I swore, Mr. Thady, that that man should be put beneath the sod before the time came round that Tim should be out agin; an' this very night I war a grieving in my heart to think that he war out of the country safe an' merry—ready agin to play the same bloody game with them among he war going; an' that I should let him go without so much as making one effort to keep my word with him! By G—d, Mr. Thady, quare as you may think it, who are now so low within yerself with what you've done, that thought was heavy on my heart this night. Had I known what way he war to travel, I'd followed him, had it been for days an' nights, till I had got one fair blow. By dad, he would niver have wanted a second. Corney what's the owld hag doing since her two sons is in gaol along with Tim?"

"Ah! thin, she's doing badly enough; she war niver from her bed since. Faix, Joe, they'll niver be out in time to bury her."

"Is it starving she is?"

"Well thin, I b'lieve that's the worst of it; that an' the aguy, an' no one to mind her at all, is enough to kill an owld woman like her."

"Niver mind," replied Joe, "it will be a comfort to her any way to hear that Ussher's gone before her; not but what they'll go to different places, though." And then, after a time, he added, "Ussher's black soul has gone its long journey this night with more curses on it than there are stones on these shingles. But come on, lads, we mustn't be standing here; we must be in Aughacashel before sunrise, or else they'll be stopping us as we pass through the counthry."

And again they went through the clear bright moonlight. They passed Loch Sheen, and soon afterwards another little lake, lying also to the left of the road, and then they found themselves in the small village of Cashcarrigan. This they passed through silently and quickly and without speaking a word, and having proceeded about half a mile on the road towards Ballinamore, they again left it and took to the fields. They went along the northern margin of Loch Dieney, running where the ground was hard enough, at other times stepping from one dry sod to another, through gaps and fences, which seemed as well known to Thady's guides as the cabins in which they had passed their lives. They left Drumshambo to their left, and at about four in the morning they came to Loch Allen. Here they got upon a road which for some way skirts the eastern side of the lake, along which they ran for about a mile and a half, and then turned into a small boreen or path, and began to ascend the mountains.

"Asy boys, now," said Corney; "we're all right when we're here; an', by the powers! I'm hot," and the man began wiping his brow with his sleeve.

"What, Corney, you're not blown yet!" said the other, "an' here's Mr. Thady as fresh as a four year old. Come along, man; the sooner he's got a snug room over his head the better he'll be. You forget he's not accustomed to be out all night, and take his supper of moonshine, as you are. Come along, Mr. Thady; you'll soon be where you'll get as good a dhrop as iver man tasted, an' you'll feel a deal better when you've got a glass or two of that stuff in you."

Thady, who, in spite of Joe's compliment as to his freshness, was so weary that he could hardly drag his legs along, and who had seated himself for a moment upon one of the big loose stones which were scattered over the side of the hill, again rose, and they all resumed their journey. They soon lost the track of the boreen, but they still continued to ascend, keeping by the sides of the loose built walls with which the land was subdivided. It was astonishing what labour had seemingly been wasted in piling wall after wall in that barren place, and that even in spots where no attempt had been made at tillage, and where the only produce the land afforded was the food of a few miserable sheep and goats, which it might be thought could have grazed in safety without the necessity for all those numerous fences. These, however, after a time, ceased too; but just at the spot where the open mountain no longer showed any signs of man's handiwork, Dan Kennedy's lime-kiln was built, and immediately behind it were the two cabins of which we have before spoken.

It was at the door of the furthest of these two that Joe—did not knock—but raised the latch and rattled it. The old man within well knew the sign, and, getting out of bed, drew the wooden bolt, and admitted the three into the cabin. Though he did not expect Joe or Corney, and had not an idea who Thady was; and though Thady's dress, which was somewhat better than those worn by his usual associates, must have struck him as uncommon, he made no remark, but hobbled into bed again, merely saying, in Irish, "God save ye kindly, boys! it's a fine night ye've had, the Lord be praised!" There was a second bed in the place—if a filthy, ragged cotton tick filled with straw, and lying on the ground, could be called a bed—in which the old man's daughter was lying. It was nearly dark now out of doors, for the moon had disappeared, and it was hardly yet six o'clock; but one of the men lighted a candle, of which there were two or three hanging against the wall. The girl was not asleep, for her eyes were wide open, looking at the party, but she seemed not at all surprised by their entrance, or at the addition to their usual numbers, for she lay quite quiet where she was, as if such morning guests in her bed-chamber were no unusual thing.

Joe now got a stool for Thady; and he and Corney sat down opposite the fire, while Reynolds drew a stone jar out from beneath the old man's bed—he seemed well to know the place where it was to be found—and reaching a cracked cup down from a shelf which was fixed into the wall over the fire-place, filled it with spirits and handed it to Thady. He swallowed a considerable portion of it and returned it, when Joe filled it again, finished the contents

R

himself, and gave it again full to Corney, who in a very short time did the same.

"By gor," said the latter, "I wanted that; an' I tell you that's not bad work. Why, Mr. Thady—"

"Have done with your Misthers, Corney," said Joe, in a whisper, "let them find out who he is theyselves. They'll know soon enough, divil doubt them! there's no good telling them yet, any how."

"That's thrue, Joe; but as I was saying, that's not bad work; why, Mr. Thady—"

"Sorrow saze yer tongue, thin, ye born idiot!"

"Well, by dad, it comes so natural to me, Joe, to call him by his own name, that one can't help it; but it war only four o'clock when we left this, this blessed afthernoon—that is, yesterday afthernoon—an' since that we wor down at Mulready's, an' then at Drumleesh, an' now we're here agin; why how many miles is that?"

"Niver mind the miles; he"—and Joe pointed to Thady—"he has done a deal more than that in the same time—an' whatever comes of it, he did a good deed. Howsomever, if you'll take my advice, you'll take a stretch now. Meg!—I say, Meg,"—and he turned round to the girl who was lying in the corner—"get out of that, an' make room for this man to lie down. You've been asleep all night; make room for yer betthers now."

The girl, without grumbling, turned out of bed, and burthened with no feeling of conventional modesty, commenced and finished her toilet, by getting into an old ragged calico gown, and tying up, with a bit of antique tape, her long rough locks which had escaped from their bondage during her sleep. Thady for a long time resisted, but Joe at last was successful in persuading him to take advantage of the bed which Meg had so good-humouredly relinquished.

"I an' Corney have still-work to do afore daylight, an' we won't be back afore it's night," said Joe, "but do you bide here, an' you'll be safe. You must put up with the pratees this day, for there's nothing better in it at all; but I'll be getting something fitter for you by night; an' av' you feel low, which you'll be doing when you wakes, mind, there's the sperrits in the jar there undher the bed; a sup of it won't hurt you now an' agin, for indeed you'll be wanting it, by yerself here all day. An' look you,"—and he led him to the door as he spoke, and pointed to the two within—"they'll soon know who you are, an' all about it; but you needn't be talking to them, you know; an' you may be quite certain, that even should any one be axing about you, they'll niver 'peach, or give the word to the police, or any one else. Av you like to go out of this during the day, don't go further than the kiln; an' av you lie there, you could easily see them miles afore they war nigh you, even av anything should put it into their heads to think of coming afther you to Aughacashel."

The two guides then took their leave of him, and Thady laid himself down on Meg's bed, and, after a time, from sheer fatigue and exhaustion, he fell asleep.

CHAPTER XXIII.

AUGHACASHEL.

At what hour he woke Thady did not know, but it was broad day, and the sun was high in the heavens; he would have slept again if he could, that he might again forget the dreadful deed which had made the last night so horrible, but he could not; he was obliged therefore to get up, and when he did so he felt himself weak for want of food. Meg it appears had gone out. The old man could not speak a word of English; but Thady could talk Irish, and he had no difficulty in getting plenty of potatoes from him, and as he was eating them the old man pulled out the jar of whiskey. Thady took part of another cup full, and then felt less sad than he had done before. After his breakfast he sat for a long time over the fire, smoked his pipe till he had no tobacco left in it, got up and sat down again, walked to the door and then again returned to his seat. At last he became dreadfully fatigued; he felt all the misery which a man, usually active, always feels when condemned for a time to idleness; he sat watching the turf, as though he could employ his mind, or interest himself in observing the different forms which the sods took, or how soon they would reduce themselves to ashes; then he counted the smutty rafters on which the crazy roof was supported, and then the different scraughs of which it was composed; he next endeavoured to think how the old man got through the tedium of his miserable existence. There he sat on the bed, quite imperturbable; he had not spoken ten words since Thady had got up, and seemed quite satisfied in sitting there enjoying the warmth of the fire, and having nothing to do. How Thady envied his quiescence! Then he began to reflect what had been this man's life; had he always been content to sit thus tranquil, and find his comfort in idleness? At last he got almost alarmed at this old man; why did not he speak to him?

why did he sit there so quiet, doing nothing—saying nothing—looking at nothing—and apparently thinking of nothing? it was as sitting with a dead body or a ghost—that sitting there with that lifeless but yet breathing creature. Every now and again, as he endeavoured to fill his mind with some idea that was not distressing to him, the thoughts of the horrors of his own position would come across him—the almost certainty of detection—the ignominy of his future punishment—the disgrace to his father and his sister; and even if not detected, if left in his present concealment, the horrors of such a life as he was now leading, a few hours of which had already nearly made him frantic, nearly overwhelmed him.

He got up, and leaving his companion to himself, he went to the lime-kiln and laid himself on the top of it, looking down the mountain towards Loch Allen and Drumshambs, that he might see if any of the police were coming in search of him. The open air was for a time pleasanter than the close heat of the burning turf, and solitude by far preferable to the company of that silent old man,—but it was only for a short time that he felt the relief. The horrid inactivity of the day, joined to the weight that was on his mind, nearly drove him mad; as long as he had work to do,—while he had to dispose of the dead man's body,—while he had his father and his sister near him,—as long as he was hurrying through the country with Reynolds,—the energy of whose character had for a time relieved him,—as long as the sweat was pouring down his face, and his legs had been weary under him,—he had borne much better the misery, which he felt now he was always doomed to bear; for he had then thought less of the past and the future; but now he could occupy his mind with nothing but the remembrance of the death he had inflicted, and the anticipation of the death he was to suffer. He tried to sleep, but it was in vain; he tried to imitate that old man, and let his mind sleep, but no, he could only think—he could not but think. Oh! he said to himself, that it were all over—if it were only done—if he could only swallow up the next six months and be dead and forgotten! If he had got past that dreadful trial—that cold unfeeling prison, with the harsh noise of the large key and the fetters, the stern judge, and the twelve stern men sworn to hang him if he deserved it! If he could escape the eyes of the whole country which would then be on him; the harsh, cold, solemn words which would then be addressed to him—the sorrow of his father—the shame of his sister—and, last and worst, the horrid touch of that dread man with the fatal rope! It was not death he feared—it was the disgrace of death, and the misery of the ignominious preparations. He knew in his heart that heaven could not call it murder that he had done; but he felt equally sure that man would do so.

He lay there on the lime-kiln till the sun had already set, and then he was again driven into the cabin by the cold.

There sat that silent, still old man. He had not moved from his former position, his bare feet thrust into old ragged shoes, which in some former generation had been made for some strong man double his size, and hanging down so that his toes just reached the floor—his hands resting on the quilt on each side of him, and his head dropping on his chest. Oh, what an easy, quiet mind, thought Thady, must that man have—how devoid of care and fear must he be, to be able to sit there motionless all the live-long day, and not feel it dreary, long, endless, insupportable, as he did.

The girl was still absent, and Thady again sat himself down by the fire, the blazing turf on which gave the only signs that the old man had moved. Again he counted the rafters, counted the miserable scraps of furniture, counted the sods of turf, speculated where the turf was cut—who cut it? who was the landlord of the cabin? what rent was paid? who collected it? But a minute—half a minute sufficed for the full consideration of all these things, and again he began to reflect how long it would be before the police would find him, and drag him forth from that dreary place; how long it would be before he should feel the handcuffs on his wrist; and before the first day of his concealment had passed over, he had become almost impatient for that time; and looked forward to the excitement of his capture, which he knew must sooner or later take place, with something like a wish that it might soon occur, to relieve him from the weight of his present condition.

At last he determined to speak to his companion, and after considering for some time what he should say to him, he asked him what his name was; but Thady had spoken in his usual language, and the old man, looking up, answered that he had no English.

"What's your name?" asked Thady, in Irish.

"Andy McEvoy."

"And is this cabin your own?"

"Yes."

"And who's your landlord?"

"The mountain belongs mostly to Sir Michael."

"But don't you pay any rent?"

"No."

"And what is it you do all day long?"

"Why then mostly nothing; I'm very old."

"And what does your daughter be doing?"

"Why then I don't rightly know; she's mostly out for Dan Kennedy."

"And where do you be getting the pratees?"

"'Deed I b'lieve Meg gets them mostly from Dan's garden."

"Who does Dan pay his rent to?"

"Why then I can't be saying."

It was useless carrying on a conversation any longer with such a man. He neither interested himself about his house, his food, his landlord, or his family, and Thady again held his tongue.

Soon after dusk Meg returned; she had in the folds of her gown a loaf of bread and a very small piece of bacon, and it was evident to Thady that whatever had become of Joe and the other, they had not forgotten him or their promise to provide him with some better food than the lumpers which sufficed for Andy McEvoy and his daughter.

When the old man saw the provisions his eyes glistened a little, and he clutched the dirty quilt somewhat faster, and by the eagerness he evinced for the food it was a relief to see that he had some human feeling left. Meg boiled the bacon and some potatoes together, and when they were ready, put them on the dirty deal table before Thady; she did not seem much more communicative than her father, but she asked him civilly if he would eat, and evidently knew he was of a higher rank than those with whom she was accustomed to associate, for she went through the ceremony of wiping the top of the table with the tail of her gown. Thady eat a portion of what was given him; and as he did so he saw the old man's greedy eyes glare on him, as he still sat in his accustomed seat; it was quite horrible to see how greedy and ravenous he appeared. Thady, however, left much more than he consumed, and the girl carefully putting the bit of bread away, for his breakfast in the morning, divided the remnant of the bacon with her father.

Then the man's apathy and tranquillity vanished, and the voracity with which he devoured the unaccustomed dainty showed that though he might have no demon thoughts to rack his brain, the vulture in his stomach tortured him as violently.

Joe Reynolds and Corney returned about an hour after dark, and requested Thady to come out with them, which he did. They then told him that it was necessary that he should now take the oath, which they before warned him that he would have to take if he accompanied them to their haunts at Aughacashel. He at first felt inclined to declare that he had again changed his mind, and that instead of taking this oath and joining himself in any league with them, he was prepared to return home to Ballycloran, and give himself up to the police; but his courage failed him now that he was, as it were, in their own country, and particularly after the kindness and attention that Reynolds had showed him. He therefore followed them, and they entered together the other cabin belonging to Dan Kennedy. Dan and his wife, and another man, his brother, were there. Dan was a sullen, surly, brutal looking ruffian, about fifty years old, and his wife was a fitting mate for such a man; she was dirty, squalid, and meagre; but there was a determined look of passion and self-will about her, which plainly declared that whoever Dan bullied, he did not, and could not, bully his wife.

His brother Abraham was a cripple, having no use in either of his legs; but he had an appearance of intelligence and wit in his face, which his brother in no degree shared, and he was very powerful with his arms. It was he who chiefly made the spirits, while Dan and the others procured the barley—brought it up to Aughacashel, malted it, and afterwards disposed of the whiskey.

"Well, my hearty," said Dan, as Thady followed his guides into the cabin, where his family party were engaged drinking raw spirits round the fire, "so you've done for that bloody thief of the world, have you? Joe tells me you riz agin him quick enough when you found him at his tricks with yer sisther. Divil a toe though you stirred to come to mother Mulready's when we axed you, in spite of the oath you took on the holy cross; but you're quick enough coming among us now you're in the wrong box yourself."

"Asy, Dan," said Joe; "what's the use of all that bother now; an't he here? and hasn't he rid us of him that would have got clane off from us, but for Mr. Thady here, that struck the blow we ought to have struck?"

"Thrue for you, Joe," said Abraham; "so hould yer jaw, Dan, and give me hoult of the blessed book till I give him the oath."

"All's right," said Dan; "and I'm glad to see you here, my lad of wax, seeing what sent you; but business first and play after. I s'pose if you're maning to stay here wid us—an' by G—d you're wilcome—you'll not be saying anything agin giving me or Corney there, a bit of a line to some of your frinds at Ballycloran, to be sending you up a thrifle of money or so, or a few odd bits of duds, or may be a lump of mate or bacon, or a pound or two of sugar to swaiten the punch."

Thady looked very blank at this, for he by no means wished to be writing to his friends at Ballycloran, nor were the articles mentioned in Dan's catalogue at all too plentiful in that place;

however, before he could answer, Joe indignantly scoffed at his friend's shabbiness.

"D—n it, Dan, I didn't think you war that main, to be charging a boy for the morsel he'd be ating, an' the sup he'd be taking, an' him undher a cloud, an' he afther doing us sich a sarvice."

"Av he wor one of ourselves," replied Dan; "but a gintleman the likes of him, may be, would be plased not to be beholden to the likes of us."

"Nonsense, Dan," said Joe; "don't think of giving such a line at all, Mr. Thady. I'm not so bad off, but I'll not see you wanting; you're as wilcome to everything here as daylight."

"Spake for yerself; you're mighty ready, I'm thinking, to spake for others," said Dan's helpmate; "av the gintleman's willing to help a poor man like Dan for putting a house over his head in his throubles, who's to hinder him?"

Thady, however, made them understand that he would give them no such letter to his father or his sister as they proposed, and Abraham then proceeded to administer the oath to him. By this he bound himself, first of all, never to divulge to any one, particularly not to any magistrate or policeman, or in any court of law, anything that should be done or said in that place where he now was, that might be prejudicial to any of the party. Secondly, to give all aid and assistance in his power to all those now present, and to any which might be in possession of a certain pass-word, and who might be able to answer certain questions with the fit and appointed answers, and to help in the escape or concealment of any such, when they might be either in confinement, or in dread of being arrested. And thirdly, that he would aid and assist in all schemes of vengeance and punishment which would be entered into by those with whom he was now bound, against any who attempted to molest them, but especially against all Revenue officers and their men.

To all these conditions Thady bound himself, and as he finished repeating each article after Abraham, he kissed the dirty prayer-book which that man presented to him; and having done this, he made one of the party round the fire, whilst Corney, Dan, and Joe took it by turns to go out and watch that no unexpected visitor was at hand.

When the night was tolerably advanced the three left the family of the Kennedys to themselves, and returned to Andy's cabin; and Thady having refused to allow that Meg should be again disturbed for his accommodation, they all stretched themselves upon the earthen floor before the fire, and were soon asleep.

The next morning Joe and Corney again went away early, and

Thady found himself doomed to pass just such another day as the preceding one.

After giving him his breakfast Meg again also went out, and left Thady alone with her father.

By way of propitiating the old man he gave him half the bit of bread which he was eating. Andy devoured it as he had done the bacon, and then resumed the same apathy and look of idle contentment which had so harassed Thady on the previous day. This second day was more grievous, more intolerable even than the first. He walked from the cabin to the lime-kiln, and from the lime-kiln to the cabin twenty times. He went to Kennedy's cabin, to try if he could kill time by subjecting himself to the brutality of the man or his wife; but the door was locked or bolted, and there was apparently no one in it; he clambered up the hill and then down again—and again threw himself upon the walls of the lime-kiln, and looked upon the silver lake that lay beneath him. But the day would not pass—it was not even yet noon—he could see that the sun had yet a heavy space to cover before it would reach the middle of the skies. Oh heavens! what should he do? Should he sit there from day to day, when every hour seemed like an age of misery, waiting till he should be dragged out like a badger from its hole. He looked towards the village, and to different bits of road which his eye could reach, thinking that he should see the dark uniform of a policeman; but no, nothing ever was stirring—it seemed as if nothing ever stirred —as if nothing had life by day, in that lifeless, desolate spot. At length he thought to himself that he would bear it no longer; that he would not remain for a short time indebted for his food to such a man as Dan Kennedy, and then at length be taken away to the fate which he knew awaited him, and be dragged along the roads by a policeman, with handcuffs on his wrists—a show, to be gaped at by the country! No; he would return at once, and give himself up; he would boldly go to the magistrates at Carrick —declare that he had done the deed, and under what provocation he had done it, and then let them do the worst they chose with him.

After much considering, and many changes in his resolutions, he at length determined that he would do this—that as soon as it began to be dusk, he would leave the horrid mountain where he had passed the saddest hours that he had yet known, and go at once from thence to Father John, and implicitly follow the advice which he might give him.

When once he had definitely resolved on this line of conduct he was much easier in his mind; he had at any rate once more something to do—some occupation. He had freed himself from the prospect of long, weary, unending days, to be passed with that horrid man; and he was comparatively comfortable.

He determined to wait till it was nearly or quite dusk, which would be about five or half-past five o'clock, and then to leave the cabin, and making what haste he could to Drumshambo, go from thence by the road to Cashcarrigan and Ballycloran; and he calculated that he would be able to reach Father John's cottage between ten and eleven, before the priest had gone to bed; and having finally settled this in his mind, he returned to the cabin for the last time, determined manfully to sit out the remainder of the afternoon in the same apathetic tranquillity, which his enemy Andy displayed.

CHAPTER XXIV.

THE SECOND ESCAPE.

For four long hours there he remained, seated on the same stool, without moving or speaking; and for the same time there sat Andy on his bed, looking at the fire, and from time to time dragging a few sods from under the bed to throw them upon the ashes and keep up the warmth which seemed to be his only comfort. At length Thady thought it was dark enough, and without saying a word to the old man, he left the cabin and again descended the hill. He would not return by the same path by which he had come for fear he should meet Joe or Corney, or Meg—for he was unwilling that even she should see him escaping from his hiding-place. By the time that he reached Drumshambo it was dark, and it continued so till he got to Cashcarrigan, which he did without meeting any one who either recognised him or spoke to him. From thence he passed back by the two small lakes and the cabin of the poor widow who owed her misery to Ussher's energy, and across the bog of Drumleesh to the lane which would take him by Ballycloran to Father John's cottage. But before he reached Ballycloran the moon again rose bright and clear, and as he passed the spot where he more particularly wished to be shrouded by the darkness, it was so light that any one passing could not but recognise him.

He pulled his hat far over his forehead, and passed on quickly; but just as he got to the gateway he met Mary McGovery, who was on the very point of turning up the avenue to the house.

The turn in the road, exactly at the spot, had prevented him from seeing her before, and she immediately recognised him.

"Holy Virgin! Mr. Thady," she said; "and is that yerself?"

"Hist, Mary, don't spake so loud—not that I care who spakes now; you see it's me; and I'm going to the Cottage. Is Father John at home?"

"And what would you do with Father John, now? Don't you know the police is afther you?"

"What matther? it's not much throuble I'll be giving thim, looking for me. I'm going to thim myself now."

"An' what for would you do that, Mr. Thady? Don't you know they found it murdher agin you? We all hoped you were out of the counthry afore this. What for would you go to the police? Time enough when they catches you."

This was the first time that Thady had heard that a verdict of murder had been found against him before the Coroner, and though it was only what he expected, nevertheless the certainty, now that it reached him, almost made him change his mind and return to Aughacashel. The remembrance, however, of that weary day, and the feeling that even though he were there, he would assuredly be ultimately taken, strengthened his resolution, and he said,

"No, Mary, I've had enough of running away already. But tell me; how's Feemy?"

"Why, thin, Mr. Thady, she's nothing much to boast of; since she was in Carrick, yesterday, she's been very bad intirely."

"What is it ails her? It's—it's that man's death, isn't it Mary?"

"'Deed, Mr. Thady, I s'pose that war the first on it. Poor young lady! in course she feels it.—Wouldn't I feel it, av any one was to knock poor Denis on the head?—not that it's the same thing, altogether, for the Captain wasn't her lawful wedded husband.—Not that I'm saying agin you, Mr Thady, for what ye did."

"Never mind about that, Mary; what I've done is my own look out. But would Feemy see me, do you think?"

"See you, Mr. Thady! How could she see you, an' she in a raging fever in bed at Mrs. McKeons? in course she couldn't see you."

"Good God! and is she so bad as that?"

"Faith then, she is, very bad intirely; at laste, Docther Blake says so."

"It's very well, any way, that she's at Drumsna, instead of here at Ballycloran. Mrs. McKeon must be a kind woman to take her at such a time as this. And what's the owld man doing here by himself?"

"He's very quare in his ways, they do be saying; but I didn't see him meself yet; I'm going down to mind him, meself, this blessed moment."

"Why, isn't the two girls in it still?"

"Yes, they is, Mr. Thady; but they got frighted with the quare ways the owld man brought back with him from Carrick. He's wake in the head, they say, Mr. Thady, since he war up afore the gintlemen at the inquest; an' as the two girls wor frighted with 'im, an' as I am, maybe, a bit sthronger, an' a thrifle owlder nor they, Father John said I'd better step down an' mind him a bit; an' when all was settled, that he would see my expinses war paid."

"Well, Mary, good night! Be kind and gentle with the owld man, for he's enough on him jist now to unsettle his mind, av it were sthronger than it iver was; and don't tell him you see me here, for it would only be making him more onasy."

"Good night, thin, an' God bless you, Mr. Thady," said Mary. "You've a peck of throubles on yer head, this night," she added to herself, as she walked up the avenue, "an' it's little you did to desarve 'em, onless working hard night an' day war a sin. Well, God forgive us! shure you're betther off still, than the gay man you stretched the other night;" and she went on to commence her new business—that of watching and consoling Larry Macdermot in his idiotcy.

Thady pursued his road to the Cottage, without meeting any one else, and with some hesitation knocked at the priest's door. His heart palpitated violently within him as he waited some little time for an answer. It was about eleven, and he knew that at that hour Father John would still be up, if he were at home, though Judy would probably have retired to her slumbers. He was right in his calculation; for in a short time he heard the heavy step of Father John in the hall, and then the rusty door-key grated in the lock. Thady's knees shook beneath him as he listened to the rising latch. How should he meet Father John's eyes after what he had done? How should he find words to tell him that he had broken the solemn vow that he had taken on the holy scriptures, and had, in his first difficulty, flown to the disreputable security to be found in the haunts of such men as Joe Reynolds and Dan Kennedy. However, this he would have to tell him; for the door was now open, and there stood the priest, with his eyes fixed on Thady's sad face and soiled appearance.

Thady had not had his clothes off for the last two nights, and they now bore all the soil and stains of his two midnight walks; his countenance was pale in the extreme, and, never full or healthy, now seemed more thin and wan, than forty-eight hours' sorrow could possibly have made it. He was much fatigued, for his shoes had become soaked with water in the moist grounds through which he had passed and repassed, and his feet were blistered with his long and unaccustomed walks.

When Father John saw him, his heart melted within him at the sight of the young man's sad and melancholy figure. We already know that from the moment he had first heard of the catastrophe, he had made excuses in his own heart for Thady; and when he had heard, as he did at the inquest, that his sister had been with Ussher when he lifted his stick against him, he had not only acquitted him in his own estimation, from anything like the crime of murder, but he also felt certain that had he been in the same situation, he would most assuredly have done the same as Thady had done. He had been much surprised at the Coroner's verdict; he could not think how twelve men on their oath could call Ussher's death murder, when it so evidently appeared to him that the man stigmatised by that verdict as a murderer, had only been actuated by the praiseworthy purpose of defending his sister from disgrace and violence; and when, moreover, it was so plain that Thady's presence on the scene at the moment was accidental, and that the attack could not have been premeditated.

The jurors, however, had not been Thady's friends, as Father John was, nor were they inclined to look upon such a deed with the same lenient eyes. It appeared to them that Ussher was not using any violence to the young lady, who had herself admitted in her evidence, that she was a willing party to Ussher's proceedings. Doubtless, there might be circumstances, which at the prisoner's trial would be properly put forward in palliation of the murder, by his counsel; but with that the jury before the Coroner could have nothing to do; and on these considerations, the jurors with very little delay had come to the conclusion which had so surprised and grieved Father John. Still, however, he looked forward with almost absolute certainty to Thady's acquittal at his trial, and was by far more angry with the young man himself, at his folly in attempting to fly from justice, than he was at the deed which had put him under its power. Now, however, when he saw him pale, fatigued, harassed, and in sorrow at his door, his anger all turned to pity, and the only feeling left in his bosom led him to think how he could assuage his sufferings and comfort him in his afflictions.

Thady was the first to speak,—"Father John," he said, "I've come to give myself up; I thought I'd tell you, as I passed the door."

"Oh my son, my son!" said Father John. "Come in though, Thady, come in—till we think what's best to do in this sad time;"

and they went again into the little parlour, where so short a time ago Thady had made the promise which he now had to confess he had broken.

He then gave the priest, by degrees, the whole history of the affair; he told how the different events had happened; he explained how Feemy's appearance as she lay fainting in Ussher's arms, and that man's words to her, when he declared that she must come with him, had at the moment made him think that she was being dragged away by violence; and that he had had this conviction on his mind when he raised his stick to strike. He then told Father John exactly what he had done since the occurrence, the precautions which he took respecting the body—the visit which he paid to his father and his sister, and lastly, how he had fled for the sake of security, and passed two miserable days among the mountains in Aughacashel.

"Ah! my poor boy," said Father John, "that's what I have to blame you for. What made you fly there? what made you fly anywhere? why did you not with an honest face at once place yourself in the hands of the police, from whom you must know you couldn't have remained concealed?"

"Oh, Father John, av you could feel all I felt when I first knew the man was dead—when my own sisther spurned me—and when my father told me I was a murdherer, you wouldn't wonder at my flying, av it were only for an hour."

"That's true, my boy—that's very true; and I won't ask you now where you were, or who were with you—or what folly you may have done whilst there; for I haven't the heart to blame you, for what you've done in the extremity of your misery. But now, Thady, we must think of the future; of course you know, that having come to my house, and having seen me, you must at once place yourself in the hands of the police."

"In course, Father John; I was only on my way to Carrick when I called here. In truth, I wanted a kind word from you before they put me in that horrid place."

"My poor, dear boy, it's little comfort I can give you, except to tell you that we all think,—that is McKeon and I, and the rest of us,—that when the trial comes on they must acquit you—any jury must acquit you; and that till that time comes, you may be sure whatever can be done for you by the warmest friends, shall be done by us. But you know, Thady, till that time does come—till the trial is over, you must remain in prison."

"But, Father John, do you think they'll acquit me? do you think—does Mr. McKeon think, they'll not find it murder?"

"Indeed he does, Thady, and so do I; and so I'm sure does the Coroner, by what he said to the jury. I'm sure he didn't expect them to find it murder at the inquest."

"That's great comfort, Father John; but you always had comfort for me. But tell me, what's this I hear about Feemy and my father; is it thrue they're both ill?"

"I've little comfort for you in that quarter, I'm afraid; but though Feemy's ill, I don't think she's dangerously so. She will want time to bring her round; but I've no doubt time will bring her round. She has had a great deal to try her too; she was very fond of that man, though he was so unworthy of her; and it isn't easy for a girl like Feemy to get over at once the loss of him she loved so dearly."

"God send she may recover! I did it all for the best. Larry was long ailing; I fear this has knocked him up intirely; what'll the tinants do now at all? they'll have no one over thim but Keegan, I suppose: he'll be resaving the rints now, Father John; won't he?"

"Don't mind that now, my boy; you've enough on your heart now without troubling yourself about that."

"Well, then, I'll be wishing you good bye; I'll go on to Carrick."

"No, Thady, not to-night; stay here to-night. I would not have you go in and give yourself up under cover of the dark. Early to-morrow—as soon as Counsellor Webb will be up, you shall go with me to him. He'll no doubt commit you; indeed he must do so; but that will be better for you than lying all night in the guard-room at the police station, and being dragged out in the morning, cold, comfortless, and hungry."

Father John then got him supper and had a bed prepared for him, and early in the morning he sent down to Ballycloran for his linen and clothes that he might appear in a more respectable manner before the magistrate; he had his horse and car ready for them after breakfast, and at about ten they started for Counsellor Webb's.

They found the magistrate at home, and Father John sent in word to him that Mr. Macdermot having heard the verdict which had been returned at the Coroner's inquest, had come to surrender himself. Mr. Webb received the two into his study, and having explained to Thady that it was of course his duty immediately to commit him, sent to Carrick for police, in whose charge it would be necessary that the prisoner should be sent from thence.

"I'm very sorry," said Webb, "that this should be my principal duty, and that I should be obliged to hand you over to the constables; but you must have been aware that I should do so, when you came to me."

Father John then took Mr. Webb aside, and explained to him all the particulars of the case, which had not come out at the inquest; and at last it was agreed that he, Mr. Webb, should go with them into Carrick—that they would call at the police-office to inform the sergeant there that the prisoner was in custody, and that they should go direct to the gaol, and that Thady should be immediately handed over to the custody of the gaoler. This was accordingly done, and he avoided the disgrace, which he so feared, of being led through the town with handcuffs on his wrists.

Father John did not leave him until he had seen him settled with whatever comfort a prison could afford; but of these things, now that he was there, he seemed to think much less than the priest himself.

When Father John was kindly petitioning with the Governor to allow the prisoner a light in his cell, he said, " What matters ? a light won't make the time pass over quicker."

The next assizes would not take place till April, six months after the present time; and it was finally agreed that Father John should take on himself all the cares connected with his defence, and should from time to time visit him in his confinement, and give him such news respecting his father, his sister, and the affairs at Ballycloran, as he might have to bring ;—and then he took his leave.

When he was gone Thady was once more alone and in solitude; moreover, he felt strongly the gloom of the big cold walls around him—of the huge locks which kept him—the austerity and discomforts of prison discipline, and all the miseries of confinement; but yet even there, in gaol and committed to take his trial for life —though doomed to the monotony of that dull cell for six months —still he felt infinitely less wretched than he had done whilst sitting in Andy McEvoy's cabin, wondering at the torpidity of its owner. The feeling of suspense, of inactivity, the dread of being found and dragged away, joined to the horror he felt at remaining in so desolate a place, would have driven him mad. Now he knew that he had no daily accident to fear—no new misfortune to dread —and he nerved himself to bear the six long coming months with fortitude and patience. Though the time was long, and his weary days generally unbroken by anything that could interest or enliven them, still, from the hour when Father John first spoke to him at his hall-door, to that in which he was led into the Court-house dock as a prisoner to take his trial for his life, he never once repented that he had quitted Aughacashel and his mountain security, to give himself up as a prisoner to the authorities of Carrick.

CHAPTER XXV.

RETROSPECTIVE.

As story-tellers of every description have, from time immemorial, been considered free from those niceties by which all attempts in the nobler classes of literature are, or should be restrained, we consider no apology necessary for requesting the reader to leap over with us the space of four months; but still, before we continue our tale from that date, it will be as well that we should give a short outline of the principal events which produced the state in which the circumstances of the Macdermots will then be found, and we are sorry to say that they were not such as could offer much consolation to them.

It will be remembered that Pat Brady was commissioned by his master to take Ussher's body to the police station at Carrick, in Fred Brown's gig. This commission he promptly performed, and also that of restoring the gig to its owner; and after having thus completed his master's behests like a good servant, he paid a visit on his own account to Mr. Keegan.

Although it was late, he still found that active gentleman up, and gave him a tolerably accurate account of what had happened at Ballycloran, adding that "the young masther had gone off to join the boys, at laste that's what he supposed he'd be afther now." As soon as Keegan's surprise was a little abated, he perceived that the affair would probably act as a stepping-stone, on which he might walk into Ballycloran even sooner than he had hitherto thought to do; and when, as one of the jurors at the coroner's inquest, on the next morning, he saw that poor Larry had evidently fallen into absolute idiotcy, and heard that Thady had, in fact, escaped, he instantly determined to take such legal steps on behalf of his father-in-law as would put the property under his management. And this, accordingly, he did. The proper steps for proving the old man to be of unsound mind would have been attended with very great expense; instead of doing this, he got himself made receiver over the property, and determined to arrest Larry, which, in his existing state, he conceived he should have no difficulty in doing. Here, however, he found himself very much mistaken, for nothing could induce the old man to leave his own room, or so much as allow the front door to be unlocked. Mary Brady still continued to attend him every day, returning home to her husband after sunset, and she found him very easy to manage in every other particular, as long as he was allowed to have his own way in this.

He had quite lost the triumphant feeling which le
in the streets of Carrick, after leaving the inquest
escaped from Flannelly's power, and that he would
pay him another farthing; for now if he heard a st
fancied it to be a bailiff's, and if there was the slighte
house, he thought that an attempt was being made t(
by violence. It was a miserable sight to see the old ı
and worn out, sitting during that cold winter, by a fe
with the door of his own room ajar, watching the fı
morning till night, to see that no one opened it. Be
he had his bed brought down into the same room, iı
might not be betrayed into the hands of his enemies i
before he was up, and from that time no inducement
on him to leave the room for a moment.

During this time his poverty was very great; th
been served with legal notices to pay neither to him
any portion of their rents, and consequently provisi
low and very scarce at Ballycloran; in fact, had it n(
kindness of Father John, Mr. McKeon, and Counsello1
property was adjoining to Ballycloran, Larry wou
starved into a surrender. Mr. Webb went so far ;
with Mr. Keegan, and to point out to him that in al
should stay his proceedings till after Thady's trial
replied that he was only acting for Mr. Flannelly. v
mined to have the matter settled at once; that all]
his own, and that he had already waited too long.

When Keegan found that Larry Macdermot, iı
infirmities, was too wary to be caught, he endeavo
Mary to open the door to his emissaries, and to betra}
but though Mary was very fond of money, she was
this, and she replied to the attorney by telling him, "ı
money in the bank of Carrick, she wouldn't be the o
ould blood that way." Larry consequently still helc
cloran, living on the chance presents of his friends, w
one time a few stone of potatoes, at another a pound
bit of bacon or a few bottles of whiskey; this last,
confided to Mary, with injunctions not to allow him
to have recourse to the only comforter that was left t(

Though Keegan failed to gain admission into tl
could not therefore put himself into absolute possessio1
still he could do what he pleased with the lands, a1
long in availing himself of the power. In January he
on all the tenents that unless the whole arrears we:
before the end of the next month, they would be ej

many of those who held portions of the better part of the land, he sent summary notices to quit on the first of May next following. These notices were all served by Pat, who assured the tenants that he only performed the duties which he had now undertaken that he might look after Mr. Thady's interests, and as, as he said, " there could be no use in life in his refusing to do it, for av he didn't, another would, and the tenants would be no betther, and he a dale the worse."

These things by no means tended to make Keegan's name popular on the estate, particularly at Drumleesh, where the tenants were but ill prepared to pay their rent by small portions at a time, and were utterly confounded at the idea of having to pay up the arrears in a lump; but Pat assured him that although they were surly and sullen, they gave no signs or showed any determination of having recourse to violence, or of openly rebelling against the authority of their new landlord.

Pat, however, knew but little of what was going on amongst them now. Although they found no absolute fault with the arguments which he used for acting on Mr. Keegan's behalf, still he soon discovered that the tenants had withdrawn their confidence from him, and that they looked upon him rather as the servant of their new tyrant, than as the friend to whom they had been accustomed to turn, when they wanted any little favour from their old master. He had moreover discontinued his visits to Mrs. Mulready's, and had for a long time seen nothing of Joe Reynolds and his set, who spent most of their time in Aughacashel, or at any rate away from Drumleesh.

Joe Reynolds had been altogether unable to account for Thady's sudden disappearance from Aughacashel. At first he thought he must have been taken prisoner by some of the police, whilst roaming about in the neighbourhood; and although he ultimately heard that Father John and he had gone together to Counsellor Webb's, still he never could learn how Thady had fallen into the priest's hands. Joe, however, did not forget that Thady had done what he considered the good service of ridding the country of Ussher, and he swore that he would repay it by punishing the man, who in his estimation was robbing Thady of his right and his property; he had long since declared at Mrs. Mulready's, as we are aware, that if Thady would come over and join his party, Keegan should not come upon the estate with impunity, and he was now detemined to keep his word.

Keegan, trusting to the assurance of Pat, that the tenants were all quiet and peaceable, at length began to go among them himself, and had, about the beginning of February, once or twice ridden

over portions of the property. About five o'clock o[n]
that month, he was riding towards home along the li[ttle]
skirts Drumleesh bog, after having seen as much of th[e]
neighbourhood as a man could do on horseback, when
stopped by a man wrapped in a very large frieze co[at,]
face was not concealed, who asked him, " could he spak[e]
about a bit of land that he was thinking of axing aft[er the]
man that was on it was put off, as he heard war to b[e]
the man said this he laid his hands on the bridle, and K[negan knew]
from this that something was not right, put his hand
pocket, where his pistols were, and told the man to co[me to]
Carrick, if he wanted to say anything. The man, h[e con]-
tinued, " av his honer wouldn't think it too much th[en to]
come down for one moment, he'd point out the ca[bin he]
meant." Keegan was now sure from the man's contir[nuing]
his hand on the bridle, that some injury to him was [meant,]
was in the act of drawing his pistol from his pocket, [when]
knocked altogether from off his horse by a blow whic[h struck]
on the head with a large stone, thrown from the other sid[e of the]
banks which ran along the road. The blow and the fa[ll]
stunned him, and when he came to himself he was [on the]
road; the man who had stopped his horse was kn[eeling on]
chest; a man, whose face was blackened, was holding [his]
feet, and a third, whose face had also been blackened, [stood]
on the road beside him with a small axe in his han[d. His]
courage utterly failed him when he saw the sharp inst[rument in the]
ruffian's grasp; he began to promise largely if they v[vould let him]
escape—forgiveness—money—land—anything—ever[ything but his]
life. Neither of them, however, answered him, and b[efore one]
sentence he uttered was well out of his mouth, the i[nstrument descended]
on his leg, just above the ankle, with all the man's fo[rce. The first]
blow only cut his trousers and his boot, and bruised l[im,]
for his boots protected him; the second cut the flesl[and jarred]
against the bone; in vain he struggled violently, anc[l with the]
force of a man struggling for his life; a third, and a [fourth, and a]
fifth descended, crushing the bone, dividing the [flesh, and]
ultimately severing the foot from the leg. When th[ey had done]
their work, they left him on the road, till some pass[er by might]
have compassion on him, and obtain for him the means c[of returning]
to his home.

In a short time Keegan fainted from loss of blood, [but the]
frost soon brought him to his senses; he got up and h[obbled to the]
nearest cabin, dragging after him the mutilated foo[t, which still]
attached itself to his body by the cartilages and by the

his boot and trousers; and from thence reached his home on a country car, racked by pain, which the jolting of the car and the sharp frost did not tend to assuage.

At the time of which we are writing—about the first week in March—he had been entirely unable to ascertain any of the party by whom he had been attacked. The men were Dan Kennedy, Joe Reynolds, and Corney Dolan; of these, Joe alone was personally known to Keegan, and it was he who used the axe with such fell cruelty; but he had been so completely disguised at the time, that Keegan had not in the least recognised him. Dan was the man who had at first stopped the horse, and he being confident that Keegan had not even heard his name, and that he was very unlikely to be in any place where his victim could again see him so as to know him, had not feared to stop the horse, and address its rider without any disguise.

This act, which was originally proposed and finally executed more with the intent of avenging Thady, than with any other purpose, was the most unfortunate thing for him that could have happened; for in the first place it made the magistrates and the government imagine that the country was in a disorderly state generally, and that it was therefore necessary to follow up the prosecutions at the Assizes with more than ordinary vigour; and in the next place, it made Keegan determined to do all that he could to secure Thady's conviction, for he attributed his horrible mutilation to the influence of the Macdermots.

Other things had also occurred during the four months since Thady had given himself up to the authorities, which had determined the law officers of the government to follow up Ussher's murderer with all severity, and obtain if possible a conviction.

The man who had been sent to Mohill in Ussher's place was by no means his equal either in courage, determination, or perseverance; still it had been necessary for him to follow to a certain degree in his predecessor's steps, especially as at the time illicit distillation had become more general in the country than it had ever been known to be before. A man named Cogan, who had acted very successfully as a spy to Ussher, also offered his services to the new officer, by whom they were accepted. This man had learnt that potheen was being made at Aughacashel, and, dressed in the uniform of one of the Revenue police, had led the men to Dan Kennedy's cabin. Here they merely found Abraham, the cripple, harmlessly employed in superintending the boiling of some lumpers, and Andy McEvoy in the other cabin, sitting on his bed; not a drop of potheen—not a grain of malt—not a utensil used in distillation was found, and they had to return foiled and beaten.

The new officer, whose name was Foster, also received various threatening letters, and among them the following :—

"This is to giv' notis, Captin Furster, av you'll live and let live, and be quite an' pacable—divil a rason is there, why you need be afeard—but av you go on among the Leatrim boys—as that bloody thundhering ruffin Ussher, by the etarnal blessed Glory, you wul soon be streatched as he war—for the Leatrim boys isn't thim as wul put up with it."

This was only one of many that he received—and these, together with the futility of his first attempt—a tremendous stoning which he and his men received in the neighbourhood of Drumshambo—the burning of Cogan's cabin, and the fate of his predecessor, totally frightened him; and he represented to the head office in Dublin that the country was in such a state, that he was unable, with the small body of men at his command, to carry on his business with anything approaching to security.

These things all operated much against the chance of Thady's acquittal, and his warmest friends could not but feel that they did so. People in the country began to say that some severe example was necessary—that the country was in a dreadful state—and that the government must be upheld; and these fears became ten times greater, when it was generally known that Thady, a day or two before the catastrophe, had absolutely associated with some of the most desperate characters in the country.

Brady, at first, had been unwilling to divulge all that he knew to Mr. Keegan; for, though he felt no hesitation in betraying his old master, he was not desirous to hang him; but Keegan, by degrees, got it all out of him, and bribed so high that Pat, at last, consented to come forward at the trial and swear to all the circumstances of the meeting at Mr. Mehan's, and the attorney lost no time in informing the solicitor, who was to conduct the prosecution on behalf of the crown, what this witness was able to prove.

All this was sad news for Father John, and his friend McKeon, but still they would not despair. They talked the matter over and over again in McKeon's parlour, and Tony occasionally almost forgot his punch in his anxiety to put forward and make the most of all those points, which he considered to be in Thady's favour. It was not only the love of justice, his regard for the family of the Macdermots, and Father John's eloquence which had enlisted McKeon so thoroughly in Thady's interest,—though, no doubt, these three things had great weight with him,—but his own personal predilections had also a considerable share in doing so.

The three leading resident gentlemen in the neighbourhood were

Sir Michael Gibson, Mr. Jonas Brown, and Counsellor Webb; they were the three magistrates who regularly attended the petty sessions at Carrick; and as they usually held different opinions on all important subjects relative to the locality in which they resided, so all their neighbours swore by one of them, condemning the other two as little better than fools or knaves.

Sir Michael was by far the richest, and would, therefore, naturally have had the greatest number of followers, had it not been that it was usually extremely difficult to find out what his opinion was. He was neither a bad nor a good landlord—that is to say, his land was seldom let for more than double its value; and his agent did not eject his tenants as long as they contrived not to increase the arrears which they owed when he undertook the management of the property; but Sir Michael himself neither looked after their welfare, or took the slightest care to see that they were comfortable.

On the bench, by attempting to agree with both his colleagues, he very generally managed to express an opinion different from either of them; and as he was, of course, the chairman, the decisions of the bench were in consequence frequently of a rather singular nature; however, on the whole, Sir Michael was popular, for if he benefited none, he harmed none; and he was considered by many a safe constitutional man, with no flighty ideas on any side.

Jonas Brown was hated by the poor. In every case he would, if he had the power, visit every fault committed by them with the severest penalty awarded by the law. He was a stern, hard, cruel man, with no sympathy for any one, and was actuated by the most superlative contempt for the poor, from whom he drew his whole income. He was a clever, clear-headed, avaricious man; and he knew that the only means of keeping the peasantry in their present utterly helpless and dependent state, was to deny them education, and to oppose every scheme for their improvement and welfare. He dreaded every movement which tended to teach them anything, and when he heard of landlords reducing their rents, improving cabins, and building schools, he would prophesy to his neighbour, Sir Michael, that the gentry would soon begin to repent of their folly, when the rents they had reduced were not paid, the cabins which they had made comfortable were filled with ribbonmen, and when the poor had learnt in the schools to disobey their masters and landlords. Sir Michael never contradicted all this, and he would probably have become a second Jonas Brown, and much more injurious, because so much more extensive in his interests, were it not for the counteracting influence of Counsellor Webb, who was in all his opinions diametrically opposed to Mr. Brown.

Mr. Webb was a clear-headed, and a much more talented man

than his brother magistrate. He was, moreover, a kind-hearted landlord—ever anxious to ameliorate the condition of the poor—and by no means greedy after money, though he was neither very opulent nor very economical. But, nevertheless, with all these high qualities he was hardly the man most fit to do real good in a very poor and ignorant neighbourhood. He was, in the first place, by far too fond of popularity, and of being the favourite among the peasantry; and, in the next, he had become so habituated to oppose Jonas Brown in all his sayings and doings, that he now did so whether he was right or wrong.

Thady's case had been much talked of in the country, and the rival magistrates, of course, held diametrically opposite opinions respecting it.

Jonas Brown had declared at his own table, that "unless that young man were hanged, there would be an end to anything like law in the country; his being the son of a landlord made it ten times worse; if the landlords themselves turned ribbonmen, and taught the tenants all manner of iniquity, and the law didn't then interfere, it would be impossible to live in the country; he, for one, should leave it. Here had a most praiseworthy servant of the crown—a man who had merited the thanks of the whole country by the fearless manner in which he had performed his duties, here," he said, " had this man been murdered in cold blood by a known ribbonman, by one, who, as he understood, had, a few days before the murder, conspired with others to commit it; and yet he was told there were a pack of people through the country—priests, and popularity hunters, who were not only using their best endeavours to screen the murderer, but who absolutely justified the deed. By G—d, he couldn't understand how a man, holding the position of a gentleman, could so far forget what he owed to his country and himself as to dirty his hands with such a filthy business as this, however absurd his general opinions on politics might be. As for the man's sister, that was all a got up story since the business. Every one knew that the family had been trying to catch the young man for the girl; she had been allowed to walk with Captain Ussher at all hours, night and day; and he was doing no more than walking with her when he was basely murdered by her brother. As for him (Jonas Brown), he hoped and trusted the murderer would be hung as he deserved."

The purport of this piece of after-dinner eloquence was duly conveyed to Counsellor Webb, who fully appreciated the remarks about the popularity-hunting gentleman who was dirtying his hands. Up to this time these two men, though differing so widely from each other, had still kept up a show of courtesy between them; but Mr. Brown's remarks altogether put an end to it.

Counsellor Webb never again addressed him in friendly terms.

He did not, however, in the least relax his efforts on Thady's behalf, or express less strongly his opinion on the case. He told Sir Michael one morning in Carrick, after some public meeting at which all the gentry of the neighbourhood had been present, and while many of them, and among them Mr. Brown, were standing by, that " he had lately been giving a great deal of very close attention to that very distressing case of young Mr. Macdermot; he thought it was the most melancholy and heartrending case he had ever known. It was proved beyond possibility of doubt that Ussher was eloping with the young man's sister; it seemed now to be pretty certain that the girl was herself absolutely senseless at the time the occurrence took place; he believed she had changed her mind, or got frightened, or what not; it was now a known fact, that she was being dragged senseless in the man's arms, when Macdermot attacked him. And was a brother to stand by and look on at such a sight as that, and not protect his sister, and punish the miscreant who was endeavouring to dishonour her? Was Mr. Macdermot to turn his back upon the affair, and leave his sister to her fate because, forsooth, the man who did it was a Revenue officer? Let us bring the matter home to ourselves, Sir Michael," he continued. " Suppose you saw that gay young Captain Jem Boyle hurrying through the demesne at Knockadrum with one of your own fair flock in his arms, violently carrying her off, wouldn't you not only knock him down yourself, if you could catch him; but also set all your people after him, begging them to do the same? Of course, you would; and what more has this young man done? Unfortunately he struck too hard; but that, although we may deplore the circumstance, shows no criminality on his part; but only the strong indignation which he very properly felt. As to the cock and bull story of his being a ribbonman, no man of sense could entertain it. It appears that a few nights before the occurrence he went to a tenant's wedding, and unfortunately took a drop too much punch. That had been many a good man's case before his. And then he got among a lot of men who were uttering vague, nonsensical threats against different persons, whom they disliked. One, I hear, says that Ussher was threatened; and another—and, I am told, by far the more creditable witness—that it was Keegan, the attorney, whose name was mentioned; it appears, that when drunk, he promised to join these men in another drinking party, which promise he, of course, never thought of keeping after he was sober; and yet there are some who are cruel enough to say—I won't say harsh enough to believe, for they can't believe it—that when he attacked Ussher in his sister's defence, Macdermot was only carrying into execution a premeditated plan of murdering him! Premeditated indeed, when it was plain to every one, that it was by the merest accident that he happened to be in the avenue at the time. People might just as well say that it was he who cut off the attorney's foot the other day, though he was in gaol at the time. I must say," continued the Counsellor, " that should the poor young man fall a victim to the false evidence which I am aware private malice and wretchedly vindictive feeling will supply, then the basest murder will really have been committed which ever disgraced this county. I don't envy the state of mind of any gentleman who can look forward with a feeling of satisfaction to the prospect of that poor youth's being hanged for protecting his sister, merely because the seducer was in habits of intimacy with himself or his family."

Mr. Brown left the meeting, taking no immediate notice of the Counsellor's philippic. It was not, however, because he did not comprehend the latter part of it, or that he meant to overlook it.

Sir Michael was much distressed in making up his mind finally on the subject. It was reported, however, soon after the meeting above alluded to, that he had stated to some of his more immediate friends and admirers, that " he considered it highly discreditable, he might say disgraceful, for any of the more respectable classes to give any countenance to the illegal meetings, which he was afraid were too general through the country, and that there was too much reason to fear that the unfortunate man in prison had been guilty in doing so; but that there could be no doubt that every one was justified—he might add, only performed his bounden duty—in protecting the females of his family from injury or violence."

Now Tony McKeon was a tenant both of Sir Michael and of the Counsellor; he also held land from other landlords, but he had no connexion whatever with Mr. Brown: he was not at all the sort of tenant that Jonas liked; for though he always punctually paid his rent to the day, he usually chose to have everything his own way, and would take no land except at a fair rent and on a long lease.

Mr. Webb, however, was his chief friend and principal ally in the country. Sir Michael was altogether too grand for him, seeing that Tony had no idea of being a humble dependent; but Mr. Webb would occasionally come and dine with him—and often asked him in return. Mrs. Webb too was civil to his wife and the girls—always lent them the Dublin pattern for their frills, frocks, and other frippery—and seldom drove into Drumsna without calling. The consequence was, that the Counsellor was a man after Tony's own heart. Though they were of different religions, they had, generally speaking, the same political feelings and opinions—the same philanthropical principles—and the same popular prejudices; and after a few years intimacy in each other's neighbourhood, Mr. Webb well knew where to find a powerful recruit for any service in which he might wish to enlist one.

Tony declared that if any one spoke ill of Feemy's character, he should make it personal with himself; that he was ready, willing, and moreover determined to quarrel with any one who dared to apply the opprobrious name of murderer to Thady; and he had even been heard, on one or two occasions, to stand up for Larry himself, and to declare that although he might be a little light-headed or so, he was still a deal better than those muddy-minded blackguards at Carrick who had driven him to his present state.

For a long time Feemy had been very ill, but after Christmas she had apparently got a little stronger; she would sit up in her bed-room for a few hours in the day; but still she would talk to no one. Mrs. McKeon endeavoured more than once to lead her to the subject which she knew must be nearest her heart, thinking that if she could be got to speak of it, she would be relieved; but in vain. In vain she tried to interest her in her brother's fate—in vain she tried to make her understand that Thady's safety—that his acquittal would, in a great degree, depend on her being able to prove, at the trial, that at the time when the occurrence took place, she was herself insensible. She shuddered violently at the idea of being again questioned, and declared with sobs that she should die if she were again dragged to that horrid place. When Mrs. McKeon asked her if she would not make a struggle to save her brother's life, she remained mute. It was evident that it was for her lover that she was still grieving, and that it was not the danger or ignominy of Thady's position that afflicted her.

Mrs. McKeon, however, conceived it to be her duty to persevere with her—and, at last, told her how wrong it was of her to give way to a grief, which was in its first stage respected. Feemy answered her only with tears; and on the next morning told her that she had determined to return to Ballycloran, as she thought she would be better there, at home with her father.

To this, however, Mrs. McKeon would not consent, and Feemy was told that the doctor had forbidden her to be moved. She was, therefore, obliged to remain satisfied for the present, as she had no means of escaping from Drumsna; but she soon became more sullen than ever—and, at last, almost refused to speak to any one.

Things went on in this way till about the middle of March,

Feemy constantly requested to be allowed to go home, which request was as constantly refused; when different circumstances acting together gave rise to a dreadful suspicion in Mrs. McKeon's mind. She began to fear that Ussher, before his death, had accomplished the poor girl's ruin, and that she was now in the family way. For some few days she was determined to reject the idea, and endeavoured to make herself believe that she was mistaken; but the more close her observations were, the more certain she became that her suspicions were well founded. She was much distressed as to what she should do. Her first and most natural feelings were those of anger against Feemy, and of dismay at the situation into which her own and her husband's good nature had brought herself and her daughters; and she made up her mind that Feemy should at once have her wish and return to Ballycloran. But then, she might be mistaken—or even, if it were too true—how could she turn the poor girl, weak, ill, and miserable, out of her house, and send her to an empty unprovided barrack, inhabited by an infirm, idiotical old man, where she could receive none of that attention which her situation so much required?

She communicated her suspicions to the doctor, and after a few days' observations, he told her that there was too much reason to fear that the case was as she supposed. He, however, strongly advised her to speak to Miss Macdermot herself on the subject. This she did, at last, most tenderly, and with the greatest gentleness—but still imploring Feemy to tell her the truth. Feemy, at first, could not speak in reply; she threw herself on her bed sobbing most violently, and fell from one fit into another, till Mrs. McKeon was afraid that she would choke herself with the violence of her emotion. At last, however, she declared that the accusation brought against her was untrue—protested on her most solemn word and honour that it was not the case—and ended by saying how thankful she was to Mrs. McKeon for her kindness and protection, but that she must now beg her to allow her to return to Ballycloran.

Feemy's denial of the charge against her was so firm, and so positively made, that it very much shook her friend's suspicions. When Feemy begged to be sent home, she told her not to agitate herself at present—that they would all see how she was in a day or two—and then speaking a few kind words to her, left her to herself.

CHAPTER XXVI.

THE DUEL.

Mr. Jonas Brown was in a towering passion, when he left the meeting at which he had listened to, but had not ventured to answer, Counsellor Webb's remarks respecting Thady Macdermot and the supposed intimacy between Ussher and the inmates of Brown Hall. He had so openly expressed his wish that the young man might be capitally punished—and this joined to the fact that Ussher had not been as intimate at any other house as he had been at Brown Hall, could leave no doubt on the mind of any one who had been present, that Webb's allusion had been intended for him. His first impulse was to challenge his foe at once; but his ardour on that point soon cooled a little, and he came to the conclusion of sleeping on the matter, or, at any rate, of drinking a bottle or two of wine over it with his sons.

As soon as the servant had withdrawn after dinner he began his grievance.

"By G—d, Fred, that ruffian Webb is passing all bounds. He's not only forgotten the opinions and notions of a gentleman, but he has lain down the manners of one too."

"Why, what has he done now? With all his queer ideas, Webb can be a gentleman if he pleases," said Fred.

"I must say," said George, "the Counsellor is a good fellow on the course. I don't care how seldom I see him anywhere else."

"I don't know what you may call being a good fellow or a gentleman," replied the father; "but I know he has insulted me publicly, and that in the most gross way, and before half the country. I don't know whether that's your idea of acting like a gentleman or a good fellow."

"It's what many a gentleman and many a good fellow has done before him," said George; "but if he has insulted you, of course he must apologize—or do the other thing."

"What—let it alone?" rejoined Fred.

"No; fight—and that's what he's a deal the most likely to do," said George.

"Be d—d," said old Brown, "but I think both of you seem glad to hear that your father has been insulted! you've neither of you a grain of proper feeling."

"It's with a grain or two of gunpowder, I'd take it," said George, "and I'd advise you, father, to do the same; a precious deal better thing than good feeling to settle an insult with."

"But you've not told us what it's all about?" said Fred; "what was the quarrel about?"

"Quarrel! there was no quarrel at all in the matter—I couldn't quarrel with him for I wouldn't speak to him. It was about that infernal friend of yours, Fred, that Ussher; I wish he'd never darkened this door."

"Poor devil!" answered Fred; "there's no use abusing him now he's dead. I suppose the row wasn't his fault."

"It was about him though, and the low blackguard that murdered him. Webb was talking about him, making a speech in the public-room, taking the fellow's part, as I'm told he's always doing, and going on with all the clap-trap story about protecting his sister;—as if every one in the country didn't know that she'd been Ussher's mistress for months back. Well, that was all nothing to me—only he'll be rightly served when he finds every man on his estate has become a ribbonman, and every other tenant ready to turn murderer. But this wasn't enough for him, but at the end of the whole he must declare—I forget what it was he said—but something about Ussher's intimacy here—that it was a shameful thing of me to be wishing on that account that this Macdermot should be hanged, as he deserves."

"Did he actually mention Brown Hall?" asked Fred.

"No; but he put it so that there could be no mistake about it; he said he didn't envy my state of mind."

"Well, tell him you don't envy his. I don't think you could call him out for that," said George.

"By heavens you're enough to provoke a saint!" continued the father. "Can't you believe me, when I tell you, he made as direct a cut at Brown Hall as he could, because I can't repeat all his words like a newspaper? By G—d the pluck's gone out of the country entirely! if as much had been said to my father, when I was your age, I'd have had the fellow who said it out, if he'd been the best shot in Connaught."

"Don't say another word, father," said George, "if that's what you're after. I thought, may be, you'd like the fun yourself, or I'd have offered. I'd call him out with a heart and a half; there's nothing I'd like better. May be I'd be able to make up a match between Diamond and the Counsellor's brown mare, when it's done. He'd be a little soft, would Webb, after such a job as that, and wouldn't stand for a few pounds difference."

"That's nonsense, George," said the father, a little mollified by the son's dutiful offer. "I don't want any one to take the thing off my hands. I don't want to be shelved that way—but I wish you to see the matter in the right light. I tell you the man was cursedly insolent, Fred; in fact, he said what I don't mean to put up with; and the question is, what had I better do?"

"He didn't say anything, did he," asked Fred, "with your name, or Brown Hall in it?"

"No, he didn't name them exactly."

"Then I don't think you can call for an apology; write him a civil note, and beg him to say that he intended no allusion to you or your family in what he said."

"Fred's right for once," said George, "that's all you can do as the matter stands now. If he won't say that, call him out and have done with it."

"I've no wish to be fighting," said the father; "in fact, at my time of life I'd rather not. I was ready enough once, but I'd sooner settle it quietly."

"Why, there's no contenting you," answered Fred; "just now nothing but pistols and coffee would do for you; and then you were in a passion because one of us wouldn't take a challenge for you at once, without knowing anything about it; and now you're just the other way; if you don't like the business, there's George will take it off your hands, he says."

After a considerable quantity of squabbling among this family party it was at last decided that a civil note should be sent to Ardrum, in which Mr. Webb should be desired to state that he had made no allusion to Brown Hall; accordingly a servant on horseback was dispatched on the Monday morning with the following missive:—

"*Brown Hall,*
  "*Sunday Evening.*

"Mr. Brown presents his compliments to Mr. Webb, and begs to inform him that certain expressions which fell from him at the meeting at Carrick on Saturday respecting the murder of Captain Ussher, have been thought by many to have had reference to the family at Brown Hall. Mr. Brown feels himself assured that Mr. Webb would not so far forget himself, as to make any such allusion in public to a neighbouring gentleman and magistrate; but as Mr. Webb's words were certainly singular in their reference to Captain Ussher's intimacy with some family in the neighbourhood, and as many conceive that they were directly pointed at Brown Hall, Mr. Brown must beg Mr. Webb to give him his direct assurance in writing that nothing which fell from him was intended to apply either to Mr. Brown or his family."

"*To* W. WEBB, *Esq.*,
  "*Ardrum.*"

Mr. Webb was at home when the servant arrived, and, only detain˙g him two minutes, sent him back with the following answer :—

"*Ardrum,*
"Monday Morning.

"Mr. Webb presents his compliments to Mr. Brown. Mr. Webb regrets that he cannot comply with the request made in Mr. Brown's letter of yesterday's date."

"*To* Jonas Brown, *Esq.,*
"*Brown Hall.*"

The conclave at Brown Hall, on receipt of this laconic epistle, unanimously declared that it was tantamount to a declaration of war, and that desperate measures must at once be adopted.

"The sod's the only place now, father," said George; "by heavens I like him the better for not recanting."

"He's a cursed good shot," said Fred. "Would you like to send for Keegan before you go out?"

"Keegan be d—d!" said George; "but have Blake by, for he'll wing you as sure as Moses."

"May be not," said Fred. "Webb's a d—d good shot in a gallery; but may be he won't allow for the wind on the sod; but it'll be as well to have the sawbones."

"No fear of your legs, governor, for he'll fire high. The shoulder's his spot; you may always tell from a man's eye where he'll fix the sight of a pistol. Webb always looks up. If his tool lifts a little, he'll fire over you."

"Yes, he might," said Fred; "or take you on the head—which wouldn't be so pleasant. I'm not particular—but I'd better run my chance myself with a chap that fired low."

"There you're out," answered the brother. "The low shot's the death-shot. Why man, if you did catch a ball in the head, you'd get over it—if it was in the mouth, or cheek, or neck, or anywhere but the temple; but your body's all over tender bits. May heaven always keep lead out of my bowels—I'd sooner have it in my brains."

The father fidgetted about very uneasily whilst enduring these pleasant remarks from his affectionate children, which, it is needless to say, they made for his particular comfort and amusement at the present moment. At last he lost his temper, and exclaimed—

"D— your brains, you fool—I don't believe you've got any! what's the use of the two of you going on that way—you that were never out in your life. I tell you when a man's standing to be fired at, he doesn't know, nine times in ten, whether he fires high or low. Who'll I get to go out with me?"

"Yes, and take your message," said Fred; "you've a deal to do yet before you're snug home again."

"Well, who'll I get to go to him?"

"Why wouldn't I do?" suggested George. George, at any rate, had the merit of being a good son.

"Nonsense," said Fred; "if the governor got shot you'd be considered a brute if you were cool; and a man should be cool then."

"Cool," said George; "I'd be as cool as a cucumber."

"Nonsense," said the father; "of course I couldn't go out with my own son; there's Theobald French; I went out with his cousin just after Waterloo."

"He can't show—he's on his keeping. He'd be nabbed before he was on the ground."

"Then I'll have Larkin; I've known him since I was a boy."

"Larkin's too old for that game now; he'd be letting them have Webb up with his back to the sun."

"Murphy, of Mullough; he's used to these things—I'll send over to him."

"Murphy's up to snuff; but since the affair of the bill he forged Dan Connolly's name to, he's queerly thought of. It wouldn't do at all, governor, to send any one that Webb's friend could refuse to meet."

"I'll tell you, father, who'd be proud of the job—and he's quite a gentleman now, since he got an estate of his own—and that's Cynthy Keegan. It'd be great fun to see him stepping the ground, and he only with one foot."

"By heavens, George, you're a born fool; must you have your d—d joke, when I'm talking so seriously?"

"Upon my soul, then, if it were myself, I'd send for Keegan. He'd think the compliment so great, he wouldn't refuse, and it'd be such a joke to see him on the ground with his crutches. But if you don't like the attorney, send to Fitzpatrick."

"He's so young," said the father; "he'd do very well for either of you; but I'd want some one steadier."

"Besides," said Fred, "Webb and Fitz are bosom friends. I wouldn't wonder if Fitz were Webb's friend himself."

"I tell you, father—Major Longsword's exactly the boy," said George; "send to Boyle for him; he wants to get a name in the country, and the job'll just suit him."

"You're right for once, George," said Jonas, "Longsword's just the man that will answer." And accordingly it was at last

T

decided that Major Longsword was to be the honoured individual. He had dined once or twice at Brown Hall, and therefore there was some excuse for calling upon him; and a note was accordingly written to him, with a great deal of blarney about his station and experience, and the inexpediency of entrusting affairs of honour to inexperienced country gentlemen. This had the effect of immediately bringing him over to Brown Hall, and on the Tuesday morning he was dispatched to Ardrum, to make what arrangements he pleased with Mr. Webb.

To give Major Longsword his due, Mr. Brown could not have made a much better choice; for though he was a disciple of that school, which thoroughly entertained the now antiquated notion that the world—that is, the world of men in broad cloth—could not go on without duels, or a pretence of duels; still he was one who, as a second, would do all in his power to prevent an absolute effusion of lead. He was a great hand at an apology, and could regulate its proper degree of indifference or abjectness to the exact state of the case; he could make it almost satisfactory to the receiver, without being very disagreeable to the giver; he could twaddle about honour for ever without causing bloodshed; and would, if possible, protect a man's reputation and body at the same time.

He started on his mission of peace with the determined intention of returning with some document in his pocket which would appease Mr. Brown's irritated feelings, and add another laurel to the wreath which he considered his due as a peace-maker.

He was shown into Mr. Webb's parlour, where that gentleman soon joined him, and he was not long in making known his business. Major Longsword plumed himself on his manners in such embassies, and to-day he was perfect.

"Now, Mr. Webb," he continued after a long preamble, "of course I am not to judge of the propriety of any words you may think fit to use; but, I am afraid I must admit in this case, a somewhat—I must say a somewhat unwarranted allusion was made to my friend. Such I can assure you is the general opinion. Now, if you will allow me to say as much, I think,—I cannot but think, you were right—perfectly right—in not disclaiming such an allusion, having once made it; but I trust, indeed I feel confident, that a man of your acknowledged sense, and general character as a man of the world, will not object to give me a line—a mere line will suffice—addressed to myself; I wouldn't ask you in such a matter to write to Mr. Brown—a mere line, just stating that you regret having said anything in your fervour which should hurt any one's feelings. The matter you know is now in my hands, and I pledge myself that shall suffice; I really think such a bagatelle as that cannot be objectionable to you. Were I in your place, I can assure you, Mr. Webb, as a man of honour, I should be delighted to do the same."

"Were you in my place, Major Longsword," replied the Counsellor, "you would, no doubt, act with more judgment than I shall do; but without wishing to say anything offensive to you, I may as well assure you at once that I will give no letter to any one on the subject."

"But, Mr. Webb, you cannot deny or justify the allusion—the very pointed allusion?"

"I certainly shall not deny it; indeed to you, Major Longsword, I have no objection to acknowledge it."

"And yet you'll not just state your regret—in a note to myself mind! Why, Mr. Webb, you can't but regret it; you can't desire bloodshed."

"Indeed, Major, I do not regret it. Your friend considered himself at liberty to accuse me in private—not by name, but by allusion, as you say—of certain feelings and opinions derogatory to me. I have retaliated in public. I believe now you will own that I consult your convenience best by telling you that Major Macdonnel, of Tramore, is my friend in this matter. He will make all arrangements with you for the immediate termination of this affair."

"I shall be proud to see the Major; but still let me hope, Mr. Webb, that this little affair may be arranged. As a magistrate, and as a man, I may say, not exactly in your *première jeunesse*—"

"As a magistrate, and as a man not exactly, as you say, in my *première jeunesse*, for I was fifty yesterday, let me assure you that if Mr. Brown intends to call me out, I shall go out. If he intends to let me alone, I shall be better pleased to be let alone; as for a word, or a line of retractation or apology, I will not give it."

"But, Mr. Webb—"

"Forgive me for interrupting you, but allow me to suggest that any further remarks you may have to make on the subject had better be made to my friend, Major Macdonnel."

"Would you allow me to put it to you in another light? Suppose now—"

"Major Longsword, the idea of being uncourteous to any man in my own house is particularly grievous to me; but with your pardon I must say that I cannot continue this conversation with you. If you will allow me the honour of considering the remainder of your visit one of compliment, I shall be proud to increase my acquaintance with a gentleman for whom I entertain so profound a respect."

The baffled Major was obliged to take the hint, to move himself

off, and have recourse to his brother major. Maj[or]
received his visitor with a very long face, assured
principal had left him nothing to do but to arrange
and that however willing he might be to agree to pa[y]
himself, he had no power to do so. The Boyle M[ajor]
found a more willing listener in his colleague than in t[he]
and made many eloquent dissertations; but it was all t[o]
he was obliged to return to Brown Hall, signally defe[ated]
himself, and with the tidings that a place had been a[greed]
that the meeting was to take place at eight, A.M., the [next]

"I had really hoped, Mr. Brown, to have been abl[e]
little matter amicably; indeed I had no doubt about i[t]
say a more impracticable gentleman to deal with than
was never my lot to meet upon such an occasion."

The Major dined at Brown Hall, and could not b[ut]
solicitude which the two sons expressed for their fathe[r]
the filial manner in which they comforted him. Duri[ng]
was somewhat silent and moody; but when he got t[o]
recovered his spirits, and seemed tolerably happy.
conducted himself wonderfully well, considering tha[t]
whole evening Fred and George would talk of nothing
skulls, false knee-caps—cork legs—bullets that had
men's backs ten years after they had entered men's belli[es]
knives—pincers and tourniquets—wills—attorneys—[]
and the family vault. George expressed a great des[ire to]
see his parent shot. Fred said that eight o'clock was
early, or else he'd be happy. George was so warm in
that in spite of his father's declining this mark of hi[s]
insisted on attending him to the ground; and it w[as]
Major Longsword gravely assured him that if he, Geo[rge]
he, Major Longsword, would not be there too, that th[e]
was prevailed on to give up his project.

The affair was to come off in the County Roscom[mon]
mile and a half from Carrick, at the edge of a small [a]
mile on the left hand side of the Boyle road. A mess[age]
conveyed to Doctor Blake to be near the spot with
instruments that had been so freely named on the prev[ious]
At the hour appointed, the military Major and his frie[nd]
the Brown Hall chariot, and a few minutes afterw[ards]
military Major and his man appeared on the Counsello[r]
any one walked about the ground with very scrutinis[ing]
might have espied Doctor Blake snugly ensconced und[er]
a cigar in his mouth, and a small mahogany box lying

The carriages had been left a few hundred yards

the two servants, well knowing what was going to happen, discussed cosily and leisurely the chance they either of them had of carrying home a dead master.

"Faix, Barney," said the Brown Hall whip, "I believe we stand a baddish chance; they do be saying the Counsellor's mighty handy with the powdher; would you plaze to try a blast this cowld morning?" and he handed him his pipe.

"And thank ye kindly too, Dan; it's a mighty cowld place. Why thin it's thrue for you,—the masther is handy with the powdher; more power to his elbow this morning."

"But whisper now, Barney, did he iver shoot many now to your knowing? did he shoot 'em dead? I wonder whether Mr. Fred will be keeping on the chariot; he's more taste in the gig way, I'm fearing."

"Why thin, the Counsellor mayn't shoot him dead; that is, av he behaves himself, and don't have no blusthering. Was old Jonas much afeard, now, Dan?"

"Afeard, is it! the divil wouldn't fright him. Maybe, after all, it's the Counsellor 'll be shot first."

"Oh, in course he may," said Barney; "oh musha, musha, wirrasthrue, how'd I ever be looking the misthress and the young ladies in the face, av I was taking him home dead and buried as he's likely to be, av he don't hit that owld masther of yours in the very first go off;" and then the man's air of triumph at the idea of his master's shooting Jonas Brown, turned to despondency as the thought struck him that the Counsellor might be shot himself. But he soon cheered up again at a brighter reflection.

"But that'd be the wake, Dan! My; there'd have been nothing like that in the counthry, since old Peyton was waked up at Castleboy; not a man in the county but would be there, nor a woman neither; and signs on, there's not another in the counthry at all like the masther for a poor man."

At this moment two shots were heard.

"Virgin Mary!—there they are at it," said Dan; "now they're oncet began in arnest, they'll not lave it till they're both dead, or there's not a grain of powdher left. Bad cess to them Majors for bringing thim together; couldn't they be fighting theyselles av they plazed, and not be setting the real gentry of the counthry at each other like game cocks?"

"Had they much powdher I wonder, Dan? Was there a dail of ammunition in the carriage?"

"Faix their war so; that Major, bad luck to him, had his own and Master George's horns crammed with powdher, and as many bullets in a bag under his coat-tail as he could well-nigh carry."

"Then they're one or both as good as dead; they're loading again now, I'll go bail. Och! that I'd thrown the owld horse down coming over the bridge, and pitched the masther into the wather. I'd be a dail readier getting him out of that, than putting the life into him when he's had three or four of them bullets through his skin."

"It's thrue for you, Barney," said the good-natured Dan; "and as Mr. Fred couldn't well be turning an owld servant like me off the place av he didn't keep up the chariot, I wish it mayn't be the Counsellor's luck to be first kilt, for he's as good a man as iver trod."

In the meantime the two Majors had paced the ground with a good deal of official propriety, loaded the pistols, and exchanged a quantity of courtesies.

"Not so agreeable an occasion as when we last acted together in the field, Major Macdonnel; I'd sooner be clearing the course for my friend's horse, than measuring the ground for his fire."

"True, indeed, Major Longsword; true, indeed. Don't you think you're putting your friend a leetle too much under the shade? I don't know—perhaps not—but a foot or two off the trees gives a more equal light; that's it."

"I believe we're ready now—eh, Major?"

"Quite ready, Major. We'll have it over in two minutes."

"I say, Major," and the other Major whispered; "Blake's just under the small bush there, I hope you won't want him."

"Thank ye, Major, thank ye—I hope not."

"And, Major, there can be no necessity for a second shot, I think—eh? Brown won't want a second shot, will he?"

"Not at all, Major, not at all; a trifling thing like this—we'll have it over now in a double crack, eh?"

"True, Major, true; put your man up, and I'll give the word."

And the Majors put up their men with great dexterity, and the word was given. They both fired, each at his adversary, but each without attempting to cover the other. Brown's ball whistled harmlessly away without approaching within any dangerous proximity of the Counsellor's body; but not so Webb's; it was very evident Jonas was hit, for his body gave a spasmodic jerk forwards, his knees bent under him, and his head became thrown back somewhat over his shoulders. He did not fall himself, but his hat did; he dropped his pistol to the ground, and inserted both his right and his left hand under the tails of his coat.

Mr. Brown indulged a notion, whether correctly or not I am unable to say, but one which I believe to be not uncommon, that by presenting his side instead of his front to his adversary's fire, he exposed fewer vital parts to danger; and if destiny intended him to be wounded, he certainly, in the present instance, was benefited by the above arrangement, for he received the bullet in perhaps the least dangerous part of his body.

Mr. Brown was a stout, compact man, well developed and rounded in the fuller parts of his body; he piqued himself somewhat on the fair proportions of his nether man; he was also somewhat of a dandy; and had come out this morning, as, I believe, was the custom on such occasions, nearly full dressed; he had on a black dress coat, black waistcoat, and black well fitting trousers; and as he turned his side to the Counsellor, he displayed to advantage the whole of his comely figure.

But, alas! its comeliness was destined for a time to be destroyed. Mr. Webb's fire passed directly under the tails of his coat; the ball just traversed along his trousers about a foot beneath the waistband, cutting them and his drawers and shirt, as it were, with a knife, and wounding the flesh in its course to the depth of perhaps the eighth part of an inch.

Directly Major Longsword perceived that his man was hit, he vociferously called for Blake.

From the position which Mr. Brown assumed on receiving the fire, it was the general opinion of all the party that he was not mortally wounded. Blake was immediately on the spot, and lost no time in supporting him.

"Where is it, Mr. Brown, where is it? Can you stand? Can you walk? Allow me to support you to the bank. You can get a seat there; we must sit down at once. My dear sir, the first thing is to get you to a comfortable seat."

"Comfortable seat, and be d—d to you!" was the patient's uncivil reply. "Go to hell, I tell you!" as Blake continued to lift him. "I'm well enough; I can walk to the carriage!"

"My dear sir," continued the doctor, "the ball must be in your side; at any rate allow me to discover where it is."

"Ball be d—d, I tell you!" and he hobbled a little way off from his tormentor; the portion of his trousers on the part affected annoyed him sorely when he attempted to walk.

"Permit me to hope," said the Counsellor, coming up—"permit me to hope, now that this affair seems to be over, that you are not seriously hurt. Had you not better allow Doctor Blake to ascertain whether the bullet still remains in you? had you not better sit down?"

"Bother Doctor Blake, sir," said Mr. Brown, with his hands still under his coat tails.

"Ah! I see now," said the Doctor, stooping down; "I see the

wound, I think. It's bleeding now—and I think I may guarantee that there's no danger; allow me one minute, for the ball may be lodged," and he proceeded to lift up the tails of the coat.

"Doctor Blake, if you touch me again, by heavens I'll kick you! when I want you, I'll send for you. Major Longsword, will you do me the honour to accompany me to my carriage—ugh, d—n it!"

This last exclamation was occasioned by his renewed attempt to walk. He managed, however, at last, to get to his carriage, and in that to Brown Hall. Major Longsword, who accompanied him, declared afterwards to his brother officers at Boyle, that Mr. Brown's efforts to support himself by the arm-straps in the carriage were really disagreeable to witness. He got home safely, however; and though he was not competent to attend to his public duties for some considerable time, it is believed he was not a great sufferer. The Brown Hall livery servant was seen in the chemist's shop the same morning, asking for a yard and a half of diaculum, which was supplied to him; and a new pair of dress trousers, somewhat fuller than the last, was ordered from the tailor. Doctor Blake was not called in, for Mr. Brown found himself, with his son's assistance, equal to the cure of the wound he had received.

CHAPTER XXVII.

FEEMY RETURNS TO BALLYCLORAN.

It will be remembered that Father John had promised to take upon himself all the trouble attendant upon the preparation for Thady's trial; and with the view of redeeming this promise he went up to Dublin and spent a week among the lawyers who were to be engaged for the young man's defence. The chief among these was one Mr. O'Malley, and the priest strove hard to imbue that gentleman with his own views of the whole matter. The day after that on which Father John returned, he saw both Mr. McKeon and the Counsellor, and explained to them as nearly as he could all that had passed between himself and O'Malley. Though they were both greatly interested on Thady's account, they did not feel the same intense, constant anxiety, which now quite oppressed the priest; and, moreover, trusting more to their own judgment than he did, they were not so inclined to alter their pre-conceived opinion. They both, therefore, assured Father John that they were still quite sanguine as to Thady's acquittal. This raised his hopes again a little, but nevertheless, from that time till the trial, he was so absorbed by his strong feeling on the subject, that he was almost totally unable to attend to the usual duties and employment of his life. It was decided that Mr. Webb should use all his endeavours to obtain tidings of Corney Dolan, and ascertain whether, in the event of his being summoned, he would be able to give any evidence respecting the meeting at Mrs. Mehan's, which would be of use to Thady at the trial. In this he was successful, and he learnt from that respectable individual that he could swear that Ussher's name was not mentioned at all.

It must be owned that Mr. Dolan's manner was not such as to inspire the Counsellor with any great admiration for his veracity, and his opinion in this respect was strengthened when the witness added "that by Garra, av his honor thought it'd be any use in life to Mr. Thady, he'd swear as how he was asleep all the time; or for the matther of that, that he was out along wid de gals dancing the livelong night." It was with difficulty that Mr. Webb made him understand that he was only to swear to what he believed to be the truth, and that if he told a single lie in answer to the numerous questions which would be asked him, he would only be endangering Mr. Macdermot's life.

Father John undertook the more difficult task of explaining to Feemy what it was she was expected to do at the trial, and of making her understand that her brother's life depended on her making an effort to give her evidence in the court clearly and firmly. On reaching Drumsna he was much distressed to find that she was no longer at Mrs. McKeon's. For two days after the conversation which had passed between that lady and her charge, in which she declared her suspicions that Feemy was *enceinte*, the latter had made a great effort to recover her health, or at any rate the appearance of health. She left her bed earlier in the morning than she had ever done for the last five months; she dressed herself with great care, and—for alas, Mrs. McKeon's suspicion was but too true— fastened her dress with a most dangerous determination to prove that the charge was unfounded. Patiently she endured all the agonies which this occasioned her during the first day and during the whole evening, till the house was at rest and she was secure from being again visited. On the next morning she went so far as to come down to breakfast, and to undergo Tony's somewhat rough congratulation as to her convalescence, without betraying her sufferings. After breakfast, when he was gone out, she again opened the subject of her return home, and begged Mrs. McKeon to allow her to have the car to return to Ballycloran. Mrs. McKeon again put her off, telling her that it would be necessary first to consult the doctor, and that he would not be likely to call till the following day.

In the afternoon Mrs. McKeon, with Lyddy and Louey, went out for a drive, and as Feemy was apparently so much better, they asked her to accompany them, but this she declined.

"It's as well for her not to go out before the trial," whispered Mrs. McKeon to her daughters. "Poor girl; she has a great deal, a great deal, indeed, to go through yet." Indeed she had a very great deal to go through; a very heavy atonement to pay for her folly and her crime.

As soon as the car was gone from the door, she hurried up stairs, put on her bonnet and cloak, took a letter which she had already prepared, and opening the door of Mrs. McKeon's own room, put it on the table. She then crept noiselessly down stairs, opened the front door, and passed into the street, without having been seen or heard by either of the servants, who were alone left with her in the house. The following is the letter, which, to her great grief and surprise, Mrs. McKeon found on her table when she returned:—

"Dear Mrs. McKeon,

"It is because I know you'd never let me go back to Ballycloran, that I've now gone away without telling you what I was going to do. Pray don't be angry with me. Indeed I'm very unhappy; but I should be worse if you were to be angry with me. I'm only a bother and a throuble to you here, and I hav'n't spirits left even to let you see how very much obliged I am to you for all your throuble; but indeed I am in my heart, my dear Mrs. McKeon, both to you and to dear Lyddy and Louey, who have been so very kind to me. It is a deal better for me to be at home with my father, my heart's nearly broken with all I've gone through; but he'll bear with me, for he's used to me. Give my compliments to Doctor Blake. Pray beg him not to come to Ballycloran. I am in his debt a great deal already, and how will I ever pay him? Besides, I'm a deal better now, as you see, in health; it's only the heart now that ails me. Give my kind love to Lyddy and Louey. I felt their kindness when the sorrow within me wouldn't let me tell them so. Now good bye, dear Mrs. McKeon; don't be throubling yourself to come to Ballycloran; it'll be a poor place now. I'll send Katty for the things.

"I remain, dear Mrs. McKeon,
"Very, very faithfully yours,
"Feemy.

"P.S.—Indeed—indeed—it isn't the case, what you were saying."

When Mrs. McKeon found the letter on her return, she was greatly vexed; but she could do nothing; she couldn't go to Ballycloran and fetch Feemy by force. The falsehood with which the letter concluded was not altogether disbelieved; but still she felt by no means certain that her former suspicions were not true, and if so, perhaps it was better for all parties that Feemy should be at home. She determined to call at Ballycloran when Feemy might be supposed to have settled herself, and content herself for the present with hearing from the girl who came for the clothes that she had got home safe.

When Father John called on the Saturday, she talked over the subject as fully with him as she could without alluding to the matter respecting which she was so much in doubt. He declared his intention of seeing Feemy on the following Monday, and of speaking to her strongly on the subject of the trial which was so soon coming on; and he begged Mrs. McKeon to do the same afterwards—as perhaps having become latterly used to her interference, Feemy might bear from her what she had to be told, with more patience than she would from himself.

"Indeed I will, Father John, but do you be gentle with her She's broken-hearted now; you'll find her very different from the hot-headed creature she was before her sorrows began."

"I fear she is—I fear she is; but, Mrs. McKeon, has she ever shown a feeling of regard—a spark of interest, for her noble brother?—it's that so annoys me in Feemy; I could feel for her—weep for her—and forgive her with all my heart—all but that."

"Ah, Father John," answered the lady; "it's not for me to preach to you: but where would we all be at the last, if our Judge should say to us, 'I can forgive you all but that?'"

"God forbid I should judge her; God forbid I should limit that to her, which I so much need myself. But isn't her heart hardened against her brother? Oh, if you could have seen him as I have done this morning—if you could believe how softened is his heart! He had never much false pride in it—it is nearly all gone now! If you could have heard how warmly, how affectionately he asks after the sister that won't mention his name; if you could know how much more anxious he is on her account and his father's, than on his own, Feemy's coldness and repugnance would strike you as it does me. I'm afraid her chief sorrow is still for the robber that would have destroyed her, and has destroyed her brother."

"Of course it is, Father John—and so it should be. I'm a woman and a mother, and you may take my word respecting a woman's heart. No wife could love her husband more truly than Feemy loved that man: unworthy as he was, he was all in all to her.

Would it not, therefore, show more heartlessness in her to forget him that is now dead, than the brother who killed him? Of course she loved him better than her brother, as every woman loves the man she does love better than all the world. How can she forget him? Be gentle to her, Father John, and I think she will do what you desire."

Father John promised that he would comply with Mrs. McKeon's advice, and he was as good as his word.

On reaching the hall-door of Mrs. McKeon's house Feemy looked cautiously about her, but seeing that no one belonging to the house was in sight, she passed on through the little garden into the street. She pulled her old veil down over her face, and walked on through the village as quickly as she could. She felt that every one's eye was on her; that all the country was looking at her; but she had made up her mind to go through it all, and she persevered. The last time she had been out of the house was the day she had been taken from Ballycloran to the inquest. That was a horrid day, but the present seemed worse; she had now a greater sorrow than any of which she was then conscious, and she had to bear it alone, unpitied and uncomforted. Indeed, her only rest, her only respite from absolute torture was now to consist in being alone; and yet bad as the present was, there was a worse,—she felt that there was a worse in store for her. She already anticipated the tortures of that day, when she would again be dragged out from her resting-place before the eyes of all mankind, and placed in the very middle of the crowd, conspicuous above the rest, to be stared at, bullied, and questioned horridly about that dread subject, which it even racked her mind to remember. Would she be able on that long, long day—days, for what she knew—to conceal her shame from all who would be looking at her, and to bear in patience the agonies which it would be necessary for her to endure? She walked on quickly, and was soon out of Drumsna, and in the lane leading by the cottage to Ballycloran. By the time she had walked half a mile she was in a dreadful heat, although it was still in March, for she was so weak and ill that her exertion in proportion to her strength, had been immense. She sat down by the side of the road for a time, and then continued; and then again sat down. Her sufferings were soon so great that she was unable to walk above two hundred yards at a time, and she began to fear that she would be utterly unable to get to the house. Once when she was sitting, panting on the bank by the road-side, one of the labouring peasants recognised her—saw she was ill—and offered to get her a country car. Oh, what an agonising struggle she made to answer the man cheerfully, when she assured him that she was quite well—that she was only sitting there for her pleasure—that she required no assistance, and that she should walk home directly. The man well knew that she was not there for her pleasure—that her brother was in gaol, her father on the point of losing his property, and that she was weak and in need of rest; but he saw that she would sooner be alone, and he had the good tact to leave her, without pressing his offer for her accommodation.

At length she reached the avenue, and had to pass the spot where she had sat so long on that fatal night listening for the sound of her lover's horse, and watching her brother as he stood swinging his stick before the house. She shuddered as she did so, but she did walk by the tree where she had then sat shivering, and at last once more stood on the steps of her father's house.

The door was fastened inside, and she had to knock for admittance. This she did three times, till she thought she should have fainted on the flags, and at last the window of her own sitting-room was raised, and Mary McGovery's head was slowly protruded. Feemy was sitting on the low stone wall, which guarded the side of the flags, as she heard Mary say in a sharp voice—

"Who's that?—and what are ye wanting here? Oh! by the mortials, but av it aint Miss Feemy herself come back I declare!"

And Mary ran round, and began to draw the bolts of the front door. Up jumped Larry at the unwelcome sound, from his accustomed seat by the fire.

"What in the divil's name are ye afther? What are ye doing? Ye owld hag, will ye be letting the ruffians in on me?" And he caught violently hold of Mary's gown to drag her back, before she had accomplished the liberation of the rusty bolts.

"Now go in, sir, and sit down," said Mary. "Go in, sir, will you; I tell you it's yer own daughter, and no ruffian whatever. Dra— the owld man, but he'll have every rag off the back of me! Don't I tell you, it's Miss Feemy. Will you be asy now?—do you want to have me stark naked?"

"Come away, woman, I tell you; don't I know Feemy's gone off, away from me; she'll niver, niver come back; it's Keegan and his hell-hounds you're letting in on me."

By this time Mary had accomplished her object of undoing the door in spite of the old man's exertions, and Feemy entered weary and worn, soiled with the road, and pale and wan in spite of the hectic flush which reddened a portion of her cheek.

"Father," she said when she saw the old man standing astonished and stupified in the hall, "father, don't ye know me—won't ye spake to me?"

"Why thin, Feemy, is it yer own self in arnest come back again?

And where's yer lover? the man ye married, ye kn
his name?—why don't ye tell me? Mary, what's t
Captain Feemy married?"

"Asy, sir, asy; come in thin," and Mary led him int
and Feemy followed in silence with her eyes already f

"Where's yer own husband thin, Feemy dear?
—Captain Ussher—it's he'd be welcome with you
and he began stroking his daughter's shoulders an
had still her bonnet on her head. "Thady's not
brow-beating and teasing him; it's we'll be comfo
cowld long nights—for the Captain 'll be bringing t
the groceries with him, won't he, darling? and Th
guard's out along wid Keegan, and they can't get
door, for it's always locked;" and then turning to
"why don't you put the locks back, you d—d jade
them to be catching me the first moment I'm seeing 1
girl here?"

Feemy could not say a word to her father: his a
and the manner in which he referred to Ussher, quite
she sat down and wept bitterly.

"What ails you, pet?" continued the old man, '
alanna? they shan't touch him, dear—there, you se
closed now; he'll be safe from Thady now, darling.'

"Oh, Miss Feemy," said Mary, "he's quite besid
now, sir, asy, and don't be talking such nonsense;
the Captain got kilt—months ago—last October?"

"Killed—and who dared to kill my darling's husbar
to touch him? why wasn't he here? why wasn't he
lock?"

"Why, don't you know," and Mary gave the old
shake to refresh his memory; "don't you know
him in the avenue?"

"May his father's curse blisther him then! May
they wor telling me about that before. Eh, Feemy?
with a sigh, "it's a bad time I've been having of it
woman since you were gone; she don't lave me a
from morning to night; bad 'cess to her, but I wis
out of the house. I'll have you to mind me now—
be bawling and shaking me as she does; but she's a
he added in a whisper.

Feemy could bear this no longer; she was oblige
escape from the room into her own, in which she fo
had taken up her temporary residence during so mu
as she could spare from bawling at, and shaking, po

dinner time, she again went into her father's room, but he took no farther notice of her, than if she had been there continually for the last four months. He grumbled at his dinner, which consisted of nothing but potatoes, some milk, and an egg, and he scolded Feemy for having no meat; after dinner she mixed him a tumbler of punch, for there was still a little of Tony's whiskey in the house; and whether it was that she made it stronger for him and better than that which Mary McGovery was in the habit of mixing, or that the action to which he had been for so many years accustomed roused some pleasant memory within him, when he tasted it, he said—

"Heaven's blessing on you, Feemy, my daughter; may you live many happy years with the man you love."

Feemy soon left him, and went to bed, and Katty, who had been dispatched to Drumsna, returned with her mistress's small box, and a kind message from Mrs. McKeon:—" Her kind love to Miss Macdermot; she hoped she had felt the walk of service to her, and she would call some time during the next week." She had asked no questions of the girl which could lead her to imagine that her mistress's departure from Drumsna had been unexpected, nor had she said a word to her own servants which could let them suppose that she was surprised at the circumstance.

For five or six days Feemy remained quiet at Ballycloran—spending the greater part of her time in her own room, but taking her meals, such as they were, with her father; she had no books to read, and she was unable to undertake needlework, and she passed the long days much as her father did—sitting from breakfast till dinner over the fire, meditating on the miseries of her condition. There was this difference, however, between them—that the old man felt a degree of triumph at his successful attempt to keep out his foes, whereas Feemy's thoughts were those of unmixed sorrow. She had great difficulty too in inducing Mary to leave her alone to herself. Had that woman the slightest particle of softness in her composition, anything of the tenderness of a woman about her, Feemy would have made a confidant of her, and her present sufferings would have been immeasurably decreased; but Mary was such an iron creature—so loud, so hard, so equable in her temper, so impenetrable, that Feemy could not bring herself to tell her tale of woe, which otherwise she would have been tempted to disclose. She had, therefore, the additional labour of keeping her secret from Mary's prying eyes, and Mary was nearly as acute as Mrs. McKeon.

About noon, on Monday, Feemy was horror-struck at being told by Katty that Father John was at the back door asking for her.

"Oh, Katty, tell him to wait awhile; say I'm ill, can't you—do, dear!"

"Why, Miss, I towld him as how you war up, and betther, thank God, since you war home."

It was clearly necessary that she should see the priest; but she insisted on his not being shown in till she had dressed herself; and she again submitted herself to those agonies which she trusted, for a time, would hide her disgrace, which at last must become known to all. When this was done, she seated herself on the sofa, and plucked up all her courage to go through the painful conversation which she knew she was to endure. She did not rise as he entered, but remained on the sofa with the hectic tint on her face almost suffused into a blush, and her hands clasping the calico covering of the cushion, as if from that she could get more strength for endurance.

Father John shook hands with her as he seated himself by her; the tears came into his eyes as he observed the sad change which so short a time had made in her. The flesh had fallen from her face, and the skin now hung loose upon her cheek and jaw bones, falling-in towards the mouth, giving her that lean and care-worn look which misery so soon produces. Her healthy colour, too, had all fled; part of her face was of a dull leaden paleness, and though there was a bright colour round her eyes, it gave her no appearance of health. She looked ten years older than when he had seen her last. No wonder Mrs. McKeon pitied her so deeply; she appeared even more pitiable than her brother, who was awaiting his doubtful fate in gaol—though with nervous anxiety, still with unflinching courage.

"I am glad to hear you're better, Feemy. Mrs. McKeon thinks you a great deal better."

"Thank ye, Father John; I believe I'm well enough now."

"That's well, then; but you must take care of yourself, Feemy, no more long walks; you should have waited for the car to come home that day. Mrs. McKeon's not the least angry; if you are more at ease here than at Drumsna, she's glad for your sake you're here now, and she bids me tell you how sorry she is she didn't give you the car the day you asked for it."

"Oh, Father John, Mrs. McKeon's been too kind to me. Indeed I love her dearly, though I could never tell her so. Give her my kind love. I never thought she was so kind a woman."

"I will, Feemy; indeed I will. She is a kind woman; and it will please her to the heart to hear how you speak of her. She sends you all manner of loves, and Lyddy and Louey too. She is sending up a few things for you too. Patsey'll bring them, just till affairs are settled a little. She wishes me to tell you she'll be up herself on Thursday; she wouldn't come before, for she thought you'd be better pleased to be alone a few days."

"Tell her not to come here. This is no place for her now. They never open the front door now. This is no place for any one now, but just father and me. But tell her how I love her. I'll never forget her; no, not in my grave!"

"But I've another message for you, Feemy."

"Is it from her?"

"No, not from her, well as she loves you; it's from one who loves you better than she does; it is from one who loves you better than any ever did, since your poor mother died."

Feemy raised her eyes, and clasped her hands, as she listened to Father John's words, and marked his solemn tones. No thought of Thady entered her mind; but some indefinite, half-conceived idea respecting Ussher—that he had not been killed—that he had come to life again—that some mysterious miracle, such as she had read of in novels, had taken place; and that Father John had come with some blessed news, which might yet restore her to happiness and tranquillity. The illusion was but for a moment, though during that moment it completely took possession of her. It was as speedily dispelled by Father John's concluding words—

"I mean from your brother."

Feemy gave a long, long sigh as she heard the word. She wished for no message from her brother; he had robbed her of everything; she could not think of him without horror and shuddering.

"He sends his kindest love to you. I told him you were better, and he was very glad to hear it. Though he has many heavy cares of his own to bear, I have never seen him but he asks after your health with more anxiety than he thinks of his own prospects. Now you are better, Feemy, won't you send him some message by me?—some kind word, which may comfort him in his sorrow?"

Feemy was no hypocrite; hypocrisy, though she did not know it herself, was distasteful to her. She had no kind feelings for her brother, and she did not know how to make the pretence which might produce kind words; so she remained silent.

"What! not a word, Feemy? you who spoke so well, so properly, so affectionately, but now of that good friend of yours— have you not a word of kindness for a most affectionate brother?"

Feemy still remained silent.

"Why, Feemy, what is this? Don't you love your own brother?"

U

She said nothing in reply for a moment or tw[o]
bursting into tears, she exclaimed,

"Don't scold me, Father John!—don't scold me [as I] die! I try to forgive him—I am always trying! [But] he—why did he—why did he—" She was unable [to finish the] sentence from the violence of her sobs and the difficu[lty of] the words which should have concluded it. She [said,] "Why did he kill my lover?"

"Don't agitate yourself, Feemy. I don't mean t[o— I] don't mean even to vex you more than I can possib[ly, but I] must speak to you about your brother. I see th[at he] is in your mind, and I will not blame you for it, fo[r it is] natural; but I beseech you to pray that your hear[t be soft]ened towards your brother, who instead of repugn[ance merits] from you the warmest affection. But though I wi[sh you] to control your feelings, I must tell you that you [will be] wicked if you allow them to interfere with the [performance of] your duties. You know your brother's trial is com[ing on,] not?"

"Yes."

"Wednesday fortnight next is the day fixed, I [also] know you will have to be a witness?"

"I believe so, Father John."

"Certainly you will; and I wish you now to list[en, that] you may know what it is that you will then have [to say. In the] first place you will be asked, I presume, by one gentl[eman, if] you were willingly eloping with Captain Ussher?" [She shud]dered as the name was pronounced. "And of co[urse you must] answer that truly—that you were doing so. Then a[nother gentle]man will ask you whether you were absolutely wa[lking with] him when the blow was struck which killed Captai[n Ussher.] Feemy, you must also answer that truly. Now th[ink well—] can you remember what you were doing when [the blow was] struck? Tell me now, Feemy, can you remember?"

"No, Father John, I remember nothing; from t[he time] he took me by the arm, as I sat upon the tree, till [I knew] he was dead, I remember nothing. If they kill [him I'll tell] them nothing."

"Feemy, dear, don't sob so! That's all you'l[l say.] Merely say that—merely say that you were sitti[ng there.] Were you waiting for Captain Ussher there?"

"Yes."

"And that whilst you were there you saw Thady;[?]"

"Yes."

"And Usslier then raised you by the arm, and then you fainted?"

"I don't know what happened to me; but I heard nothing, and saw nothing, till Thady lifted me from the ground, and told me he was dead."

"That's all, Feemy. Surely there's no great difficulty in saying that—when it'll save your own brother's life to say so; and it's only the truth. You can say as much in court as you've just said to me, can't you? Mrs. McKeon'll be there with you—and I'll be there with you. You'll only have to say in court what you've just said to me."

"I'll try, Father John. But you don't know what it is for one like me to be talking with so many horrid faces round one—with the heart dead within—to be asked such horrid questions, and everybody listening. I'll do as you bid me; I'll go with them when they fetch me—but I know I'll die before I've said all they will want me to say."

Father John tried to comfort and strengthen her, but she was in great bodily pain, and he soon saw that he had better leave her; she had at any rate shown him by her answers to his questions, that the evidence she could give would be such as would most tend to Thady's acquittal; and, moreover, he perceived from her manner, that though the feelings which she entertained towards her brother were of a most painful description, she would, nevertheless, not be actuated by them in any of the answers she might give.

On the Thursday following Mrs. McKeon and one of her daughters called at Ballycloran, and in spite of the bars and bolts with which the front door was barricaded, they contrived to make their way into Feemy's room. She remembered that Father John had told her that they would call on that day, and she was therefore prepared to receive them. Mrs. McKeon brought her some little comforts from Drumsna, of which she was sadly in want; for there was literally nothing at Ballycloran but what was supplied by the charity of those who pitied them in their misfortunes; and among other things she brought two or three volumes from the library. She was very kind to her, and did and said all in her power that could in any way console the poor girl. Though Father John had been gentle in his manners and had endeavoured to abstain from saying anything hard, still Mrs. McKeon was more successful in her way of explaining to Feemy what it was that she would have to do. She promised, moreover, to come to Ballycloran and fetch her, and to remain with her and support her during the whole of the painful time that she would either be in the court itself, or waiting in the neighbourhood till she should be called on to give her evidence. She did not allude either to the manner in which Feemy had left Drumsna, or to the suspicions which she had formerly expressed. Her whole object now was to relieve as much as possible the despondency and misery so plainly pictured in the poor girl's face. As she put her arm round her neck and kissed her lips, Feemy's heart yearned towards her new-found friend with a kind of tenderness she had never before felt. It was as though she for once experienced a mother's solicitude for her in her sorrows, and she longed to throw herself on her knees, hide her face in her friend's lap, and confess it all. Had she been alone with her she would have done so; but there sat Louey in the same room, and though her conduct to Feemy had been everything that was kind, she felt that it was not as if she had been absolutely alone with her mother. She could not at the same time confess her disgrace to two.

Mrs. McKeon went away, after having strongly implored Feemy to return with her to Drumsna, and remain there till the trial was over. But this she absolutely refused to do—and at last it was settled that Mrs. McKeon should come for her on the morning on which the trial was to come on, and that she should hold herself ready to attend on any day that she might be called for after the commencement of the assizes.

The time now wore quickly on. When Mrs. McKeon called it had only wanted a fortnight to the first day on which the trial could take place; and as it quickly slipped away, day by day, to that bourn from which no day returns, poor Feemy's sorrow and agonies became in every way more acute. At last, on the Wednesday,—the day before that on which she was to be, or at any rate, might be fetched,—she was in such a state that she was unable to support herself in a chair. Mary McGovery would not leave her for a moment. The woman meant kindly, but her presence was only an additional torment. She worried and tortured Feemy the whole day; she talked to her, intending to comfort her, till she was so bewildered, that she could not understand a word that was said; and she kept bringing her food and slops, declaring that there was nothing like eating for a sore heart,—that if Ussher was gone, there were still as good fish in the sea as ever were caught,—and that even if Thady were condemned, the judge couldn't do more than transport him, which would only be sending him out to a better country, and "faix the one he'd lave's bad enough for man and baste."

About seven in the evening Feemy was so weak that she fainted. Mary, who was in the room at the time, lifted her on the sofa, and when she found that her mistress did not immediately come to herself, she began stripping her for the sake of unlacing her stays, and thus learnt to a certainty poor Feemy's secret.

Mary had a great deal of shrewd common sense of the coarser kind; she felt that however well inclined she might be to her mistress, she should not keep to herself the circumstance that she had just learnt; she knew it was her duty as a woman to make it known to some one, and she at once determined to go that evening to Mrs. McKeon and tell her what it was she had discovered.

As soon as Feemy had come to herself, she got her into bed, and having performed the same friendly office for the old man, she started off for Drumsna; and having procured a private audience with Mrs. McKeon, told her what had occurred.

Mrs. McKeon was not at all surprised, though she was greatly grieved. She merely said,—

"You have done quite right, Mary, to tell me; but don't mention it yet to any one else; after all this affair is over we'll see what will be best to do. God help her, poor girl; it were almost better she should die," and as Mary went down stairs she called her back to her. "Take my silk cloak with you, Mary. Tell Miss Macdermot I've sent it, because she'll be so cold to-morrow —and Mary," and here she whispered some instruction on the stairs, " and mind I shall come myself for her—but let her be ready, as may be there mayn't be a minute to spare."

Father John was certainly right when he said that Mrs. McKeon had a kind heart.

CHAPTER XXVIII.

ASSIZES AT CARRICK-ON-SHANNON.

AND now the assize week in Carrick-on-Shannon had commenced, and all was bustle and confusion, noise, dirt, and distraction. I have observed that a strong, determined, regularly set-in week of bad weather usually goes the circuit in Ireland in company with the judges and barristers, making the business of those who are obliged to attend even more intolerable than from its own nature it is always sure to be. And so it was in this case.

On Tuesday afternoon Mr. Baron Hamilton and Justice Kilpatrick entered Carrick-on-Shannon, one after the other, in the company of the high sheriff, and a tremendous shower of rain, which drenched the tawdry liveries of the servants, and gave a most uncomfortable appearance to the whole affair.

The grand jury had been in the town since Monday morning—settling fiscal business—wrangling about roads—talking of tolls—checking county cesses—and performing those various patriotic offices, which they would fain make the uninitiated believe, require so much talent, industry, and energy; and as they were seen stepping over the running gutters, and making the best of their way through the splashing streets, their physiognomies appeared ominous of nothing good to the criminals, whose cases had in the first instance to come before them.

Every lodging in the town was engaged, beds being let, sometimes three in a room, for the moderate sum of a guinea each for the week. The hotels, for there are two, were crowded from the garrets to the cellars. Happy the man at such a period, who enjoys a bed-room which he can secure with a key—for without such precaution the rightful possessor is not at all unlikely, on entering his own premises, to find three or four somewhat rough looking strangers, perhaps liberated jurors, or witnesses just escaped from the fangs of a counsel, sitting in most undisturbed ease on his bed, eating bread and butter, and drinking bottled porter. Some huge farmer with dripping frieze coat will be squatted on his pillow, his towel spread as table-cloth on the little deal table which has been allotted to him as the only receptacle for his jug, basin, looking-glass, brushes, and every other article of the toilet, and his carpet-bag, dressing-gown, and pantaloons chucked unceremoniously into a corner, off the chairs which they had occupied, to make way for the damp friends of the big farmer, who is seated on the bed. This man is now drawing a cork from a bottle of porter, the froth of which you are quite sure from the manner in which the bottle is held, will chiefly fall upon the sheets between which you are destined to sleep,—unless some half drunken ruffian, regardless of rights of possession and negligent of etiquette, deposits himself there before the hour at which you may think good to retire to rest.

Fruitless and vain would it be for you to endeavour to disturb that convivial party. Better lock up your bag, above all things not forgetting your brushes; and, as you are a witness yourself, go down to the court and admire the ingenious manner in which the great barrister, Mr. Allewinde, is endeavouring to make that unfortunate and thoroughly disconcerted young man in the witness box, swear to a point diametrically opposite to another point to which he has already sworn at the instigation of counsel on the other side,—and thereby perjure himself. Never mind the bustling of eager, curious countrymen; never mind those noisy numerous policemen with their Sunday brass-chained caps; push on through them all, make your way into the centre of the court—go down there right on to the lawyers' benches; never mind the seats being full—plunge in; if you hesitate, look timid—ask question, or hang back—you are lost, thrust out, expelled, and finally banished with ignominy into the tumultuous sea of damp frieze coats, which æstuates in the outer court. But go on with noise, impudence, and a full face; tread on people's toes, and thrust them back with "by your leave," and you will find yourself soon seated in direct view of the judge, counsel, witness and prisoner. You will be taken for an attorney, or, at any rate, for an influential court witness. If you talk somewhat loud, and frown very angrily in the face of the tallest policeman, you may by the ignorant even be taken for a barrister.

In fact, into court you must come, there is no other place open to receive you. The big room at the hotel, in which we have been three times on such different occasions, the long big room where McKeon presided over so many drunken spirits—where poor Feemy made her last arrangements with her lover at the ball —and where so soon afterwards she was brought forward to give her evidence touching his death, while his cold body was lying dead on the table before her,—this long big room is now set apart for yet another purpose. The grand jury are to dine there, and already the knives and forks are laid out upon the long deal table. The little coffee-room—so called, though whiskey-room, or punch-room, or porter-room would be much the more appropriate name, unless indeed there is a kind of "*lucus a non lucendo*" propriety in the appellation—is full nearly to suffocation. There is not an unoccupied chair or corner of a table to be found.

Large men half wet through—reeking, smelling most unwholesomely as the rain steams up from their clothes—are keeping the cold out of their stomachs by various spirituous appliances. The room is half covered with damp straw, which has been kicked in from the passage; the windows are closed, and there is a huge fire burning on the other side of that moist mass of humanity. On entering the room you feel that you breathe nothing but second-hand rain; a sojourn there you find to be impossible; the porter drinkers are still in your bed-room, even on your bed up-stairs. What are you to do? where are you to go? Back home you cannot. You have a summons in your pocket; you have been unfortunately present when Mr. Terence O'Flanagan squeezed the fair hand of Miss Letitia Murphy; false Mr. Terence O'Flanagan would not come to the matrimonial altar when required; fair Miss Letitia Murphy demands damages, and you must swear to the fact of the hand having been squeezed as aforesaid. Who can tell when the case may come on? Rumour comes from the clerk of the peace, town clerk, or some other clerk who sits there in pride of place, always conspicuous under the judge's feet, and whispers that Letitia Murphy, spinster, is coming on next. Attorneys' clerks have been round diligently to all witnesses, especially as it seems to yourself, warning you that the important hour is at hand—that on no account may you be absent, so much as ten minutes' walk from the court. Vainly you think to yourself that it can hardly be of such vital import that you, her father's friend, saw little Letty Murphy's hand ensconced one evening in the brawny palm of that false Lothario O'Flanagan; yes, of serious import is it—if not to Letty, or to Terence—yet to that facetious barrister, Mr. O'Laugher, who, at your expense, is going to amuse the dull court for a brief half-hour,—and of importance to yourself, who are about to become the laughing-stock of your county for the next twelve months. It is, therefore, evident that you cannot leave the filthy town with its running gutters—the filthy inn with its steamy stinking atmosphere, and bed-room porter drinkers for good and all, and let Lothario O'Flanagan, Spinster Letty, Lawyers Allewinde and O'Laugher, with Justice Kilpatrick, settle the matter by themselves their own way; but that you must, willy nilly, in spite of rain, crowd, and offensive smell, stay and help to settle it with them. Into court therefore return, unfortunate witness; other shelter have you none; and now being a man of strong nerves,—except when put into a chair to be stared at by judge, bar, grand jury, little jury, attorney, galleries, &c., &c.,—you can push your way into a seat, and listen with attention to the quiddities of the legally erudite Mr. Allewinde, as on behalf of his client he ingeniously attempts—nay, as he himself afterwards boasts to the jury, succeeds in making that disconcerted young gentleman in the witness chair commit perjury.

Mr. Allewinde is a most erudite lawyer. He has been for many years employed by the crown in its prosecutions, and with great success. He knows well the art of luring on an approver, or crown witness, to give the information he wants without asking absolutely leading questions; he knows well how to bully a witness brought up on the defence out of his senses, and make him give evidence rather against than for the prisoner; and it is not only witnesses that he bullies, but his very brethren of the gown. The barristers themselves who are opposed to him, at any rate, the juniors, are doomed to bear the withering force of his caustic remarks.

"No, really, I cannot suffer this; witness, don't answer that question. The learned gentleman must be aware that this is irregular; my lord, I must appeal to you. Stop, stop; that can never be evidence," and so on:—the unfortunate junior, who fondly thought that with the pet witness now in the chair, he would be surely able to acquit his client, finds that he can hardly frame a question which his knowing foe will allow him to ask, and the great Mr. Allewinde convicts the prisoner not from the strength of his own case, but from his vastly superior legal acquirements.

How masterly is he in all the points of his profession as evinced in a criminal court. With what "becks, and smiles, and wreathed nods," he passes by his brethren on the prosecuting side, and takes his seat of honour. How charmingly he nods to the judge when his lordship lays down the law on some point in conformity with the opinion expressed by himself. How rapidly he throws to the wind the frivolous excuses of some juror wishing to escape the foreseen long night's confinement. How great is he on all points of panels—admissible and inadmissible evidence—replying and not replying. How thoroughly he knows the minute practice of the place; how he withers any attorney who may dare to speak a word on his own behalf, whilst asking questions of a witness on behalf of an otherwise undefended prisoner. How unceremoniously he takes the word out of the mouth of the, in his opinion, hardly competent junior barrister who is with him. How Demosthenic is his language when addressing the jury on the enormity of all agrarian offences; with what frightful, fearful eloquence does he depict the miseries of anarchy, which are to follow nonpayment of tithes, rents, and taxes; and with what energy does he point out to a jury that their own hearths, homes, and very existence depend on their vindicating justice in the instance before them.

Mr. Allewinde was never greater than in the case now before the court. A young farmer of the better class had been served with some disagreeably legal document on account of his non-payment of an arrear of rent; he had at the time about twenty acres of unripe oats on the ground for which the arrear was due; and he also held other ground for which he owed no arrear. On ascertaining that a distraint was to be put on the ground which owed the rent, he attended there with a crowd of countrymen, and would not allow the bailiff to put his foot upon the lands; the next day the bailiff came again with police in numbers at his heels, and found the twenty acres which had yesterday been waving with green crops, utterly denuded. Every blade had been cut and carried in the night, and was then stacked on the ground on which no distraint could be levied. In twelve hours, and those mostly hours of darkness, twenty acres had been reaped, bound, carted, carried, uncarted, and stacked, and the bailiff and the policemen had nothing to seize but the long, green, uneven stubble.

The whole country must have been there—the field must have been like a fair-green the whole night—each acre must have taken at least six men to reap—there must have been thirty head of cattle, of one sort or other, dragging it home; and there must have been upwards of a hundred women and children binding and loading. There could at any rate be no want of evidence to prove the fact. One would think so, with two or three hundred people with their tools, horses, and cars. But yet, when the landlord determined on prosecuting the tenant, there was not a person to be found who had seen the corn removed;—not one. In fact people who had not seen, as the bailiff had, the corn covering the broad field one day, and the same field bare the next, began to think that the fact was not so; and that the miraculous night's work was a fable. It was certain that the bailiff had been deterred from entering on the ground, but it was also certain that nothing but words had been used to deter him; he had not been struck or even pushed; he had only been frightened; and it seemed somewhat plain that his faint heart only had prevented him from completing his seizure—either that or some pecuniary inducement. Things were going badly with the bailiff, particularly when in answer to Mr. O'Laugher, he had been obliged to confess that on the morning on which the seizure should have been made he had taken—a thrifle of sperrits! a glass, perhaps—yes, maybe, two—yes he had taken two; three, suggested Mr. O'Laugher with a merely raised eyebrow; he couldn't say that he had not taken three; four? again inquired Mr. O'Laugher; he didn't think he had taken four. Could he swear he had not taken four? He would not swear he hadn't. He would not even swear he had not taken five;—nor even six, so conscientious a bailiff was he; but he was nearly sure he hadn't, and would swear positively he had not swallowed seven. Whereupon Mr. O'Laugher most ill-naturedly put down his morning dram at three quarters of a pint, and asked the unhappy bailiff whether that quantity was not sufficient to make him see a crop of oats in an empty field. It was going badly with the landlord and bailiff, and well with the energetic, night-working, fraudulent tenant;—and would have gone well with him, had he not determined to make assurance doubly sure.

A young man had been dining out, and had returned home at twelve o'clock on the night of the supposed miraculous reaping; he had at that hour walked home along the lane which skirted the field, and had seen no men—heard no noise—nor perceived either reapers, cars, horses, or any signs of work; yet he had passed the very gate of the field through which the corn must have come out, had it come out at all. Such was the effect of this young gentleman's evidence, when he was handed over to Mr. Allewinde by Mr. O'Laugher, with a courteous inquiry of his brother whether he wished to ask that gentleman any questions. Mr. Allewinde said that he would ask him a few questions, and the young gentleman began to tremble.

"Mr. Green, I think your name is," began Mr. Allewinde.

"Yes sir."

And then it appeared that Mr. Green absolutely remembered the night of the 12th September; had heard the rumour of the corn having been removed, but had not observed it growing there when he went to dinner; had dined at the house of the prisoner's father, about a mile beyond the field; had certainly passed the very field; could positively swear he was perfectly sober; was certainly not carried by drunk; had not observed the field especially; could not say he had looked at the field as he passed; had heard of the bailiff's retreat that morning; did not think to look at the ground where the mob had been; did not observe the place; will positively swear he heard nothing; was not walking in his sleep; could not swear whether the oats were standing at the time or not —whether the gate was open or shut—whether or no men were in the field; only he saw none; he believed it was moonlight.

"Why man! what did you see?" asked Mr. Allewinde.

"Nothing particular."

"Had you your eyes open?"

No answer.

"Now by virtue of your oath were your eyes open?"

No answer.

"Come, sir, I must, and will have an answer; on your solemn oath were your eyes open when you walked by that field?"

At last, after various renewed questions, the witness says, "No."

"Did you shut them by accident?"

After that question had been sufficiently often repeated, the witness again said, "No; he had been blinded;" and in the same way it was at last extracted from him that his ears had been stopped also, and that he had been led along the road by the field, that he might be able to swear that he had passed the place during the night without either seeing or hearing what was at the moment taking place there.

Oh that miserable witness! One could swear from the glassy look of his eyes that then also, during those awful questions, he could see nothing. The sweat rolled down his miserable face. That savage barrister appeared to him as a devil sent direct

from the infernals, for his express behoof; so unme
tear him, and lacerate him; twenty times did he mal
his own shame in twenty different ways. Oh! wha
clever, sharp, ingenious, triumphant Counsellor A
wicked false witness, with his shallow, detected devic
with him like a cat does with a mouse—now letting
moment, with the vain hope that he was to escap
pouncing on him, and giving him a fresh tear; till
the young man was desired to leave the chair, one
clined to detest the ingenuity of the ferocious lawyer
iniquity of the false witness.

This case was now over; the bailiff again held up
landlord gained his cause; the farmer was sent to p
blind and deaf witness sneaked out of town in shame
This came of not letting well alone.

The Wednesday was now advanced, and it wa
there would not be time for the great murder case, a:
affair was called. Besides, Mr. Allewinde was also t
and he wanted some rest after his exertions; and as
with triumph, some minor cases were brought forwar
and Mr. O'Laugher rushed into the other court to d
O'Flanagan before Mr. Justice Kilpatrick, agains
made upon his pocket by that willow-wearing sp
Murphy.

In rushed also all the loungers from the other cc
a place as Carrick-on-Shannon, a breach of promis
case is not an every day treat, and, consequently, m
mined to make the most of it. Counsellor O'Lau
hands through his dark grey hair, opens wide his l
pulls out the needful papers from that bottomless ba
but the other moment so signally defeated in the oth
sure trust in his own resources prepares for victory.

The case is soon stated. Mr. Terence O'Flanag
hundred a-year, profit rents, out of the town and ne
Mannhamilton, has, to the palpable evidence of the v
baronies, been making up, as the phrase goes, to L
for the last six months. This has been no case of B:
wick, but a real downright matter of love-making o1
and love made on the other. Letters, too have bee
are now to be read in court, to the great edification of
jury, and amusement of the whole assemblage; and
culprit has gone so far as to inform the father, M1
has a thousand pounds saved to settle, if he, the fathe
to add to it. All these things Mr. O'Malley pu1

behalf of the injured Letty, in his opening speech, and then proceeds to bring evidence to prove them.

In the first place the father gives his evidence, and is cross-examined with great effect by Mr. O'Laugher; then the letters are read, and are agreed by all to be very affectionate, proper, agreeable love-letters; there is no cross-questioning them, for though answered, they will not answer; and our friend, who escaped but just now melancholy from the porter drinkers in his bed-room, is brought forward to prove the love-makings of the delinquent.

All Mr. O'Malley's questions he answers with great readiness and fluency, for it was for the purpose of answering them that he came forward. He states without hesitation that love-making to a considerable extent has been going on; that to his knowledge, and in his presence, most particular attentions have been paid by Mr. Terence to Miss Letty; that they have sat together, talked together, walked together, and whispered together to such an extent, that in his, the witness's, mind, they had for some time past been considered to be a regularly engaged couple; and that, moreover, he had himself seen Mr. Terence O'Flanagan squeezing the hand of Miss Letty. Having declared so much on behalf of the lady, he also was handed over to Mr. O'Laugher to be made to say what he could on behalf of the gentleman.

In answer to different questions, he stated that he himself was a middle-aged gentleman, about forty—a bachelor moving in good society—sufficiently so to be acquainted with its usages; that he was in the habit of finding himself in company with ladies —married ladies and single; he confessed, after some interlocutions, that he did prefer the company of the latter, and that he preferred the good-looking to the plain—the young to the old; he would not state whether he had made up his own mind on the subject of matrimony, and had a very strong objection to inform the jury whether he was engaged. Was his objection insurmountable? Yes, it was; whereupon it was decided by the court that the witness need not answer the question, as he could not be called on to criminate himself. He had, probably, however, been in love? suggested Mr. O'Laugher; but he wouldn't say that he had. A little smitten, perhaps? Perhaps he had. Was, perhaps, of a susceptible heart? No answer. And accustomed to Cupid's gentler wounds? No answer. Hadn't he usually in his heart a prepossession for some young lady? Mr. O'Laugher must insist on having an answer to this question; as it was absolutely necessary the jury should know the nature of a witness's temperament, whose evidence was chiefly one of opinion, and not of facts; how

could they otherwise know what weight to give to l
Hadn't he usually a prepossession in his heart for son
There was a great deal of hesitation about this qu
last he was got to inform the jury on his oath that
fact always—did entertaim such a prepossession. W
of conversing with the lady who for the time might
of this feeling? He supposed he was. Of walki
No, not particularly of walking with her. Did he n
his loved one? He didn't think he ever did, excep
Weren't such happy accidents of frequent occurr
might be. Weren't they gratifying accidents when tl
Why, yes; he supposed they were. Then he *was* f
with his loved one? Why, taking it in that way
he was. Mr. O'Laugher supposed so too. Did he
to this loved object? No, never. What, never? I
could he swear that he had never whispered to the
of his adoration? He had no object of adoration.
object of love? He had no object of love; that i
say whether he had or not. He thought it very
should be asked all these questions. Well, then,
possession. Could he swear that he had never whis
present object of his prepossession? Never—exc
that was to say, he couldn't tell. Never except in
walk with her except by accident! Mr. O'Laugher
the witness was a very cautious fellow—quite an ol
be caught with chaff. Did he never sit by her?
By the object of his prepossession? He supposec
dinner, or at a party, or a concert or a ball.

"What! sit by the object you love best at a co
whisper to her between the tunes—and you a Con
said Mr. O'Laugher. "Come, mend your reputa
wasn't that a slip you made, when you said no
whispered to her at a concert?" Perhaps he had
"Well, now, I thought so. I thought by your co
wouldn't sit by a pretty girl, and take no notice of
never squeeze a girl's hand while you were whispe
He couldn't remember. "Now, on your oath did you
a girl's hand?" He might have done so. "Did
your arm round a girl's waist?" At last the witi
might have done even that. "And now, one que
done. Did you never kiss a girl?" No answer. "C
last. After all you've owned you needn't haggle at
it, man, it must come at last. Did you never kiss a
for the sake of morality, the witness was at leng

own that he had perpetrated the enormity. "And," asked Mr. O'Laugher with a look of great surprise, "were you never proceeded against for damages? Was an action for breach of promise of marriage never brought against you?"

No, never; the witness had never been in such a predicament.

"What, never? You who have declared, I won't say unblushingly, for heaven knows you have blushed enough about it, but openly and on your oath, that you have always some different object of affection, with whom you walk, sit, talk, and whisper; whose hand you squeeze, round whose waist you put your arm (a crime, by the by, never imputed to my client), whom you even confess that you kiss; and yet you sit here secure, unassailed, unsolicited for damages, unengaged, as you lead us to suppose. What are the fathers and brothers of Connaught doing to let such a hydra-headed monster as thou near their doors—such a wolf into their sheep-pens? Go down, thou false Lothario. Go down, thou amorous Turk, and remember that a day of retribution may yet come for yourself."

The unfortunate witness hurried out of court—ran through the pelting rain to the inn—crammed his brushes and pantaloons into the carpet-bag in spite of damp, farmers, and burly porter drinkers —paid a guinea for the bed in which he had never slept, and hiring a post-car, hurried from the scene of his disgrace, regardless of the torrents which were falling.

On the Wednesday morning, for it had been forgotten till then, a summons was served on Hyacinth Keegan to attend as a witness at Thady's trial, on the prisoner's behalf; and as he was living in the town the service was quite in sufficient time, and there was no possible means by which he could avoid the disagreeable duty which was thus imposed upon him. He was much annoyed, however, for he felt that there were no questions, which he could be asked on the subject, which it would not annoy him to answer. He had been out but little since the day on which he had been so savagely treated at Drumleesh—indeed he had not been able to go out till quite lately; and he now most thoroughly wished that he was bad enough to obtain a medical certificate, which would prevent the necessity of his attending in court. That, however, was impossible, and he, therefore, sat himself to consider what answers he would give to the questions they would be most likely to ask him. Regard for his oath he had none; but there were some most disagreeable questions which, if asked him, he would be obliged to answer with the truth, for on those subjects he would be unable to lie without detection. His rancour against Thady was unabated. Unless young Macdermot were hung he would be unable to avenge the mutilated stump which crippled all his exertions, and now rendered his existence miserable.

He flattered himself, however, that Brady's evidence would render that event certain; and whatever annoying questions might be put to himself on the defence, he was determined that Brady should swear to enough on the direct examination to ensure his purpose.

On the Wednesday evening it was decided that Thady's case was to come on first in the criminal court on Thursday morning, and on the same Wednesday evening Keegan sent for Brady into his office.

Pat was now regularly installed as the attorney's managing man on the property, and there was therefore nothing very remarkable in his sending for him, although he was going to be a witness on the morrow.

"Did you hear, Brady," said the master, "that they've summoned me for the trial to-morrow?"

"Iss, yer honour; they war telling me so up at the court; there's Dolan is summoned too."

"Who's Dolan?"

"He's one of the boys, Mr. Keegan, as war in it that night at Mrs. Mehan's."

"Well, and what can he say? he can't say Macdermot wasn't there. He can't do any harm, Pat; for if he was to swear that he wasn't there, there's enough to prove that he was."

"No, yer honour, it isn't that he'll be saying, but he'll be saying Captain Ussher's name wasn't mentioned, or may be that the boys were merely taking their drink, innocent like; that's what I be afeared—and that's what Corney'll say; you'll see av he don't; he's the biggest liar in Drumleesh."

"Oh, they'd soon knock all that out of him; besides, isn't he one of these potheen boys?"

"Faix he is so, Mr. Keegan."

"Then they'll not believe him—they'll believe you a deal sooner than him that way; but you must be plain about this, Brady, that they were talking about Ussher that night—d'ye hear? Be d—d but if you let them shake you about that you're lost. D'ye hear? Why don't you answer me, eh?"

"Oh! shure, your honour, I'll be plain enough; certain sure the Captain's name war mentioned."

"Mentioned! yes, and how was it mentioned? Didn't you tell me that Reynolds and young Macdermot were talking broadly about murdhering him? Didn't they agree to kill him—to choke him in a bog hole—or blow his brains out?"

"It war your honour they war to put in a bog hole."

"D—n them! I'll have 'em before I've done. But don't you know that Macdermot, Reynolds, and the other fellow agreed to put an end to Ussher? Why you told me so twenty times."

"I b'lieve they did; but faix, I ain't shure I heard it all rightly myself, yer honour; I warn't exactly one of the party."

"That won't do, Brady; you told me distinctly that Reynolds and Macdermot swore together to kill the man; and you must swear to that in court. Why the barrister has been told that you can prove it."

"But, Mr. Keegan, do you wish me now to go and hang myself? You would not wish a poor boy to say anything as'd ruin hisself?"

"Be d—d, but some one has been tampering with you. You know you'll be in no danger, as well as I do; and by heavens if you flinch now it'll be worse for you. Mind, I want you to say nothing but the truth. But you know Ussher's death was settled among them; and you must say it out plainly—d'ye hear? And I tell you what, Brady, if you give your evidence like a man you'll never be the worse of those evenings you spent at Mohill at Mrs. Mulready's, you know. But if you hesitate or falter, as sure as you stand there, they'll come against you; and then I'll not be the man to help you out of the scrape."

"But, Mr. Keegan, yer honour, they do be saying that iv I brings out all that, it'll hang the young masther out and out, and then I'll have his blood upon my conscience."

"Have the divil on your conscience. Isn't he a murderer out and out? and, if so, shouldn't you tell the truth about it? Why, you fool, it's only the truth. What are you afraid of? after telling me so often that you would go through with it without caring a flash for any one!"

"But you see there's so much more of a ruction about it now through the counthry than there war. Counsellor Webb and all thim has made Mr. Thady's name so great, that there'd be no pace for a boy at all av he war to say a word agin him."

"Then it's a coward you are afther all, Brady?"

"No, yer honour, I'm no coward; but it's a bad thing living in a counthry, where all the boys is sworn to stretch you."

"Nonsense, Pat; did they ever stretch me? and haven't I done as bad and worse to them twenty times. They're trying to frighten you out of your duty, and you're going to let them. Any way, I see you are not the man for me. I thought you had more pluck in you."

x

"Why thin, Mr. Keegan, I've pluck enough; but faix, I don't like hanging the young man thin—and now it's out."

"Very well—then you'll be transported for perjury, that's all; all the things you've to swear to have been sent written out to the Counsellor; and when you contradict in court what you have already declared to be the truth they'll prosecute you for perjury, and a deal of good you'll do young Macdermot afther all!"

After a few more arguments of a similar nature, Brady was again reduced to his allegiance, and at last was dismissed, having promised to swear stiffly both that Ussher's death had been agreed on at the meeting at Mrs. Mehan's, and also that in private conversation with him (Pat Brady) Macdermot had frequently expressed his determination of being revenged on Ussher for the injury he was doing to his sister. And Hyacinth Keegan betook himself to the company of the fair partner of his prosperity and misfortunes, comforting himself with the idea that he was sure of success in his attempts to secure Thady's conviction, and flattering himself that Mr. O'Malley could at the worst only ask him some few teasing questions about the property.

CHAPTER XXIX.

THADY'S TRIAL IS COMMENCED.

On the same evening, namely that immediately before the trial, Father John visited Thady in prison, and it was the last time that they were to meet before the fate of the latter was decided. The priest had constantly visited the young man in his confinement, and had done all in his power to support and cheer his spirits under the horrible circumstances in which he was placed, and not without success. Thady had borne his incarceration and distress with the greatest courage. When remaining at Aughacashel among the lawless associates with whom he had so foolishly looked for safety, he had completely lost his fortitude and power of endurance; he was aware that he was doing what was in every sense culpable, and he then could not but look on himself as a murderer flying from justice; but now he had learned to see what was really criminal in what he had done, and what was venial; and though the last five months had been spent in prison, and though he felt by no means sanguine of his acquittal, he had, nevertheless, never regretted that he had given himself up.

Father John had again to-day seen Mr. O'Malley, who now that he had the affair thoroughly at his fingers' ends, seemed to be almost sanguine of success, and consequently the good priest himself was correspondingly elated.

"I trust in God, Thady," said he, "I confidently trust you will be with me at the Cottage to-morrow night, or at any rate the next. The Cottage shall be your home for some time, my boy, if they allow you any home in the country. I don't want to give you false hopes, but I don't think any jury can convict you. I'm sure Mr. O'Malley thinks so too."

"I don't think so, Father John; it may be so, but I don't think so; it's a comfort to me to know I never meant his death, although he was doing what might have tempted me to shoot him, av I'd had a pistol in my hand; for as I sit here he was dragging her down the avenue by the waist. But I never thought to kill him, and though I think they will hang me, I feel that I haven't the weight of murdher on my hands."

"You haven't, Thady; indeed you may say you haven't. I that should teach you to repent your sins, not to hide them from your own heart, tell you that you haven't. But should they condemn you, there are those that will have. But God forbid—may God in his great mercy forbid it."

"But, Father John, what'll Feemy do? what will the owld man do when I am—when I'm gone? Keegan 'll have all now. She'll be turned out to beg across the world; and what'll ever become of her?"

"Your father'll be cared for, Thady. Though no one else should see to him, I will, for your sake. He's very infirm; you'll be astonished when you see him; but while he lives and while I have a bit of bread to share with him, or a roof to shelter him, for your sake, he shall never want it."

Thady pressed the priest's hand between his own.

"What a thing it is to have a friend like you! but Feemy—who'll provide for Feemy? she'll be the only one left of the name when I'm gone; there'll be nothing left but her; house and family 'll be gone then, and except for poor Feemy, there'd be an end of the whole concern."

"Don't go on that way," said Father John, with tears in his eyes. "You'll be able to see after, and live with your own sister yet; and who knows but you may yet beat Keegan out of Ballycloran?"

"Oh, no, Father John! av they don't hang me out and out—av they don't put an end to me altogether, I'll be transported, or sent back here to gaol. I'll never be at Ballycloran again. Bad as the place is, I loved it. I think it's all the throuble I had with it,

and with the tinants, that made me love it so. Go(
I was hard enough to some of them!"

Father John remained with him till the evenir
vanced, and then left him, promising to be in court (

"Let me see you there, Father John," said he.
me whilst it's going on ; it'll be a comfort to me to]
near me among so many strangers, and at such a ti

"I will, my boy. I must leave the court whe
come, for I've promised to be with Mrs. McKeon w
her in ; but excepting that, I'll stand as near yor
me."

The priest then left his friend, and Thady was o
in his cell, about to pass the last of many long, tec
suspense. There he sat, on his iron bedstead in h
with his eyes fixed upon vacancy, thinking over the
of his past life, and trying to nerve himself for the
too truly believed, was in store for him. Thad
had not been prone to hope ; he had never been
never sanguine enough. From the years to wh
memory could fall back, he had been fighting an
battle with the world's cares, and though not th
quished, he had always been worsted. He had nev
what men called luck, and he therefore never expe
men in any rank of life had known so little joy as l
had so little pleasure ; his only object in life had be
wolf from his father's door and to keep a roof ove
sister.

Had patient industry and constant toil been able t
this, he would have been, perhaps not happy, but y
tented ; this, however, circumstances had put out of
he felt that the same uncontrollable circumstances ha
him into his present position. He knew little of
doctrine of necessity; but he had it in his heart th
he felt himself innocent, and was at the same time ɑ
the kind efforts of his friends would not save him fr
hangman's rope and the county gallows.

There he sat the greater part of that night alo
bedside, not knowing whether he was warm or cold—
whether it was light or dark ; and no one but God n
thoughts that passed through his untutored brain,
which kindled his warm, though rugged heart. Di
that though honest, industrious, and patient, ignom
should be his probable doom ? Had he bitter hatr

for those who had driven him to his fate? Did he still love those who had evinced so little sympathy with him? Sympathy! Ah! how could he miss that which he had never felt, till Father John had blessed him with his kind words! His love had not been that conscious love which requires kindness to nurture it, and love again to keep it warm. He was not aware himself how well he loved his father and his sister. His lot had been thrown with them; he had passed his life with them, and the feelings, which in a selfish man are given up to self, had with him been turned on those to whose care it had seemed that his life should be dedicated.

I do not say that he looked forward to a probable death without a shudder, or to so speedy a termination of his career, without a wish that, unfortunate as it had been, it might be prolonged; but it was the disgrace, and the circumstances of his fate, which made by far the greater portion of his misery. Could he be but once quiet in his grave, and have done with it all—be rid of the care, turmoil, and uneasiness, he would have been content. Could he have been again unborn—uncreated! He had once repined to Father John, that existence had been for him a necessary evil; and though checked by the priest for the impiety of the thought, was it odd if he often thought, that he was one of those for whom it would have been better had they never been born?

About three or four in the morning, he fell asleep, and was awakened by Father John about eight; he dressed himself in his best clothes—those in which he had been accustomed to go to mass —ate his breakfast, and about ten o'clock was led out of gaol, handcuffed, into the court-house. The gaol at Carrick-on-Shannon is not far from the court-house, and as they are both built on a neck of land running into the river, no portion of the town has to be traversed; but yet there was a great crowd collected to see the poor fellow pass by. This was the first of the bitter moments to which he had so constantly looked forward for the last few months. At length, however, he was in the dock, and here the high wooden palings, twelve feet above the ground on which he had to stand, would screen him from the view of all, save the miserable prisoners beside him and the policemen who had brought him in,—until he should be called on to take his place at the bar.

After waiting there for about half an hour, sitting on the rude benches which surrounded the interior of the dock, with his eyes fixed on the red lappets of the gaoler's coat which hung over the palings as he sat upon the bar, he heard the noise of steps in the court suddenly increased, and the sound of voices hushed; the judge was taking his seat. Mr. Baron Hamilton, accompanied by a fashionably dressed young gentleman with a white wand, entered the court at a side-door, passed behind the jury-box, and sat down on the seat of judgment, under the dusty red canopy which for many years had nodded over the wisdom of Ireland's soundest lawyers.

Had that piece of red moreen been gifted with an ear to hear, and a tongue to tell, what an indifferent account would it give of the veracity of judges and of the consciences of lawyers! How many offences had it heard stigmatised by his lordship as the most heinous that had ever been brought before him in his judicial capacity! How many murderers, felons, and robbers, described as poor harmless, innocent, foolish boys, brought into trouble by a love of frolic! How many witnesses, vainly endeavouring to tell the truth, forced by the ingenuity of lawyers into falsehood and perjury! What awful denunciations and what light wit, almost in the same breath! Of what laughter hardly suppressed by judicial authority would it tell—what agonizing sobs altogether unsuppressable would it describe—how many a clever, smiling, self-sufficient barrister would it, from long knowledge, have learnt to laugh to scorn—of how many a sharp attorney would it declare the hidden ways! But yards of red moreen are fitting witnesses for judicial gravities and legal exercises. They hang profoundly, gravely—nay, all but solemnly—over the exposition of the criminal. They lend authority to the wrath, and protection to the wit of the wigged. They awe the criminal, repress the witnesses, inspire the juror, silence the spectator, absorb the dust, and tell no tales.

And now the judge having taken his place, the lesser men in office being duly seated beneath him, and the contending barristers having sufficiently dived into their blue bags, the prisoner is summoned, under various indictments, to take his trial for the murder of Myles Ussher; whereupon Thady is called upon by the gaoler, and, rising from his seat, takes his stand at the bar. In his position there, he is just enabled to raise his arm to the railing of the dock, and to rest his hand upon it during the ten long, horrid, wasting hours which he is destined to pass in his present painful position. His face is pale, and—always thin and sad—now thinner and sadder than ever; his eyes wander round the court, and as they at length alight on Father John, who is seated next to Mr. McKeon on the attorneys' benches, a kind of gentle smile softens his features, and shows how great a relief he feels the presence of a friend to be. In answer to the clerk of the crown, he declares himself not guilty, professes himself ready for his trial, and the business of the day commences.

The first thing that has to be done is to call over the long panel, and the names of all competent persons in the county, from whom the jury is to be selected. But even preparatory to this, the counsel for the defence commence their fight. Mr. O'Laugher, who, as the phrase goes, is with Mr. O'Malley, begins by declaring that the list from which the names are read is an illegal list—a foolish, useless, unauthoritative list—nothing but balderdash, moonshine, and waste paper—all empty sounds, and consisting of a string of names as little to the purpose in the present case as a regimental roll-call. The sub-sheriff, who with infinite clerkly care, and much sub-shrieval experience, has made out the list, opens wide his disturbed ears, and begins to feel somewhat uncomfortable. Mr. O'Laugher goes on to declare that the present list, instead of being one properly, legally, and expressly drawn out for March 183—, is only a copy of the one in use during the summer assizes in the last year, and assures the judge with much indignant emphasis, that he cannot allow his client to submit to the injustice of receiving a verdict from a jury composed under such atrocious circumstances.

The objection is listened to with as much gravity as though a statement had been made that the prisoner had been in Newfoundland at the time of Ussher's death, and Mr. Allewinde's assistant begins to argue the case. The sub-sheriff and his two clerks are put into the chair, and have to swear one thing and another. Books are lugged into court—dirty papers overhauled—thick volumes quoted and consulted—precedents urged—objections answered—a great deal of self-confidence shown. At last, after a weary hour's talk, it seems somehow decided that the sub-sheriff was in the right of it—that the list is correct, and that the prisoner may be tried. But Mr. O'Laugher is not in the least chagrined at the victory of his adversary; one would say, from his countenance, that his only object had been to delay the business for an hour, and that he triumphed in his success.

The list is accordingly read over, and the householders of County Leitrim are summoned to appear and answer to their names under a penalty of two pounds. A lamentable deficiency, however, is apparent; one only here and there answers to his name as it is called out in the sonorous and practised voice of the clerk of the crown. A notice is then given that they will be again invoked under a penalty of ten pounds, which, in spite of the fear which pervades the minds of jurymen that this will be a lock-up affair, entailing a bedless night and a meagre supper, surreptitiously supplied through the windows of the court-house, has the desired effect, and

Cornelius O'Reilly, Patrick Tierney, Anthony Reynolds, &c., &c., reply to the call, and the court becomes sufficiently full of strong, thick-set, comfortable men.

This is only the long panel. Now the jury has to be formed. To twenty names the prisoner is entitled to object from caprice, and Mr. O'Laugher is not the man to give up one of the twenty. Then he can object to as many more as he chooses, on showing cause, and you may be sure Mr. O'Laugher has a great many causes to show. One man has lived near young Macdermot all his life, has been a friend of his, must have formed an opinion on the case, and is therefore not fit; another man has been his enemy, and is therefore not fit; a third man used to drive with Captain Ussher twice a week; a fourth lived in Mohill; a fifth at Drumsna; a sixth did not live in the county at all; a seventh had not a house of his own, and so on. Why, it appeared there was not a proper juror in the county! On all these objections Mr. O'Laugher was beaten; and as he was beaten on each, he indefatigably prepared for the next.

Then the jurors themselves objected. They unblushingly declared themselves unfit;—asserted that they could not depend upon themselves to give a true verdict, and assured the judge that their minds would be improperly biassed by circumstances on one side or the other. What atrocious characters!—what self-condemned miscreants! Why does not the judge instantly, with that stern look he knows so well how to assume, turn them out of court, bid them make way for honest men, and send them home, disgraced for ever, to their sorrowing families? Does he do so? No indeed! he picks his teeth while Mr. Allewinde assures this recusant or the other that he has no doubt but that he will make a most eligible juror; and at last, with considerable delay, a little trial takes place in each case, and two other jurymen have to decide on their oaths, whether Terence Murphy stands indifferent between our Lord and Sovereign the King and the prisoner at the bar; and to enable them to decide, they have to hear all the evidence in the case.

The twelve are at last sworn—the proper officer repeating in each case those awful words, "Juror, look upon the prisoner. Prisoner, look upon the juror. You shall well and truly try, and true deliverance make, between our Lord and Sovereign the King and the prisoner at the bar—so help you God!"

As this injunction in each case reached Thady's ear, he moved his eyes upon the man who was then being sworn, as if demanding from him that true deliverance to which he felt himself entitled.

And now the prisoner having pleaded, the indictments read, and the jury armed with pen, ink, and paper, Mr. Allewinde, full of legal dignity and intellectual warmth, rises to his subject. We will not follow him through the whole of the long narrative which he, with great practised perspicuity, and in the clearest language, laid before the jury, for we already know the facts which he had to detail. He first of all described the death of Ussher; then stated that he could prove that the prisoner had killed him, and having informed the jury that doubtless the prisoner's sister was in the act of eloping with the deceased when he met his death, launched out into a powerful description of the present dreadful state of the country. He told the jury that it was in his power to prove to them that the prisoner was one of an illegal society who had often threatened Ussher, and that he had but a day or two previous to the affray met a sworn portion of his own tenants for the purpose of planning the murder. He went on to tell the jury that they were not to allow themselves to be deceived by the idea that the murder could not have been premeditated, because there existed a presumption that the prisoner was not aware of Ussher's expected presence in the avenue; for that the fact of the murder having been talked over deliberately, and then executed, afforded the strongest evidence that the prisoner was at the time lying in wait for the deceased; and that, through the servants, or from other means, he had made himself cognisant of the projected elopement. He then, preparatory to examining the witnesses, concluded in the following words,—

"Gentlemen of the jury,—You are probably all aware that the prisoner is from that rank in life to which the greatest number of yourselves belong; and you cannot but see that the fact of his being so, greatly increases the magnitude of his presumed crime. Far be it from me to urge you on this account to come to a conviction, should the evidence prove in any way deficient; but I do implore you, if you value the peace of your country—the comfort of your hearths—the safety of your houses—and the protection of your property, not to allow yourselves to be led away by a feeling of false sympathy, or to be improperly actuated by the idea that the deed was done in legitimate defence of the prisoner's sister, if the evidence do not prove that such was the case. I do implore you to divest yourselves of any such preconceived notions. Did the evidence merely go to show that Mr. Ussher was killed by the brother whilst eloping with the sister, it would doubtless be fair that the circumstance should be taken into your consideration; but when you shall have heard it proved that the death of this unfortunate man was deliberately talked over, canvassed, and decided on by the very man by whom it was executed, you will only fall into the shallow device by which the prisoner has endeavoured to deceive you, did you not clearly perceive that he has merely used the fact of his sister's elopement as a favourable opportunity for the completion of his project. Gentlemen, I shall now proceed to call the different witnesses, satisfied that when you shall have heard their evidence, you will have no difficulty in coming to a verdict in the case."

The first witness called was Dr. Blake. He stated that he had examined the body the day after Ussher had met his death; that he had no doubt death had been occasioned by two heavy blows, one of which had fractured the skull immediately over the temple, and which was of itself quite sufficient to cause instantaneous death; that he should presume these blows to have been inflicted with some heavy blunt instrument, and that he considered the stick then produced in court and shown to him was such as had probably been used on the occasion.

This witness was not cross-examined.

Biddy was next called, and took her seat in the chair with much trepidation; but her usual womanly volubility soon returned to her, and she gave her evidence fluently enough. She stated that her mistress had confided to her her intention of eloping with Ussher on the morning of the evening on which he had been killed; that in obedience to her mistress's commands, she had walked down the road towards Mohill, and had met Ussher in a gig, and had put a parcel for her mistress into it; that when she returned to the house, she believed her master—that was the prisoner—was in the house. in her mistress's sitting-room; that shortly after her return she saw him come into the hall; that he then told her to go in to his sister, and that Captain Ussher was dead. She did not know what became of him after that, and that she had not seen him from that moment till the present one.

Mr. O'Laugher then asked her, whether she had told any one of her mistress's intention of eloping with Ussher, and she replied that she had not—that she had never opened her lips on the subject to any one before she heard the prisoner say that Captain Ussher was dead. She also stated that it was her young master's habit to go out to the stables every night.

She also was then allowed to go down, and Frederick Brown was called. He proved that Ussher had revealed to him his plan of running off with Feemy, and he stated, that not thinking much about it, he had told three or four friends of the circumstance, and that he could not tell whether or not it might in that manner have got round to the ears of the prisoner.

Mr. O'Laugher in his cross-examination bothered this young gentleman considerably, but as neither the questions nor the answers are material to the story, it would be useless to repeat them.

The next witness was Pat Brady, and as the verdict to which the jury came, depended in a great degree on his evidence, it will be given as nearly as possible in detail.

Having given his name, he stated that at the time of Ussher's death he was in the employment of the prisoner; that he had been his confidential servant, and was intimate with all his habits; that on the night when the deceased was killed, at some time, he supposed, about half-past nine o'clock, his master had entered the kitchen at Ballycloran, and had desired him, Brady, to follow him out into the avenue; that his master, when in the avenue, had told him that he had killed Captain Ussher.

By this time the counsel had ceased asking questions, and as the witness was telling his own story, we will leave it in his words.

"I thought it war poking his fun at me, yer honours—for I knowed the Captain hadn't been at Ballycloran that night, and that the masther had been ating his dinner at home, so I didn't be taking much notice of what he war saying, till we war mostly half down the avenue, when Mr. Thady told me the body war there. Well, yer honours—what with the night, and what wid the trees it was a'most too dark to see; but I felt the man's body with my foot, and then I know'd it war thrue enough what the masther was afther saying. I axed no questions thin, for I knew there'd been ill blood betwixt them, and when I comed to remember myself, I wasn't that much surprised. But Mr. Thady axed me what we'd be doing wid the body, and I can't exactly take upon myself to say what I answered; but, at last, he said as how we would take it down to Mrs. Mehan's as keeps the shebeen shop beyond Ballycloran. He then told me something about Miss Feemy and the Captain—as how he was carrying her off by force like, and that war why he'd stretched him. Well, yer honours, at the bottom of the avenue, at the gate like,—though for the matter of that, there ain't no gate there,—we discovered the Brown Hall gig, and Mr. Fred's crop-tailed bay pony horse standing in the middle of the road—and the masther bid me take the body away to the police at Carrick, saying he would be off at oncet to the mountains in Aughacashel. Well, yer honours, this I did—I left the Captain's body with the police—I took the gig to

Brown Hall—and I brought home Miss Feemy's bundle as had been left there in the gig, when the Captain came out into the avenue—and that's the long and the short of what I knows about it, yer honours—at laste, all I knows about the murder."

"The prisoner then owned to you," continued Mr. Allewinde "that it was he who killed Captain Ussher?"

"Shure he made no bones about it all—but told me straight out that he'd killed him in the avenue."

"Did he say why he had done so?"

"Faix I don't remember his saying thin why he'd done it—and I didn't think to ask him. He was in a flurry like, as war nathural, and he and I carrying the dead man that'd been hearty only a few minutes afore! But shure, yer honour knows the thing had been talked over."

"What thing had been talked over?"

"Why, the Captain's death."

"You mean to say by that, that arrangements had been made by certain persons to kill Captain Ussher?"

"I don't know about arrangements; but there war boys through the counthry determined to have a fling at him."

"Now I am going to ask you a question particularly affecting the prisoner, and one to which you must give me a direct answer. Have you ever been in the prisoner's company, when he and others have expressed their determination to murder Captain Ussher?"

"Faix, I don't know about dethermination and murder, but I've heard him threatened."

"Have you heard him threatened with murder?"

"I've heard the boys say that he would be undher the sod that day six months."

"Have you heard Captain Ussher threatened with death in the prisoner's presence?"

"I don't know that they ever said death or murder; they don't spake out that way; av they war going to hole a chap, it's giving him his *quiatis* or his *gruel* they'd be talking about."

"Well, now, on you're oath, have you ever, in the prisoner's presence, heard such language used respecting Captain Ussher as made you think that he was to be killed?"

"Didn't I tell yer honour I thought all along how he'd be killed."

"Were you ever at Mrs. Mulready's in Mohill?"

"I war."

"Did you ever hear Captain Ussher's name mentioned there?"

"I did."

"Now tell the jury as nearly as you can what was said respecting him there."

"Why a lot of boys swore together over a noggin or two of sperrits, to put him undher the sod—that's all; but shure, yer honour, Mr. Thady, that's him there," and he pointed to the dock, "was niver at Mother Mulready's."

"Well, but when the boys swore to put the Captain under the sod was the prisoner's name mentioned?"

"Oh, it war ofthen."

"And what was said about him?"

"Why, yer honour it was this way—and I'll tell you all I know about it off hand—and thin you'll not be throubling yer honour's self wid all these questions. The boys war mostly tenants to Mr. Thady here—and they did be saying that av so—av Mr. Thady would jine them in putting down the peelers and the Captain—they'd undhertake Mr. Keegan 'd never put a second foot on the lands of Ballycloran; and they war the more hot about this, as they knew Mr. Thady war agin the Captain about his sisther, for he thought thim two were too thick like; and he used to be saying as how Ussher war playing his thricks with Miss Feemy. Well, along of this—and knowing as how the masther were agin Mr. Keegan too, they thought he'd jine in; and to bring him round, they swore niver to pay the rint afore he did. Well, yer honour, I was one night at the Widdy's, that's Mother Mulready's, for I'd gone there knowing as how the tenants 'd be in it, and I war noticing them to be up with the masther on Friday next about the rint. Afther I'd been telling 'em all to be up at Ballycloran, they got swearing that divil a foot they'd stir to the place, or divil a penny they'd pay any more, because Mr. Thady here war so thick with the Captain. This war jist afther the row up to Loch Sheen, when three boys war locked up about some squall—and this made the rest more bitter agin the Captain. Well, when they got swearing this way, I axed 'em, why not go to the masther like a man, and tell him what they thought. Wid that they agreed to come up to Mary's wedding—that's Mary McGovery, yer honour, as is my sisther, and who war to be married the Thursday; and so they parted, and a lot on 'em swore that blessed night that the Captain should be under the sod that day six months. Well, yer honour, the next morning Mr. Keegan called down to Ballycloran about law business, and somehow there war words atwixt him and Mr. Thady, and from that they got to blows, and I b'lieve somehow Mr. Keegan got the best of it, and Mr. Thady was a little hurted, and this made him bittherer nor iver."

"But that did not make him bitterer against Captain Ussher, did it?" asked a juror.

"Faix thin, I think it did, yer honour," answered Pat. "It seemed to make him bitther altogether agin everybody; when I war talking to him aftherwards about coming down to the wedding, he seemed to be trating all the world alike. But the Captain and Mr. Keegan especial. Well, when the supper war over, and the boys were begun dancing, Mr. Thady come down and immediately comed into the inside room, where the men war sitting dhrinking, and I war wid them: thin one of the men, a tinent to Mr. Thady, up and tould the masther all as I've tould yer honours, of what took place at the Widdy's in Mohill, and how av Mr. Thady would jine them to rid the counthry of the Captain, they'd stand to him, and wouldn't let Mr. Keegan on the lands of Ballycloran, right or wrong. Wid that there war a dale of shilly-shallying—but at last the masther said as how he would jine the boys in ridding the counthry of the Captain, and he thin agreed to come down to the Widdy's the next night, or that afther, to get the secret signs and the pass-words, and to take the oaths they war to swear him to. Wid that he tuk an oath thin niver to tell nothin' of what had passed that night. After that, I don't remember rightly how it war, but he got up to look for Miss Feemy, and she war out walking in the road wid the Captain. Well, Mr. Thady went down the road afther thim—and there war a ruction in the road betwixt thim two; but as I warn't there I can't say exactly what was said one side or the other. By the time they come agin to Mrs. Mehan's door, Father John, that's Father Magrath, you know, war there, and made the pace betwixt 'em; and that's all I can tell yer honours about it av I war to sit here till doomsday."

"You said just now," said Mr. Allewinde, "that the prisoner agreed to join the men assembled at Mrs. Mehan's in ridding the country of Captain Ussher; now what was meant by ridding the country of him?"

"Why isn't it ridding the counthry of him? yer honour knows what that means as well as ere a boy in the barony."

"Perhaps I do; but you must tell the jury what you mane by it."

"Is it I? I didn't mane nothin' at all: it warn't I as said it—or as war ever a going to do it."

"What did you suppose was the meaning of those who did make use of the phrase?"

"I 'sposed the boys did mane to get rid of the Captain out of the counthry; jist that, yer honour."

"But how did you suppose they were to get rid of him?"

"Oh, yer honour, I niver heard the particklars; I niver knew nothin' of the plan. I warn't one of them, you know."

"But the prisoner agreed to join them in any plan, or in some plan for ridding the country of Captain Ussher?"

"He did, yer honour; shure I said that before."

"Now, you said some time ago, that when you first discovered that Captain Ussher had been killed by the prisoner, and that when you came to remember yourself, you weren't much surprised. Now, thank God! it is, at any rate in this county, a very uncommon thing to find that one man has killed another. Can you tell the jury why you were not surprised at such an event as that?"

"Becase I knowed there war ill-blood betwixt the two."

"But men do not kill one another whenever they quarrel, do they?"

"Faix, they do sometimes."

"Did you ever, of your own knowledge, know a man before who killed another?"

"Oh dear! yes; shure I did."

"Well, tell us an instance."

"Why there war ould Paddy Rafferty, who war in the Cavan Militia in the Rabellion—av he didn't kill scores of the French at Ballinamuck, he's the biggest liar I ever heard; but he's dead now, yer honour."

"Supposing that the death of Captain Ussher had happened a fortnight before—that the prisoner had killed him a fortnight before the day on which he did kill him, would you not have been surprised then?"

"Why I don't know that a fortnight makes much difference."

"Answer my question. In such a case as that, would you not have felt more surprise than you did when the affair did occur?"

"Why, yer honour, I can't answer that—becase, you see, it didn't happen then, and I couldn't exactly be saying what my feelings might be."

"At any rate, you were not surprised?"

"Oh yes, I war surprised; in course it war a surprise to me when I kicked the dead body; but when I come to think over all about the Captain, I warn't that much surprised."

"After what had taken place at Mrs. Mehan's, you did not expect Captain Ussher would be very long lived?"

"Faix, he lived longer than I expected—seeing the way he war going on through the counthry."

"Do you remember telling me some time ago, speaking of Captain Ussher's death, that the thing had been talked over?"

"I b'lieve I said as much."

"What did you mean by that?"

"Why just that the job had been talked about."

"What job?"

"Why this job."

"What job? Tell the jury what job."

"Faix, they all know well enough by this time," and the witness looked up to the jury, "—or else they oughtn't to be there, any way."

"Tell them what job you mean—never mind what they know."

"'Deed thin, you're bothering me so entirely with yer jobs, I don't rightly know myself which I'm maning."

"Think a little then, for you must tell them; you said the job had been talked over; what was it that had been talked over?"

The witness gave a stolid look at the counsel, but answered nothing.

"Come," continued Mr. Allewinde, "what was the job that had been talked over?"

"Bad manners to the likes of me; but I war niver cute, and now I'm bothered intirely."

"You mean to tell the jury then that you don't know what you meant when you said the thing had been talked over, do you?"

"Why, I s'pose it was this thing about Captain Ussher. Weren't we talking of that then?"

"That's for you to say. Was it Captain Ussher's death that had been talked over?"

"Witness, don't answer that question," said Mr. O'Malley. "I'm sure my learned friend will not press it; it's very seldom he makes such a slip as that."

Mr. Allewinde had asked a leading, and therefore an unallowable question.

"Why the witness had just said that he supposed it was this thing about Captain Ussher," said Mr. Allewinde.

"I'll say no more about it," continued Mr. O'Malley, "feeling perfectly certain that you will not press the question."

"Well," said Mr. Allewinde to the witness, "tell the jury at once what was the thing that had been talked over."

"Why, yer honour knows well enough. Shure weren't you saying it yourself, only the gentleman here wouldn't let you."

"Well, now do you say it."

"Say what?"

"Say what was the thing that had been talked over."

"Talked over when, yer honour?"

"You told the jury some time since that the prisoner owned to you in the avenue that he had killed Captain Ussher, did you not?"

"Faix, I did—and it was thrue for me—he made no bones about it at all."

"And you then added that the thing had been talked over; what thing was it that had been talked over?"

"Ah, that's what you're wanting, is it? 'Deed thin I'm axing yer pardon for keeping yer honours all this time in suspinse. Faix thin, Captain Ussher war the thing what war talked over; and divil a lie in it, for he war talked over ofthen enough."

"Captain Ussher had been talked over in such a manner as to prevent your feeling much surprise, when you found that the prisoner had killed him, isn't that it?"

"Jist so—faix, I'd have no difficulty in discoursing wid yer honour, av the other gentleman wouldn't put in his say."

"You'll find by and by he'll have a great deal more to say."

"In course; and no objection on arth on my part so long as it's one at a time."

"Now I think I have only two more questions to ask you, if you will give me direct answers to them."

"Twenty, av you plaze, yer honour."

"You have said that the tenants of the prisoner had sworn together to put Captain Ussher under the sod, and also that the prisoner had agreed to join the tenants in ridding the country of him; was the former phrase, that of putting the Captain under the sod, used in the prisoner's presence on the evening of the wedding?"

"There war a lot of thim phrases used—ridding the counthry—sodding him—and all thim sort of disagreeable sayings; but I can't swear to any one exactly at Mrs. Mehan's—thim's the sort of words."

"Very well. Now I think you told us that when the prisoner desired you to take the dead body to the police at Carrick, he told you he was going to some place: where did he say he was going to?"

"To Aughacashel."

"Where's Aughacashel?"

"It's a mountain behind Drumshambo."

"And did he tell you why he was going to Aughacashel?"

"That he mightn't be tuk, I s'pose."

"I don't want your supposition. Did the prisoner tell you why he was going to Aughacashel?"

"There war some of the tinants there, I b'lieve, and he thought he'd be safe may be."

"Did the prisoner tell you that he was going to Aughacashel because he thought he'd be safe there?"

"I'll tell you how it war thin. We were jist talking together about what he'd betther be doing, which was nathural, and he with the dead body there, he'd been jist afther killing. Wid that, says he, 'Pat,' says he, 'where's the stills mostly at work now?' 'Faith,' says I, 'I don't exactly be knowing;' for, yer honour, I niver turned a penny that way myself—'but,' says I, 'sich a one'll tell you,' and I mintioned one of the tinants; 'and where's he?' said the masther; 'why I heard tell,' says I, 'that he's in Aughacashel, but av you'll go down to Drumleesh, you'll find out, and wid that he went down the road to Drumleesh, and I druv the body off to Carrick."

"That'll do," said Mr. Allewinde. "I've done with this witness, my lord."

CHAPTER XXX.

THE PRISONER'S DEFENCE.

MR. O'MALLEY then rose, but before he began to cross-examine the witness, he addressed the judge.

"There's a witness in court, my lord, whom I shall have to examine by and by on the defence, and I must request that he may be directed to absent himself during my examination of the witness now in the chair. It is material that he should not hear the answers which this witness may give, I mean Mr. Hyacinth Keegan, my lord, who is sitting beneath me."

Keegan was sitting on the bench immediately under that of the barrister, among the attorneys employed in court. When he heard Mr. O'Malley's request to the judge, he rose up on his one leg, and the judge having ordered him to leave the court, he hobbled out with the assistance of his crutch.

"Your name is Pat Brady, I think," commenced Mr. O'Malley.

Pat did not reply.

"Why don't you answer my question, sir?" said the counsellor, angrily.

"Why I towld what my name war afore. Thim gintlemen up there knows it well enough, and yourself knows it; why'd I be saying it agin?"

"Well, my friend, I tell you to begin with, I shall ask you many questions you'll find considerably more difficult to answer than that, and you'd better make up your mind to answer them; for I mean to get an answer to the questions I shall ask, and you'll sit in that chair till you do answer them, unless you're moved from it into gaol."

"Fire away, sir; I'm very well where I am, and I'm thinking I can howld out agin the hunger longer nor yer honer."

"Your name is Pat Bady?"

"It is."

"Whose servant are you?"

"Whose servant?"

"Don't you understand what I say? whose servant are you?"

"Faix thin, I don't call myself a servant at all."

"Who's your master then?"

"Mr. Macdermot here was my masther afore this affair."

"I didn't ask who was your master; who is your master now?"

"Why, Mr. Keegan."

"Mr. Hyacinth Keegan, that's just gone out of court; he's your master, eh?"

"He is."

"And a very good master—isn't he?"

"Betther, maybe, than yer honour'd be, and yet perhaps none of the best."

"Answer my questions, sir; isn't he a good master?"

"Faix, he is so."

"How long have you been in his employment?"

"How long!"

"Yes, how long?"

"Why, I can't jist say how long."

"Have you been a year?"

"No."

"Six months?"

"No."

"Will you swear that you never were in Mr. Keegan's pay before six months ago?"

"I will."

"You never received any money from Mr. Keegan before six months ago?"

"I did not say that."

"Why, if you received his money weren't you in his pay?"

"No; maybe he gave me a Christmas-box or so; he's very good to a poor boy like me in that way, is Mr. Keegan."

"In whose employment were you six months ago?"

"In Mr. Macdermot's; yourself knows that well enough."

"And Mr. Macdermot and Mr. Keegan were great friends at that time; weren't they?"

"Faix they were not; I never seed much frindship betwixt 'em."

"Did you ever see any enmity between them—any quarrelling—or what you very properly call bad blood?"

"Indeed I did then."

"I b'lieve Mr. Macdermot—that's the prisoner—had great trust in you; hadn't he?"

"I believe he had."

"You knew all the affairs about the estate?"

"I b'lieve I did."

"He told you all his troubles—all his money difficulties, didn't he?"

"One way or other, I b'lieve I knew the most on 'em."

"Particularly as to the money due on his father's property, which Keegan had to receive; he used to talk to you confidentially about those things?"

"Well, and av he did?"

"But he did so; didn't he?"

"Faix, but I don't know what you're afther; I b'lieve he towld me all about everything."

"I believe he did indeed; and now I'll tell you what I'm after. Mr. Macdermot, unfortunately believing you to be an honest man, told you all his plans and secrets, which you, in consideration of certain pay, which you call Christmas-boxes, sold to the man whom you knew to be your master's enemy; isn't that the fact now?"

"No, it a'nt."

"Ah, but I say it is the fact; and now do you suppose any jury will believe a word you've said, after having shown yourself guilty of such treachery as that. Do you expect the jury to believe you?"

"'Deed I do—every word; Lord bless you, they knows me."

"Now, then, tell me. Can you recall any conversation between yourself and Mr. Keegan since the death of Captain Ussher, relative to this trial?"

"I can."

"More than one, perhaps?"

"Oh, lor yes; twenty maybe."

"Will you tell us any particulars you may remember of the last?"

A long conversation then ensued, but Mr. O'Malley could only elicit that Brady had, of his own accord, informed his master of all he knew on the subject, and that he had done so because he thought it right. He admitted, however, that Mr. Keegan had expressed a desire that the prisoner might be hung. A great many questions were then asked as to the present holding of Ballycloran, to which Brady answered, stating with tolerable accuracy the manner in which Larry at present lived on the property, and the hold which Keegan had upon it. He, moreover, stated that the house was in a very bad state of repair, and that most of the tenants who were left on the property were unable to pay their rent. He then, after much hesitation, owned that he had overheard what had taken place between Keegan and Thady in the avenue, on the day when the attorney had called at Ballycloran—that he had heard the name which Keegan had applied to Feemy, and that he had seen the manner in which Thady had been struck.

He was then asked whether he himself had not cautioned Thady against Ussher, telling him the reports that were going through the country as to Ussher's treatment of his sister. This he denied, stating that it wasn't probable that "the likes of him should go to speak to his masther about such things as that." He was repeatedly questioned on this point, but Mr. O'Malley could not shake his evidence. Brady, however, owned that in talking to Thady about Ussher, he had called the latter "a black Protestant," and that he had always spoken ill of him; "and now," continued Mr. O'Malley, "I don't wish to ask you any questions by answering which you will criminate yourself; but you have already said that you have been a visitor at Mrs. Mulready's shop?"

"Oh yes, I've been there."

"And you have been there when certain persons swore that before twelve months were passed, Captain Ussher should be under the sod?"

"Yes; I swear I heard thim words, and saw the boys take the oath."

"But to the best of your belief the prisoner was never at this house when such an oath was taken?"

"Is it Mr. Thady? He was niver at mother Mulready's at all."

"But he met the party who had taken this oath at your sister's wedding?"

"He did."

"And the same subject was spoken of there; was it?"

"What subject?"

"The propriety of sodding Captain Ussher?"

"I don't know about propriety."

"Well, then, the advisability of doing so?"

"Oh, yer honer, I aint no scollard. I can't make nothin' of thim long words."

"At any rate, they talked of sodding Captain Ussher at the wedding—didn't they?"

"I niver said so."

"Well, but did they?"

"Talk of sodding him! Faix I don't know; I don't think they said sodding."

"Did they say killing?"

"I won't say they did."

"Or murdering?"

"No; they did not say nothin' about murdher."

"Oh; they did not say anything about murder,—or doing for him? perhaps the prisoner and the other boys agreed to do for him?"

"Maybe they did—maybe you were there; only if so I disremember you; but thim's not the words I swore to."

"Well, they didn't agree to sod him, or kill him, or murder him, or do for him; what was it they were to do for him?"

"They were to rid the counthry of him."

"What—make the country too hot to hold him? eh, is that what you mean?"

"It don't matter what I mean; that warn't what they meant."

"And how do you know what they meant?"

"Why, they meant to kill the man; you know that as well as I."

"But I don't know it—nor do I think it; nor what is more, do you think it; for you are sharp enough to know that where there are so many figurative terms in use to signify murder, it is not probable that had they, on this occasion, wished to signify murder, they would have used a phrase which every one knows expresses an intention to drive a man out of the country. Yes, sir, you know that not one of the party would have dared to propose to Mr. Macdermot to have a share in murder. You and they talked of murder at Mrs. Mulready's, but you know that for your life you would not have dared to mention it before Mr. Macdermot. Now tell me how long was the prisoner at the wedding party?"

"Maybe three hours."

"Was he sober when he came in?"

"He war."

"Was he sober when he went out?"

"Sober when he went out?"

"Yes, sir; was he sober when he went out?"

"I don't think he war—not to say sober."

"Wasn't he mad drunk?"

"Mad dhrunk?"

"Don't repeat my words, sir; wasn't he mad drunk?"

"Faix, that's thrue for you, sir—they're not worth repeating; no, he war not mad dhrunk."

"Was he drunk? and mind, sir, you are on your oath—and there were many others present there who will prove whether you answer this question truly or falsely; was he drunk when he left the wedding party?"

"'Deed then I don't know; you can ask thim as war there besides me."

"But I choose to ask you, and I choose that you should answer me; was he drunk?"

"Don't I tell you that I don't know?"

"On your oath you don't know whether he was drunk or not?"

"He war screwed; divil a doubt of that; but thin, he could walk—I wouldn't call him dhrunk."

"Wasn't he nearer being so than you'd seen him for many months?"

"Faix, he war. I didn't see him so bad since Leitrim fair, two years back."

"And now you say, that at the wedding, the prisoner promised in a day or two to meet the same boys at Mrs. Mulready's, to settle their plans of ridding the country of Ussher?"

"Yes; about that and other things."

"And the prisoner never kept that appointment?"

"No, Mr. Thady niver went there."

"Did you ever say anything to him about not going there?"

"Oh, I did; we were discoursing about it."

"And what did you say to him on the subject?"

"Why, I towld him av he guv the boys a promise, he ought never to go back from his word."

"That is to say, you endeavoured to persuade him to go?"

"By-dad, I don't know about persuading; it warn't for the likes of me to persuade him."

"On your oath, sir, didn't you endeavour to induce the prisoner to go to Mrs. Mulready's?"

"I towld him he ought to be as good as his word."

"Yes, you did; and you think he ought to have gone?"

"May be av he'd gone there, he'd never have stood here this day."

"You wanted him to go to Mrs. Mulready's, then?'

"Wanted! No, I didn't want nothing about it."

"You only asked him to go?"

"Jist as I towld you; I said av he guv the boys his word, as a man he shouldn't go from it."

"Did you say anything to him about Mr. Jonas Brown?"

"Jonas Brown?"

"Yes, Mr. Jonas Brown, the magistrate?"

"Faix, I don't know. I can't rightly say."

"Think now, my man; when you were trying to persuade your master to go to the widow Mulready's, did you mention Mr. Jonas Brown's name?"

"D'ye think I do be counting my words that way; how am I to say all the names I mintioned four or five months back?"

"On your solemn oath don't you remember mentioning that gentleman's name to the prisoner with reference to his visit to Mrs. Mulready's?"

"What, Jonas Brown's name?"

"Yes."

"Faix I may."

"Don't you know you did?"

"Faix I don't."

"Didn't you threaten your master, that if he did not attend the meeting, some of the boys would swear against him, before Mr. Brown, for having joined the party and taken the oath at the wedding?"

"What av I did?"

"But did you?"

"Maybe I did—maybe I didn't; I disremember thim little things."

The cross-examination continued for a considerable time; but nothing further that was material could be drawn from Brady. He seemed even more unwilling to answer Mr. O'Malley, than he had been in replying to Mr. Allewinde, and at last he was sent off the table.

The next witness called was McGovery, who had been summoned on behalf of the prosecution. He was asked whether he had not suspected that some foul play was intended against Ussher, and he stated in what manner he had, in the first place, cautioned Ussher himself—then that he had told the same thing to Father John—and that after overhearing a portion of the conversation at Mrs. Mehan's, he had gone to Father Cullen, for the purpose of informing him that he feared there was a conspiracy against Mr. Keegan. Little, however, could be learnt from him, for he owned that he had no substantial grounds for his suspicions in the first case, and that he had chiefly been led to fear an attack upon Ussher, from knowing his unpopularity and the bad character of many of the guests expected at the wedding. Mr. O'Laugher tried to make him say that the conversation at Mrs. Mehan's had been confined to Keegan, and the threats which he had heard uttered against him; but McGovery would not say as much as this; he stated positively that he had never heard Ussher's name mentioned, but that during a considerable portion of the evening he had been entirely unable to hear a word that the men said; he declared, however, positively that Thady was drunk when he left the room, and that it appeared to him that he, Thady, had taken very little part in the conversation before he was drunk.

When this witness went off the table, Mr. Allewinde declared that the case for the prosecution was finished—stating at the same time that he abstained from feelings of delicacy and respect from putting the prisoner's sister into the witness box; and that he should trouble her with no questions unless she were placed there by the counsel for the defence.

Mr. O'Malley then rose to address the jury on behalf of the prisoner, and spoke to the following effect:—

"Gentlemen of the jury, it now becomes my duty to address to you such words as may best suit to point out to you the weakness of the evidence against the prisoner—to explain to you the different objects we had in our lengthened cross-examination of the witnesses—to inform you what we intend to prove on behalf of the prisoner from further witnesses—and, in fact, to put the case before you in a light, and point of view, differing as widely as I can make it do from that in which my learned friend has presented it to you. This you are aware is the general duty and constant object of a counsel endeavouring to obtain a verdict of acquittal from a jury. It is a duty in which long practice has made me familiar, if not skilful; and I never undertook that duty with the same assurance of its facility, as that which I now feel, after having heard the evidence which has been brought forward on the prosecution. I knew beforehand, as surely as one can trust to human knowledge, that the evidence would fail; but knowing the acute legal abilities of my learned friend, and the extraordinary avidity which exists among a large class of men for a verdict against the prisoner in this case,—remembering, I say, these things, I did not expect such a total break down, such an exposure of weakness as that which has been just made before you. Were my object merely to rescue the prisoner from an ignominious death—had it been my mere duty on this occasion to obtain an acquittal, I should feel no hesitation in requesting his lordship at once to send the case before you, with such remarks as the evidence would call forth from him; and I should consider that I was only wasting the time of the court in pointing out to you the insufficiency of the evidence, in which each of you must perceive that nothing whatever is proved against the prisoner; but I have been employed with another object; and I must own to you that so great is my own personal anxiety—so terrible and so undeserved the present position of that unfortunate young man, and so essentially necessary is it for his future happiness, that I should effect my present object;—I must own to you, I say, for these reasons, that from the time when I first found myself standing in a crowded court to address a jury, up to the present moment, I have never felt so little self-confidence, or experienced so total a prostration of that assurance, which is a lawyer's first requisite, as I do at present.

" I have said my object in addressing you is not merely that of obtaining an acquittal; and I said so because a mere acquittal will serve that unfortunate young man but little. Unless he can walk out of this court with such a verdict as, damning as it may be to others, will altogether cleanse his name from the stain of guilt in this matter; unless he can, not only save his neck from the halter, but also entirely clear his character from the gross charges which have been brought against him,—he would as lief go back to the cell whence he has come, as return to his father's house acquitted by the voice of law, but condemned by that of opinion.

" On this account I am debarred from many of the usual resources of counsel pleading for a prisoner; I am forbidden to make use of legal points in his favour; I am forbidden to effect an escape by the numerous weak points in the enemy's plan of attack; I am desired to meet him face to face in the open field—to fight under no banner but that of truth, and not to strike my adversary below the belt. You are aware that this is a line of conduct as rare as it is difficult in a criminal court—when an advocate has to contend for his client against the law—where every possible means of success which legal ingenuity can devise is taken in the prosecution, and where you are accustomed to hear every legal technicality used in the defence.

" Had I not received instructions of so peculiar a nature, I should point out to the jury that no proof has been given direct or circumstantial, that the prisoner was the person by whose hands Ussher fell; instead of doing so I am to declare that he did, as he is supposed to have done, kill the deceased in the avenue of Ballycloran, by striking him twice with his stick. I am to justify that deed, and disprove the charge of his having entered into a conspiracy to murder the man, whom he did kill.

"The prisoner, you have been told, and are probably all aware, is above the rank of men whom you are mostly accustomed to see placed in that dock. He is the only son of a gentleman, living on his own small estate, and has for some years past acted as his father's sole agent and manager.

"I must now tell you a few particulars respecting that estate; and though, of course, you cannot receive as evidence what I tell you, still this course will be necessary, as I shall thereby be enabled to explain to you my object in obtaining answers to certain questions which I have asked, or shall ask, the answers to which you will take as evidence.

"In the time of the prisoner's grandfather, a house was built on this estate by a Mr. Flannelly, of this town, and the price of the building not having been paid, this man, the builder, obtained a mortgage on the estate for the amount of the debt. This is still due, though the house, as you have heard, is falling to the ground; and it has so been increased by interest not paid up and by legal charges, that it has completely embarrassed the present proprietor, who is even now unable to leave his house for fear of arrest. Mr. Keegan, whose name has often come before you in the evidence, and who, by and by, will be examined himself, is the son-in-law of this Mr. Flannelly, and owns, as I have no doubt I shall be able to prove to you, the whole interest in the estate of Ballycloran arising from this mortgage.

"The prisoner's time, since he ceased to be a boy, has been employed in futile endeavours to satisfy the legal claims of this man; and I shall prove to you by most undoubtable evidence that his industry in this object has been unceasing, and that his conduct as a son and a brother has been beyond all praise. But he has failed—times have been against him—legal costs have so swelled the legal interest as to consume the whole rents—those rents he has been unable to collect, and his life has been one manful struggle against poverty and Mr. Keegan;—and I could not wish my worst foe two more inveterate enemies.

"Some few days before Ussher's death—and now I am going to confine myself to that which I am in a position to prove—Mr. Keegan called on the Macdermots for the purpose of proposing certain terms for the adjustment of the debt, which were neither more nor less than that he should have the whole estate, paying a small weekly stipend for life to the prisoner's father. The prisoner was willing to agree, providing some provision should be made for his sister; but the father indignantly spurned the offer, and turned Mr. Keegan out of the house in no very gentle manner. The prisoner followed him into the avenue—still wishing to come to some arrangement; but the attorney was so enraged at the conduct of the father, that instead of listening to the son, he began abusing the whole family, and, as you have heard, applied the most shameful epithet to the sister with which the tongue of a man can defile the name of a woman. He afterwards struck the prisoner, who was unarmed, heavily with his stick; and I have no hesitation in telling you, that that quarrel, in which no blame appears to have been attributable to the young man, placed him in that dock.

"Brady, the confidential servant of the prisoner, both saw and overheard what took place at this interview, as he has told you, and he afterwards,—as he will not deny, though he will not confess it,—incited his master, during the period of his natural irritation, to go down to the wedding party, to meet a number of his tenants who would be willing to assist him in revenging himself against his enemy Keegan, the attorney, if he would assist them against their enemy, Ussher, the Revenue officer. And here my client made the one false step—and the only one which I can trace to him—and committed that folly from which this bitter foe has thought to ruin him. Irritated by the blow—his ear still ringing with the infamous name applied to his loved sister—full of his father's wrong, and his own hard condition, he consented to meet men whose object he knew was illegal; though what their plans were he was entirely ignorant.

"With reference to what took place at the wedding, I have, in the first place, to remark that from the character of this man Brady, I could confidently call upon you to reject every word of his evidence; and I shall presently show you in what respects and why you are bound to do so. But, in the present instance, I am satisfied to tell you that my client did attend that meeting. But mind, that was no illegal meeting—it was not secret; the door was not locked, nor even closed; it was a party of men met at the wedding of one of their own station. The woman to be married was a sister of the prisoner's servant, and it was natural that he should be present. He directs me positively to tell you that he did attend that meeting; though I also tell you, with confidence, that he committed no crime in doing so, and his lordship will corroborate what I tell you.

"It was, however, a part of the plan organised against the prisoner that he should be induced to commit an illegal act, and he was, as you have heard, brought when drunk to promise that he would go down to Mrs. Mulready's, to take upon himself illegal oaths and obligations.

"On the following day he was invited by this same Brady to come on a certain evening; but Macdermot was no longer drunk; he was no longer infuriated by the gross outrages he had received; and what did he do then? Did he go to Mrs. Mulready's to settle the particulars of this murder which he is said to have premeditated? Did he join these outlaws of whom he is represented to have been the leader? Did he even send them an encouraging message—a word of fellowship? No! Even by the testimony of this man, now so anxious to hang his benefactor—this man, who by his own showing was at the same time in the pay of the prisoner and of his enemy Keegan—he indignantly repudiated the idea; he at once informed this wretch—equally a traitor to his confederates and to his master—that he would have nothing in common with them or their schemes; and although threatened with the vengeance of the party, and with the authority of a magistrate, steadily refused even to enter the house in which they were accustomed to assemble. Why, from what I can learn of the young man and of his daily habits, I do not conceive that there is one of yourselves who would not be as likely to join an illegal society as he would. Patient under poverty—industrious under accumulated sufferings—he has led a life which would not have disgraced a priest; he has been ever found sincere in his thoughts, moral in his conduct, and most unselfish in his actions. Is this the man to join a set of senseless rioters, furious at the imprisonment of their relatives, and anxious only to protect their illicit stills? And this is no empty praise. That what I have said of the prisoner is no more than is his due, will be proved to you by evidence which I defy you to doubt. Well, he did not go to Mrs. Mulready's; but he did go to his friend and priest, Mr. Magrath; and not as a penitent to his confessor, but as a friend to a friend, told him exactly what had passed, lamented his indiscretion, and declared his determination never to put himself in the way of repeating it.

"Up to this time my chief object has been to show to you the enmity existing between Keegan and the prisoner,—the object which the former had in view in ruining the prisoner, and that Brady was a paid spy employed to entrap him.

"I shall now come to the deed itself, and I shall afterwards refer to what absolutely did take place at the meeting at the wedding. I have told you that young Macdermot did kill the deceased. He struck him with the stick which has been shown to you in court, and as he was rising from the blow he struck him again; and no doubt the medical witness was right in his opinion that the second blow occasioned instant death.

"You are, however, aware that circumstances might exist which would justify any man in taking the life of another. If a man were violently to attack you, and you were to strike him on the head and kill him, you would be justified. If you were to kill a man in a fray, in fair defence of a third party, you would be justified. If you were to kill a man by a blow in the quarrel of a moment, you would not be guilty of murder. But I can fancy no case in which death, however much it may be lamented, can lay less of the murderer's stain upon the hand that inflicts it, than one in which a brother interferes to rescue a sister from the violent grasp of a seducer. Such was precisely the case in the instance now before us. My learned friend on the other side has truly told you that Miss Macdermot, the prisoner's sister, had consented to elope with Captain Ussher on the evening on which that man was killed. You have learnt, from evidence which you have no reason to doubt, that she had prepared to do so. In fact, you cannot doubt that she left the house of Ballycloran for that purpose; this has been proved—but there are circumstances beyond this on which it is essentially necessary that you should have evidence, and this evidence can only be given by the young lady herself. I shall therefore have to bring her before you. When my learned friend told you that he would not call upon her, nor question her unless placed in that chair by me, he forgot his usual candour, and assumed to himself credit for humanity to which he has no title. He himself has nothing to learn from her, as he will prove to you if he attempts to cross-examine her. Moreover, he was as fully aware as I am myself, that the prisoner must rely on her alone for anything like a true account of the affray.

"The brother and the sister are the only living witnesses of that scene. He has within him that high consciousness of innocence and rectitude of intention which has enabled him to bear his sufferings, his imprisonment, and the misery of his position, with a fortitude which I not only admire, but envy. But that can avail nothing with you; from the sister's lips you must hear the only account which you can receive, and if we find that she has been unable to recall the dreadful circumstances of that night, that fact will bear me out in the history of the occurrence which I am now going to give you."

Mr. O'Malley then gave as exact an account of the occurrence as he had been able to collect from Thady, from Feemy's evidence before the coroner, and from such words as Mrs. McKeon had been able to extract from Feemy on the subject. He then continued,

"When the prisoner struck Ussher, he had come to the knowledge of what the burden was which this man was dragging, solely from the words which the man had used. Miss Macdermot was lying senseless in his arms, and, supporting her by her waist, he was forcing her down the avenue. The words he used were, 'This is damned nonsense,—you must come now.' Then the brother perceived the fate to which this man was—not alluring—but forcing his sister. At that moment—and it was the only one in which the prisoner had to judge of the circumstances of the case—she was not in the act of eloping willingly; she had seen her brother's form, and had refused, or been unable, to rise from the timber on which she was seated. She was forced from thence by this man, whose death protects him from the language in which his name would otherwise be mentioned. She fainted in his arms, and only came to her senses to find her lover dead, and her brother standing beside her, red with his blood. Yes; he had avenged her!—he had punished the ruffian for his barbarity towards her, and saved his sister from the ignominy to which Mr. Frederick Brown told you with so much flippancy that she had been doomed.

"If this was the young man's conduct, was there anything in it that you can even blame? Which of you would have done otherwise? Which of you will tell me that in avenging the wrongs of a sister, or of a daughter, he would pause to measure the weight of his stick, or the number of his blows. Fancy each of you that you see the form of her you love best in the rough grasp of a violent seducer! Endeavour to bring home to yourselves the feelings to which such a sight would give rise within you! and then, if you can, find that young man guilty of murder, because his heart was warm to feel his sister's wrongs and his hand was strong to avenge them.

"But you have been told that as the prisoner had met certain persons for the purpose of entering into a conspiracy of murdering Ussher—and that that fact would be proved to you—you are bound to consider that his coming across Ussher was not accidental, and that the manner in which he attacked that man whilst carrying off his sister was a part of his preconcerted plan. I first of all deny that any credible evidence, any evidence worthy of the slightest belief, has been brought before you to induce you to suppose that the prisoner had even joined any such conspiracy; instead of which you have strong circumstantial evidence that he had never done so.

"You have most of you, no doubt, heard, on various occasions, from different learned judges seated on that bench, that a crown approver's evidence is to be taken with the greatest caution, and only to be believed in detail, when corroborated by other evidence or by circumstances. Now this man, Brady, on whose sole evidence you are desired to convict the prisoner, has shown himself an approver of the very worst description. You are aware that he was the prisoner's servant; that he is now Mr. Keegan's; that there has been long enmity between these men; that the former has been an oppressed debtor — the latter a most oppressive creditor. Mr. Keegan's spirit towards the prisoner's family you may learn from the scandalous and unwarrantable language which has been proved to you to have been used by him towards them. Mr. Keegan's acerbity has been increased by the mutilation he has undergone, and which he conceives he owes to his interference with the Ballycloran property. This man and the witness Brady have, as you have heard, constantly been talking over this trial, and the attorney, it seems, has repeatedly expressed to his servant his ardent wish that the prisoner might be hung. This is his expressed eager desire; and then this new servant, but long-used spy, comes forward boldly to swear away the prisoner's life! Why it would be ridiculing you to suppose you could believe him. Then look at the man's character. He was a constant attendant at that scene of villany into which he vainly endeavoured to seduce the prisoner at Mrs. Mulready's. It is plain enough that Ussher's death was a constant theme of discourse at that haunt; it is plain enough that a project did exist there to accomplish his murder; and is it not plain enough that this man was one of the conspirators—one of the murderers? Would he have been admitted to their counsels—to their dangerous secrets—unless he had been an active participator in their plans? Would they have taken in his presence a solemn oath to put this unfortunate Revenue officer under the sod, unless he had joined in that oath? Of course they would not! And this is the man whom they expect you to believe with such confidence, that on his unsupported evidence you should condemn the prisoner! What I have said to you respecting this respectable witness, and his not less respectable master, will perhaps be made somewhat plainer to you when you shall have heard the evidence which I hope to extract from the latter. Now, as to the meeting at Mrs. Mehan's, even were you to believe Brady, I maintain that nothing whatever has been proved against the prisoner. Brady states that at Mrs. Mulready's certain men swore together that at a certain period Captain Ussher should be under the sod. This phrase brings to the mind of every one the conviction that they meant to express murder. The man could not be under the sod unless he were dead.

"But at the wedding, when young Macdermot was present, even by the showing of Brady himself, the men were afraid to use any such phrase. They implored their landlord's assistance to help them to rid the country of him; to frighten him off; to make the place too hot to hold him. As I told that wretched reptile, whilst in the chair, they would have no more dared to propose a scheme of murder to young Macdermot, even in his drunkenness, than they would have to you or to me.

"Now as to the probability of the prisoner's having been aware of his sister's project for eloping, and having made use of that opportunity for the safe execution of a scheme of murder,—and this perhaps is the most material point of all; for were there good grounds to suppose that he knew that this elopement was to take place —that he took no precautionary steps to prevent it—but that having this previous knowledge, he rushed out at the time, and killed the man, I should be very far from telling you that he was perfectly justified, as I do now. But I must positively maintain that you cannot come to such a conclusion. It has, to a degree, been proved to you, and will be so more clearly, that the prisoner had all along shown himself averse to the intimacy which existed between Ussher and his sister; it is therefore to be presumed that both of them took every means in their power to prevent the prisoner from learning their intention; and there is every reason to suppose they were successful.

"Two persons appear to have been told, as their services were required, both of whom have been examined before you—the servant girl and Mr. Frederick Brown. The former has sworn that she mentioned it to no one, and there is no reason to disbelieve her. The latter proved himself not so trustworthy. It seems that with that foolish flippancy which distinguishes him he told his friend's secret to other friends of his as a good joke. But you must remember that Mr. Brown's friends were not the prisoner's friends —that they rather were in such different circles, that what was said in one, would be very little likely to find its way into the other; and above all, that those to whom Mr. Brown or his friends communicated it, would think that the brother was the last person who should be told of it. Again, had the prisoner known the projected elopement, and intended to make use of it for the perpetration of a preconcerted murder, would he—could he have acted as he did? Could he have waited for such an unexpected accident as

z

his sister's fainting before he drew near to his victim. His sister had walked down the avenue, and after waiting some time in the road, returned and sat down upon a fallen tree; it was whilst so seated that she heard the brother open the hall-door; had she, as she expected, met her lover at the hour appointed, they would have been far beyond the prisoner's reach before he had left the house;—would he have allowed this to be the case, had it been his intention to take advantage of the opportunity? It is absurd to argue on such a point. It is unnecessary almost to call your attention to things which must so manifestly present themselves to you. The whole of this case has received additional weight and importance from official authority. It has been considered worthy of especial government interference. My learned friend has come express from the metropolis for the purpose of conducting it;—a rumour has been spread abroad that most conclusive evidence would be produced to prove that a prisoner from the better orders of society had joined, and headed one of those illegal bodies of men whose existence is supposed to be the cause of the troubles of this distracted country; and that he had, in unison with these schemes, committed a foul and deliberate murder; and my learned friend has not hesitated to tell you that it is essentially necessary to use the utmost extent of legal severity, that an end may be put to the agrarian outrages which are now becoming so frightfully prevalent in the country. Has anything been proved to warrant this official zeal—this government interference? No, nothing; not one iota; but still these paraphernalia of office, this more than ordinary anxiety to obtain a verdict, may have an effect upon your minds most prejudicial to my client. I have no doubt as to your actual verdict. I have no doubt that you will—nay, I know that you must—acquit that young man of murder. But I beseech you to remember that, though in the indictment he has been charged with murder only, he has been by the servant of government, by my learned friend on the other side, accused of other grievous crimes; and I implore you by your verdict, to purge his character of the stain which has been so unjustly attached to it, if you find, on examination of the evidence, no cause to suppose that he had been a participator in the councils of such societies. I beseech you to do him that justice, which can now only be done by the strong expression of your unanimous assurance of absolute innocence. I beseech you to reject from your minds those pre-conceived opinions so injurious to the prisoner, with which the present unfortunate state of your country may so naturally have influenced you, and to remember that it is your duty, as jurors, to confine yourself to the individual case before you; and that the doctrine laid down by my learned friend, that you should make an example in one case for the sake of prevention of crimes in others, is most unconstitutional, and would imply, that whilst the solemn oath you have taken is still vibrating in your ears, your object should be far wide from that for which you have been assembled—that of making a fair and true trial between your sovereign and the prisoner. I shall now call a few witnesses, and then leave the case, with confidence, in your hands."

CHAPTER XXXI.

THE LAST WITNESS.

When Mr. O'Malley had finished his address to the jury, it was past seven o'clock, and the judge suggested that as it would be evidently impracticable to finish the case that night, so as to release the jury, they might as well at this point adjourn it till the morrow. To this Mr. Allewinde readily assented; but Mr. O'Malley declared that though he was most unwilling to detain his lordship and the court at that late hour, he must request permission to be allowed to examine one of his witnesses, as otherwise his caution in having had him ordered out of court, would have been in vain. It was most essential, he said, that his examination of Mr. Keegan should take place before that man could have an opportunity of conversing with his servant, Brady; whereupon the judge consented to hearing Keegan's evidence that evening, and forthwith the name of Hyacinth Keegan was called out in a loud voice by the crier, and was repeated by every policeman in court, till a stranger to the proceedings would have thought that Hyacinth Keegan's society was the one thing desirable in Carrick-on-Shannon.

It would be drawing this trial out to a weary length to give the whole of his evidence; but Mr. O'Malley's questions were such as the attorney found it almost impossible to answer. He was asked in the first place whether he at present received the rents from Ballycloran, and then whether he received them on his own behalf; the latter he denied, but when told that if he denied the fact Mr. Flannelly would be brought forward to prove it, he at last owned that Mr. Flannelly had promised to make over that property to him; he then denied that any conversation had passed between him and Brady as to the nature of the evidence the latter was to give at the trial, or that he had expressed any anxiety on any occasion that a verdict might be given against the prisoner; he confessed that he might, in conversation, have attributed the loss of his foot to the influence of the prisoner; but he could not remember that he had ever said that Macdermot should pay for it with his life. In answering the different questions put to him, he hesitated and blundered so much—stammered so often, and spoke so low, that every one in court was convinced that he was perjuring himself; but still he persisted in denying everything. The only good effect Mr. O'Malley could get from his evidence was, that the master frequently contradicted what had been said by the servant. But then Brady had shown so much confidence and self-assurance in his replies, and Keegan so much hesitation and confusion, that it was much more probable that the jury would believe the former, than the latter; and if so, Keegan's contradicting the statements made by Brady, would not serve to invalidate the material evidence given by that man.

When Mr. Keegan came down from the chair, the court broke up for the night, and the jury were informed that the sheriff would afford them all the accommodation in his power;—and with long faces they were marched away to durance vile.

The court, which, during the trial, had been so densely crowded, again became desolate and silent. Baron Hamilton, with his brother Kilpatrick, retired to their dinner, which they had well earned; and the coffee-rooms at the hotels again became crammed with hungry guests, clamorous for food; and the evening was passed in speculations as to what would be the verdict in the case to which they had all been listening.

In the barristers' mess-room all the feuds of the day were forgotten, and a most jovial party was assembled. As each bottle of claret succeeded the other, fresh anecdotes were told, and innumerable puns were made. Mr. Allewinde was quite great; his forensic dignity was all laid aside, and he chatted to the juniors with most condescending familiarity.

Mr. O'Laugher became the originator of incessant peals of laughter; all that had taken place during the day he turned into food for merriment; not for one moment did he hold his tongue, nor once did he say a foolish thing. He was the pet of the bar-room. The Connaught bar was famous for Mr. O'Laugher; and they knew it, and were proud of him.

Of all of them assembled there but one seemed to have any memory of the sadness of the scene that they had that day witnessed. How should they? Or rather how miserable would be a barrister's life, were he to be affected by the misery which he is so constantly obliged to witness in a criminal court. On this occasion, however, the anxiety which Mr. O'Malley had expressed when addressing the jury had not been feigned, and the doubt which he felt as to the fate of his client lay heavy on him. He was aware that he had failed in shaking Brady's testimony, and he feared that in spite of all he had done to prove the depravity of that man's character, the jury would be too much inclined to believe him.

It had been decided that Feemy was not to be brought into Carrick from Drumsna till such time as Mr. O'Malley sent out word that she would be required; and when he found how late it was before he began his speech, he had told Father John in court that she would not be wanted on that day. She had, therefore, been left tranquilly at Mrs. McKeon's, who had fetched her to her own house from Ballycloran on the morning of the trial.

When Larry Macdermot saw the car at the door, in which Feemy was to go away, he was dreadfully wrath. He first of all declared that his daughter should not be taken away to Mr. Keegan's—that his own son had deserted him and tried to sell the estate, and that now they meant to rob him of his daughter! And he wept like a child, when he was told that unless she went of her own accord, the house would be broken open, and she would be taken away by force. It was in vain that Mary McGovery endeavoured to make him understand that Feemy's presence was necessary in Carrick, and that she had to appear as a witness at her brother's trial.

Whenever Thady's trial was spoken of;—and Mary, by continually recurring to the subject, had made the old man at last comprehend that his son was to be tried;—but whenever it was spoken of now, he merely expressed his approbation, and a wish that Thady might be punished, for making friends with such a reptile as Keegan—for deserting his father, and planning to cheat him out of his house and his property. Mary took great pains to set him right, and bellowed into his ear as if he were deaf instead of stupid, twenty times a day, that Thady was to be tried for Ussher's death; but Larry couldn't be got to remember that Ussher was dead, and would continually ask his daughter when her lover was coming back to live with them, and defend them and the property against the machinations of Keegan and her brother.

All the Thursday Feemy remained at Drumsna, every moment expecting that she would be immediately called in to go to Carrick. She sat the whole day in the drawing-room, close by the fire, with her friend's cloak around her, without speaking to any one. The girls had come and spoken kindly to her when she first arrived; but their mother had told them that they had better not attempt to converse with her. Mrs. McKeon herself sat with her the whole day, and spoke to her a gentle word now and again; but she purposely abstained from troubling her, and she made no allusion whatever to the subject on which she had thought so much, and on which her own suspicions had been corroborated by Mary's information. Necessary as it was that the poor girl should tell some one, this was not the time to press her.

There sat Feemy. Ah! how different from the girl described in the opening of this tale. Her cheek was pale and wan, and the flesh had gone, and the yellow skin fell in from her cheekbone to her mouth, giving her almost a ghastly appearance; her eyes appeared larger than ever, but they were quenched with weeping, and dull with grief; her hair was drawn back carelessly behind her ears, and her lips were thin and bloodless. Two or three times during the day Mrs. McKeon had given her half a glass of wine, which she had drank on being told to do so, and she had once tried to eat a bit of bread. But she had soon put it down again, for it seemed to choke her.

About five o'clock Mrs. McKeon learnt that Feemy would not be called for that day, and the poor girl was then induced to go to bed; but nothing could persuade her to allow any one to assist her. It was wonderful how she could have undressed herself, and dressed herself the next morning, she seemed so weak and powerless!

Tony and Father John got home to dinner about eight. They were both in good spirits, for Mr. O'Malley's speech had been so convincing to them, that they conceived it could not but be equally so to the jury. They forgot that they had previously assured themselves of Thady's evidence, and that therefore they were prepared to believe every word said on his behalf; but that this would by no means be the case with the jury. They were very sanguine, and Tony insisted that Counsellor O'Malley's health should be drunk with all the honours.

On the morning they went early into town; they had obtained from the clerk of the peace permission to make use of a small room within the court, and here Feemy and Mrs. McKeon were to remain undisturbed till the former was called for; then that lady was to bring her into court, and even undertook to go upon the table with her, and repeat to the jury, if she would be allowed to do so, the evidence, which they were all sure Feemy herself would not be able to give in a voice loud enough to be heard by any one.

When the car stopped at the court-house in Carrick-on-Shannon, it was found absolutely necessary to carry her into the room, for she had apparently lost all power of action. She neither cried nor sobbed now; but gazed listlessly before her, with her eyes fixed upon vacancy, as the two strong men lifted her from the car, and supported her between them by her arms up the steps into the court-house.

"This will never do," said Tony to his friend after leaving her in the room; "this will never do; she'll never be able to say a word on the table; it's only cruelty, Father John, bringing her here."

"But O'Malley says she must come," said Father John; "he says, if she can take the oath, and speak but three or four words to Mrs. McKeon, that will do."

"She'll never do it; she'll never be able to take the oath; she'll have to be carried on the table, and when there, she'll faint. Poor Thady! if he's acquitted, the first thing he'll have to learn will be her disgrace. You must tell him of that, Father John; no one else can."

"Poor fellow; it will be worse to him than all. But she brought him to this, and she must save him if she can."

"I tell you," said Tony, "she'll never speak a word upon that table; we'd better tell O'Malley at once; 't would be only cruelty to put her there."

They both accordingly went to O'Malley, who was now in court, and told him that they thought Feemy Macdermot could not be safely brought there. He, however, still declared that it was imperative for her brother's safety that she should appear, even if it were utterly impossible to get her to speak; and that as she had been the person in fault, and has he had had all the suffering, the cruelty would be to him, if she were not brought forward.

Father John returned to the private room, and tried to make her speak. He kneeled down before her, and again began explaining to her the purpose for which she was there, and implored her to exert herself to save her brother. She once or twice opened her mouth, as if speaking, but uttered no sound. She understood, however, what the priest said to her, for she gently pressed his hand when he took hold of hers, and nodded her head to him, when he begged her to exert herself.

In the meantime Mr. O'Malley was continuing the examination of his witnesses. The first who appeared on this the second morning of the trial was Corney Dolan, who unfortunately came prepared to swear anything which he thought might benefit the prisoner. He said he remembered the evening of the wedding, he remembered the conversation at which the prisoner had been present, that he was quite sure Ussher's name wasn't mentioned—or at any rate that if mentioned, it was not accompanied by any threat—that the only plan of violence alluded to during the evening was that one or two of the boys said that they would duck Keegan in a bog hole if he came to receive rents at Ballycloran.

This was all very well, as long as the questions were put to him by Mr. O'Malley; but he was forced to tell a somewhat different tale when examined by Mr. Allewinde, by whom he was made to own that there had been projects abroad for murdering Ussher, though he still maintained that none of them had been alluded to by the party at Mrs. Mehan's. He was also made to give himself so bad a character that it was more than probable that the jury would not believe a word he had said.

Father John was the next; he was only called on to prove that Thady had been intoxicated when he left the party at Mrs. Mehan's, and to speak as to character. With tears in his eyes he corroborated all that the barrister had said in his speech in praise of his poor young friend; he described him as honest, industrious, and manly—patient under his own wrongs, but unable to endure quietly those inflicted on his family.

Tony McKeon was the next, and with the exception of Feemy, the last; and he too had only to speak as to character.

Just as Father John had been getting into the chair, a policeman had come into court and whispered to Doctor Blake, who was sitting in one of the lower benches; and the Doctor immediately got up from his seat and went away with the man.

Father John had not observed the occurrence; but when he was leaving the table, and as Tony was getting up, the latter whispered to him,

"Blake has been called out. Just look to Feemy."

And at the same moment Mr. O'Malley said out aloud:

"Mr. Magrath, if I might trouble you so far, would you have the kindness to bring Miss Macdermot into court? I do not anticipate that we shall have much delay with Mr. McKeon's evidence."

Father John immediately hurried into the room, where Mrs. McKeon had been left with her charge; and his heart trembled within him as he remembered the death-like look the poor girl had when he left her but an hour since, and reflected that it was too probably to her aid that Doctor Blake had been called.

And so it was. When he entered the room, round the door of

which a lot of frieze coats had crowded, but which was kept shut, he found Feemy on the ground, with her head supported on Mrs McKeon's lap, and Blake kneeling beside her, endeavouring to pour something into her mouth. There was another woman standing in the room, and an apothecary, whom the doctor had sent for; but Father John was soon made to understand that medical skill could avail but little, and that all the aid which Feemy could now receive from her fellow-creatures was to come from him.

To describe the scene which immediately followed would be to treat so sacred a subject much too lightly. The priest, however, found that neither life nor reason was extinct; she acknowledged the symbol of salvation in which she trusted, and received that absolution from her sins which her church considers necessary. Who can say how deeply she had repented of her misdeeds during the many hours of silent agony which she had endured!

Her arm was stretched out from her body, and her hand was clasped tightly in that of Mrs. McKeon's. The moment before she drew her final breath, she felt and tried to return the pressure; she made one great struggle to speak. "Myles" was the single word which her lips had strength to form; and with that last effort poor Feemy died.

In the meantime McKeon had given his evidence in the court and had left the table—Mr. Allewinde having declined to cross-examine either him or Father John. There was then a pause of some little duration in court, during which Mr. O'Malley, addressing the judge, said that Miss Macdermot, the witness now about to be brought forward, was unfortunately in a very weak state of health, so much so, that had her evidence not been essential to her brother, he should be most unwilling to have troubled her; he then apologised for the delay, and asked for and obtained permission for Mrs. McKeon to be on the table and repeat the answers of the witness to the jury: the judge merely premising that it would be necessary that that lady should be sworn to repeat the true answers.

There was still some further delay after Mr. O'Malley had sat down. Mr. McKeon got up to go and help to bring her into court, but just in the doorway he met a man who whispered to him; he did not return however, but hurried on to the room where he had left his wife, and reached it just as the breath left the poor girl's body. In spite of their distress it was apparent to all that the truth must be immediately made known in the court, and Mr. McKeon was leaving for the purpose of telling Mr.

O'Malley, when Father John laid his hand upon his friend's shoulder, and said—

"Poor Thady, it will break his heart to hear it. It must be kept from him. But heaven only knows what's best; he must hear it at last. Go, McKeon, and tell O'Malley; he'll know what's best to do."

McKeon returned into court, and making his way with difficulty close up to the barrister, whispered in his ear that his witness was no more.

Mr. O'Malley, who had been standing, instantly sat down, as if appalled by the suddenness of the event. Every one in the court who had seen McKeon's face as he entered, felt aware that something had happened to Feemy.

The judge leaned forward over his desk, addressing himself particularly to Mr. O'Malley, and said,—

"Is Miss Macdermot too unwell, Mr. O'Malley, to be brought into court?"

"My lord," said he again, rising from his seat, "she has already gone before another judgment-seat. Macdermot," and he turned round to the prisoner in the dock, "you have borne your sorrows hitherto like a man; you must try and bear this also—your sister is dead. She has fallen the first victim—God forbid that another should be sacrificed. My lord, my cause is now done; there is now no living witness, but the prisoner, of that scene which I described to you. The case must go to the jury as it is."

During the time of the whole trial, Thady had stood upright at the bar, with his elbow leaning on the wooden rail, and his face resting on his arm. He had almost constantly kept his eye upon the speakers, occasionally turning his gaze to the place where Father John had sat during the trial, to see that he had not deserted him. During the speech which Mr. O'Malley had made on his behalf, he had brightened up, and looked more cheerful than he had done for many months. When that was finished he had felt more sanguine as to his acquittal than he had done at any time since he had first given himself up as a prisoner. During the short pause which occurred in court immediately after McKeon left the table, he had once or twice looked round to learn if Feemy were coming, though the high woodwork of the dock would effectually prevent him from seeing her till she was at the table.

It will be remembered that Feemy's extreme illness had never been made known to her brother,—much less her lamentable situation. Father John had told him that she was unwell, but he had not thought it necessary to frighten him at the present time by letting him know how very ill she was. The doctor's departure from court he did not notice at all. Father John was sent for to his sister in a manner which caused him no apprehension,—and even when McKeon went out to see whether she was coming, it never occurred to Thady that the delay in his sister's appearance was occasioned by ill health. It was only when he saw O'Malley sit down, after hearing some whispered tidings from McKeon, that he felt alarmed. When the barrister told the judge that his witness had gone before another judgment-seat, it was still evident from his face that he did not perfectly comprehend what had happened; but there was no misunderstanding the language in which the tidings were immediately afterwards communicated to himself. He seemed to make one attempt as if to say something; but the feeling of his situation, and the paraphernalia of the court awed him into silence, and he sank down within the dock to hide his sorrow from the crowd that were gazing at him.

There was some considerable delay in the court after this, as though all the parties concerned felt unwilling to commence business after the shock which Feemy's death had occasioned. The judge sat back in his chair, silent and abstracted, as if, valuable as he must know his own and the public time to be, he felt unable to call on any one to proceed with the case immediately after so sad an event.

At last Mr. Allewinde rose and said that no one could regret more than himself the dreadfully tragical manner in which the prisoner had lost the benefit of the evidence, which it was expected his sister would have been able to give on his behalf; that he conceived that it would be anything but mercy to the prisoner to delay the proceedings in their present stage on account of what had happened; moreover, he considered that doing so would be illegal. He would suggest to the judge, to his learned friend on the other side, and to the jury, whether any legal and available use could be made of the evidence which had been given by the prisoner's sister before the coroner.

This, however, Mr. O'Malley declined, alleging that the questions put to Miss Macdermot by the coroner, were merely intended to elicit evidence that Captain Ussher had been killed by her brother, and that the answers she then gave were of course not such as would be favourable to the prisoner; nor were such as could prove those facts which Mr. O'Malley had intended to prove. Mr. O'Malley finished by stating that as far as he was concerned the case was ready to be submitted by his lordship to the jury.

Mr. Allewinde, however, still had the right of reply, and he was not the man to allow any chance circumstance to prevent him making use of it. He accordingly again got up to address the jury. He told them that what he had to say would not keep them long, and considering that he was a lawyer and a barrister, he kept his word with tolerable fidelity. He remarked that the evidence of Brady had in no degree been shaken. That the subjects in which Keegan had been examined had had no reference to the case; and that it was quite plain that Dolan had come forward to swear to anything which he thought might tend to the prisoner's acquittal. He made no allusion whatever to Father John and Tony McKeon, and then ended by saying, that "the unexpected and melancholy death of Miss Macdermot was an occurrence which could not but fill the breast of every one present with most profound sympathy for the prisoner,—that he should abstain from saying a word which might be unnecessarily disagreeable or painful to the feelings of any one—but that the jury must feel that the prisoner would lose nothing from the loss of her evidence. Of course," he continued, "in a point of law you are bound to look on the case as if Miss Macdermot had died at the same moment with her betrothed husband, for you are aware that you cannot allow anything which my learned friend has told you to be taken into consideration by you in finding your verdict. But it will lessen the pain which more or less you must suffer in this sad case, to reflect what strong grounds you have for supposing that the sister, had she lived, could have proved nothing favourable to the brother; for had she been able to do so, she would have done it when examined before the coroner. I shall now trouble you no further. His lordship in submitting the case to you will give you doubtless the necessary caution against allowing excited feelings to have any influence over the verdict to which you shall come."

Mr. Allewinde then sat down, and after the lapse of one or two minutes the judge turned to the jury, and spoke his charge to them upon the question. He went deliberately through the whole evidence—dwelt upon various minor points in the prisoner's favour —told them that the prisoner could not be considered as guilty of murder, if there was ground to believe that he had committed the act whilst the deceased was forcibly carrying off his sister; and that if they believed that the prisoner had never before premeditated the death of the man he killed, he could not be considered to have been guilty of the crime for which he was now tried. He then went at length into all the points; he showed the jury that no evidence whatever had been brought up to prove that the girl was in a senseless state when Ussher was attacked; and that for anything they had heard proved, she might have been walking quietly with him. He then went into the evidence given by Brady, and he stated it as his own opinion, that the man was in the main to be believed; he argued that his whole evidence, both on direct and cross-examination had been given in a manner which seemed to him to show an unwillingness to give more information than he could possibly help on either side—but still with a determination not to forswear himself. But at the same time he told them that this was a question on which each juror should form his own opinion; in fact that it was to judge of the value and credibility of evidence that they were summoned. It was, also, he said, for them to decide whether the death of the revenue officer was premeditated by the party at Mrs. Mehan's when they talked of ridding the country of him. He passed very slightly over the remaining evidence, merely saying that this was a case in which character could not weigh with them, as, if the prisoner were guilty, his former apparent good character only aggravated his sin. He then concluded by telling the jurors that they were bound by solemn oaths to allow nothing to interfere with the truth of their verdict—that they must all deplore the untimely death of the young woman who was to have appeared before them, and sympathise with the brother for the loss of his sister—but that his misfortune in this respect, could not lighten his guilt if he were guilty, or diminish the sacredness of the duty which each juror owed to his country.

When the judge had finished, the jury retired to consider their verdict; and the other business of the assizes was proceeded with, as if nothing peculiar had happened to check the regular routine duties of the court.

CHAPTER XXXII.

THE VERDICT.

IT was not very late in the day when the jury retired, and it was generally thought that they would come to a verdict in time to escape being immured for a second night; but they did not.

Immediately after hearing the judge's charge, Father John, McKeon, and Webb agreed among them that it was absolutely necessary that old Macdermot should be acquainted with his daughter's death; but who was to take upon himself the sad errand! Father John had for the last few days been so harassed, so worn down by anxiety, and was now so depressed by, as he conceived the unfavourable tone of the judge's charge, that he looked like the ghost of himself; and yet the duty of seeing old Macdermot could fall on no one but himself. Neither Webb nor McKeon knew the ways of the old man, and it was more than probable that neither of them would be admitted into the house. Father John therefore put himself on a car and hurried off to Ballycloran, making his friend promise that he would wait in Carrick for him till his return.

Father John soon found himself in the presence of Larry; but he could with difficulty find words to tell him of his bereavement. The old man was seated on his bed—he always slept now in the parlour—he had his legs thrust into a tattered pair of breeches, and had worn-out slippers on his feet; and an old and ragged coat, into which he had been unable or unwilling to thrust his arms, hung over his shoulder; but he had no stockings on—no cravat round his throat; his long-worn shirt was unbuttoned over his breast; and his face was not only unshorn, but was also, as well as his hands and feet, unwashed and filthy. When Father John entered the room he was seated on his bed, which had not been made since he rose from it. He had a pipe in his mouth, and a glass of grog in his hand. The smell of the room was most offensive, and it seemed from the dreadfully close atmosphere, that no window had been opened in it for weeks past. Mary McGovery followed the priest's steps into the room, running through numerous apologies as to the state in which the old man was found, and assuring him that Macdermot was so stupid and so obstinate that it was impossible to get him to do or to understand anything; and she forthwith took hold of his shoulders, and began shaking him, and scolding him—bawling into his ear, till the poor idiot shook in her grasp.

Father John at last succeeded in rescuing him from her hands, and, seating himself in a chair immediately opposite to him, he began his sad tale. He told him by degrees that his daughter had been taken very ill—that she had got worse and worse—that Doctor Blake had been sent for—that she was found to be in imminent danger. But it had no effect on Larry; he kept on continually thanking Father John for his friendly visit, saying how kind it was of him, to come and sit with an old man like him—how hard it was to be shut up alone with such a d—d old jade as Mary; and then he began telling Father John a history of the ill-treatment and cruelty he received from her,—which to do Mary justice, was in the main false; for, excepting that she shook him and bawled to him, by way of rousing his dormant intellect, she had always endeavoured to be as kind to him as the nature of her disposition would allow. He begged of Father John to tell him when Ussher and Feemy would come back to take care of him; asked if Feemy hadn't gone away to marry her lover; and complained that it was cruel in his own dear girl not to let her old father be present at her wedding.

At last the priest saw it was no good trying to break this bad news, by degrees, to such a man as Larry; and he told him that his daughter was dead. The old man remained silent for a few minutes staring him in the face, and Father John continued—

"Yes, Mr. Macdermot, your poor daughter died in Mrs McKeon's arms."

"Is it Feemy?" said Larry. "My own Feemy?"

"It is too true, Mr. Macdermot; and indeed, indeed, I feel for you."

"But it aint true, Father John," said the idiot, grinning. "Shure didn't I see her myself, when she went away on the car to the wedding?" And then the old man paused as if thinking, and the stupid smile passed off from his face, and the saddest cloud one could conceive came over it, and he said, "Ah, they're gone away from me; they're gone away to Thady, and now I'll never see them agin." He then paused for a moment, but after a while a fire came into his eyes and he began again, "but curse her—curse—"

This was too horrid; Father John got up and held his hand before the father's face, as if to forbid him to finish the curse which he was about to utter; and the old man trembled like a frightened child upon his seat, and sat silent with his eye fixed on the priest.

Mary had not been present at this interview; Father John, however, now found it necessary to call her, and to commission her if possible to make the father understand that he had been bereaved of his daughter. Poor Mary was dreadfully distressed herself, and for a long time sat sobbing and weeping. But by degrees she recovered her tone, and commenced the duty which Father John had enjoined her to perform; but nothing could convince Larry of Feemy's death; he felt assured that they were all trying to deceive him, and that Feemy and her lover had now deserted him as well as Thady.

When Father John returned to Carrick, anxious, yet fearing to hear the verdict, he found that the jury had not yet agreed. Even this was some comfort, for it made it evident that there was doubt on the subject; and surely, thought he, if a man doubts on such a subject as this, he must ultimately lean to the side of mercy. He remained with Tony McKeon in court till about eight, when they went to the hotel and got their dinner—for they would not leave the town till the jury were locked up for the night.

Soon afterwards Webb joined them, and the three sat together till eleven o'clock, when it was signified to them that the judge would not receive the verdict that night; and that the jury were, therefore, again to be locked up. Webb then went home, and the priest and his friend both returned to Drumsna to sleep.

Thady had remained in the dock that he might be ready to hear the verdict, till the judge left the bench. He was then conducted back into the prison, and it was so late that the prison regulations did not allow him to see any friend or visitor; he was, therefore, debarred from the comfort which a few kind words from Father John would have afforded him. After he had heard the news of his sister's death he never once raised himself from the position into which he almost fell rather than sunk. During the whole of the long afternoon he remained crouched down in one corner of the benches within the dock. When the judge commenced his charge to the jury, he had once attempted to rise; but he felt that he could no longer endure the gaze of those around him, and he remained on his seat till he was taken back to gaol.

Father John and McKeon agreed that the cause of Feemy's death should not be told to Thady—at any rate till after the verdict had been given. If he should be condemned it would only be a useless cruelty to increase his sufferings by telling him of his sister's disgrace. Should he be acquitted, it would then become a question whether or no he might still be suffered to live in ignorance of that which, if known, would so deeply embitter the remainder of his life.

On the Friday morning the two friends again took their seat in court, waiting anxiously till the jury should send in word that they had come to a unanimous decision.

Thady was again in the dock, and Father John was just enabled to say one word to him over the wooden paling;—to bid him still keep up his courage, and to press his hand closely within his own.

Hour after hour passed on, and the dull stupid work of the week went on. Mr. Allewinde's eloquence, Mr. O'Malley's energy, and Mr. O'Laugher's wit, sounded equally monotonous to the anxious priest and his good-natured friend. Though they seemed to listen, and indeed endeavoured to do so, yet at the close of each trivial case that was tried, they had no idea impressed upon them of what had just been going on. One o'clock struck—two—three—four—five—and yet they remained in the same position; and still the jury who had been considering the subject remained undecided.

The business in the Record Court had been closed on the Thursday, and therefore both the judges heard criminal cases during the whole of Friday; and by six o'clock the business of the assizes was finished, and the prisoners are all disposed of with the exception of poor Thady. It was absolutely necessary that the judges should commence their business at Sligo on the following Saturday, and if the jury did not agree to a verdict before eleven on that morning, they would have to be discharged, and the case must stand over for a fresh trial at the summer assizes. This now seemed almost desirable to Father John and McKeon. Immediately after hearing Mr. O'Malley's defence they had felt sure of success; but the judge's charge had dreadfully robbed them of their hopes, and they began to fear the arrival of the foreman.

At six Baron Hamilton left the court, saying that either he or his brother would be within call till twelve o'clock to receive the verdict, and that he would remain in town till eleven the next morning, should the jury not have decided before then. Thady was yet once more taken back to prison in doubt, and whilst McKeon went to the inn again to get some dinner ready, Father John went up to the prison to visit the prisoner in his cell.

The young man had to a great degree recovered his self-possession. He told Father John that he had given up all hope for himself—that he believed he had made up his mind perfectly to face death like a brave man. He then talked about his sister, and lamented grievously that she, ill as she was, should have been dragged into court with the vain object of saving his life. He asked many questions about the manner of her death—her disease—the state of her feelings towards himself—all which Father John found it most difficult to answer; and he was just beginning to inquire how his father had borne all the griefs which had accumulated themselves upon him, when one of the turnkeys opened the door of the cell, and told him that he was to return immediately into court—that the jury had agreed—and that the judge was now going into court to receive the verdict.

Father John turned deadly pale, and leant against the wall for support. A hectic red partially suffused the prisoner's face, and his eyes became somewhat brighter than before. A slight shudder passed over his whole frame; in spite of all that he had suffered—all that he made up his mind to suffer—it was evident that there

A A

was a fearful degree of anxiety in his bosom, a painful hope still clinging to his heart.

The fetters were again fixed on to his legs, and he was led away in the midst of a body of policemen into court. Father John hurried to the same place, where he found Mr. McKeon already seated on one of the dark benches. There were but very few there, as every one had left it after the business of the day had been concluded; some of those who were in town and had heard that the jury were at last unanimous, had hurried down; but the generality of the strangers who were still remaining in Carrick, preferred the warmth of the hotel fires to paddling down through the rain, dirt, and dark, even to hear the verdict in a case in which every one was so much interested.

The barristers' and attorneys' seats were wholly deserted by their customary learned occupants; there was but one lawyer present, and he, probably thinking it unprofessional to appear to take more than a lawyer's interest in any case, was standing by himself in the dark obscurity between the dock and the bottom of one of the galleries. This was Mr. O'Malley—and though he would not be seen in court after his business there was really over, he felt so truly anxious in the matter that he could not wait to hear the verdict from a third party.

At length the judge took his seat, and the clerk of the crown sat beneath him ready to record the decision of the jury. A few lighted candles were stuck about in different parts of the court; but they were lost in the obscurity of the large, dark, dismal building. The foreman stood ready with a written and signed paper. The judge asked him if they had all come to a unanimous verdict, and he answered in the affirmative; and handed the paper to the clerk of the peace, who glancing his eye upon it, and half turning round to the judge said in his peculiar, sonorous voice—

"My lord, the prisoner has been found guilty."

"Gentlemen, is that your verdict?" said the judge; and they said it was.

The prisoner stood up at the bar erect without moving. He neither shook nor trembled now. If it were not that his lips were pressed quite close together, he would have appeared to have heard the verdict without emotion. Not so Father John; he had been leaning back, anxiously waiting till the one fatal word met his ear; and then his head fell forward on the desk, and he sobbed like a woman.

Baron Hamilton immediately placed the black cap on his head, and proceeded to pronounce the dreadful sentence of death. As he did so, his voice seemed like some awful, measured tone proceeding from an immovable figure or statue placed beneath the dusky canopy; so dark was it—and so cold and stern; so slow and clear were his words and manner; he must have felt, and felt strongly, as he doomed that young man to a sudden and ignominious death, for he was no heartless man; but so powerfully had he schooled his emotions, so entirely had he learnt to lay aside the man in assuming the judge, that had he been the stone he looked like, he could not have betrayed less of the heart within him.

He dwelt at considerable length on the enormity of the offence of which the prisoner had been found guilty; he stated his own conviction that the verdict was a just and true one; alluded to the irreparable injury such illegal societies as that to which the prisoner too evidently belonged, must do in the country; assured him that he had no hope for mercy to look for in this world, and recommended him to seek it from Him who could always reconcile it with his justice to extend it to the repentant sinner. He concluded by ordering that he should be taken back to the place from whence he came, and be brought from thence to the place of execution on the Monday week following, and then and there be hung by his neck till he should be dead.

The assizes were then finished—the judge immediately left the court—the prisoner was taken back to his cell—the lights were extinguished—and when the servants of the sheriff came to lock the door, they found Mr. McKeon still vainly endeavouring to arouse the broken-hearted priest from his ecstasy of sorrow.

CHAPTER XXXIII.

THE END.

On Saturday morning the little town of Carrick-on-Shannon again became quiet and, comparatively speaking, empty. The judges left it very early; most of the lawyers had taken wing and flown towards Sligo, seeking fresh quarries, on the previous evening. The jury were released, and had returned weary to their homes; the crowds of litigants and witnesses who had filled the Record Court had also left on the Thursday evening; and now those who had been wanted in the criminal court were gone, and peace and quiet were restored. At eleven o'clock neither of the hotels were open; the waiters and servants who, during the last week had literally not known what a bed was, and who, during that week, had snatched their only disturbed naps before the kitchen fires, or under the kitchen dressers, were taking their sleep out for the past week. It was still raining hard, and the long, narrow, untidy street was still as dirty and disagreeable as ever; otherwise there was no resemblance in it to the street of the last few days. There was no crowd around the court house, nor policemen with cross chains on their caps, nor sheriffs' servants with dirty, tawdry liveries. The assizes were over; and till next July—when the judges, barristers, jury, &c., would all return, Carrick was doomed to fall back to its usual insignificance as a most uninteresting county town.

As Father John left the town on the previous evening, he sent word up to the governor of the gaol that he would see young Macdermot early on the following morning. He did not go home to the Cottage, but again passed the night at Mr. McKeon's, at Drumsna; and a most sad and melancholy night it was. After witnessing Feemy's death, and seeing that the body had been decently and properly disposed, Mrs. McKeon had returned home, and her husband had found her quite ill from the effects of the scene she had gone through.

Soon after the two men had made their apology for a dinner, Mr. Webb, who had had the verdict brought to his own house, called, and the three sat for some time talking over what possible means there might be still left for saving the young man's life. It was at last agreed that Webb should go up to Dublin on the morrow, and make what interest he could to see the Lord-Lieutenant himself, as well as the Under Secretary; and endeavour, by every means in his power, to obtain a pardon.

After what had been said by the judge whilst pronouncing the sentence, they all felt that there could be no reasonable ground for hope; but still they would leave no chance untried, and it was therefore settled that the counsellor should start by the morning coach.

Early the next morning the priest left Drumsna for Carrick, to see Thady for the first time since his condemnation. McKeon offered to go with him; but he declined the offer, saying, that this morning he would sooner be left alone with his doomed friend. He refused, too, the loan of McKeon's car. He wanted to collect his thoughts and his energy by the walk, for he felt that he had much to do to school his own feelings before he could make his visit a comfort instead of a cause of additional distress to Macdermot.

About ten o'clock he passed through the town, and rang the governor's bell at the gaol door. He was a well-known visitor there now, and when the door was opened he expected at once, as usual, to be shown the prisoner's cell; but instead of that he was taken into the governor's house.

This officer had always been extremely civil to Father John; and had shown all the kindness in his power, and that was no little, to the prisoner. He expressed himself to the priest greatly distressed at the verdict, and the consequent fate of Macdermot.

"It's four years, Father John," said he, "since I had a prisoner in my charge condemned to die. It's four years since there was an execution here, and then the victim was a criminal of the blackest dye—a man who had undoubtedly committed a cold-blooded, long-premeditated murder. And then his death weighed heavy on me; but I cannot but believe that this young man is innocent,—at any rate so much more innocent than he was,—my heart has failed me since he was brought back last night condemned."

"More innocent than he was!" said Father John. "Ah, indeed he is! If we were all as innocent of guilt as this poor fellow is, it would be well for most of us. I promised to see him early this morning. Will you let me go up to him now? though God knows I know not what to say to him!"

"Yes, of course. You shall go up now immediately; and God grant you may be able to comfort him! But you know you cannot see him as you have done always. That is, you may see him as often as you please, but you cannot see him alone."

"Not alone!" said Father John.

"Not now," said the governor. "When brought back capitally condemned, he was of necessity put into the condemned cell; and when once there, no visitor may be left alone with him."

"How is he to receive—how am I to perform the sacred duties of my profession?"

"When the prisoner is about to confess, the turnkey will step outside the door, which you can close. You know, Father John," continued the governor, "it is not from my own heart I give these orders; you know I would give him every indulgence I could; but you also know that I must obey the rules of my office, and they imperatively forbid that any visitor shall be left alone with a condemned prisoner."

"I know it isn't your fault; and if it must be so, it must. But will you desire the man to be sent for, for Macdermot will be expecting me?"

In a minute or two the gaoler arrived with his huge keys, and, with a palpitating heart, Father John followed him to the condemned cell.

The priest, during his walk from Drumsna, had made up his mind exactly as to what he would say on seeing Thady; how he would mix pity with condolence; how he would use such words as might strengthen him in his determination to bear his sufferings with resignation; how he would teach him to forget the present in the thoughts of his future prospects. But when the iron door was opened, and he saw Macdermot seated on the one small stone seat in the wall beneath the high, iron-barred window; when his eye rested on the young man's pale and worn face, he forgot all his studied phrases and premeditated conduct, his acute grief overcame his ideas of duty, and falling on the prisoner's bosom, he sobbed out, "My boy—my boy—my poor murdered boy!"

It would be useless to attempt to describe at length the scene between them. Father John remained with him nearly the whole of that day,—the patient, silent turnkey leaning up against the corner of the cell during the whole time. For a long time Thady was the most tranquil of the two; but at length the priest regained his composure, and was able to listen to the various requests of his friend, and to say all that could be said to comfort and strengthen him.

Thady's first request was that he might see his father. This, Father John felt, would be impracticable, and if accomplished would only be in the highest degree painful. Larry was now so perfectly a lunatic, and at the same time so resolute in his determination not to put himself in the way of being arrested by Keegan, that it would be impossible either to make him understand the fate which awaited his son, or to induce him, by any means short of force, to leave his own room. Besides, were a meeting to be effected, the idiotical father would probably not cease to abuse his son, and would certainly not comprehend his tenderness and affection. It was difficult to tell the son that his father had so utterly lost his intellects as to be unable to be brought to see him; but even this was better than allowing him to think that he was to see him, and then deceive him.

Thady bore this blow even worse than Father John had expected that he would do; it made him feel so desolate—so alone in the world! Stupid and cross as his father had been for years past—cruel and unjust as he had been on the last time they met,—still, the long time which had passed since that meeting, and the manner in which the interview had been passed by Thady, made him forget his father's treatment, and only remember that he was his last surviving relative. He submitted, however, to Father John's advice, and consented not to urge his request.

He then talked of his sister, and began to speak more feelingly of Ussher, and to allude to the deed which had brought him to his dreadful doom, with more freedom than he had ever done before. The facts of his last month's residence at Ballycloran seemed to be made less obscure than they had been, to his mind's eye, by the distance through which he looked at them. He appeared to comprehend more clearly both Feemy's conduct and that of her lover, and he spoke with the greatest affection of the former, and with justice to the latter.

"Oh! Father John," he continued, after they had been talking together for hours, and when they had become so habituated to the presence of the turnkey as almost to forget it, " no one but yourself can ever know how far murder was from my thoughts that day!—nor all that I had suffered for having listened for one moment to the plots which them boys were making for his death. But who can wonder that I hated him! God knows I have forgiven him for all that he has brought on us—both me and Feemy; but who can wonder that I didn't love him then? I knew in my heart he never meant to marry her. And oh! Father John, av I hadn't seen her that night, what would she have been now? I did hate him then;—and hadn't I cause? And for that one night at the wedding, when I was mad with the name they had called my sisther; I did think I'd be glad av the boys that hated him so should murther him at last. But when I woke in the morning and remembered that the sounds of murther had been in my ears, I felt as though I could never more be quiet or at ase in this world. And I never was; every man's hand was against me since then, Father John, except yours. I felt, as I walked through the fields that morning, that it was here I should spend my last days, and here I am. And I was warned of it too; I was warned of what would come of it, av I meddled with them boys that night at Mrs. Mehan's. He himself called me out that night when I first got there, and tould me what it was Brady was afther. And I believed him, and yet I went; for my heart was full of hatred for the man who warned me. Oh! why, Father John, could he not let us alone. We were poor, but we were no worse; but there's an end of us now altogether, and perhaps it's for the betther as it is!"

He then earnestly begged Father John to attend to his sister's burial, and to take some little heed of his father during his few remaining years; and all this the priest promised. He spoke of the property, and of the chance there might be of saving something out of it for the old man's support. Father John, however, told him that for his, Thady's sake, and for the love he bore him, his father should never want till he wanted himself; and though this promise, for many long months, entailed a heavy burden on the priest, he most religiously kept his word.

Thady then spoke of his own coming death; and though he had made up his mind to die, and could think, without regret, of leaving the world where he had known so many sorrows and so few joys, still he shuddered when he remembered the gaping crowd which would be assembled to see his expiring convulsions, and the horror which he could not but feel, when the executioner's hands should touch his neck, and the dreadful cap should be drawn over his eyes. Oh! that that horrid moment might be over—when he would still be alive—still sensible to the thoughts of life—but when the light of the sun would have been for ever excluded, and his last thoughts would be wandering between doubtful hopes of Heaven's mercy, and awful fears of his coming agony.

The cold sweat stood upon his brow as he endeavoured to explain his feelings to the priest. And assiduously, patiently, warmly, and kindly, did that friend endeavour to allay his sufferings, and make him feel as confident of God's pardon for his sins as he was of the executioner's doom. He told him also that, if possible, no crowd should be assembled to gaze at his death; and he promised himself to stand by him, and hold his hand to the last moment of his life.

At six the priest left him promising to see him again on the Sunday, and on every day till it was all over. He then returned to McKeon's, where he dined.

At about ten they were sitting together with Mrs. McKeon by the fire talking over the affairs of Ballycloran, and consulting as to what had better be done with Larry after the execution, when the girl entered and said a man was waiting outside wishing to speak to Mr. McKeon. Tony accordingly went out; and standing at the back-door, for he would not enter the kitchen, with his hat slouched over his face, he found Pat Brady. He was very much astonished at seeing this man; more especially so, as since the trial Brady's name had been mentioned with execration by almost every one, and particularly by those, who like McKeon, had taken every opportunity of showing themselves Macdermot's friends; and it would have been thought therefore that McKeon's house was one of the last places to which he would be likely to come.

Pat was the first to speak.

"There's a word or two I want to spake to you, Mr. Mc Keon."

"To speak to me," said Mr. McKeon; "well, what is it?"

"I couldn't just be telling you here; av you wouldn't mind stepping out, a minute or so—it's not five minutes I'd be keeping you."

McKeon accordingly went out into the dark yard, about thirty paces from the house, and Brady continued—

"It's about the young masther, yer honor."

"You've said enough about him; you've hanged him; now, what more have you?"

"May I niver see the Blessed Virgin in glory av I towld a word of a lie agin the masther. Av I iver towld the truth it was that day; an' worse luck—av I'd lied then maybe it'd been betther for Mr. Thady."

"It wasn't to tell me that, you came here;—if you've anything to say, let me hear what it is."

"Why then, yer honor, is Mr. Larry, the owld man, a going to see the young masther?"

"And what if he is?"

"Why jist this thin; av he do, Keegan's boys is to saze him as he comes out on the road from Ballycloran."

"Gracious God! would he arrest the man coming to see his own son for the last time!"

"Faix, he will, Mr. McKeon; so don't let him do it; I heard him telling the bailiff."

McKeon seemed lost in astonishment, at this fresh instance of the attorney's relentless barbarity, and Brady turned round to go away. But after having walked a few yards, he came back, and said, in a hesitating whisper—

"You'll be seeing Mr. Thady afore it's all over, Mr. McKeon?"

"Well; I shall see him."

"Would you mind axing him to pardon a poor boy, Mr. McKeon?"

"May God pardon you, Brady. Your master that was, has been taught before this to forgive all his enemies; but I wouldn't dirty my mouth with your name the last time I see him."

"Sorrow a word of a lie thin I towld, Mr. McKeon."

"Never mind; truth or lies it's much the same." And McKeon returned to the house, and told Father John what he had heard from Brady; and the priest and he agreed together that it would be by far the best course to make Thady understand that his father could not leave his home to see him, for fear of falling into the hands of the attorney.

On the next day, Sunday, Father John performed mass and preached as usual in the parish chapel. When the service was over, he addressed his congregation from the altar on the subject of Thady's approaching execution, and he begged them all, as they valued his good opinion, not only not to be present at it themselves, but also to do all in their power to prevent others from being so. The same thing was done in Carrick, where the priest moreover begged his parishioners not to open their shops on that morning until the execution should be over.

The ensuing week passed slowly away. Father John was with the doomed man constantly, and McKeon saw him two or three times. On the Wednesday Mr. Webb returned from Dublin, but his journey had been a fruitless one; he had seen the Lord-Lieutenant, and had been kindly received by him; but at the same time he was informed that he could not exercise his privilege of mercy in this case, as he had been strongly advised not to do so, both by those in office under him and by the judge.

Macdermot kept up his heart wonderfully through the whole week. He never repined, nor once even alluded to Keegan. Father John spent the whole of Sunday with him. It was to be his last in this world; the last time he was to watch the light growing out of the darkness—and the darkness following the light. As the minutes flew by, his face became gradually paler, and his hand occasionally trembled. The brave soldier goes to meet Death, and meets him without a shudder when he comes. The suffering woman patiently awaits him on her bed of sickness, and conscious of her malady dies slowly without a struggle. A not uncommon fortitude enables men and women to leave their mortal coil, and take the dread leap in the dark with apparent readiness and ease. But to wait in full health and strength for the arrival of the fixed hour of certain death—to feel the moments sink from under you which are fast bringing you to the executioner's hand;—to know that in twelve—ten—eight—six hours by the clock, which hurries through the rapid minutes, you are to become—not by God's accomplished visitation—not in any gallant struggle of your own—but through the stern will of certain powerful men—a hideous, foul, and dislocated corse;—to know that at one certain ordained moment you are to be made extinct— to be violently put an end to;—to be fully aware that this is your fixed fate, and that though strong as a lion, you must at that moment die like a dog;—to await the doom without fear—without feeling the blood grow cold round the heart,—without a quickened pulse and shaking muscles, exceeds the bounds of mortal courage, and requires either the ignorant unimaginative indifference of a brute, or the superhuman endurance of an enthusiastic martyr.

Thady was neither the one nor the other; and the blood did grow cold round his heart—his pulse quickened, and his nerves shook within him; but these were involuntary signs of his human nature. He spent the day in the performance of his religious duties, and made continual efforts to fix his mind on those subjects to which it was directed by the priest; and at last he received from him final absolution for his sins, with a full assurance in its efficacy. And if true and deep repentance can make absolution available, the priest's assurance was not ill grounded.

Father Cullen, at Drumsna, and different priests in the neighbouring parishes again desired their congregations to absent themselves from the execution, and on the Sunday evening before the fatal day it was thoroughly understood through the country, that it was the wish of the priest that no one should be present.

The Monday morning came. Though Father John had not been allowed to remain all night in the prisoner's cell, he did not leave it till eleven, and was with him again at six. When the gaoler turned the key in the door, Father John found the prisoner still sleeping on his pallet. Even the loud noise of the key in the lock, and the dropping back of the heavy bolt had failed to awaken him. Before he left him on the previous evening he had insisted on his partially undressing, and he now found him exactly in the position in which he had left him.

Eight was the hour fixed for the execution, and though it seemed cruel to rob him of his last human comfort, still as so few minutes of life remained, the priest thought it better to rouse him. He laid his hand on his shoulder, and calling out his christian name, gently shook him. It was wonderful how soundly the poor fellow slept; and at last he jumped up with a smile on his wan face, uttering those confused words of acknowledgment which so readily come to the lips of any one conscious of being caught sleeping too late, to the neglect of his worldly duties. He had been dreaming—and in his dreams he was again at Ballycloran—again sitting over the warm turf fire, talking with his father, after his hard day's work, of their lands, and their rents, and their difficulties. Father John's presence—the cold close white wall and his own memory soon made him again conscious of the truth; and as he pressed his hands to his forehead, remembering that he should never again feel the luxury of sleep, the expression of his face was dreadful to be seen.

There is nothing further to relate respecting him. As the clock struck eight he was standing on the iron grate over the front entrance into Carrick gaol. He had supported himself firmly—though evidently with difficulty. The cap was over his face—his hands were tied behind his back—and the rope was round his neck. The last sound that met his ear was the final prayer which Father John sobbed forth that God would receive him into his mercy; the bolt was drawn—and Thady Macdermot was soon no more.

Not one human form appeared before the gaol that morning. Not even a passenger crossed over the bridge from half-past seven till after eight, as from thence one might just catch a glimpse of the front of the prison. At the end of the bridge stood three or four men guarding the street, and cautioning those who came, that they could not pass by; and as their behests were quietly obeyed the police did not interfere with them. Among them were Joe Reynolds and Corney Dolan, and they did not leave their post till they were aware that the body of him to whom they showed this last respect had been removed. The shops were closed during the whole day; but it was many days before the sad melancholy which attended the execution of Thady Macdermot wore away from the little town of Carrick-on-Shannon.

www.ingramcontent.com/pod-product-compliance
Lightning Source LLC
Chambersburg PA
CBHW020221240426
43672CB00006B/376